An Introduction to Cyberpsychology

C000258352

An Introduction to Cyberpsychology is the first book to provide a student-oriented introduction to this rapidly growing and increasingly studied topic. It is designed to encourage students to critically evaluate the psychology of online interactions, and to develop appropriate research methodologies to complete their own work in this field.

The book is comprised of four main sections:

1   An overview of cyberpsychology and online research methodologies.
2   Social psychology in an online context.
3   The practical applications of cyberpsychology.
4   The psychological aspects of other technologies.

Each chapter includes:

- Explanations of key terms and a glossary to facilitate understanding.
- Content summaries to aid student learning.
- Activity boxes, discussion questions and recommended reading to guide further study.

Further resources for students and instructors are available on the book's companion website, including audio and video links, essay questions, a multiple-choice test bank, and PowerPoint lecture slides (www.routledge.com/cw/connolly).

Uniquely combining a survey of the field with a focus on the applied areas of psychology, the book is designed to be a core text for undergraduate modules in cyberpsychology and the psychology of the Internet, and a primer for students of postgraduate programmes in cyberpsychology.

Irene Connolly is Lecturer in Developmental and Educational Psychology at Dun Laoghaire Institute of Art, Design and Technology, Ireland.

Marion Palmer is Head of the Department of Technology and Psychology at Dun Laoghaire Institute of Art, Design and Technology, Ireland.

Hannah Barton is Lecturer in Psychology at Dun Laoghaire Institute of Art, Design and Technology, Ireland.

Gráinne Kirwan is Lecturer in Psychology at Dun Laoghaire Institute of Art, Design and Technology, Ireland.

An Introduction to Cyberpsychology

Edited by Irene Connolly, Marion Palmer, Hannah Barton and Gráinne Kirwan

Routledge
Taylor & Francis Group

LONDON AND NEW YORK

First published 2016
by Routledge
2 Park Square, Milton Park, Abingdon, Oxon OX14 4RN

and by Routledge
711 Third Avenue, New York, NY 10017

Routledge is an imprint of the Taylor & Francis Group, an informa business

© 2016 selection and editorial matter, Irene Connolly, Marion Palmer, Hannah Barton and Gráinne Kirwan; individual chapters, the contributors

The right of the editors to be identified as the authors of the editorial material, and of the authors for their individual chapters, has been asserted in accordance with sections 77 and 78 of the Copyright, Designs and Patents Act 1988.

All rights reserved. No part of this book may be reprinted or reproduced or utilised in any form or by any electronic, mechanical, or other means, now known or hereafter invented, including photocopying and recording, or in any information storage or retrieval system, without permission in writing from the publishers.

Trademark notice: Product or corporate names may be trademarks or registered trademarks, and are used only for identification and explanation without intent to infringe.

British Library Cataloguing in Publication Data
A catalogue record for this book is available from the British Library

Library of Congress Cataloging in Publication Data
Names: Connolly, Irene, editor.
Title: An introduction to cyberpsychology / [edited by] Irene Connolly, Marion Palmer, Hannah Barton and Gráinne Kirwan.
Description: 1 Edition. | New York : Routledge, 2016. | Includes bibliographical references and index.
Identifiers: LCCN 2015040925| ISBN 9781138823785 (hardcover) | ISBN 9781138823792 (softcover) | ISBN 9781315741895 (ebk)
Subjects: LCSH: Cyberspace—Psychological aspects. | Virtual reality— Psychological aspects. | Telematics—Social aspects.
Classification: LCC HM1017 .I58 2016 | DDC 303.48/34—dc23
LC record available at http://lccn.loc.gov/2015040925

ISBN: 978–1–138–82378–5 (hbk)
ISBN: 978–1–138–82379–2 (pbk)
ISBN: 978–1–315–74189–5 (ebk)

Typeset in Bembo and Univers
by Florence Production Ltd, Stoodleigh, Devon, UK.

Dedicated to our families

Contents

Part 4   Psychology and technology   239

Chapter 18 Human–Computer Interaction   241
Andrew Errity

Chapter 19 Gaming   257
Andrew Errity, Brendan Rooney and Conall Tunney

Chapter 20 Psychological applications of Virtual Reality   271
Gráinne Kirwan

Chapter 21   The psychology of Artificial Intelligence   286

Gráinne Kirwan

Illustrations

FIGURES

TABLES

Contributors

Dr Irene Connolly is a lecturer of Developmental and Educational Psychology at Dun Laoghaire Institute of Art, Design and Technology (IADT) and a member of the Psychological Society of Ireland. Irene holds a Ph.D. in Educational Psychology from Trinity College Dublin, specialising in the area of bullying. Her research has focused on areas such as the role of the bully, and longitudinal research regarding the persistence of bullying and victimisation across the lifespan. Recent research has examined the complex world of cyberbullying. Irene is the Psychological Society of Ireland's Irish representative on the European Federation of Psychologists Associations (EFPA) Consultation Group 'Psychology and Internet', which is a coalition to make the Internet a safer place for children. She is also an affiliated researcher with the Anti-Bullying Research and Resource Centre, Trinity College Dublin (TCD)/Dublin City University (DCU).

Dr Marion Palmer is Head of the Department of Technology and Psychology at IADT and until recently was the chair of the Institute's Teaching and Learning Committee. Marion has worked on the M.Sc. in Cyberpsychology since its inception with a particular focus on learning in cyberspace. She researched teaching in Irish Institutes of Technology for a doctorate in education from Queen's University Belfast and was a national Award of Teaching Excellence winner in 2011. Marion is a member of the Board of the National Forum for the Enhancement of Teaching and Learning, www.teachingandlearning.ie.

Hannah Barton holds an MA in Psychology from University College Cork and is a previous coordinator of the M.Sc. in Cyberpsychology. She has been lecturing in personality and social psychology in IADT for over twelve years, teaching on both the B.Sc. (Hons) in Applied Psychology and the M.Sc. in Cyberpsychology degrees. Her research has included altruism and positive psychology, mobile learning (podcasting) and group dynamics in both online and offline settings.

Dr Gráinne Kirwan is a Chartered Psychologist with the British Psychological Society and a lecturer in Psychology in IADT. She teaches on both the B.Sc. (Hons) in Applied Psychology and the M.Sc. in Cyberpsychology. Gráinne holds a Ph.D. in Criminology as well as an M.Sc. in Applied Forensic Psychology, a Postgraduate Certificate in Third Level Learning and Teaching and an M.Litt. in Psychology. She has co-authored two books on forensic cyberpsychology with Dr Andrew Power: *Cybercrime* (Cambridge University Press, 2013) and *The Psychology of Cybercrime* (IGI Global, 2012) as well as co-editing *Cyberpsychology and New Media* (Psychology Press, 2014). She is a member of the Editorial Board of the *Cyberpsychology, Behaviour and Social Networking* journal.

Dr Andrew Errity holds a B.Sc. (Hons) in Computer Applications and a Ph.D. in Speech Signal Processing from Dublin City University. Andrew lectures in computer science, software engineering and human–computer interaction at IADT. Andrew has presented his work at a number of international conferences and has acted as a reviewer for conferences in fields including signal processing and human–computer interaction. Andrew is currently the programme co-ordinator for IADT's Special Purpose Award courses.

Cliona Flood is a Lecturer in Psychology at IADT at both Undergraduate and Masters levels. She is the current programme co-ordinator for the M.Sc. in Cyberpsychology. She studied Psychology at the Open University, and Work and Organizational Psychology with Dublin City University. Cliona has also studied Psychotherapy and has an interest in mental health issues.

Nicola Fox Hamilton holds an M.Sc. in Cyberpsychology from IADT, and is currently completing a Ph.D. at the University of Wolverhampton. Her current research examines the connection between language, personality, culture and attraction, and the consistency of expression of personality in online platforms. Nicola was founding secretary of the Psychological Society of Ireland's Special Interest Group for Media, Art and Cyberpsychology.

Dr John Greaney is a lecturer in Applied Psychology at IADT. He holds a B.Sc. (Hons) in Mathematics and Psychology and a Ph.D. in Psychology, and has worked for the Royal National Institute for the Blind, Hewlett Packard Labs and Frontend. He has held lectureships at the universities of Birmingham and Manchester, and is an Associate Fellow of the British Psychological Society.

Dr Olivia Hurley holds an M.Sc. and Ph.D. from University College Dublin in Sport Psychology. She is a Lecturer on the B.Sc. (Hons) Applied Psychology programme in IADT. Olivia is a sport psychologist for the Irish Institute of Sport and is also a Registered Psychologist with the Psychological Society of Ireland. Olivia has acted as a reviewer for the *International Review of Sport and Exercise Psychology*. She has also published in a number of peer-reviewed journals and texts.

Dr Brendan Rooney is a lecturer at University College Dublin. Brendan is a previous lecturer on the M.Sc. in Cyberpsychology at IADT. He was also the founding chairperson of the Psychological Society of Ireland's Special Interest Group for Media, Arts and Cyberpsychology. Brendan's research interests include the psychological processes of cognitive and emotional engagement with film and other virtual or fictional worlds.

Conall Tunney is currently undertaking a Ph.D. by research at University College Dublin in the area of technology for well-being. He works on the Pesky Gnats project, which designs and develops technology-based Cognitive Behavioural Therapy interventions for children who are experiencing anxiety or low mood. His research uses mixed methods, including systematic reviews and meta-analyses, qualitative focus groups and randomised controlled trials. He also lectures part-time at IADT on the Psychology of New Media and Entertainment and on Gaming and Media Psychology. Conall maintains a clinical focus in psychology with a part-time post as an assistant psychologist at the Children's University Hospital, Temple Street, Dublin.

Foreword

It is a privilege to introduce this work by Irene Connolly, Marion Palmer, Hannah Barton and Gráinne Kirwan. They have successfully created a comprehensive, objective and authoritative account demonstrating for us the promise, as well as the peril, that cyberpsychology possesses. No existing account of cyberpsychology has contained the breadth and detail we find within these pages.

I am Editor-in-Chief of a Medline-indexed journal entitled *CyberPsychology, Behavior & Social Networking* (*CYBER*). When *CYBER* was founded in 1998, the term 'cyberpsychology' was so new that we felt a subtitle was needed. We decided on 'the impact of the Internet, multimedia and virtual reality on behavior and society' to explain the journal's purpose. The term cyberpsychology – encompassing all psychological concepts associated with or influenced by emergent technologies – was novel and exciting. Now, almost two decades later, we see enormous change – the journal is indexed in Medline and PsycINFO and cyberpsychology is a commonly used term, with many of the first technologies reported at its origin now quite conventional. In addition, technologies and tools such as Facebook, Twitter and Snapchat, which did not exist in 1998, have populated the research landscape.

Technology, as opined by Carl Jung, is neutral. It is how we use that technology that determines whether it will be positive or negative. On the positive side, we now see technology offering new opportunities for scientific research to be conducted more efficiently, social isolation relieved by networking tools and healthcare transitioned into the home and office. On the negative side, we see Internet gaming addiction, cyberbullying and cybercrime. We also face a constant struggle to maintain a proper work–life balance in this age of constant connection, distractions and multitasking demands.

For two decades, I have explored questions about the nature of cyberpsychology and how it differs from more traditional psychology. I have always taken the position that any application of psychological theory or practice is first and foremost psychology. The concepts and techniques of psychology create the core competence. One then builds on this proficiency and learns to integrate, for instance, technology into their area of expertise, often enriching one's scope and abilities. In each discipline, we see specialisation and mastery in subsets that branch off from the foundation. So the selective mastery of segments of psychology, or in this case cyberpsychology, creates sets of specialists who communicate with perhaps somewhat different terminology, while still remaining understood by the larger collective. This publication does a magnificent job of weaving in psychological constructs, personality theory and communication theory, explaining to us how they apply in cyberspace. We are guided through the fundamentals of online research and methodologies, their nature and nuances. And we are asked to consider the ethical dilemmas spawned by cyberspace.

Many of the chapters in this publication could easily be expanded into complete books. There are, in fact, already books about some of the chapter topics (e.g. *Cybercrime* by Kirwan and Power published in 2013). However, the presentations here are informative and comprehensive, while being concise enough so that they can be read for an overall understanding of cyberpsychology. With its activities, practical applications, illustrations and thought-provoking questions, this book will serve to excite students and postdoctoral trainees planning for careers in cyberpsychology. It will also engage psychologists preparing to start their careers and experienced psychologists wishing to educate themselves about the implementation of new technologies in psychology and new disorders they may encounter in their patient population. At this state of human–computer interaction, continuing education and information updates are essential for us all.

With its clear and readily accessible manner, this book will also be a valuable resource suitable for policy makers, decision makers and anyone interested in an unbiased interpretation of technology's impact on individual behavior, interpersonal relationships and society in its entirety, as well as how new interactive technologies can be incorporated into existing treatment programmes and protocols to improve psychological health and well-being.

This text, primarily intended for use by students in cyberpsychology, has done a brilliant job of compiling a wealth of knowledge in which thought leaders have contributed chapters on various aspects of cyberpsychology, reflecting both the positive and negative side of technology's use. Claims and beliefs of researchers and clinicians have been critically reviewed and probingly challenged. The present book, with its unparalleled scope, quality and sophistication, invites us to see anew what lies ahead as we evolve and incorporate new technologies into our daily existence. As technology becomes more ubiquitous, it needs to be embraced with an eye towards ethical and responsible implementation, and this book is vital and timely in helping us to examine that need. It is important that we not only consider meaningful research questions, but that we also begin to discuss solutions and gain understanding of these phenomena. This book can be a reference and guide for us all as we embark on this important journey.

Professor Dr Brenda K. Wiederhold,
Ph.D., MBA, BCB, BCN

A licensed psychologist in California and Belgium, Brenda has been a leader in employing virtual reality (VR) treatment for anxiety, stress and trauma for 20 years. She completed the first clinical trial to provide VR treatment for post-traumatic stress disorder (PTSD) and works with first responders to provide stress innoculation training prior to deployment. Working to inform and educate policy makers, the scientific community and the general public on technology and healthcare, she has given invited lectures on VR in 24 countries and has published more than 150 scientific articles and 14 books.

Brenda is a Professor at the Catholic University in Milan, President of Virtual Reality Medical Institute in Belgium, Executive Vice-President of Virtual Reality Medical Center in California, and CEO of Interactive Media Institute. Founder of the CyberPsychology, CyberTherapy & Social Networking Conference, she also publishes CyberTherapy and Rehabilitation magazine, is Secretary General of the International Association of CyberPsychology, Training, and rehabilitation, and Editor-in-Chief of CyberPsychology, Behavior, and Social Networking journal.

Acknowledgements

As an editorial team, we are very grateful to all of those who helped us at each stage of the book's development. In particular, we would like to extend our gratitude to Michael Strang, Libby Volke and the rest of the editorial team at Taylor & Francis/Routledge for their enthusiasm for this project, their guidance and the many cheerful answers that they provided to our queries.

We would also like to thank each of the chapter authors. Their expertise in their respective fields and their dedication to teaching combine to form chapters that are rich in content and full of engaging pedagogic material. We know that the preparation of these chapters required a great deal of time, effort and patience, and we appreciate the authors' adherence to our schedule and quick responses to our requests, despite so many conflicting demands on their time.

While textbooks such as this can be read by people from many backgrounds, they are primarily developed with students in mind. Over the years, our own students on both the M.Sc. in Cyberpsychology and our undergraduate programmes have helped us to develop our ideas, push beyond our perceived capabilities, and view online behaviour in new ways. We hope that this textbook will help future generations of students to become as excited about online interaction as they have made us.

We would also like to make some individual acknowledgements.

From Irene: To my husband Tom, my children Lauren, Jamie and Tom, and to my parents, Ita and Michael, a huge thank you for everything you do. To my fantastic colleagues, each of you is simply brilliant.

From Marion: I'd like to thank my co-editors for all their work on the textbook both as an author and a co-editor. I appreciated the generous feedback and support, and hope that I did as much in return. Thank you.

From Hannah: To Ashling for being you, and to my friends and colleagues for unlimited patience, good humour and endless cat jokes.

From Gráinne: To my mother, Marie Kirwan, for decades of encouragement in all things academic, and for cat-sitting for a year. To Glen Lockhart, for infinite patience.

1 | Introduction

1 Introduction to cyberpsychology

Gráinne Kirwan

CHAPTER OVERVIEW

Cyberpsychology is a relatively new field within applied psychology, although there is now a growing library of research and writing examining the topic. As an area of study, it assesses how we interact with others using technology, how we can develop technology to best fit our requirements, and how our behaviour and psychological states are influenced by technology. The most commonly studied technology in cyberpsychology research is the Internet, although the area considers human interactions with many devices, including mobile computing, games consoles, virtual reality and artificial intelligence. This chapter provides a brief overview of some areas of research in cyberpsychology, including a short introduction to each of the chapters that follow.

KEY TERMS

Cyberpsychology is the branch of psychology that examines how we interact with others using technology, how our behaviour is influenced by technology, how technology can be developed to best suit our needs, and how our psychological states can be affected by technologies. Much research in cyberpsychology has been driven by the World Wide Web, and in particular the advent of **social media**. However, other technologies have also been closely examined, including **gaming** (both online and offline), **mobile computing, artificial intelligence, virtual reality** and **augmented reality.**

CYBERPSYCHOLOGY: A BRIEF SYNOPSIS

Psychology as a discipline does not stand still for long. It changes and adjusts as new research, theories and developments arise, and it has never been afraid of facing new advances while challenging concepts that were previously widely accepted. It is not surprising that the advances in technologies, especially those over the past twenty years, have drawn the interest of so many academics and practitioners in the area. Probably the most significant change in human behaviour and interaction in the past two decades has been the rise in popularity of the Internet (in a general sense) and online **social networking** and interactions (in a more specific sense). It is unsurprising that psychologists have not only embraced these technologies as methods of improving general well-being, but have also been drawn to examine how these technologies can impact our behaviour and our relationships with others. The research of psychologists in this field complements the research of other social scientists across the globe who also examine online interactions.

Cyberpsychology is a broad topic, and it encompasses many aspects of research, some of which have been in existence for some time, and some of which are more recent. Generally, cyberpsychology encompasses three main aspects. First, it assesses how we interact with others using technology. This has been of particular interest since the advent of social media technologies, but our interactions with others have been affected by technologies for a considerably longer period of time through the use of communication mechanisms such as email and websites. To consider this for a moment, think about one of the people that you communicate with the most often. Now imagine under what circumstances you might talk to them in person, or when you might send them a text message, or instant message, or email. What would be different about your communications with them in each of these contexts? Also, take a moment and think about someone who you communicate with online fairly regularly, but have never met offline. What is your impression of that person? Do you think that this might change if you met them offline now? Do you think that you might have a different impression of them if you had met them offline in the first instance, and only later started communicating with them online?

A second aspect of cyberpsychology considers how we can develop technology to best fit our requirements and desires. Some attributes of this type of cyberpsychology often come under the heading of **Human–Computer Interaction**, although this is also considered as an entire specialism in itself. One example of advances in this area involves programming the recording of programmes from television channels. Up until fairly recently this was a complex affair – blank video cassettes needed to be purchased and placed in the video cassette recorder (VCR), the television guide needed to be consulted to determine the start time, end time, day and channel that a programme was on, the VCR clock needed to be checked to ensure that it was accurate, the appropriate option within the VCR's menu needed to be identified, and all the date, time and channel details needed to be inputted correctly. An error at any stage, or a change in the scheduled time of the programme, meant that the recording would fail. Now, most digital television providers include all the necessary hardware, including storage space, and allow users to select a programme from the on-screen listings and record that episode with a single button press. Not only that, but also all remaining episodes in a season can be set to record with one more tap of a button. Changes in running schedule are no longer a problem as the system can compensate for it.

Of course, there are many other ways in which research in Human–Computer Interaction makes our daily lives easier – we only need to briefly look at a computer's operating system, or the difference in mobile phones over the past ten years, to identify such improvements. Another key example is the touchscreen – this technology was very rare before the advent of smartphones, but has become a common feature of daily life. Interacting with a computer in this way requires a different set of skills from using other interface methods, such as keyboards. One of the goals of Human–Computer Interaction includes determining which interface methods are the most appropriate for a given situation, realising that one approach does not answer all problems.

The third key aspect of cyberpsychology examines how our behaviour and psychological states can be affected by technologies. Again, there are many examples of this, but one that many will have experienced is a distorted sense of time when using technologies, particularly when gaming. This phenomenon is one of several characteristics of a 'flow' state, as identified by Csikszentmihalyi (1990), and applied to interactions with technology by many researchers (see, for example, Webster *et al.*, 1993; Voiskounsky, 2008). Of course, technology can affect us in many other ways as well. For example, theorists and researchers have identified the aspects of online communication that can result in our feeling closer to others whom we are interacting with online (see, for example, Walther's hyperpersonal model, 1996, 2007, which is discussed in more detail in Chapter 3). This may result in our disclosing our innermost thoughts in what might be unsuitably public settings. Others have identified the core psychological reasons why it is easier for people to be hostile or harassing online (see, for example, Suler, 2004; Lapidot-Lefler & Barak, 2012). These disruptive behaviours are evident through a variety of online actions, such as cyberbullying, trolling and flaming. A deeper understanding of these psychological principles can help us to advise Internet users of safer and more appropriate behaviour online – simply being aware of why we might engage in certain activities can often give us the tools we need to make wiser decisions regarding our online interactions. It can also provide us with the skills to manage such behaviours should we find ourselves on the receiving end of a hostile communication.

Much research in cyberpsychology also examines how we manage the impressions that others form of us based on our online personae, and the roles of anonymity and self-disclosure in this area (see, for example, Joinson *et al.*, 2010; Joinson *et al.*, 2007; Marder *et al.*, 2015). In some online fora (such as online gaming) we have the opportunity to create entirely new personas, even choosing to act as a different gender from our own if we wish. In others, such as **social networking sites**, we will normally adopt our own persona – we use our own name and photograph, and we will generally include our offline friends as our primary contacts. And so in these settings we do not tend to use pretence or change much about ourselves. However, we will tend to present ourselves in a more positive light than we normally would – we emphasise the good things that happen to us, and the exciting activities that we engage in, without focusing on the more mundane or negative aspects of our lives. As such, on social networking profiles our impression management is usually relatively minimal, but we still put a positive spin on our communications.

Another time when we might engage in very careful impression management is if we are considering seeking a romantic partner using an online dating application. While once these applications involved the completion of a relatively simple profile, as technology has advanced, these applications have become more complex in some cases (including the possibilities of multiple photographs, audio messages and many more). But in other cases the technology has simplified – smartphone dating applications often show a minimal profile along with a single image, and the user can decide whether or not they are interested in the individual with a simple swipe to the left or the right. While online dating has resulted in countless romantic relationships and marriages, there are many risks involved, and care must be taken (see Buchanan & Whitty, 2014 for a description of some of these risks).

The Internet has also become a rich territory for research in linguistics. While abbreviations and acronyms are not new, the frequency of use in modern times, and the rate at which new instances are noted, have resulted in these becoming a much more prevalent aspect of modern parlance. Similarly, the use of emoticons (or emoji /smileys) is of particular interest – the development of new methods of communicating emotion and mood when the primary methods by which these are normally communicated (facial expression and tone of voice) are absent (see, for example, Fullwood et al., 2013). The presence of an emoticon can completely change the meaning of a sentence, so their importance in modern linguistics must not be ignored.

Much research has also examined 'applied' cyberpsychology. This refers to any application of our online behaviours to other aspects of our daily lives. For example, emerging technologies allow us to stay in touch with our workplace, even when we cannot be there. Being geographically distant from our workplace no longer means that we cannot immediately respond to any matters that require our attention. Of course, there are negative aspects to this as well – we may feel pressure to respond to emails throughout the night, or at weekends, resulting in negative effects on our home and family lives, and in the long term, potentially negative effects on our health. That said, cyberpsychology can also have positive effects on our health – we now have access to more information on well-being, medicine and healthy living than ever before. This, coupled with support from others online who might be facing the same health problems as ourselves (see, for example, Sillence, 2013), can greatly enhance resilience and resources for an individual facing a worrying situation. Of course, seeking such support and information can also hold risks – such as distinguishing between useful and irrelevant (or even harmful) information, knowing who to trust with our personal details, and even unnecessary escalation of worry. Using insights from both psychology generally and cyberpsychology specifically can help users to make good decisions regarding their online behaviours, so that their online actions can be beneficial to them, while avoiding harmful consequences.

Another important aspect of online life is our increased tendency to use the Internet to purchase goods and services, or to manage our financial arrangements. Trust is particularly important in understanding consumer behaviour online. A thorough understanding of how and why we trust, and what features might cause us to lose trust, is essential in building a consumer base, and ensuring the continuance of online commerce. The affordances of technology also allow online retailers to provide each consumer with the modern equivalent of a personal shopper – artificially intelligent interfaces that compare your prior purchases and viewing behaviour to all those who have gone before you, and, using this information, suggesting the next product that you are likely to desire, even though you never knew of its existence. These personalised recommendations can result in increased revenue for the retailer, a more interesting experience for the consumer, and a healthier long-term prospect for economies.

The very nature of technology has also been harnessed by psychologists to improve well-being. We can see this in particular with regard to gaming – terms like serious games, gameful design and gamification all refer to methods by which game elements and gaming principles can be applied to help people and organisations to reach goals, while also adding some entertainment value. Many of these draw from other areas of psychology, such as positive psychology and learning theories. One of the key tasks in cyberpsychology is determining when our online behaviour is fundamentally similar to our offline behaviour (in which case, we can draw from the vast literature in psychology as a whole), but also determining when online behaviour differs significantly from our offline responses (in which case, new theories may need to be developed and new research conducted to fully understand the ways in which the technology has changed us).

Unfortunately, along with the good that technology brings, there are also negative aspects. Recently, the American Psychiatric Association (2013) updated their *Diagnostic and Statistical Manual* (DSM). In this most recent fifth edition, they include 'Internet gaming disorder' as a phenomenon which requires further research. Similar to other behavioural control problems, Internet gaming disorder is partially diagnosed based on the impact that the behaviour has on the individual's life (rather than the actual amount of hours spent playing games). So, if an individual plays video games to the extent that they experience tolerance and withdrawal, they relapse if they try to stop playing, they have pervasive thoughts about playing, or their playing impacts on their family, work or education, then it may be something that needs professional attention. It is not without a certain degree of irony that someone with such a problem can in fact seek help online – Internet-mediated therapy (sometimes called 'cybertherapy') is offered by an increasing number of practitioners. Such therapy offers advantages for both clients and therapists, including ease of access and increased confidentiality.

Another fear that has risen with the proliferation of our daily interactions with technology is cybercrime victimisation. There are many dangers online for all users, although understandably we pay particular attention to the Internet activity of children and adolescents who can be at particular risk for sexual exploitation (Quayle et al., 2014; Quayle & Ribisi, 2012; Quayle & Taylor, 2011). Cyberpsychology can provide insights into why some individuals who would never engage in criminal activity offline might be attracted to such behaviours online (Kirwan & Power, 2013). Researching this field can provide insights into the tactics used by offenders to ensnare their victims and the aspects of human behaviour which can make us more vulnerable to such attacks. Finally, we can also design educational programmes to help users to protect themselves and their loved ones against victimisation.

Part of such protection involves the consideration of the careful maintenance of our privacy. Much recent research in cyberpsychology examines how and why we share information with others (Joinson et al., 2011; Kirwan, in press; Paine et al., 2007; Vasalou et al., 2015). This becomes even more important as we carry an increasing amount of personal data with us in the form of mobile devices. These mobile devices may also result in our sharing information about ourselves unwittingly – such as our previous or current locations. The more that we use technology and share information about ourselves, the more we risk. However, the benefits in such sharing often outweigh the potential risks for many.

As mentioned, cyberpsychology examines technologies other than the World Wide Web. This includes common activities, such as gaming, and less common activities, such as the use of virtual reality, augmented reality and robotics. But use of these technologies is increasing as they become more affordable, and as larger companies take more of an interest in creating consumer-level versions. Also of interest in cyberpsychology is human behaviour when interacting with artificial intelligence, whether or not it is coupled with a robotic device. There is an increase in the use of artificially intelligent chatbots as a frontline in customer service, as well as understanding the potential use of artificially intelligent robots as caregivers and companions. Of course, we interact with some forms of artificial intelligence much more regularly, such as the artificial intelligence within certain websites, and that which controls non–player characters in games. While human interaction with robots is still at an early stage, it is the role of cyberpsychology research to determine how we can aid a transition into greater levels of interaction when necessary.

CYBERPSYCHOLOGY JOURNALS, CONFERENCES AND RESEARCH GROUPS

While cyberpsychology is a relatively new field, there are many resources available for students and scholars to further their knowledge of this important area.

Several journals focus primarily on cyberpsychology, or welcome papers with such a focus. These include: *Cyberpsychology, Behavior, and Social Networking* (previously *Cyberpsychology and Behavior*); *Computers in Human Behavior, Journal of Computer Mediated Communication; Behaviour & Information Technology; New Media & Society; Human Computer Interaction; Interacting with Computers; International Journal of Human-Computer Studies; Virtual Reality* and *Games for Health*.

Similarly, there are many academic conferences which focus on or include cyberpsychological research, including the Cyberpsychology, Cybertherapy & Social Networking Conference (organised by the International Association of Cyber-Psychology, Training & Rehabilitation – iACToR), the Social Networking in Cyberspace Conference (organised by the Cyberpsychology Research at the University of Wolverhampton research group) and the Internet Research Conference (organised by the Association of Internet Researchers).

There are also other excellent research groups internationally, such as the Oxford Internet Institute at the University of Oxford and the Research Centre for Virtual Environments and Behavior at the University of California Santa Barbara. Finally, if you would like to consider a structured academic programme within this area, there are various options, including the M.Sc. in Social Science of the Internet (at the Oxford Internet Institute) and the M.Sc. in Cyberpsychology (at the Institute of Art, Design and Technology in Ireland).

AIMS AND STRUCTURE OF THE BOOK

This book aims to provide readers with an introduction to the field of cyberpsychology, with a particular focus on applied aspects of the field. It is designed to encourage readers to critically evaluate the psychology of online interactions, and to develop appropriate research methodologies to complete their own research in this field. The book may be used as a core text for undergraduate modules in cyberpsychology or psychology of the Internet, and a fundamental reading for students of postgraduate programmes in cyberpsychology.

Each chapter of the book includes additional resources which may be useful for the reader, especially those who are using the book as part of a structured course. For example, activities are suggested that can help to illustrate the everyday applications of the content being covered. Additional readings are recommended for those who would like to know more about the content in each chapter, and definitions of keywords are provided within glossaries. Topics for discussion are also provided, and these can be used both online and offline. A variety of other resources are also available to instructors and students online.

The book comprises four main sections. The first section introduces the field, while the second examines human interactions online. The third section considers applications of cyberpsychology, while the final section considers psychology and technology. More information on each chapter is provided below.

Part 1: Introduction

The first section of the book comprises this introductory chapter, and a chapter by Dr Brendan Rooney describing the fundamentals of online behavioural research. It provides an introduction to behavioural research and reviews the main types of online research methodologies, such as experiments, self-report measures, interviews, focus groups and observational studies. The chapter also reflects on the main ethical considerations of online research.

Part 2: Human interactions online

The second section of the book concerns itself with the interactions between people online. Much cyberpsychological research draws from social psychological and cognitive psychological constructs, and so this section of the book often utilises similar topics to introduce the reader to many aspects of online life.

The second section commences with a chapter examining Computer Mediated Communication and online media. This chapter describes the history of online communication and the types of communication prevalent online, while also identifying the ways in which online communication is different to offline methods. It also demonstrates the applicability of communication theories to online interactions. Chapter 4, by Dr Irene Connolly, considers the self and identity in cyberspace. It introduces the main theories of the self-concept and personality and relates them to how we present ourselves online. It is designed to show how specific personality types use the Internet and how the Internet, especially social media, allows us to manage who we want to be online. It also focuses on impression management – our portrayal of ourselves to others online.

In Chapter 5, Hannah Barton examines the dark side of cyberspace, such as flaming, trolling, prejudice, stereotyping and harassment. Chapter 6 identifies how we are attracted to others online, and Nicola Fox Hamilton differentiates between how relationships are formed online and offline. Dr John Greaney then examines attention and distraction online, noting how recent technological developments have resulted in many individuals being in a relatively constant state of divided attention. He proposes ways in which users can overcome the difficulties that this may cause.

In Chapter 8, Dr Olivia Hurley considers the dynamics of groups online, comparing them to offline groups in terms of norms, group identity, group formation and group regulation, whereas Chapter 9 includes insights by Hannah Barton on social influence, persuasion and compliance online. The final chapter in this section considers privacy and trust online, why we sacrifice privacy in order to make other perceived gains and how we can improve our online security.

Part 3: Applied cyberpsychology

Applied psychology takes many forms, and this section identifies how each branch of applied psychology has importance in cyberpsychology. It starts by considering cybercrime, identifying different types of cybercrime, describing how forensic psychology differs from media portrayals of the area, and identifying how forensic psychology can aid our understanding of cybercriminals and their victims. In Chapter 12, Cliona Flood examines abnormal behaviour online, such as pathological Internet use. She also identifies how the Internet can be used as a therapeutic tool. Dr Olivia Hurley then examines the applications of sport psychology and health psychology in technological developments, including the influence of social media and health-promoting applications. In Chapter 14, Cliona Flood considers the modern workplace and the challenges that emerging technologies pose to organisations, including constant connectedness, work–life balance, telecommuting and organisational design.

The Internet has also changed the way that we study, teach and learn, and Dr Marion Palmer investigates this in Chapter 15. She considers both formal and informal learning, and recent developments such as Massive Open Online Courses (MOOCs). Chapter 16 considers consumer cyberpsychology, with Nicola Fox Hamilton evaluating the roles of trust and credibility in online transactions, and providing guidelines for advertising and marketing online. In the final chapter of Part 3, Dr Irene Connolly writes about young people online, particularly examining aspects of development and the risk of cyberbullying.

Part 4: Psychology and technology

This final section of the book examines the application of psychology to technologies other than the World Wide Web. It commences with a chapter by Dr Andrew Errity describing the history and current state of the field of Human–Computer Interaction. In Chapter 19, Dr Errity is joined by Dr Brendan Rooney and Conall Tunney in writing about the psychology of online gaming, which has diversified in terms of platforms and goals. They consider the impact of increased realism of graphics, the phenomenon of gamification, and the identification of Internet Gaming Disorder within the DSM-5.

Chapter 20 describes the psychological applications of virtual reality. There are a wide variety of virtual reality technologies currently available, and these are increasingly being aimed at the consumer market. The potential for such technologies in psychological treatments has been explored for many years, particularly as a component in the treatment of anxiety disorders. The final chapter examines the psychology of artificial intelligence, with particular focus on the potential for artificially intelligent robotic devices to be used as companions.

CONCLUSION

Cyberpsychology as a topic of research is expanding at an extraordinary rate, and it is not difficult to see why – more and more of our daily activities are being conducted in online environments and we cannot help but be influenced by the medium. Cyberpsychology researchers have a crucial role to play in understanding our behaviours, and determining how best to design technologies and information strategies to ensure that users can make the best possible use of such developments. The remainder of the book considers each of the points in this chapter in more detail, particularly with regard to the World Wide Web, but also other technologies such as online gaming, virtual reality and artificial intelligence.

ACTIVITY

Keep a diary of your use of Internet technologies for one week. What websites do you visit, what social media do you use, what other communication technologies do you employ? If possible, try to keep a log of how long you spend on each activity, and what the goal of each activity was. Try to determine how you would achieve these goals if Internet technologies didn't exist. How were similar goals achieved before the Internet was invented?

DISCUSSION QUESTIONS

1 When do you think cyberpsychology first became important as a field of study?
2 Are human behaviours online different to those offline? If there are differences, what are they, and why do you think they occur?
3 Should Internet Gaming Disorder have been included in the DSM 5? Why or why not?
4 Are there any technologies not listed in the chapter that should be considered by cyberpsychology? What are they?

RECOMMENDED READING LIST

Many of the chapter authors who contributed to the current book also contributed to a thematic reader which provides examples of research projects conducted across the field of cyberpsychology.

> Power, A. & Kirwan, G. (eds) (2014). *Cyberpsychology and New Media: A Thematic Reader*. Hove / New York: Psychology Press.

Sonia Livingstone's *Children and the Internet* identifies how children use Internet technologies considering important topics such as literacy, privacy and civic participation.

> Livingstone. S. (2009). *Children and the Internet*. Cambridge: Polity Press.

While now a little dated, the *Oxford Handbook of Internet Psychology* still provides an excellent overview of the breadth of Internet psychology and the difficulties inherent in Internet research.

> Joinson, A., McKenna, K., Postmes, T. & Reips, U.-D. (2007). *The Oxford Handbook of Internet Psychology*. Oxford: Oxford University Press.

Aleks Krotoski provides a very readable taster for cyberpsychological research and topics in her 2013 book, where she considers many aspects of online behaviour, from medical information seeking to memes.

> Krotoski, A. (2013). *Untangling the Web: What the Internet is Doing to You*. London: Faber & Faber.

GLOSSARY

Artificial intelligence   The creation of intelligent machines and computer systems.
Augmented reality (AR)   The visual portrayal of virtual objects over real world displays using technologies such as cameras and screens.
Cyberpsychology   The branch of psychology that examines how we interact with others using technology, how our behaviour is influenced by technology, how technology can be developed to best suit our needs, and how our psychological states can be affected by technologies.
Gaming   The use of video games online or offline.
Human–Computer Interaction   Refers to the field that studies the design and testing of interactive computer systems that exist at the point where humans and computers meet.
Mobile computing   The use of smartphones, tablets, laptops and other mobile devices as computers.
Social media   Websites, applications and online social networks which individuals use to make contact with others and to communicate and share information online.
Social networking   The use of social media.

Social networking sites See 'social media'.

Virtual reality The use of computer technologies to create three-dimensional virtual worlds or objects which users can interact with.

REFERENCES

American Psychiatric Association. (2013). *Diagnostic and Statistical Manual of Mental Disorders* (5th edn). Washington, DC: Author.

Buchanan, T. & Whitty, M.T. (2014). The online dating romance scam: Causes and consequences of victimhood. *Psychology, Crime & Law, 20*(3), 261–283.

Csikszentmihalyi, M. (1990). *Flow: The Psychology of Optimal Performance.* New York: Cambridge University Press.

Fullwood, C., Orchard, L. & Floyd, S. (2013). Emoticon convergence in Internet chat rooms. *Social Semiotics, 23*(5), 648–662.

Joinson, A.N., Houghton, D.J., Vasalou, A. & Marder, B.L. (2011). Digital crowding: Privacy, self-disclosure, and technology. In S. Trepte and L. Reinecke (eds) *Privacy Online: Perspectives on Privacy and Self-disclosure in the Social Web.* New York: Springer.

Joinson, A.N., Reips, U.-D., Buchanan, T. & Paine Schofield , C.B. (2010). Privacy, trust, and self-disclosure online. *Human-Computer Interaction, 25(1),* 1–24.

Joinson, A.N., Woodley, A. & Reips, U.-D. (2007). Personalisation, authentication and self-disclosure in self-administered internet surveys. *Computers in Human Behavior, 23*(1), 275–285.

Kirwan, G. (2015). Psychology and security: Utilising psychological and communication theories to promote safer cloud security behaviours. In R. Ko and K-K.R. Choo (eds) *The Cloud Security Ecosystem: Technical, Legal, Business and Management Issues* (pp. 269–281). Waltham, MA: Syngress.

Kirwan, G. & Power, A. (2013). *Cybercrime: The Psychology of Online Offenders.* Cambridge: Cambridge University Press.

Lapidot-Lefler, N. & Barak, A. (2012). Effects of anonymity, invisibility and lack of eye-contact on toxic online disinhibition. *Computers in Human Behavior, 28*(2), 434–443.

Marder, B., Joinson, A., Shankar, A. & Archer-Brown, C. (2015). Any user can be any self that they want so long as it is what they 'ought' to be: Exploring self-presentation in the presence of multiple audiences on social network sites. In L. Robinson Jr (ed.) *Marketing Dynamism & Sustainability: Things Change, Things Stay the Same . . .: Proceedings of the 2012 Academy of Marketing Science (AMS) Annual Conference* (pp. 621–626). New York: Springer.

Paine, C., Reips, U.-D., Stieger, S., Joinson, A. & Buchanan, T. (2007). Internet users' perceptions of 'privacy concerns' and 'privacy actions'. *International Journal of Human–Computer Studies, 65*(6), 526–536.

Quayle, E., Allegro, A., Hutton, L, Sheath, M. & Lööf, L. (2014). Rapid skill acquisition and online sexual grooming of children. *Computers in Human Behavior, 39,* 368–375.

Quayle, E. & Ribisi, K.M (2012). *Understanding and Preventing Online Sexual Exploitation of Children.* New York: Routledge.

Quayle, E. & Taylor, M. (2011). Social networking as a nexus for engagement and exploitation of young people. *Information Security Technical Report, 16(2)*, 44–50.

Sillence, E. (2013). Giving and receiving peer advice in an online breast cancer support group. *Cyberpsychology, Behavior, and Social Networking, 16*(6), 480–485.

Suler, J. (2004). The online disinhibition effect. *CyberPsychology & Behavior, 7*(3), 321–326.

Vasalou, A., Joinson, A.N. & Houghton, D. (2015). Privacy as a fuzzy concept: A new conceptualization of privacy for practitioners. *Journal of the American Society for Information Science and Technology, 66*(5), 918–929.

Voiskounsky, A. (2008). Flow experience in cyberspace: Current studies and perspectives. In A. Barak (ed.) *Psychological Aspects of Cyberspace: Theory, Research, Applications* (pp. 70–101). New York: Cambridge University Press.

Walther, J.B. (1996). Computer Mediated Communication: Impersonal, interpersonal and hyperpersonal interaction. *Communication Research, 23*, 3–43.

Walther, J.B. (2007). Selective self-presentation in Computer Mediated Communication: Hyperpersonal dimensions of technology, language and cognition. *Computers in Human Behaviour, 23*, 2538–2557.

Webster, J., Trevino, L.K. & Ryan, L. (1993). The dimensionality and correlates of flow in human–computer interactions. *Computers in Human Behaviour, 9*, 411–426.

2 Conducting online research

Brendan Rooney

CHAPTER OVERVIEW

The chapter will begin by briefly considering the key characteristics of good research. Next, this chapter will review the main types of online research methods (online observational studies, online interviews and focus groups, Web experiments, and online questionnaires and surveys) and provide key considerations for researchers seeking to choose an online method. Finally, the chapter will consider how the main ethical issues that apply when collecting data online can (and must) be considered.

KEY TERMS

The **research population** is the entire group of people (or animals or other things), with the characteristic(s) a researcher wishes to explore; the whole group of interest. The **research sample** is a subset of the population, from which the researcher can collect data so as to make claims about the population.

INTRODUCTION: GOOD RESEARCH

Research is the systematic process of collecting and analysing information in an effort to make a contribution to knowledge on a particular phenomenon; it is looking for an answer to a research question. It typically involves (a) considering what is currently known about a topic and articulating a specific question about it, (b) designing a way to collect information, (c) executing the information-finding strategy, (d) analysing the findings, and (e) communicating the results so as to make a contribution to knowledge.

The important thing to remember about research is that any or all outcomes (from good research) constitute a contribution to knowledge and can be equally valuable to discovery. Research students can often feel like their research project needs to produce a specific outcome, such as a significant difference between groups, in order for it to be worthwhile. This is not the case. Sometimes very bad research can produce seemingly novel and exciting findings, but it is still bad research. So how do we know what makes research good or bad? If we don't evaluate research by its findings, then how might we evaluate research?

All good research builds upon what has come before and aims to pave the way for more research. Any single research project is conducted in the context of many other questions and studies. It is part of a bigger process; part of a community of knowledge making. To evaluate research, reviewers should scrutinise the *claims* that are being made about the phenomenon in question and whether or not there is sufficient basis for these claims. In short, producing good research requires careful consideration and design.

THE INTERNET AND RESEARCH

Throughout history various developments in society and technology have afforded researchers the opportunity to conduct better quality research in line with the characteristics described above. One of the most influential developments was the rise of the Internet. Since the start of the millennium, Internet use has seen a 741 per cent increase to over 3 billion Internet users (over 42 per cent of the world's population) by 30 June 2014 (InternetWorldStats.com, 2015). This exponential penetration of the Internet into daily life has revolutionised the way in which research is conducted. This chapter explores this revolution and considers some of the associated issues for researchers wishing to collect data online.

SECONDARY RESEARCH ONLINE

Using the Internet researchers can more easily communicate with each other, collaborate in teams and coordinate their research activities. This efficient communication can facilitate multidisciplinary and international collaborations on bigger research projects using larger skill sets and greater expertise. Researchers can also more successfully and efficiently disseminate their work using online journals, interactive websites, and social and e-learning media. In turn, researchers can search and access this existing body of published work much more efficiently than before using the Internet. When a researcher collects, reviews or synthesises existing research, when they assimilate and evaluate previous theory and findings, it is referred to as **secondary research**. High quality research is built upon a systematic and thorough review of what has been done before and the Internet allows researchers to conduct this secondary research at an enormous rate using search engines and specialist databases. (See the activity section of this chapter for some advice on conducting your own online literature search.)

When researchers conduct and report a formal structured and transparent review of the literature in a particular area, it is referred to as a systematic review. A systematic review attempts to collate and analyse the findings from an entire set of research studies that fit a particular criteria (e.g. all studies exploring workplace cyberbullying, conducted in the past 10 years). By including multiple studies from different research groups, while minimising bias, systematic reviews can present a more reliable picture of the current findings and knowledge of a particular topic (Green *et al.*, 2011). By using predefined search and inclusion criteria, the systematic reviews can be replicated by other researchers and thus are available for scrutiny and peer review (one of the most important quality control checks for research). In many cases, systematic reviews can also use statistical techniques, referred to as meta-analysis, so as to combine data from multiple studies and provide more precise estimates of the size of statistical effects than individual studies (Glass, 1976). For these reasons, systematic reviews make powerful and important contributions to our understanding of phenomena. Thus, using the Internet, researchers can access and synthesise previous research but importantly, they can do so using a quantifiable and transparent system that can then be disseminated widely.

PRIMARY RESEARCH ONLINE

In addition to allowing researchers to access previous research more efficiently, it also allows them to collect their own data for new research (referred to as **primary research**) more efficiently. As mentioned earlier, so much of modern human life is lived online. People use smart phone apps to take pictures, navigate cities and monitor daily food intake or physical activity. They use the Internet to socialise and date, to study, bank and shop. High quality rich quantifiable data about all these activities can be accessed by researchers and explored. Thus, researchers can efficiently access immeasurable amounts of information about human communication, behaviour and social interactions, by observing them directly as they happen.

Observation

While some form of observation is present in all research, here 'observation' refers to a method by which researchers can collect data about participants' behaviour as they naturally go about or live through particular experiences. These methods have also been referred to as '**Non-Reactive Data Collection**' (NRDC; Janetzko, 2008) because typically, it is the participants' normal behaviour that is observed in an unobtrusive or non-invasive fashion, rather than their response to questions or their performance in a specifically designed task.

There are so many ways in which researchers can observe human behaviour online. Every time you log in to a social network, you can see people talking to each other, things they shared or liked, places they visited. This information can be collected by researchers and analysed. These sorts of behaviours are supplemented with all sorts of 'site stats' and summaries that websites display as integrated features. For example, websites such as Facebook display the number of people who have 'liked' something and the number of 'friends' someone has, while other sites might display the number of times a page was visited or the number of times a video was watched. Further to this, there are various websites, such as Akamai.com that monitor Internet use and provide publically available real-time statistics about Internet traffic (see www.akamai.com/html/technology/dataviz1.html). All of this information can be recorded and analysed for research in online observation studies.

The use of observation and NRDC studies is characterised by its directness – that is, they allow for direct observation of how people are behaving online. This means that people's reactions to events can be observed as they occur and in some cases rare behaviours can be documented. For example, in 2004, Michael Cohn and colleagues reported the results of a study that used the contents of over a thousand US citizens' online journal entries surrounding the September 11 New York terrorist attack in 2001 (Cohn et al., 2004). Specifically, they were able to use linguistic analysis to describe people's psychological experiences with unprecedented precision. This directness of NRDCs is most characteristic when the researchers are hidden, when participants never know they are being observed. However, it is important to note that this sort of research comes with ethical dilemmas and, as discussed later, researchers need to give careful consideration to the implications of the way in which they collect data.

Thus, the increased human presence and activity online has facilitated researchers in their efforts to directly observe human behaviour. But it has also facilitated the recruiting of people to participate in research that uses more explicit forms of data collection – that is, research where participants are engaging in activities that have been designed so as to collect data, such as research interviews, questionnaires and experiments.

Interviews, questionnaires and experiments

Interviews are one of the most flexible tools available to researchers, but when used for research, it is important that they are conducted using a predefined or systematic approach. Research interviews can vary along a spectrum from extremely structured interviews that follow a strict inflexible schedule, perhaps with closed-response questions (where responses have been predefined), to extremely unstructured discussions that allow for any topic to be discussed in any way. Typically, in order to allow the researcher to efficiently probe a specific topic, while allowing for unanticipated responses, researchers will carefully design and use an interview schedule that guides the agenda of the discussion. Usually interviews are conducted by a researcher with an individual participant and offer researchers a way to collect rich quality data with in–depth information about a topic. A variant of the interview method conducted with small groups of people has become a useful research tool. These **focus groups** allow the researcher to conveniently collect data from more than one person at a time and they allow for the examination of group interaction.

Another way to ask questions in research is by using a survey or questionnaire. **Questionnaires** are one of the most commonly used methods for data collection (Berends, 2006), and this is also true online where increasingly researchers are using online surveys and questionnaires (T. Buchanan, 2007; Gosling et al., 2004). Questionnaires allow researchers to collect rich data similar to the interview technique, but can also be used to identify quantified patterns and relationships that emerge in the data. If researchers want to make claims that go beyond patterns and relationships, if they want to test causal hypotheses and explore the *influences* or *causes* of events, thoughts or behaviour, then they often collect data using an **experiment**. Experiments allow researchers to hold many variables constant while manipulating only one or two factors, thus allowing the researcher to identify the role of various possible causes. By conducting experiments and questionnaires online, all sorts of things from questions or stimuli to execution of the design and testing can be precisely constructed, manipulated, automated and delivered to large numbers of participants all over the world.

Considerations for online data collection

The characteristic features of the Internet that have redefined the way people communicate are the very same features that have supported online researchers in their ability to collect data online. Online methods provide several advantages over traditional delivery. Executing research online can be faster and cheaper than traditional offline methods (Bandilla *et al.*, 2003; T. Buchanan & Smith, 1999; Cantrell & Lupinacci, 2007; Dillman, 2000; Gosling *et al.*, 2004; Kwak & Radler, 2002). Furthermore, using online research methods like these can give a researcher greater control of the design, greater flexibility and functionality (Bandilla *et al.*, 2003; Boyer *et al.*, 2002; Kwak & Radler, 2002). Researchers can conduct interviews with participants using video calls (such as Skype) or they might decide to conduct an interview through text by exchanging email messages. Thus, participating in an online study can be a more comfortable experience (e.g. Naus *et al.*, 2009). The increased comfort and convenience can help participants feel trusting of the research, which in turn encourages them to answer questions around sensitive topics (Tourangeau, 2004), to disclose more information about themselves (Weisband & Kiesler, 1996) and respond with reduced social desirability (Frick *et al.*, 2001; Joinson, 1999). (See Reips (2000) for further discussion of the benefits of using online methods.)

Online research methods provide researchers with the opportunity to access large samples of participants which can in turn increase the statistical power of the research (T. Buchanan & Smith, 1999; Cantrell & Lupinacci, 2007; Gosling *et al.*, 2004). In addition to large samples, the Internet provides an opportunity for researchers to access diverse or difficult-to-reach populations, giving a voice to some previously under-represented populations. Some research even suggests that conducting interviews and discussions online (referred to as Computer Mediated Communication or CMC) is superior to face-to-face communication (Jonassen *et al.*, 1999; G. G. Smith *et al.*, 2011). However, other researchers criticise the lack of context and non-verbal cues in CMC (Liu, 2002; Rovai, 2000). Importantly, these strengths and weaknesses vary depending on whether the CMC is synchronous (e.g. video chat, instant messaging) or asynchronous (e.g. email, SMS) (Abrams *et al.*, 2014) and whether it is an audio–visual display (e.g. talking face display) or text-based (Walker *et al.*, 1994). This point highlights that despite apparent benefits, online research methods also have some characteristic challenges that require consideration and attention if they are to be used successfully. Without such careful consideration issues might arise in terms of the quality of the data that is collected using online methods.

One major criticism of online research concerns the quality of the data collected and whether or not it is equivalent to data collected offline. Some researchers have reported that online questionnaires produced different responses to their offline counterparts (Gosling *et al.*, 2004) and even different psychometric properties (T. Buchanan, 2002). While others have argued, based on early studies, that online methods are generally valid (Krantz *et al.*, 1997; Krantz & Dalal, 2000) and sometimes generate higher quality data than offline studies (Birnbaum, 2001). A potential threat to the quality of the data in online research is 'drop-out' – that is, when a participant decides to abandon the research before it has been completed. Drop-out can be particularly problematic if it is systematic – that is, if it does not occur randomly, but rather it affects certain conditions or groups unequally. If so, then it might distort comparisons or bias inferences that come from the data. In one early study, Musch and Reips (2000) reported that, on average, Internet experiments are subject to an average drop-out rate of about 34 per cent, but for individual studies drop-out might range anywhere from 87 per cent to as low as 1 per cent. They argue that researchers can reduce drop-out dramatically within this range by giving careful consideration to the design of the study. Researchers have suggested various techniques for reducing drop-out that may suit various research projects such as using rewards or incentives for completion (Frick et al., 2001; Musch & Reips, 2000). For further suggestions on how to improve design of Web experiments and questionnaires, see Lumsden and Morgan (2005) and Reips (2002).

Related to the issue of drop-out, self-selection to participate has also been discussed as a potential threat to the quality of online data. This is because the group of people who decide to participate (called the research sample) might not be very representative of the group of people we want to study (the research population). This problem is not unique to online research, but what is unique is the magnitude to which this issue can be escalated online, due to typically large samples recruited. Whereas in offline research, increasing the sample size typically improves the quality of the data, issues such as self-selection challenge this assumption with online research (Bethlehem, 2010; Lumsden & Morgan, 2005).

The issue of self-selection draws attention to the need for researchers to consider their recruitment procedures. Various researchers have compared online with traditional recruitment procedures and present mixed findings about their equivalency (e.g. T. Buchanan & Smith, 1999; Cole et al., 2006; Davis, 1999; Hewson & Charlton, 2005; Lewis et al., 2009; McDonald & Adam, 2003; M. A. Smith & Leigh, 1997; Stanton, 1998; Whittier et al., 2004) demonstrating that failure to consider important design issues can lead to problems with the quality of the data collected. In the case of recruitment procedures, a particular problem is the occurrence of what Dillman (2000) refers to as 'coverage errors', which are errors that result from a biased or unrepresentative sample. In the past many have argued that online recruitment is problematic, as it excludes those who do not have Internet access (e.g. Bethlehem, 2010). However, more recently various user analyses have shown that, in developed economies such as Western Europe and the USA, the population of Internet users are very similar to the general population in all surveyed characteristics (e.g. Internet Society, 2014; Pew Research, 2014). The pace at which the online population profile is converging with the offline population may serve as an important advantage of Internet research over offline methods. However, it is important to note, as mentioned above, that just because a normal population are using the Internet does not means that the sample derived from an online study is representative and free from bias.

Finally, there has been much discussion and concern raised about the varied setting in which people participate in online research (e.g. T. Buchanan & Smith, 1999; Fouladi et al., 2002; Heath et al., 2007; Hewson & Charlton, 2005; Lewis et al., 2009; Nosek et al., 2002; Whittier et al., 2004). Some people might participate in research while watching TV or talking on the phone, while others might be more seriously attentive and considerate of their responses. As with drop-out and many other potential problems in research design, the varied research setting is particularly problematic if it systematically differs between conditions or groups of people. Otherwise, the potential problems with this issue might be regulated using carefully worded instructions, by asking participants to provide a note about the context in which they participated so that it can be reported or by recruiting a large sample (to balance or average out the issue).

Overall, it appears as though conducting research online brings advantages that balance out the scientific and practical disadvantages. Converging evidence shows that online research methods result in qualitatively comparable findings to traditional research methods (Cole *et al.*, 2006; Deutskens *et al.*, 2006; Krantz & Dalal, 2000; Luce *et al.*, 2007; Smither *et al.*, 2004; Weigold *et al.*, 2013) and where differences in online and offline are found, there is often an obvious explanation in the way in which the study was designed or the sample were recruited. For this reason, it is important to remember that while the Internet can become an increasingly more efficient choice of research context, careful design is still, if not more, important.

INTERNET RESEARCH ETHICS

As the Internet became more popular for data collection, ethicists and researchers attempted to apply traditional offline research ethics protocols to online research. However, the Internet has some particular features that have presented researchers with unique ethical dilemmas. For example, Bakardjieva and Feenberg (2001) point out that the way in which online electronic records of discussions are freely accessible constitutes an unprecedented ethical problem for researchers. When data is openly accessible to all online, its use in any and all research might be seen as acceptable. Yet for a number of reasons, researchers cannot rest on this assumption without fear of breaching ethical principles. King (1996) presents an illustrative case of a researcher who publishes research based on the discussions of an online support group, and when the members of the group learn of the way their discussions were used, they discontinue participation in the group and the support group dissolves. Bakardjieva and Feenberg (2001) also discuss research that uses people's online stories and communications. They argue that, what is even worse than invasions of privacy, is that such research *alienates* people and objectifies their lives in a way that is unethical. They go on to argue that this is particularly unjust as 'cyberspace provides unique opportunities for empowering subjects [participants] by involving them as *contributors* in the research project' (p. 233). Conducting research online has also raised important discussions about ethical dissemination and children's rights to online protection (for a more in-depth discussion of online ethical issues and guidelines for researchers, see E. A. Buchanan & Zimmer, 2013; Social Sciences and Humanities Research Ethics Special Working Committee, 2008; and the additional resources for this chapter). As the Internet, technology and society evolves, so too do the issues surrounding Internet research ethics and researchers therefore need to stay continuously sensitive, considerate and informed about current debates and best practice.

CONCLUSION

Technological developments continue to shape the Internet and society, and the ways in which they are shaping research needs to be seen as a dynamic process that requires continuous reconsideration. While much of the research exploring features of online data collection methods suggest that the advantages outweigh the challenges, researchers need to give careful consideration to the way in which they use the Internet and design online research if they are to obtain high quality data from appropriate samples of individuals. In addition, the use of online research methods requires additional ethical considerations if the principles of ethical research are to be maintained. While conducting research online brings issues that are unique, two trends are worth noting. First, because the Internet provides researchers with increasing efficiency of data collection and researchers are improving their online data collection skills, Internet research is becoming more and more commonplace (Reips, 2008; Denissen *et al.*, 2010). Second, as the Internet develops, many features of the offline and online worlds are converging. For example, research has demonstrated that users of online virtual worlds operate under the same non-verbal social norms (such as eye-gaze and personal space) that exist offline (Yee *et al.*, 2007). For both of these reasons, the particular features of Internet research may soon be indistinguishable as unique from 'traditional' offline research.

ACTIVITY

The capacity to access previous research online is one of the main ways in which the Internet has revolutionised research. Indeed, the amount of research literature online can be overwhelming and for this reason it is important to filter and select the relevant and credible information from the rest. When conducting a review of the current literature it is important to plan your approach.

Try to conduct an online search of the literature on a particular topic of interest. Start by articulating the main keywords for your topic (e.g. 'mobile phone' and 'addiction'). As part of your plan, consider alternative terms or cultural variants of keywords (e.g. 'cell phone', 'dependency', 'obsession', 'nomophobia'). Your plan might start with a broad search by superficially scanning a large number of potentially relevant findings. After this, you can narrow the search to a more manageable number of highly relevant articles. To get a broad sense of an area, course syllabi (can be searched online) or websites such as Wikipedia can offer helpful situational context. For more detailed information, the use of up-to-date review articles on a topic or special issues of relevant journals can be particularly helpful. Many databases also feature particular tools to support your search such as Boolean operators (i.e. combining keywords together with words such as 'AND' or 'OR').

DISCUSSION QUESTIONS

1 Can you think of any other advantages or disadvantages to conducting research online?
2 Do you think the Internet provides greater advantage to observation studies or other types such as questionnaires and experiments?
3 Are there certain types of topics that are better suited to online research than offline research?
4 Discuss the idea that, if someone posts something online, and it is publically accessible to everyone, then researchers should be allowed use it for their research.

RECOMMENDED READING LIST

This article gives an overview of how the Internet has had an impact on society, science and cyberpsychology in particular. It also includes a comprehensive discussion of various issues and recommendations for researchers.

Denissen, J. J. A, Neumann, L. & van Zalk, M. (2010). How the Internet is changing the implementation of traditional research methods, people's daily lives, and the way in which developmental scientists conduct research. *International Journal of Behavioral Development, 34*(6), 564–575.

Ulf-Dietrich Reips has published extensively on the nature of online research methods. In this book chapter he gives an overview of some of the ways in which online research has changed science.

Reips, U.-D. (2008). How Internet-mediated research changes science. In A. Barak (ed.), *Psychological Aspects of Cyberspace: Theory, Research, Applications* (pp. 268–294). Cambridge: Cambridge University Press.

This paper gives useful practical tips about designing online research.

Reips, U.-D. (2002). Internet-based psychological experimenting: Five dos and five don'ts. *Social Science Computer Review, 20*(3), 241–249.

These guidelines published by the British Psychological Society provide an excellent overview of some of the main ethical issues surrounding online research.

British Psychological Society (2013). Ethics Guidelines for Internet-mediated Research. INF206/1.2013. Leicester: Author. Available from: www.bps.org.uk/system/files/Public%20files/inf206-guidelines-for-internet-mediated-research.pdf.

GLOSSARY

Experiment   A research situation or activity that has been specifically designed and controlled so as to allow researchers to establish causal inference – i.e. the role of some condition or characteristic in causing some outcome.

Focus groups   A variant of the interview method conducted with small groups of people that allows for discussion to answer the interviewer's questions.

Interviews   A method of data collection where questions are asked by the interviewer so as to collect information from the interviewee.

Non-Reactive Data Collection (NRDC)   When the researcher collects data using an unobtrusive observation method.

Primary research   When the researcher collects original data, specifically for their research project.

Questionnaire   A series of predefined questions or other statements distributed so as to collect information from respondents.

Research   The systematic process of collecting and analysing information in an effort to make a contribution to knowledge of a particular phenomenon.

Research population   The entire group of people (or animals or other things), with the characteristic(s) a researcher wishes to explore; the whole group of interest.

Research sample   A subset of the population, from which the researcher can collect data so as to make claims about the population.

Secondary research   When the researcher collects, reviews or synthesises existing research.

REFERENCES

Abrams, K., Wang, Z., Song, Y. J. & Gonzalez-Galindo, S. (2014). Data richness tradeoffs between face-to-face, online audio-visual, and online text-only focus groups. *Social Science Computer Review, 33*(1).

Bakardjieva, M. & Feenberg, A. (2001). Involving the virtual subject. *Ethics and Information Technology, 2*(4), 233–240.

Bandilla, W., Bosnjak, M. & Altdorfer, P. (2003). Survey administration effects? A comparison of Web-based and traditional written self administered surveys using the ISSP environment module. *Social Science Computer Review, 21*, 235–243.

Berends, M. (2006). Survey methods in educational research. In J. L. Green, G. Camilli & P. B. Elmore (eds), *Handbook of Complementary Methods in Education Research* (pp. 623–640). Mahwah, NJ: Erlbaum.

Bethlehem, J. (2010). Selection bias in web surveys. *International Statistical Review, 78*, 161–188.

Birnbaum, M. H. (2001). A web-based program of research on decision making. In U.-D. Reips & M. Bosnjak (eds), *Dimensions of Internet Science* (pp. 23–55). Lengerich, Germany: Pabst.

Boyer, K. K., Olson, J. R., Calantone, R. J. & Jackson, E. C. (2002). Print versus electronic surveys: A comparison of two data collection methodologies. *Journal of Operations Management, 20*, 357–373.

Buchanan, E. A. & Zimmer, M. (2013). Internet research ethics. In E. N. Zalta (ed.), *The Stanford Encyclopedia of Philosophy* (vol. Fall 2013 edition).

Buchanan, T. (2002). Online assessment: Desirable or dangerous? *Professional Psychology: Research and Practice, 33*, 148–154.

Buchanan, T. (2007). Personality testing on the Internet: What we know, and what we do not. In A. Joinson, K. McKenna, T. Postmes & U.-D. Reips (eds), *Oxford Handbook of Internet Psychology* (pp. 447–459). Oxford: Oxford University Press.

Buchanan, T. & Smith, J. L. (1999). Using the Internet for psychological research: Personality testing on the World Wide Web. *British Journal of Psychology, 90*, 125–144.

Buchanan, T., Ali, T., Heffernan, T. M., Ling, J., Parrott, A. C., Rodgers, J. & Scholey, A. B. (2005). Nonequivalence of on-line and paper-and-pencil psychological tests: The case of the prospective memory questionnaire. *Behavior Research Methods, 37*, 148–154.

Cantrell, M. A. & Lupinacci, P. (2007). Methodological issues in online data collection. *Journal of Advanced Nursing, 60*, 544–549.

Cohn, M. A., Mehl, M. R. & Pennebaker, J. W. (2004). Linguistic markers of psychological change surrounding September 11, 2001. *Psychological Science, 15*, 687–693.

Cole, M. S., Bedeian, A. G. & Feild, H. S. (2006). The measurement equivalence of web-based and paper-and-pencil measures of transformational leadership: A multinational test. *Organizational Research Methods, 9*, 339–368.

Davis, R. N. (1999). Web-based administration of a personality questionnaire: Comparison with traditional methods. *Behavior Research Methods, Instruments & Computers, 31*, 572–577.

Denissen, J. J. A., Neumann, L. & van Zalk, M. (2010). How the internet is changing the implementation of traditional research methods, people's daily lives, and the way in which developmental scientists conduct research. *International Journal of Behavioral Development, 34*(6), 564–575.

Deutskens, E., de Ruyter, K. & Wetzels, M. (2006). An assessment of equivalence between online and mail surveys in service research. *Journal of Service Research, 8*, 346–355.

Dillman, D. A. (2000). *Mail and Internet Surveys: The Tailored Design Method*. New York: Wiley & Sons.

Fouladi, R. T., McCarthy, C. J. & Moller, N. P. (2002). Paper-and-pencil or online? Evaluating mode effects on measures of emotional functioning and attachment. *Assessment, 9*, 204–215.

Frick, A., Bächtiger, M. T. & Reips, U.-D. (2001). Financial incentives, personal information and drop-out in online studies. In U.-D. Reips & M. Bosnjak (eds), *Dimensions of Internet Science* (pp. 209–219). Lengerich: Pabst.

Glass, G. V. (1976). Primary, secondary and meta-analysis of research. *Educational Researcher, 5*, 3–8.

Gosling, S. D., Vazire, S., Srivastava, S. & John, O. P. (2004). Should we trust Web-based studies? A comparative analysis of six preconceptions about Internet questionnaires. *American Psychologist, 59*, 93–104.

Green, S., Higgins, J. P., Alderson, P., Clarke, M., Mulrow, C. D. & Oxman, A. D. (2011). What is a systematic review? In J. P. T. Higgins & S. Green (eds), *Cochrane Handbook for Systematic Reviews of Interventions Version 5.1.0, Section 1.2.2.*: The Cochrane Collaboration.

Heath, N. M., Lawyer, S. R. & Rasmussen, E. B. (2007). Web-based versus paper-and-pencil course evaluations. *Teaching of Psychology, 34*, 259–261.

Hewson, C. & Charlton, J. P. (2005). Measuring health beliefs on the Internet: A comparison of paper and Internet administrations of the Multidimensional Health Locus of Control Scale. *Behavior Research Methods, 37*, 691–702.

Internet Society (2014). Global Internet User Survey 2014. Retrieved from: www.internet society.org/sites/default/files/Global_Internet_Report_2014_0.pdf.

InternetWorldStats.com (2015). Internet Usage and World Population Statistics for June 30, 2014. Retrieved from: www.internetworldstats.com/stats.htm.

Janetzko, D. (2008). Nonreactive Data Collection on the Internet. In N. Fielding, R. M. Lee & G. Blank (eds), *The SAGE Handbook of Online Research Methods* (pp. 161–174). London: SAGE Publications.

Joinson, A. (1999). Social desirability, anonymity, and Internet-based questionnaires. *Behavior Research Methods, Instruments & Computers, 31*, 433–438.

Jonassen, D., Prevish, T., Christy, D. & Stavulaki, E. (1999). Learning to solve problems on the Web: Aggregate planning in a business management course. *Distance Education, 20*(1), 49–63.

King, S. (1996). Researching Internet communities: Proposed ethical guidelines for the reporting of results. *The Information Society, 12*(2), 119.

Krantz, J. H., Ballard, J. & Scher, J. (1997). Comparing the results of laboratory and World-Wide Web samples on the determinants of female attractiveness. *Behavior Research Methods, Instruments, & Computers, 29*, 264–269.

Krantz, J. H. & Dalal, R. (2000). Validity of Web-based psychological research. In M. H. Birnbaum (ed.), *Psychological Experiments on the Internet* (pp. 35–60). New York: Academic Press.

Kwak, N. & Radler, B. (2002). A comparison between mail and web surveys: Response pattern, respondent profile, and data quality. *Journal of Official Statistics, 18*(2), 257–274.

Lewis, I. M., Watson, B. C. & White, K. M. (2009). Internet versus paper-and-pencil survey methods in psychological experiments: Equivalence testing of participant responses to health-related messages. *Australian Journal of Psychology, 61*, 107–116.

Liu, Y. (2002). What does research say about the nature of Computer Mediated communication: Task-orientated, social-emotion-orientated, or both? *Electronic Journal of Sociology, 6*(1), A1.

Luce, K. H., Winzelberg, A. J., Das, S., Osborne, M. I., Bryson, S. W. & Taylor, C. B. (2007). Reliability of self-report: Paper versus online administration. *Computers in Human Behavior, 23*, 1384–1389.

Lumsden, J. & Morgan, W. (2005). Online-questionnaire design: Establishing guidelines and evaluating existing support. Paper presented at the 16th Annual International Conference of the Information Resources Management Association (IRMA'2005, 15–18 May), San Diego, CA.

McDonald, H. & Adam, S. (2003). A comparison of online and postal data collection methods in marketing research. *Marketing Intelligence & Planning, 21*, 85–95.

Musch, J. & Reips, U.-D. (2000). A brief history of Web experimenting. In M. H. Birnbaum (ed.), *Psychological Experiments on the Internet* (pp. 61–88). San Diego, CA: Academic Press.

Naus, M. J., Philipp, L. M. & Samsi, M. (2009). From paper to pixels: A comparison of paper and computer formats in psychological assessment. *Computers in Human Behavior, 25*, 1–7.

Nosek, B. A., Banaji, M. R. & Greenwald, A. G. (2002). E-research: Ethics, security, design, and control in psychological research on the Internet. *Journal of Social Issues, 58*, 161–176.

Pew Research (2014). Internet project: Internet user demographics. Retrieved from: www. pewinternet.org/data-trend/social-media/social-media-user-demographics/.

Reips, U.-D. (2000). The web experiment method: Advantages, disadvantages and solutions. In M. H. Birnbaum (ed.), *Psychological Experiments on the Internet* (pp. 89–114). San Diego, CA: Academic Press.

Reips, U.-D. (2002). Internet-based psychological experimenting: Five dos and five don'ts. *Social Science Computer Review, 20*, 241–249.

Reips, U.-D. (2008). How Internet-mediated research changes science. In A. Barak (ed.), *Psychological Aspects of Cyberspace: Theory, Research, Applications* (pp. 268–294). Cambridge: University Press.

Rovai, A. P. (2000). Building and sustaining community in asynchronous learning networks. *The Internet and Higher Education, 3*, 285–297.

Smith, G. G., Sorensen, C., Gump, A., Heindel, A. J., Caris, M. & Martinez, C. D. (2011). Overcoming student resistance to group work: Online versus face-to-face. *The Internet and Higher Education, 14*(2), 121–128.

Smith, M. A. & Leigh, B. (1997). Virtual subjects: Using the Internet as an alternative source of subjects and research environment. *Behavior Research Methods, Instruments & Computers, 29*, 496–505.

Smither, J. W., Walker, A. G. & Yap, M. K. T. (2004). An examination of the equivalence of Web-based versus paper-and-pencil upward feedback ratings: Rater- and ratee-level analyses. *Educational and Psychological Measurement, 64*, 40–61.

Social Sciences and Humanities Research Ethics Special Working Committee (2008). Extending the spectrum: The TCPS and ethical issues in internet-based research. Ottawa: Interagency Advisory Panel on Research Ethics.

Stanton, J. M. (1998). An empirical assessment of data collection using the Internet. *Personnel Psychology, 51*, 709–725.

Tourangeau, R. (2004). Survey research and societal change. *Annual Review of Psychology, 55*(1), 775–802.

Walker, J., Sproull, L. & Subramani, R. (1994). Using a human face in an interface. Paper presented at the Proceedings of the Conference on Human Factors in Computers, Boston, MA.

Weigold, A., Weigold, I. K. & Russell, E. J. (2013). Examination of the equivalence of self-report survey-based paper-and-pencil and internet data collection methods. *Psychological Methods, 18*(1), 53–70.

Weisband, S. & Kiesler, S. (1996). Self-disclosure on computer forms: Meta-analysis and implications. Paper presented at the CHI96, Vancouver, British Columbia, Canada.

Whittier, D. K., Seeley, S. & St Lawrence, J. S. (2004). A comparison of Web- with paper-based surveys of gay and bisexual men who vacationed in a gay resort community. *AIDS Education and Prevention, 16*, 476–485.

Yee, N., Bailenson, J. N., Urbanek, M., Chang, F. & Merget, D. (2007). The unbearable likeness of being digital: The persistence of nonverbal social norms in online virtual environments. *The Journal of CyberPsychology and Behavior, 10*, 115–121.

2 | Human interactions online

3 Computer Mediated Communication and online media

Gráinne Kirwan

CHAPTER OVERVIEW

This chapter will consider the variety of communication tools used online, as well as the history of Computer Mediated Communication (CMC), with particular focus on how the Internet has become an increasingly interactive medium in recent years. The language used online will be examined, especially in relation to abbreviations, acronyms, paralanguage and emoticons. The chapter will consider how various communication theories can be used to understand online communications, especially considering Walther's hyperpersonal communication model. It will also examine how other psychological theories, such as flow theory, can inform our understanding of online communication. Finally, the chapter will provide a brief introduction to the concepts of impression management, anonymity, disinhibition and privacy that will be considered in more detail in the following chapters.

KEY TERMS

While **Computer Mediated Communication** (CMC) is a term that most individuals may not have heard of, it describes a great deal of what they do on a daily basis. Put simply, it encompasses all communications that use computers as a medium. So every time that you send an email, or a message on social media, or comment on an online video, you are engaging in CMC. Indeed, it is even broader than that – for example, it can include text messages (or Short Message Services – SMS) from mobile phones and 'VoIP' (Voice over Internet Protocol) or videoconferencing.

Crystal (2011) suggests that CMC incorporates all forms of communication online, including music, photos, drawings, video and language.

Within these types of online communication we often engage in **paralanguage**. In general parlance, this refers to methods of modifying meaning through the use of volume, intonation or other adjustments. For example, even the simple expression 'fascinating' could be interpreted as its literal meaning if it is said in an enthusiastic, high volume manner with the accompaniment of a gasp. Alternatively, it could be interpreted as the complete opposite if said in a dull, subdued intonation and accompanied by a sigh. In CMC such distinctions might be expressed via punctuation or other devices to enrich the communication – turning the CMC from a **lean medium** into a more nuanced and sometimes playful experience. Other methods of increasing nuance can include the use of abbreviations, acronyms, excessive punctuation or even the inclusion of indicators of facial expressions, such as **emoticons** (variations of which are sometimes referred to as **emojis** or **smileys**).

Many communication theories have been proposed to help us to develop a deeper understanding of what occurs within a communication, and in some cases to give us an ability to predict the future path which that communication will take. Several of these communication theories are considered in this chapter. Some theories are specific to mediated communication, such as **hyperpersonal communication** (Walther, 1996; 2007), which examines how the formation and development of relationships can be affected by the characteristics of CMC. Other psychological theories also have relevance for our online interactions, such as **Flow Theory** which examines optimal experience (Csikszentmihalyi, 1990).

COMMUNICATION TOOLS ONLINE

Think for a moment about your online communications. Do you use email to contact lecturers? Perhaps you contact your classmates via a virtual learning environment, but use instant messaging or other CMC devices on social media to stay in touch with closer friends and family. Maybe you enjoy online gaming and use the variety of voice and text messaging systems that are used to communicate with fellow gamers. It could be that you stay in touch with family members using videoconferencing, while you use text messages to arrange meet-ups with your closest friends. Perhaps you're a member of an email discussion list (or **listserv**) that allows you to communicate with others with similar interests, or perhaps you use online forums or boards to fill that purpose. Perhaps you write a blog, or keep a Twitter account. Maybe you contribute to a wiki or other collaborative online environment. You might even share files with friends and colleagues using a system that permits **Computer Supported Co-operative Work** (CSCW).

There are some important concepts to consider when using CMC. For example, is our usage **synchronous** or **asynchronous**? Synchronous refers to a communication medium where all communicators are simultaneously exchanging messages. This might include voice communications in gaming, or chat facilities within virtual learning environments. Asynchronous communications refer to situations where it is expected that the users are not simultaneously communicating – for example, email or forums. There can sometimes be confusion regarding these, especially due to the popularity of smartphones which allow constant access to communications. An individual may become upset if they feel that they are in a synchronous communication medium, but the person that they are communicating with does not respond immediately.

The **fluidity** of online communication tools is also an important factor for consideration. Printed media, such as this book, remains static – it is not possible to change or edit the content once printed (although the information may be revised in newer editions). In contrast, online resources can change in very short periods of time. Consider, for example, an entry on particle physics in an online encyclopaedia – as new developments are made, this article can be updated to keep up, so the content is fluid when compared to a printed encyclopaedia article on the same topic. This can make online encyclopaedias extremely useful for staying abreast of modern developments, although it is worth noting that unless the entries are maintained by reliable experts in the area it is possible for intentional or unintentional errors to creep in.

A related concept is the distinction between whether we consider our communications to be most like written language or oral speech. Historically, it required a great deal of effort for most people to publish a piece of written content in a medium where it could be read by many others – for example, they needed to publish a book or have an article included in a newspaper. Even one-to-one written communication such as business and personal letters had a tone that was very different from speech. But modern online communication tends to be much more similar to spoken expression, using relaxed tone and informal language even with individuals who we do not know, or celebrities who we otherwise would not get the opportunity to interact with.

Our changed use of communication tools has also led to many academic researchers and social commentators raising worries about societal changes. For example, Sherry Turkle (2011) discusses how such technologies might have detrimental effects on our interpersonal relationships, and how people may become increasingly lonely despite greater interconnectedness. There have also been fears that the changes in language, such as increased use of abbreviations and acronyms, might have a detrimental effect on literacy although research findings in this field have been very mixed (see, for example, De Jonge & Kemp, 2012; Drouin, 2011; Plester et al., 2009). However, changes in literacy or research discrepancies may be due to other factors, such as educational systems. Of course, it must be remembered that language is constantly in a state of flux, with words being added and removed from dictionaries on a regular basis. It would be interesting to know what writers such as Geoffrey Chaucer and William Shakespeare would think of even formal modern English. Similarly, there are differences in our language in other contexts – for example, we are likely to use different language when speaking to a close friend than when speaking to our employer. Also, different types of online communication utilise different types of language, with some (such as emails or professional blogs) using more formal styles of writing than others (such as text messages or forum posts).

A VERY SHORT HISTORY OF COMPUTER MEDIATED COMMUNICATION

Computers and online communication are such a prevalent part of modern society that it is difficult for many to imagine life without them. Yet as recently as twenty years ago many offices had a very small number of Internet-enabled computers, which were frequently shared among many staff and used for specific purposes (such as bank transfers or payroll).

One of the first books considering CMC was written by Hiltz and Turoff (1978). In particular, it examined the business use of email, and described how early users of this technology noted that many non-verbal cues were lost – an early acknowledgement of the **lean medium** (as noted above), or alternatively a **cues-filtered out** situation. Hiltz and Turoff noted that many early users would attempt to re-establish this information by using a visit or a telephone call to supplement their email.

Soon users started to identify ways of including socioemotional content into their online communications (see, for example, Rice & Love, 1987). However, it was noted that this was not always appropriate in online communications (in a similar way that it is not always appropriate in offline communications). Indeed, Derks *et al.* (2008) noted that online communication has similar emotional content to offline communication.

Of course, there have been many changes in the way that online communication occurs since the work of earlier writers such as Hiltz and Turoff (1978) and Rice and Love (1987). Most notably, the much wider variety of methods used in more recent times demonstrates how we use CMC for a mixture of mass communication (to a wide group of people) and personal communication (to a smaller group or individual). While the Internet has allowed communication via computers for around five decades, the **World Wide Web** as a method of linking documents online is a much more recent phenomenon (it was conceptualised by Tim Berners-Lee in 1989). Most of the early webpages were relatively static – users could visit them and follow links on their pages, but could rarely interact with them. The concept of **Web 2.0** refers to the increased interactivity which has become prevalent online since the early 2000s, particularly in relation to social media and other user-generated content.

While images and video existed online prior to such increased interactivity levels, this development has also resulted in an increase of **multimodality**. Instead of simply reading text on a page, we often now have such text supplemented or replaced by other modes of communication, such as audio files, images or video files, among many others. The impact of this is evident in terms of the changes in social media – early versions simply allowed text updates, but more recently images and videos have become the norm, with several newer social media platforms being specifically created for the sharing of such content. It is now possible to document our own lives, and the lives of others, in ways previously impossible.

LANGUAGE AND ONLINE COMMUNICATION

The complexity of communication is seldom clearer than when you travel to a country where you do not speak the native language. Disorientation and frustration can be common, although eventually a few words are learned, and gradually communication becomes easier. One of the main reasons why this occurs is because language is symbolic. A word does not have a meaning until it is given one, and that association between the word and its meaning is accepted by the communicators involved.

Similarly, communication is not restricted to verbal language. Meaning can be altered through intonation, facial expression, gestures and context. Despite the increase in multimodal communication indicated above, the majority of CMC still occurs in the form of written language. The role of this medium can have an effect on how the messages are interpreted (this is considered in more detail in the section on hyperpersonal communication below), but various mechanisms have been adopted to add non-verbal cues to written communication online, thus reducing the lean medium effect. One method of doing this, as already mentioned, involves the use of punctuation or other cues to illustrate paralanguage. Other communication strategies online include the use of abbreviations, acronyms and emoticons.

Paralanguage

We may not be conscious of our own use of paralanguage in our verbal communications. We may often gasp, sigh or make noises indicative of hesitancy or uncertainty without realising that we're doing it. Writers of fiction have developed many ways of including cues for such paralanguage in the conversations of their characters, often through the use of punctuation or grammar. Many of these cues have been adopted or adapted by users of CMC to illustrate nuances to their own expressions. For example, ellipses (a series of dots such as '. . .') might be used to indicate a pause or that something is being left unsaid. Extra letters or exaggerated punctuation might be used to indicate strong emotional reactions, and capital letters can also be used for this purpose, or to indicate shouting. In some cases an approximation of the actual sound used might be typed, such as 'Ummm', 'Hmmm' or 'Eh'. Finally, the paralanguage may be so subtle that it is easily missed by a user who is unfamiliar with online communication. For example, the inclusion of a full stop after 'OK' can indicate frustration or anger in the writer in response to a request from their communication partner (the absence of the full stop indicates a more amicable acceptance of the request).

Acronyms and abbreviations

Acronyms and abbreviations are popular communication tools for many reasons. They can speed up response times and use fewer characters in communications where space might be limited (for example, Twitter) or where longer messages incur additional costs (such as in text messaging). They also avoid the need for repetitive writing or reading of frequently occurring longer terms or phrases. Acronyms and abbreviations may be spontaneously invented by groups or individuals as required.

The usefulness of such acronyms and abbreviations is dependent on the familiarity of the receiving communicator with the term. While some are pervasive across many types of online communication (for example, LOL – an extremely common acronym which stands for 'laugh out loud'), others might be rarely seen outside of a specific type of online communication (for example, ELI5 – seen on particular bulletin-board type systems and meaning 'Explain like I'm 5 [years old]'). Other examples might only be seen in communications that consider particular topics – the acronym 'FMIL' (future mother-in-law) makes frequent appearances on forums dedicated to wedding planning, while 'PEBKAC' (problem exists between keyboard and chair) is used by the software engineering community to indicate user error.

There are also cultural differences in the use of acronyms and abbreviations. A popular Malaysian one, 'TCSS' (talk cock, sing song – derived from 'cock and bull story'), refers to hanging out and chatting (C. Teoh, personal communication, 2 December 2014), while 'FFK' (Fong Fei Kei) is a Cantonese acronym whose literal translation approximates 'leaving on an aeroplane' but is used to indicate being stood up for a planned meeting or date (R.H.C. Goh, personal communication, 21 April 2015). A Thai alternative to 'LOL' is '5555', as '5' is pronounced 'ha', but in Cantonese '555' means 'fast fast fast' (A.J. Jegathesan, personal communication, 3 December 2014).

Several authors, such as De Jonge and Kemp (2012) have developed typologies and taxonomies of such abbreviations, acronyms and other 'textisms'. Some of the most common types include 'initialism' (which primarily describes acronyms), 'contraction' (where letters within words are omitted), 'shortening' (where letters are omitted from the start or end of words) and 'combined letter/number homophones', such as 'GR8' in place of 'great'. For many, it is these types of textisms which generate the worries relating to decreased literacy skills among users, especially children and adolescents, outlined above.

Emoticons/graphic accents/smileys/emojis

While many modern online communications allow text to be easily supplemented with video or images, the early Internet was not capable of managing such files easily, and they were used with much less frequency. When users wished to indicate an emotional expression with the message they were sending they were restricted to a basic set of characters, including letters, numbers, punctuation and commonly used mathematical symbols. Using these characters, Internet users began creating miniature facial expressions, termed emoticons, with the most common one being the 'smiley' – :-) .

Variations of emoticons have been given different designations, including 'graphic accents' and 'emojis', depending on their origin and type. As with paralanguage, different emoticons can adjust the meaning of a message. Consider the following two communications:

- Looking forward to seeing you tonight :-)
- Looking forward to seeing you tonight ;-)

The second communication is more flirtatious than the first, despite using a very similar emoticon. Emoticons of various types can also be used to denote irony, sarcasm, anger, sadness, humour, and many other emotional states.

Many researchers have examined the use of emoticons. For example, Derks, Bos and von Grumbkow (2007) noted that socioemotional discussions evoke more use of emoticons than task-oriented discussions. A later paper by the same researchers (2008) described findings that emoticons are mostly used in the expression of emotion and humour, particularly in positive contexts (rather than negative ones) and with friends. Similarly, Kato, Kato and Scott (2009) found that fewer emoticons were used when there were strong negative emotions (such as anger and guilt) present.

Some research has focused on the use of emoticons across genders. For example, Tossell et al. (2012) found that in text messages, females sent more emoticons but males had more diversity in the range of emoticons sent. This was similar to the findings of Fullwood, Orchard and Floyd (2013), who also identified women as more likely to use emoticons, but identified no difference in range.

COMMUNICATION THEORIES

So far, this chapter has concerned itself with describing online communication and aspects of it which are different from offline communication. However, it is useful to examine theories of communication relating to both online and offline interactions to gain an understanding of why online interactions take the form that they do. We shall examine a selection of these theories now.

Hyperpersonal communication

Several theories have attempted to examine CMC specifically, and the most famous of these is probably Walther's **hyperpersonal** model. This suggests that emotion and levels of affection developed through CMC can sometimes surpass those developed through offline interactions. Specifically, Walther felt that there were four elements that influence this: the receiver, the sender, feedback and the asynchronous channels of communication.

The receiver may assume positive and idealised characteristics about their communication partner when there is uncertainty. This relates to another model known as the Social Identity model of Deindividuation Effects (SIDE) which suggests that a social identity might replace individual identity in CMC (the potential positive and negative effects of which are investigated by Postmes et al., 1998). Walther also suggests that the sender of CMC messages can selectively choose what aspects of themselves they present, carefully editing and curating the information disseminated to enhance others' opinions. As many online communications are asynchronous, there is a reduction in the time constraints normally evident in offline tasks, permitting social interactions to occur without having a detrimental effect on task completion. Finally, the importance of any feedback received during the interaction is magnified, which might lead to idealisation.

Many researchers have examined the hyperpersonal model in experimental studies. For example, Jiang, Bazarova and Hancock (2011) had participants communicate with a confederate who made either high or low intimacy self-disclosures either face to face or in a CMC condition. CMC was found to lead to intensified disclosures and perceived intimacy compared to offline interactions.

The Shannon–Weaver mathematical model

Not all communication theories include strong psychological focus, but they may still have considerable psychological implications. The mathematical model proposed by Shannon and Weaver (1949) is one such model. Fundamentally, it focuses on the mechanical exchange of information from a source to a destination via a transmitter, channel and receiver. However, it also considers how other factors, such as noise, entropy, redundancy and channel capacity can affect the quality of the message received (or whether it is received at all). If we think about the various things that can go wrong during a communication exchange using computers, it is clear that the Shannon–Weaver model is important. This is probably particularly the case in video-conferencing technologies, where some computers and Internet connections struggle to keep up with the volume of information that is being communicated. The video image may become distorted, the sound may be muffled or there may be considerable lag. It is easy for information to be lost, and in some cases, for frustration to occur as a result.

While the Shannon–Weaver model has an important part to play in understanding communication, it does not consider many different aspects that are important in interpreting and responding to a message. For example, it does not consider the relationship between the communicators, the context of the communication, or how the receiver of a message extracts the meaning from the communication. Thankfully, these gaps have been identified by other researchers and theorists.

Rules theory/co-ordinated management of meaning (CMM)

Pearce and Cronen (1980) suggested rules theory and the co-ordinated management of meaning to help understanding of human communication in a broad sense (i.e. not restricted to CMC). Their theory suggests that human communication is guided by rules and the social patterns of our culture.

Pearce and Cronen proposed that there is a hierarchy of meanings which needs to be borne in mind when interpreting a communication. At the lowest level there is the literal content of the expression. Using the 'fascinating' example from earlier, the literal meaning is just that. But at the next level, 'Speech Act', the word indicates further meaning – for example, indicating interest in the information. Other levels of meaning include episodes, relationships, autobiography and cultural patterns. For example, use of the word 'fascinating' in a particular tone and manner could be employed by fans of the original *Star Trek* series to denote humour, relationships and cultural group.

Different levels in the hierarchy are co-ordinated by rules, and these rules form two main types – constitutive rules and regulative rules. Constitutive rules refer to what certain communications mean – for example, if someone provides instructions or mentoring, they are demonstrating leadership, while if they offer sympathies during a crisis this often demonstrates affection and care. Regulative rules tell us when it's appropriate to do certain things and what we should do next in an interaction. For example, if a person stops speaking, we should pick up the conversation unless it has been drawn to a close.

It is easy to see how communications in various online settings are regulated by the hierarchy of meaning, constitutive rules and regulative rules. But it must also be noted that different settings have different rules, and what is acceptable in some online groups is highly offensive in others.

Herb Clark's grounding theory

In a series of papers, Herb Clark outlines how conversation is collaborative, and requires shared understanding by building common ground based on mutual knowledge (see, for example, Clark & Brennan, 1991). This process is referred to as grounding, and participants collaborate to add information to their common ground. We can easily see this as we teach young children new words – by repeating the word and indicating what it means by pointing to a picture or engaging in an action, it provides the child with the common ground to use the word in future conversations.

It should be noted that making an utterance in itself does not automatically add to the common ground. If the adult repeatedly says the word 'computer' to a child, but does not show them what a computer is or explain what it does, then the child cannot absorb the information effectively. However, when a child understands what a computer is, and can identify or describe one, then they have provided evidence of sufficient understanding.

The applications of grounding theory to CMC are particularly clear in terms of the use of abbreviations, acronyms and emoticons. It is easy for a novice user to be confused or misunderstand a communication which includes these components. For example, there have been several anecdotal instances of individuals telling a friend or family member about a recent bereavement via text message, signing off with 'LOL'. As noted above, this is generally accepted as meaning 'laugh out loud', but the senders in these cases confused the meaning for 'lots of love'.

Flow Theory

Flow Theory (Csikszentmihalyi, 1990) is not a communication theory, but rather a positive psychology concept often discussed in relation to CMC due to its descriptions of a sense of immersion and a deep sense of enjoyment which develops from being in an activity. It is a subjective experience, including factors such as a merging of action and awareness, a loss of reflective self-consciousness, a distortion of temporal experience and a sensation of the activity as being intrinsically rewarding. Flow Theory has been applied to many different types of online activities (see, for example, Webster et al., 1993; Voiskounsky, 2008) and can help to explain exploratory and gaming behaviours in online environments.

Other theories of communication

In addition to the above, there are many other theories of communication which can help us to understand both online and offline communications. For example, Paul Watzlawick proposed the interactional view of communications (Watzlawick et al., 1967) which proposes several axioms, including how it is impossible not to communicate (even silence is a communication in itself), how the nature of relationships depends on how the communicators punctuate the sequence, and how power is asserted within communications. Berger (1979) suggested that when strangers commence communicating there is a high level of uncertainty between them, and in order to progress the relationship this uncertainty needs to be reduced. A similar concept is Altman and Taylor's (1973) social penetration theory, which suggests that intimacy is reached as communicators progress through disclosure of information at various layers, progressing from superficial layers (such as liked aspects of popular culture), through middle and inner layers (such as social attitudes, deep fears, hopes, spiritual values, etc.) and finally to the core personality. Even established relationships may run into problems, however, and Baxter and Montgomery's Dialectical Theory (e.g. Baxter, 1988; Baxter & Montgomery, 1996) examines how internal conflicts can affect communication patterns within relationships. Of course, it is also possible that we adjust our communication patterns to accommodate others, a position taken by Howard Giles in Communication Accommodation Theory (see, for example, Giles, 2008).

It should be noted, of course, that all these theories, as well as all those listed above, are partial – none completely describe all human communication. Most specialise in one particular area of communication (e.g. information transfer, relationship development) and few integrate different aspects together. Few of the theories directly compete with each other and most provide new insights not present in others. It is only when we consider several theories together that we can hope to gain an overview of the complexity of human communication in both online and offline arenas.

RELATED CONCEPTS

It is important to note that communication does not occur in a vacuum. Many other factors impact on what is said, who it is said by and how it is said. It is not possible to cover all these within this chapter, so it is recommended that the reader also consults other related chapters in this text, depending on their area of interest. For example, authors of online communications often attempt to manage the impressions that others form of them, and carefully control their online self and identity, and this is considered in the next chapter. This is particularly the case for those seeking to find potential romantic partners online, and Chapter 6 examines this phenomenon. Chapter 5 considers the disruptive sides of online behaviour, including communication behaviours such as flaming and trolling, while the methods by which persuasion occurs online are described in Chapter 9. Factors relating to privacy, trust and anonymity are described in Chapter 10, including Communication Privacy Management theory – another communication theory that describes how and why we share information that we deem private. Finally, communication in online gaming is considered in Chapter 19.

CONCLUSION

This chapter has provided an introduction to CMC, considering how our communications have changed as computers have become more popular, and examining the range of communications that we now engage in. It has identified how language can be different online from offline, particularly focusing on paralanguage, abbreviations, acronyms and emoticons. Finally, online communication was considered in the light of communication theories, both those specifically developed for online communication and ones developed with offline communication in mind, but which have applications for online interaction. Despite all this, communication in itself is a complex topic – by its very nature the vast majority of our communications are discussing something else, or are made to reach a goal. Any consideration of online communication must also consider the context, topic and aim of that communication, and many of the following chapters consider these aspects of online life.

ACTIVITY

Look for a few examples of interesting conversations on publicly accessible forums online (for ethical reasons, please ensure that you do not need to log in to the relevant websites to see the conversations, and protect the individuals' anonymity and confidentiality if discussing this activity with others). It is best if the conversations include several communications by one or more of the writers. Consider how each of the communication theories outlined above help us to form insights into the process of the communication, the relationship between the communicators and the eventual outcome.

DISCUSSION QUESTIONS

1   What do you use online communication for? Do you use different communication methods to communicate with different people or to discuss different topics?
2   Which of the communication theories mentioned do you think provides the greatest understanding of CMC? Is it necessary to combine different theories to get a better overview of the phenomenon?
3   During what computer-based activities do you experience flow? What do you think it is about these activities that results in flow?
4   Does CMC have an adverse effect on interpersonal relationships?

RECOMMENDED READING LIST

David Crystal has written extensively in the area of online communication, with a particular focus on linguistics. *Internet Linguistics* is a very accessible read with many examples and observations on how language is used online.

Crystal, D. (2011). *Internet Linguistics: A Student Guide*. Abingdon, Oxford/New York: Routledge.

Communication also has cognitive elements. This book by Richard Jackson Harris and Fred Sanborn examines this, particularly in relation to mass communication channels.

Harris, R.J. & Sanborn, F.W. (2014). *A Cognitive Psychology of Mass Communication* (6th edn). New York: Taylor & Francis.

Many excellent research studies examine usage of the various types of language online. For example, in this paper, Fullwood, Orchard and Floyd examine the use of emoticons in online chat rooms, with particular focus on gender differences (and similarities).

Fullwood, C., Orchard, L. & Floyd, S. (2013). Emoticon convergence in Internet chat rooms. *Social Semiotics, 23*(5), 648–662.

Sherry Turkle (2011) examines the effects of increased use of communication methods, with particular focus on how people may become increasingly lonely despite greater interconnectedness.

Turkle, S. (2011). *Alone Together: Why We Expect More from Technology and Less from Each Other*. Philadelphia, PA: Basic Books.

GLOSSARY

Asynchronous communication   Communications where it is expected that the users are not simultaneously communicating.

Computer Mediated Communication (CMC)   Human communication that relies on the medium of computer technology.

Computer Supported Co-operative Work (CSCW)   The use of computing technology to support work by groups.

Cues-filtered out   A description of CMC as a medium where there are limited non-verbal cues available (see also lean medium).

Emojis   Variation of emoticons

Emoticons   The use of symbols to demonstrate facial expressions in communication.

Flow Theory   A positive psychology theory proposed by Csikszentmihalyi (1990) which can help to explain optimal experience online. A flow state is a heightened state of engagement with a video game activity (or other activity) that is characterised by feelings of presence, energised focus and enjoyment, and being at one with the game. Flow typically involves distortions of time perception.

Fluidity   In CMC, refers to content that can be changed easily and frequently.

Hyperpersonal communication   A model by Walther (1996) describing how Computer Mediated Communication can lead to enhanced feelings of intimacy.

Lean medium   A description of CMC as a medium where limited non-verbal cues are available.

Listserv   Email discussion list.

Multimodality   The use of multiple modes of communication, such as text with video, images or sound.

Paralanguage Modifying meaning through the use of volume, intonation or other adjustments.

Smileys Variation of emoticons.

Synchronous communication Communications where it is expected that users are simultaneously communicating, such as instant messaging.

Web 2.0 A term used to describe the increased interactivity online, particularly in relation to social media and other user-generated content.

World Wide Web An application of the Internet which allows the linking of documents online.

REFERENCES

Altman, I. & Taylor, D. (1973). *Social Penetration: The Development of Interpersonal Relationships.* New York: Holt, Rinehart & Winston.

Baxter, L.A. (1988). A dialectical perspective on communication strategies in relationship development. In S. Duck (ed.), *Handbook of Personal Relationships* (pp. 257–273). New York: Wiley.

Baxter, L.A. & Montgomery, B.M. (1996). *Relating: Dialogues and Dialectics.* New York: Guilford.

Berger, C.R. (1979). Beyond initial interaction: Uncertainty, understanding and the development of interpersonal relationships. In H. Giles & R. St Clair (eds), *Language and Social Psychology* (pp. 122–144). Oxford: Blackwell.

Clark, H.H. & Brennan, S.A. (1991). Grounding in communication. In L.B. Resnick, J.M. Levine & S.D. Teasley (eds), *Perspectives on Socially Shared Cognition* (pp. 127–149). Washington, DC: APA Books.

Crystal, D. (2011). *Internet Linguistics: A Student Guide.* Abingdon, Oxford/New York: Routledge.

Csikszentmihalyi, M. (1990). *Flow: The Psychology of Optimal Performance.* New York: Cambridge University Press.

De Jonge, S. & Kemp, N. (2012). Text-message abbreviations and language skills in high school and university students. *Journal of Research in Reading, 35*(1), 49–68.

Derks, D., Bos, A.E.R. & von Grumbkow, J. (2007). Emoticons and social interaction on the Internet: The importance of social context. *Computers in Human Behavior, 23*(1), 842–849.

Derks, D., Bos, A.E.R. & von Grumbkow, J. (2008). Emoticons in computer mediated communication: Social motives and social context. *CyberPsychology & Behavior, 11*(1), 99–101.

Derks, D., Fischer, A.H. & Bos, A.E.R. (2008). The role of emotion in Computer Mediated communication: A review. *Computers in Human Behavior, 24*(3), 766–785.

Drouin, M.A. (2011). College students' text messaging, use of textese and literacy skills. *Journal of Computer Assisted Learning, 27*(1), 67–75.

Fullwood, C., Orchard, L. & Floyd, S. (2013). Emoticon convergence in Internet chat rooms. *Social Semiotics, 23*(5), 648–662.

Giles, H. (2008). Communication accommodation theory. In L.A. Baxter & D.O. Braithewaite (eds), *Engaging Theories in Interpersonal Communication: Multiple Perspectives* (pp. 161–173). Thousand Oaks, CA: Sage Publications.

Hiltz, S.R. & Turoff, M. (1978). *The Network Nation: Human Communication via Computer*. New York: Addison-Wesley.

Jiang, L.C., Bazarova, N.N. & Hancock, J.T. (2011). The disclosure–intimacy link in Computer Mediated Communication: An attributional extension of the hyperpersonal model. *Human Communication Research*, *37*(1), 58–77.

Kato, S., Kato, Y. & Scott, D. (2009). Relationships between emotional states and emoticons in mobile phone email communication in Japan. *International Journal on E-Learning*, *8*(3), 385–401.

Pearce, W.B. & Cronen, V.E. (1980). *Communication, Action and Meaning: The Creation of Social Realities*. Westport, CT: Praeger.

Plester, B., Wood, C. & Joshi, P. (2009). Exploring the relationship between children's knowledge of text message abbreviations and school literacy outcomes. *British Journal of Developmental Psychology*, *27*(1), 145–161.

Postmes, T., Spears, R. & Lea, M. (1998). Breaching or building social boundaries? SIDE-effects of Computer Mediated Communication. *Communication Research*, *25*(6), 689–715.

Rice, R.E. & Love, G. (1987). Electronic emotion: Socioemotional content in a Computer Mediated communication network. *Communication Research*, *14*(1), 85–108.

Shannon, C.E. & Weaver, W. (1949). *The Mathematical Theory of Communication*. Urbana, IL: University of Illinois Press.

Tossell, C.C., Kortum, P., Shepard, C., Barg-Walkow, L.H., Rahmati, A. & Zhong, L. (2012). A longitudinal study of emoticon use in text messaging from smartphones. *Computers in Human Behavior*, *28*(2), 659–663.

Turkle, S. (2011). *Alone Together: Why We Expect More from Technology and Less from Each Other*. Philadelphia, PA: Basic Books.

Voiskounsky, A. (2008). Flow experience in cyberspace: Current studies and perspectives. In A. Barak (ed.), *Psychological Aspects of Cyberspace: Theory, Research, Applications* (pp. 70–101). New York: Cambridge University Press.

Walther, J.B. (1996). Computer Mediated Communication: Impersonal, interpersonal and hyperpersonal interaction. *Communication Research*, *23*, 3–43.

Walther, J.B. (2007). Selective self-presentation in Computer Mediated Communication: Hyperpersonal dimensions of technology, language and cognition. *Computers in Human Behaviour*, *23*, 2538–2557.

Watzlawick, P., Beavin, J. & Jackson, D., (1967). *Pragmatics of Human Communication*. New York: W. W. Norton.

Webster, J., Trevino, L.K. & Ryan, L. (1993). The dimensionality and correlates of flow in human-computer interactions. *Computers in Human Behavior*, *9*, 411–426.

4 Self and identity in cyberspace

Irene Connolly

CHAPTER OVERVIEW

This chapter will introduce the main theories of identity, self-concept and personality and relate them to how we present ourselves online. The role of identity in identifiable settings, where one's identity is known is compared to anonymous environments, where identity is not known. It is designed to show how specific personality types use the Internet and how the Internet, especially social media, allows us to manage who we want to be online. It will highlight how we can use self-enhancing tools to show ourselves in a positive light, using impression management.

KEY TERMS

Identity is the development of one's self-concept, including one's thoughts and feelings about oneself (Rosenberg, 1986). In the online world the role of identity is complex, as multiple versions of the **self** can be expressed (Ellison *et al.*, 2006). Further exploration of the self by Higgins (1987) proposes three domains: the 'actual self' or 'now self' (Markus & Nurius, 1986), which are characteristics an individual actually possesses, the 'ideal self', which are characteristics a person would like to possess, and the 'ought self', which are the characteristics a person feels that they should possess. Online anonymity gives people the chance to present any of these three selves and hence permits individuals to better present aspects of their true selves than they would feel capable of doing in a face to face (F2F) interaction (Ellison *et al.*, 2006). The concept of 'true selves' has been used to refer to the 'hidden aspects of what we need or wish to be' (Suler, 2002, p. 458), and 'hidden' has meant 'anti-normative' or 'deviant' in this context. Potentially, identity empowerment may occur in the online environment.

In a fully **identifiable** (Zhao, 2006) offline world (where a person's identity is known), any deviance from established social norms may be punished or ridiculed, the masks people wear in everyday life become their 'real' or known identities (Goffman, 1959) and a person's 'true' self is often inhibited (Bargh *et al.*, 2002). Zhao *et al.* (2008) challenge the distinction between 'real selves' and 'virtual selves' or 'true selves' and 'false selves'. Where 'virtual selves' commonly refer to online selves and 'real selves' to offline selves, Zhao *et al.* (2008) reported that Facebook identities are clearly real in the sense that they have real consequences for the lives of the individuals who constructed them.

In contrast, in a fully **anonymous** online world where responsibility is absent, the masks people wear offline are often discarded and their 'true' selves allowed to emerge. The identifiable online world, however, emerges as a third type of environment where people may tend to express what has been called the 'hoped-for possible selves' (Yurchisin *et al.*, 2005). Hoped-for possible selves are a subcomponent of the possible selves (Markus & Nurius, 1986) that differs from the suppressed or hidden 'true self' on one hand and the unrealistic or fantasised 'ideal self' (Higgins, 1987) on the other. Hoped-for possible selves are socially pleasing identities a person wishes to ascertain under receptive conditions such as an anonymous online environment. The materialisation of hoped-for possible selves can be hampered by the presence of physical 'gating characteristics'. These 'gating characteristics' can include gender, social status, ethnicity or even shyness. The identifiable online environment may assist these individuals to achieve a more positive interaction which they would not achieve in a first encounter in a F2F environment.

ONLINE BEHAVIOUR THEORIES

Several theories have been put forward to analyse the variation of online behaviour in anonymous and identifiable environments. Two prominent theories include the Equalisation Hypothesis and Social Identity Model of Deindividuation Effects (SIDE). In F2F interaction a person's gender, age or ethnicity are apparent and social power hierarchies all play a role in these social interactions (Allport, 1954, 1979; Hatfield & Spreacher, 1986).

Equalisation Hypothesis

The Equalisation Hypothesis suggests that with the removal of these social cues, a reduction of associated stereotypes may occur, and therefore may lead to increased social power in the online world (Kiesler *et al.*, 1984). Without this inhibitory information, it is hypothesised that individuals who hold less power in society should have increased power in the online environment. However, complete anonymity is not fundamental to the Equalisation Hypothesis (Dubrovsky *et al.*, 1991). The following research has supported the idea of the Equalisation Hypothesis. Research conducted by Siegel *et al.* (1986) investigated whether or not there were more equal amounts of participation in a group decision-making process in Computer Mediated Communication (CMC) discussions rather than in F2F discussions. Anonymity was manipulated with participants indicating their first name or remaining completely anonymous in their communications. Results indicated that there was significantly more equalisation in the CMC condition than in the F2F condition. Dubrovsky *et al.* (1991) further explored these findings by studying the effect of status as well as the effect of anonymity. This research supported the hypothesis that CMC would diminish inequality, each group member submitted an equal number of responses as the other members, regardless of status, even when the status differences of the group members were revealed to the participants in the CMC condition.

Social Identity Model of Deindividuation Effects (SIDE) Theory

The Social Identity Model of Deindividuation Effects (SIDE) Theory is a reinterpretation of the classic deindividuation theory (Zimbardo, 1969) which highlights the importance of the situational explicit variables in a social situation. SIDE Theory incorporates two components of the effect and use of anonymity in CMC. First, a cognitive element of anonymity exists which focuses on how group dynamics, and individual behaviour within groups, is facilitated by anonymity and the depth of an individual's identification with the group (Postmes *et al.*, 2001). SIDE Theory anticipates that when complete anonymity exists within a group, then group salience will be enhanced, with those members' identification with the group growing stronger. However, where an individual can identify group members, while remaining anonymous to the group, SIDE Theory predicts that the one anonymous individual will identify more strongly with him or herself. This individual's behaviour will not be advantageous to the group. Researchers such as Joinson (2000), Lea *et al.* (2001) and Postmes *et al.* (2001) on the cognitive component of SIDE Theory support these assertions by Spears & Lea (1992).

Second, the SIDE Theory comprises a strategic component, including the deliberate use of anonymity in CMC, as a method to benefit from this anonymity (Spears & Lea, 1994). It strengthens the influence of social norms and their effect when social identity is strong. Also, anonymity will lessen the effect of social norms where a person's own identity is more conspicuous (Spears & Lea, 1992). Therefore, social norms are more likely to be adhered to when the individual has a high awareness of social identity and personal identity is less. In conclusion, SIDE Theory proposes that in order to achieve goal-directed groups, where each member strives to achieve the group's goal and not their own personal goals, circumstances call for the complete anonymity of each member for the groups or complete identity transparency across the group (Spears & Lea, 1992).

IMPRESSION MANAGEMENT

Social networking communication is more closely related to F2F communication than other forms of text-based CMC (Walther, 2007). One aspect of these online environments which allows people to alter their self-representation is known as **Impression Management**. Impression management is selectively self-presenting or editing messages to reveal socially desirable attitudes and dimensions of the self (Walther, 1996). The more critical the impression is thought to be in relation to one's goal fulfilment, the more motivated a person may be to realise an anticipated impression (Leary, 1996). Leary (1996) put forward that there are three reasons why an individual manages impressions; these include attempting to persuade others to respond in desired manner, or to create and preserve one's private self-identity and self-esteem, and to standardise their emotional practices. Furthermore, Goffman (1959) suggested that people want to convince others to see them as fair, decent and ethical individuals, and also sustain established positive impressions (Lemert & Branaman, 1997). Social networking sites, one example being Facebook, are devoted to developing and handling impressions, as well as engaging in personal maintenance and relationship-seeking behaviours (Tong, 2008). The physical attractiveness of one's Facebook friends and comments made by those friends were found to be related to ratings of the profile owner's physical and social attractiveness, including the person's credibility (Walther et al., 2008). In addition, the more Facebook friends a profile owner had, the more socially attractive the person was professed to be (Walther et al., 2008). Profile owners with the highest levels of extraversion appeared to have moderate number of friends (Tong et al., 2008). Facebook identity tends to be highly socially desirable and difficult to attain offline (Zhao et al., 2008).

The role of anonymity in impression management

Impression management may be affected by several factors, including the effect of anonymous versus identifiable environment, identity and self-development. Pedersen (1979) suggested that there are six different types of privacy, which include reserve, isolation, intimacy with family, intimacy with friends, solitude and anonymity. *Reserve* refers to the reluctance to reveal personal information about one's self. *Isolation* is the wish to be alone and away from others. *Intimacy with family* and *intimacy with friends* involves the desire to be alone with either group. *Solitude* comprises being free of scrutiny from other people and *anonymity* involves interacting with others, without being scrutinised by them. Anonymity occurs when a person cannot be identified by others in a social networking situation. Within this concept there appears to be two aspects: *technical anonymity* (Hayne & Rice, 1997) or *discursive anonymity* (Qian & Scott, 2007) and *social anonymity* (Hayne & Rice, 1997) or *visual anonymity* (Qian & Scott, 2007). With the former referring to identifying material from online communication, such as names and e-mail addresses, and the latter referring to the perception of others or one's self as unidentifiable as a result of lack of signs to provide an identity for that person. The role of anonymity in the online world can have both positive and negative effects, where traditional research such as Zimbardo (1969) and Mann (1981) have highlighted the negative aspects of anonymity in relation to increases in aggressive behaviour. Anonymity can have a positive effect in the role of privacy or the amount of contact that someone has with others. While privacy can enhance psychological well-being (Werner *et al.*, 1992), the absence of it can lead to aggression and anti-social behaviour (Heffron, 1972). Anonymity can also provide autonomy, where people can try out new behaviours without fear of social consequences or the fear of reprisal. However, the online world may not be completely anonymous, as real world communities can interact with online communities, disallowing complete anonymity. While the identifiable nature of the environment does seem to make people more 'realistic and honest' (Ellison *et al.*, 2006) in their self-presentation, the reduction of 'gating obstacles' in the online setting enables the users to be more liberal with the truth (Yurchisin *et al.*, 2005). This occurs in particular when attempting to project a self that is more socially desirable and better than their 'real' offline identity.

Lying or impression management?

Within the area of impression management, a person's willingness to deceive is paramount. Research has suggested that Social Networking Sites (SNS) users possess more risk-taking attitudes than non-users (Fogel & Nehmad, 2009), where this is demonstrated largely with males in the online world (Zuckerman & Kuhlman, 2000) and also by DePaulo *et al.* (1996a) in the offline world, where male students told significantly more self-centred lies than did female students. Over half of their total lies were self-oriented, involving impression management and self-promotion in nature. There is a great variation in a person telling 'white lies' and participating in full deception of another individual (DePaulo *et al.*, 1996b; Hancock *et al.*, 2004). DePaulo *et al.*'s (1996b) taxonomy of lies proposes four main features: (1) The content of the lie, (2) the reason for the lie, (3) the type of lie, or its seriousness and (4) the referent of the lie, which is who the lie concerns. Zhao *et al.* (2008) assert that different behaviours in anonymous and identifiable online environments exist. The research found that, while anonymous environments often do support an identity closer to that of the individual's 'real' offline identity, the degree to which this is so differs across individuals.

Broadcasters and communicators

Underwood *et al.*'s, (2011) study identified differences in online social networking behaviours. An opportunity sample of 113 undergraduate students within a UK university, aged between 18 and 36, 48 males (M = 20.94 years, SD = 2.49) and 65 females (M = 20.65 years, SD = 2.57) participated in this study. The key criterion for inclusion in the study was an active Facebook account. The study has provided evidence for highlighting two clearly identifiable modes of interaction when using a SNS, termed *broadcasting* and *communicating*, and provided compelling information for the underlying behavioural characteristics in helping to explain such online activity. At one end of the continuum are group-focused *communicators* while at the other are the self-focused *broadcasters*. *Broadcasting*, one-to-many with the primary flow outwards from the one, and *communicating* involves one-to-few with reciprocal exchanges (Underwood *et al.*, 2011). Broadcasting can be identified as a public communication style depicted by an individual's self-projection (Pempek *et al.*, 2009) and can involve impression management (Walther, 1996). It can result in a low quality of interaction, particularly with regard to blogs (Instone, 2005; Zhou & Hovy, 2006). Broadcasters who engaged in such self-promotion and self-oriented lies attempt to provide a more desirable self (Ginger, 2007; Hancock, 2007; Walther, 2007). In this sense the broadcasters' behaviours are closer to those within anonymous online environments (Bargh *et al.*, 2002). They are also characterised by higher levels of out-going personality, risk-taking behaviour, mild social deviance (MSD) and a willingness to engage in lying behaviours. The risk-taking leads to a greater willingness to disclose personal information online and engage in deviant or risky behaviours (Fogel & Nehmad, 2009). However, the act of communicating between individuals who know one another and have shared interests tends to produce high quality interactions (Skinstad, 2008). *Communicators* are more likely to have anchored relationships – that is, the communicators talk to individuals who are liked and well known; to focus on maintenance of strong close-knit social friendship group; to have regular high quality interactions and to support smaller online network communities. Moreover, communicators are uncomfortable about lying even though their lies tend to be those everyday lies that oil social interaction (Skinstad, 2008). The conclusion here is that communicators are working to support group coherence and to maintain their membership of the group. This is corroborated by Zhao *et al.*'s (2008) finding that users stress group identities over personal identities in their postings on Facebook.

IDENTIFIABLE ONLINE ENVIRONMENTS

Studies have examined identity construction in Internet dating which is a unique identifiable online environment (Ellison *et al.*, 2006; Gibbs *et al.*, 2006; Yurchisin *et al.*, 2005). These vary from the Role Playing Games (RPGs) which are anonymous in nature. Internet dating sites are designed to facilitate the exchange of personal information. Individuals have to find a balance between presenting of 'the best self' on their profile and providing precise information (Ellison *et al.*, 2006; Whitty, 2007). There is a narrowed discrepancy between 'actual selves' and 'ideal selves' in people's online self-presentation when dealing with being identified in the online world. The identifiable nature of the environment, particularly the expectation of ensuing F2F encounters, had been theorised to narrow the incongruity between actual selves and ideal selves in people's online self-presentation (Ellison *et al.*, 2006). Identities produced on Internet dating sites differ from the identities produced in F2F situations, because people on the Internet dating sites tend to 'stretch the truth a bit' (Yurchisin *et al.*, 2005, p. 742) in their online self-presentations. Regardless of those 'truthstretching' behaviours, identities formed on Internet dating sites were found to be both honest and realistic, perhaps in an attempt to avoid objectionable encounters in an offline meetings that occurred (Ellison *et al.*, 2006).

Online dating

The online dating environment can use either identifiable or anonymous methods of communication, with many online dating sites using pseudonyms, with real names only being used when daters meet in other environments, including offline. Online dating is where individuals are seeking a personal relationship which would require a cohesiveness between the online presentation of self and the offline self. Perceptions that others are lying may encourage reciprocal deception, because users will exaggerate to the extent that they feel others are exaggerating or deceiving (Fiore & Donath, 2005). Ellison *et al.* (2006) examined self-presentation strategies among online dating participants, where investigations examined the methods of their online self-presentation in order to seek out a romantic partner. Qualitative data analysis proposed that participants concentrated on small cues online, mediating the tension between impression management pressures and the aspiration to present an accurate sense of self. The findings of this study suggested that participants consistently engaged in creative sidestepping tactics in their presentation of self and in their communication with others. The interview data suggested that the notion that people frequently, explicitly and intentionally 'lie' online is simplistic and inaccurate. Exploring the question of whether participants created a playful or fantastical identity online (Stone, 1995; Turkle, 1995) or were more open and honest (Rubin, 1975), Ellison *et al.* (2006) found that the online dating participants claimed that they attempted to present an accurate self-representation online, a finding also reported by Gibbs *et al.* (2006). Creating an accurate online representation of self in this environment appeared to be a multifaceted and developing process. Finally, Ellison *et al.* (2006) put forward that online representations of one's ideal self, which may be affected by the possibility of F2F interaction in the future, may in itself act as a buffer to reduce the variation between the actual and ideal selves. In the realm of online dating, participants reported using the profile to ideate a version of self they desired to experience in the future, which suggests that for some individuals online profile construction may encompass self-growth, which the aim is to diminish the difference between the actual and ideal self.

Identity and self in anonymous versus identifiable online environments

Zhao *et al.*'s (2008) research examined identity construction on Facebook, which is another identifiable online environment. The research methodology combined same-ethnic focus groups, interviews with administrators involved in student services and student organisations, structured in-depth interviews as well as online Facebook analyses. Using content analyses of 63 users, the research found that the identities devised by those in an identifiable environment does vary from those created in an anonymous environment. The authors reported that the hoped-for possible selves users projected on Facebook were neither the 'true selves' often seen in anonymous online environments nor the 'real selves' people presented in F2F communications. The Facebook selves appear to be highly socially desirable identities that people wish to have but cannot achieve. This is a similar result to the Ellison *et al.* (2006) study of Internet dating. Being identifiable in the online world seems to produce a more honest presentation of the self (Ellison *et al.*, 2006), but the lack of social cues seems to allow them to present themselves more favourably than they can offline (Yurchisin *et al.*, 2005). Zhao *et al.* (2008) have suggested some implications arising from their study, one being that identity is not an individual characteristic but is a social product. Individuals will produce identities based on the context of the environment. Hence, they put forward that true selves, real selves and hoped-for possible selves are pro-duced with regard to the environment rather than the characteristics of the person. Second, in an identifiable environment, where a person's identity can be recognised,

Zhao *et al.* (2008) found that individuals are more likely to present themselves within the normal expectations of the offline world. Whereas in an anonymous environment, either online or offline, where individuals are unidentifiable and thus cannot be held responsible, people are more likely to behave as they wish, ignoring normative restrictions (Cinnirella & Green, 2007). Third, Zhoa *et al.* (2008) suggest that there are little distinctions between online behaviour and offline behaviour and consequences. Individuals need to co-ordinate their behaviours in both environments. 'Digital selves' are real, and they can serve to enhance users' overall self-image and identity claims and quite possibly increase their chances to connect in the offline world. Finally, the researchers challenge the distinction between real selves and virtual selves or true selves and false selves. Virtual selves commonly refers to online selves and real selves to offline selves, as Zhoa *et al.* (2008) found the Facebook identities are clearly real in the sense that they have real consequences for the lives of the individuals who constructed them.

Two studies on the impact of cues to identity within anonymous online environments were carried out by Tanis and Postmes (2007). In the first study, cues to identity were manipulated by showing the participants a photo and first name of the alleged partner and themselves or not. The researchers found that more positive impressions did result minimally with the presence of cues to one's identity, this supported earlier findings by Tanis and Postmes (2003) where even the smallest identity cues had an effect on a person's impression management. Additionally, in this study, Tanis and Postmes reported that cues to identity had negative effects on variables related to assessments of the contact. People had slightly more positive impressions of their partners but they felt less certain about, and were less satisfied with, the interaction. The subsequent study by Tanis and Postmes (2007) demonstrated that when performing an online communication task (discussing a paper for college), participants felt more confident, were more pleased with the interaction, and thought they had performed better in the absence of cues to identity. Therefore, this study supports the supposition that interactions that allow the communication of cues to identity such as F2F are better, as they make the interaction more personal, but that these effects are not reflected by the appraisal of the contact. Perhaps the existence of cues to identity positively affects social perceptions, while decreasing perceptions of cohesion. The results of these studies conflict with expectations resulting from Social Presence Theory (see Short, 1974; Short *et al.*, 1976), Reduced Social Cues Approach (see Culnan & Markus, 1987), and the Cuelessness Model (see Rutter & Stephenson, 1979), all of which predict that cues to identity benefit the interaction. Certainly, Walther *et al.* (2001) suggested that in the presence of photographic identification, participants were less able to shape the impressions that others created about them (Walther *et al.*, 2001).

CONCLUSION

The role of self and identity in cyberspace is complex. A person's identity impacts their thoughts and feelings, and hence can influence the type of person they wish to associate with. Many factors in cyberspace can affect interactions, such as the anonymity or identifiable nature of sites visited. The Equalisation Hypothesis and Social Identity Model of Deindividuation Effects (SIDE) attempt to explain the impact of the anonymity in SNS on behaviour. Impression Management occurs in both anonymous and identifiable environment but to varying extents, with the issue of telling lies being linked to the personality type. Online environments appear to encourage impression management for personal gain or status; for some this may be used negatively or for others, it may be used positively.

ACTIVITY

Who am I? Provide five sentences that answer this question about yourself. Then go to your personal social networking site (whichever one you use the most). This time look at your own profile and your own comments and write down five sentences that answer the Who am I? question based on your online persona. Compare the offline life answers with those of the online persona. Does the offline you and the online you match or vary completely?

DISCUSSION QUESTIONS

1 Do you think that people are different in the online world compared to the offline world? Explain.
2 Should anonymity exist in the online world? Support your answers.
3 Is Impression Management simply a nicer way of saying that people lie online? Elaborate.
4 Can online dating be successful if people are managing their identities rather than showing their true selves? Discuss.

RECOMMENDED READING LIST

Nicole Ellison and her colleagues continue their in-depth analysis of online dating in this research, which explores how users conceptualise misrepresentation (their own and others') in a specific genre of online self-presentation.

Ellison, N. B., Hancock, J. T. & Toma, C. L. (2012). Profile as promise: A framework for conceptualizing veracity in online dating self-presentations. *New Media & Society, 14*(1), 45–62.

Rosenberg and Egbert found that personality traits and secondary goals are theoretically and empirically sound components for the conceptualisation of online impression management.

Rosenberg, J. & Egbert, N. (2011). Online impression management: Personality traits and concerns for secondary goals as predictors of self-presentation tactics on Facebook. *Journal of Computer Mediated Communication, 17*(1), 1–18.

Carolyn Cunningham offers critical inquiry into how identity is constructed, deconstructed, performed and perceived on social networking sites (SNSs), such as Facebook and LinkedIn.

Cunningham, C. (ed.). (2013). *Social Networking and Impression Management: Self-presentation in the Digital Age.* Plymouth: Rowman & Littlefield.

This article by Rosanna Guadagno and colleagues examines how the differences in expectations about meeting impacted the degree of deceptive self-presentation individuals displayed within the context of dating.

Guadagno, R. E., Okdie, B. M. & Kruse, S. A. (2012). Dating deception: Gender, online dating, and exaggerated self-presentation. *Computers in Human Behavior, 28*(2), 642–647.

GLOSSARY

Anonymous   Your identity is hidden from others.

Broadcasting   One-to-many with the primary flow outwards from the one.

Communicating   Involves one-to-few with reciprocal exchanges.

Identity   Recognition of one's potential and qualities as an individual, especially in relation to social context.

Impression management   Selectively self-presenting or editing messages to reveal socially desirable attitudes and dimensions of the self.

Identifiable   Your identity can be seen by others.

Online dating   Searching for a romantic or sexual partner on the Internet, typically via a dedicated website.

Self   A person's essential being that distinguishes them from others, especially considered as the object of introspection or reflexive action.

REFERENCES

Allport, G. W. (1954/1979). *The Nature of Prejudice.* Reading, MA: Addison-Wesley.

Bargh, J. A., McKenna, K. Y. & Fitzsimons, G. M. (2002). Can you see the real me? Activation and expression of the 'true self' on the Internet. *Journal of Social Issues, 58*(1), 33–48.

Cinnirella, M. & Green, B. (2007). Does 'cyber-conformity' vary cross-culturally? Exploring the effect of culture and communication medium on social conformity. *Computers in Human Behaviour, 23*(4), 2011–2025.

Culnan, M. & Markus, M. L. (1987). Information technologies. In F. M. Jablin, L. L. Putnam, K. H. Roberts & L. W. Porter (eds.), *Handbook of Organizational Communication: An Interdisciplinary Perspective* (pp. 420–444). Newbury Park, CA: Sage.

DePaulo, B. M., Ansfield, M. E. & Bell, K. L. (1996a). Theories about deception and paradigms for studying it: A critical appraisal of Buller and Burgoon's interpersonal deception theory and research. *Communication Theory, 3*, 297–310.

DePaulo, B. M., Kashy, D. A., Kirkendol, S. E., Wyer, M. M. & Epstein, J. A. (1996b). Lying in everyday life. *Journal of Personality and Social Psychology, 70*, 979–995.

Dubrovsky, V. J., Kiesler, S. & Sethna, B. N. (1991).The equalization phenomenon: Status effects in Computer Mediated and face-to-face decision-making groups. *Human Computer Interaction, 6*, 119–146.

Ellison, N., Heino, R. & Gibbs, J. (2006). Managing impressions online: Self-presentation processes in the online dating environment. *Journal of Computer Mediated Communication, 11*(2), article 2. Retrieved from: http://jcmc.indiana.edu/vol11/issue2/ellison.html.

Fiore, A. T. & Donath, J. S. (2005). Homophily in online dating: When do you like someone like yourself? *Computer-Human Interaction 2005*, 1371–1374.

Fogel, J. & Nehmad, E. (2009). Internet social network communities: Risk-taking trust, and privacy concerns. *Computers in Human Behaviour, 25*, 153–160.

Gibbs, J. L., Ellison, N. B. & Heino, R. D. (2006). Self-presentation in online personals the role of anticipated future interaction, self-disclosure, and perceived success in Internet dating. *Communication Research, 33*(2), 152–177.

Ginger, J. (2007). The Facebook project: Social capital and the chief. Retrieved from: www.thefacebookproject.com/research/jeff/publications/socialcapitalchief.html.

Goffman, E. (1959). *The Presentation of Self in Everyday Life*. Garden City, NY: Doubleday.

Hancock, J. T. (2007). Digital deception: When, where and how people lie online. In A. N. Joinson, K. McKenna, T. Postmes & U. Reips (eds), *Oxford Handbook of Internet Psychology* (pp. 287–301). Oxford: Oxford University Press.

Hancock, J. T., Thom-Santelli, J. & Ritchie, T. (2004*). Deception and Design: The Impact of Communication Technologies on Lying Behaviour*. In *Proceedings of the Conference on Computer Human Interaction* (vol. 6, pp. 130–136). New York: ACM.

Hatfield, E. & Sprecher, S. (1986). *Mirror, Mirror . . . The Importance of Looks in Everyday Life*. Albany, NY: State University of New York Press.

Hayne, S. C. & Rice, R. E. (1997). Attribution accuracy when using anonymity in group support systems. *International Journal of Human–Computer Studies, 47*, 429–452.

Heffron, M. H. (1972). The naval ship as an urban design problem. *Naval Engineers Journal, 12*, 49–64.

Higgins, E. T. (1987). Self-discrepancy: A theory relating self and affect. *Psychological Review, 94*(3), 319–340.

Instone, L. (2005). Conversations beyond the classroom: Blogging in a professional development course. In H. Godd (ed.), *Balance, Fidelity, Mobility: Maintaining the Momentum? Proceedings of the 22nd ASCILITE Conference* (vol. 1, pp. 305–308). Brisbane: Ascilite.

Joinson, A. N. (2000). Self-disclosure in Computer Mediated communication: The role of self-awareness and visual anonymity. *European Journal of Social Psychology, 31*, 177–192.

Kiesler, S., Siegel, J. & McGuire, T. (1984). Social psychological aspects of Computer Mediated communication. *American Psychologist, 39*, 1123–1134.

Lea, M., Spears, R. & de Groot, D. (2001). Knowing me, knowing you: Anonymity effects on social identity processes within groups. *Personality and Social Psychology Bulletin, 27*, 526–537.

Leary, M. R. (1996). *Self-presentation: Impression Management and Interpersonal Behaviour*. Boulder, CO: Westview Press.

Lemert, C. & Branaman, A. (1997) *The Goffman Reader*. Malden, MA: Blackwell.

Mann, L. (1981). The baiting crowd in episodes of threatened suicide. *Journal of Personality and Social Psychology, 41*(4), 703.

Markus, H. & Nurius, P. (1986). Possible selves. *American Psychologist, 41*(9), 954–969.

Pedersen, D. M. (1979). Dimensions of privacy. *Perceptual and Motor Skills, 48*(3), 1291–1297.

Pempek, T. A., Yermolayeva, Y. A. & Calvert, S. L. (2009). College students' social networking experiences on Facebook. *Journal of Applied Developmental Psychology, 30*, 227–238.

Postmes, T., Spears, R., Sakhel, K. & de Groot, D. (2001). Social influence in computer mediated communication: The effects of anonymity on group behaviour. *Personality and Social Psychology Bulletin, 27*, 1242–1254.

Qian, H. & Scott, C. R. (2007), Anonymity and self-disclosure on weblogs. *Journal of Computer Mediated Communication, 12*, 1428–1451.

Rosenberg, M. (1986). *Society and the Adolescent Self-Image* (revised edn). Middletown, CT: Wesleyan University Press.

Rubin, Z. (1975). Disclosing oneself to a stranger: Reciprocity and its limits. *Journal of Experimental Social Psychology, 11*(3), 233–260.

Rutter, D. R. & Stephenson, G. M. (1979). The role of visual communication in social interaction. *Current Anthropology, 20*(1), 124–125.

Short, J. A. (1974). Effects of medium of communication on experimental negotiation. *Human Relations, 27*(3), 225–234.

Short, J., Williams, E. & Christie, B. (1976). *The Social Psychology of Telecommunications*. London: Wiley.

Siegel, J., Dubrovsky, V., Kiesler, S. & McGuire, T. W. (1986). Group processes in Computer Mediated communication. *Organizational Behaviour and Human Decision Processes, 37*, 157–187.

Skinstad, M. (2008). Facebook: A digital network of friends. In paper presented at the 24th Conference of the Nordic Sociological Association, University of Aarhus, pp. 1–14.

Spears, R. & Lea, M. (1992). Social influence and the influence of the 'social' in Computer Mediated communication. In M. Lea (ed.), *Contexts of Computer Mediated Communication* (pp. 30–65). London: Harvester-Wheatsheaf.

Spears, R. & Lea, M. (1994). Panacea or panopticon? The hidden power in Computer Mediated communication. *Communication Research, 21*(4), 427–459.

Stone, A. R. (1995). *The War of Desire and Technology at the Close of the Mechanical Age*. Cambridge, MA: MIT Press.

Suler, J. R. (2002). Identity management in cyberspace. *Journal of Applied Psychoanalytic Studies, 4*(4), 455–459.

Tanis, M. & Postmes, T. (2003). Social cues and impression formation in CMC. *Journal of Communication, 53*, 676–693.

Tanis, M. & Postmes, T. (2007). Two faces of anonymity: Paradoxical effects of cues to identity in CMC. *Computers in Human Behaviour, 23*(2), 955–970.

Tong, S. T., Van Der Heide, B., Langwell, L. & Walther, J. B. (2008). Too much of a good thing? The relationship between number of friends and interpersonal impressions on Facebook. *Journal of Computer Mediated Communication*, *13*, 531–549.

Turkle, S. (1995) *Life on the Screen: Identity in the Age of the Internet*. New York: Simon & Schuster.

Underwood, J. D. M., Kerlin, L. & Farrington-Flint, L. (2011). The lies we tell and what they say about us: Using behavioural characteristics to explain Facebook activity. *Computers in Human Behaviour*, *27*, 1621–1626.

Walther, J. B. (1996). Computer Mediated communication: Impersonal, interpersonal, and hyperpersonal interaction. *Communication Research*, *23*, 3–43.

Walther, J. B. (2007). Selective self-presentation in Computer Mediated communication: Hyperpersonal dimensions of technology, language, and cognition. *Computers in Human Behaviour*, *23*, 2538–2557.

Walther, J. B., Slovacek, C. L. & Tidwell, L. C. (2001). Is a picture worth a thousand words? Photographic images in long-term and short-term computer-mediated communications. *Communication Research*, *28*(1).

Walther, J. B., Van Der Heide, B., Kim, S., Westerman, D. & Tong, S. T. (2008). The role of friends' appearance and behavior on evaluations of individuals on facebook: Are we known by the company we keep? *Human Communication Research*, *34*, 28–49.

Werner, C. C., Altman, I. & Brown, B. B. (1992). A transactional approach to interpersonal relations: Physical environment, social context, and temporal. *Journal of Social and Personal Relations*, *9*(2), 297–323.

Whitty, M. T. (2007). Revealing the 'real' me, searching for the 'actual' you: Presentations of self on an Internet dating site. *Computers in Human Behaviour*, *24*, 1707–1723.

Yurchisin, J., Watchravesringkan, K. & McCabe, D. B. (2005). An exploration of identity re-creation in the context of Internet dating. *Social Behavior and Personality*, *33*(8), 735–750.

Zhao, S. (2006). Cyber-gathering places and online-embedded relationships. Paper presented at The Annual Meetings of the Eastern Sociological Society, Boston, MA.

Zhou, L. & Hovy, E. (2006). On the summarization of dynamically introduced information: Online discussions and blogs. In Proceedings of the AAAI Spring Symposium on Computational Approaches to Analysing weblogs. Stanford, CA.

Zhao, S., Grasmuck, S. & Martin, J. (2008). Identity construction on Facebook: Digital empowerment in anchored relationships. *Computers in Human Behaviour*, *24*, 1816–1836.

Zimbardo, P. G. (1969). The human choice. Individuation, reason, and order vs. deindividuation, impulse and chaos. *Nebraska Symposium on Motivation*, *17*, 237–307.

Zuckerman, M. & Kuhlman, D. M. (2000). Personality and risk-taking: Common biosocial factors. *Journal of Personality*, *68*, 999–1029.

5 The dark side of the Internet

Hannah Barton

CHAPTER OVERVIEW

The online environment has offered many opportunities for positive interactions, from social support to keeping people connected and entertained. However, it can also facilitate much negative behaviour, which can cause all sorts of consequences and pain to those who experience them. The online experience can be just as powerful and painful as an offline one. This chapter will provide an overview on some of the more common anti-social behaviours that can be found online such as trolling, flaming, griefing and online sexual harassment. It will also examine how the online environment can facilitate prejudice and ostracism.

KEY TERMS

When we think of a troll from the fairy tales, we think of an ugly brute that hides under a bridge or in a dark cave, just waiting for an unsuspecting victim who they can then terrorise. Well, online trolls behave in a similar fashion. They frequent discussion pages and online communities' support pages and wait for an opportune moment to pounce with a provocative comment before sitting back and watching the sparks fly. To the trolls, this is just fun. **Trolling** occurs when there is 'deliberate attempts to provoke other participants into any reaction, thus disrupting communication on the forum and potentially steering the discussion from its original topic' (Hopkins, 2013, p. 5).

Trolls operate by participating in a discussion just like any other member, but then post a comment which is the bait and is designed to be upsetting. The disagreement spirals out of control with comments being directed away from the content of the posts or the topic and becoming personal insults. This is then a flame war. **Flaming** occurs when personal insults are used at the other participants in the discussion. Flaming can also be broadened to include verbal aggression through the use of swearing and offensive language. Certain sites such as YouTube seem to be popular venues for flaming (Moor *et al.*, 2010, p. 1536). It can be argued that the disinhibition characteristics of the Internet and the lack of social cues can foster flaming.

THE INTERNET AND TROLLING

It has been argued that the Internet by its nature can facilitate trolling – the fact that in many online discussions the participants do not actually see each other or, more importantly, the impact their words have on the person. This lack of visibility can lead to a dehumanising effect, making us feel detached and remote from the effects of our words and behaviours. This, coupled with the anonymity that most users feel when online, can trigger **online disinhibition** (Suler, 2004), leading us to do and say things that we would not do in a face-to-face situation. As Widyanto and Griffins (2011, p.15) describe it, 'the internet provides anonymity which removes the threat of confrontation, rejection and other consequences of behaviour'. We do not feel responsible or accountable for our behaviour. This loss of self-consciousness is akin to **deindividuation** which occurs when we become submerged in a group and which results in anti-social behaviour.

Why do the trolls do it?

To date, there has been little empirical research on trolling, but that is changing. One of the first studies to look at the motivations behind trolling examined trolling in Wikipedia and discovered that the main reasons for trolling were boredom, attention seeking and revenge. Furthermore, Shachaf and Hara's (2010) study found that the trolls found it fun to cause trouble for Wikipedia and its users. Herring's (2002) study examined trolling in online feminist discussion forums and found that certain environments and support sites are prime targets for trolling. These are ones that are regarded as non-mainstream and according to Herring (2002, p.371) provide a 'new arena for the enactment of power inequalities such as those motivated by sexism, racism and heterosexism'.

Hopkins (2013) found that trolls get entertainment from getting a reaction or rise from the other users and that their behaviour can be seen within a game frame. Flaming can be interpreted as game or contest of verbal wit. This possible explanation can be seen in terms of online communities and group behaviour, and how status and prestige is awarded. The verbal contest between the core members who retaliate against the troll turns into an online show, and the defending members are often rewarded by praise, support and respect from the other members of the community. Thus, often a troll and his/her attack on an online community can enhance cohesion in the group

FIGURE 5.1 Image of a troll

(Christos Georghiou/Shutterstock)

when the members unite to defend their community against a common enemy. Trolling and flaming can also be seen, in some cases, as a battle between out-group members (dissenters) of a community and core members (in-group members) rather than just an attack by an outsider to the community. Trolling can often serve a useful function to strengthen group cohesion, and to cement ties and bonds between the community members.

How do trolls operate?

Herring (2002) has identified three ways in which a troll operates depending on the type of message they post. Not all trolls will use the same strategy all the time. There are three types of messages which serve a different purpose but whose underlying goal of disruption is still the same.

1   Messages that appear outwardly sincere.
2   Messages that are deliberately designed to provoke a reaction.
3   Messages that are designed to waste time through fruitless argument.

The trolls get pleasure out of watching the other participants react to their bait and continue to draw them in through ever increasing provocative comments.

Hardaker (2010, p.231) describes four main characteristics of trolling. These are as follows. *Aggression* – this involves baiting the other users through the use of annoying or offensive comments. *Success* – this is whether or not the bait has been taken and has provoked an angry response from the other users. This is known as biting. The next stage is *disruption* – this is where the troll changes the course of the discussion and leads the discussion into a series of personal insults and the last one is *deception* – this is where the troll often uses a virtual or false identity created with the sole intention of disrupting the group discussion and creating conflict. These identities change when the users realise that it is a troll who is at work. The troll discards the identity and creates a new one to continue to stay in the group.

Most members when they realise that it is a troll refuse to engage or **bite**. However, some members willingly get caught up in a flame war. Trolls create personas in order to get a bite. Some exaggerate for effect and then may express a viewpoint which is extreme in order to get a reaction. Trolls can also use sarcasm, mock-respect and mock-politeness in order to ridicule the group members (Hopkins, 2013). It can be said that trolls appear to role play and move between personas during the exchange. It can be viewed as an online verbal duel to the troll who is seemingly indifferent to the chaos and pain that their comments can cause.

Flaming can also be viewed as a verbal duel. But the lack of social cues (facial expression, body language and tone of voice) can add to its intensity. Group members often communicate in particular ways to each other. They develop communication norms and some groups adopt communication styles/norms which are akin to flaming. Lea and Spears (1991) found that student groups often used insults when communicating with each other, which the student members found funny. These comments are defined as flames by third-party observers who are not actually involved in the communication. Some critics (Lange, 2005) have argued that this context should be taken into account and that it is the perceptions of the communicators that matters. Thus, some groups may use flaming as normative behaviour and other groups may not. Moor *et al.* (2010) comments that it is often the ambiguity of Computer Mediated Communication (CMC) which can frustrate users who then express themselves more explicitly. This can become aggressive or can lead to flaming. It has been suggested that often flaming starts with a disagreeing comment which is interpreted as offensive (Moor *et al.*, 2010). This shows how the media of the Internet can contribute to miscommunication, which can then become aggressive as in a flaming war.

THE INTERACTIONAL NORM FRAMEWORK OF FLAMING

The gaps in the conceptual models of flaming as mentioned above, which do not take situation or context into account when making a judgement on flaming, led to O'Sullivan and Flanagin (2003) putting forward a theoretical framework called the interactional norm cube. This theory focuses on the perceived appropriateness of a message based on the perspectives of the sender, the receiver and the context or third party. This can be visually represented in a cube which yields eight possible conditions. Each party to the communication must decide on the level of social appropriateness that the message contains. If it is deemed to be inappropriate, then it is labelled as a transgression. A flame occurs when the sender deliberately violates the norm, the receiver perceives it as a transgression and the third party or audience also sees it as a violation of the norms. This framework does set out to take culture, social norms, relationship norms and the dynamic nature of these over time into account, as well as the interactions between parties when judging the appropriateness of communications between the parties. The framework could lead to better understanding of harassment and hate speech.

PREJUDICE AND STEREOTYPING ONLINE

Prejudice has been traditionally an umbrella term that covers discrimination, negative attitudes and stereotyping. They are interrelated but separate topics. **Prejudice** is a negative attitude towards a social group and its members. It works by viewing the targets as being less than human. This dehumanisation of a group can then make discrimination and other unacceptable behaviours seem acceptable as the targets are falsely considered as 'less than human'. Traditionally, Allport (1954) viewed prejudice as being composed of three components. These are: the cognitive – the beliefs about the person; the affective, which are the strong feelings, usually negative, about the person; the conative which is the intention to behave in a certain way towards the person.

We know from a classic experiment conducted by LaPiere in 1934 that often the *attitude* (prejudice)–*behaviour* (discrimination) relationship is not as straightforward as we may think. LaPiere spent two years travelling around the United States with a young Chinese-American couple and visited 250 hotels, caravan parks and restaurants. They were refused service only once during the tour. When they finished, LaPiere contacted 128 of the places that they had visited and asked them 'Would you accept members of the Chinese race in your businesses?' The response was that 92 per cent said no, they would not, 7 per cent were uncertain and 1 per cent said yes, they would accept them. So the expressed prejudice was not actually encountered during the tour. From this, we can take it that many people do not actually act or behave overtly in line with their attitudes. That is not to say that discrimination cannot be expressed in subtle ways or indirectly. Often people may not show explicit prejudice but may still have implicit prejudice which can be revealed through the use of the **Implicit Association Test** (IAT) by Greenwald *et al.* (1998). This is a reaction time test that measures attitudes and can detect attitudes that people might try to hide due to their unpopularity. It works by looking at the underlying stereotypical associations that people form due to social categorisation. Our attitudes and behaviours towards others are consequently influenced by this categorisation, even when we are unaware of this influence. This is called implicit biases. These can occur online as well as offline.

How widespread is prejudice online? Some researchers such as Tynes, Giang and Williams (2008) have found that participants had a 59 per cent chance of experiencing or witnessing racial prejudice in unmonitored chat rooms and a 19 per cent chance in a monitored chat room. Other researchers have commented on the abundance of white avatars in virtual environments. There have been accusations of 'white dominance' against avatar-based virtual worlds (Kafai *et al.*, 2010). Real world prejudice has been found in the virtual world. Participants with greater negative implicit prejudice kept a greater distance from a dark-skinned avatar (Dotsch & Wigboldus, 2008). Requests are more likely to be complied with if they come from a light-skinned avatar compared to a dark-skinned avatar. We judge and treat avatars using the same criteria and rules that people are judged with in the real world. This can make the virtual world rather threatening to minorities. Research by Lee and Park (2011) into how avatar-based cues can shape ethno-racial minorities have shown that white dominance cues can signal threat to non-white individuals and therefore they feel disconnected and detached from the virtual world. In other words, non-white individuals do not feel comfortable being who they are in the virtual world. They do not feel a sense of belonging and do not feel they can participate.

Stereotyping

Stereotyping is an over-generalised belief about an individual based on their group membership. Stereotypes are culturally defined, and knowledge of a stereotype does not indicate agreement. This is due to our tendency to put people, just like we do with objects, into groups, based on a perceived or actual similarity. This is social categorisation and is a mental shortcut or heuristic. Indicators of social group identification, such as physical features indicating gender or race, can activate concepts or stereotypes relating to those social groups. Stereotypes are culturally created from our tendency to categorise.

This idea of forming categories of people into groups such as in-group (like me/us) and out-group (not like me/us) as a natural and universal one, is one of the core tenets of **Social Identity Theory** devised by Tajfel and Turner. This theory also suggests that our group membership is an important source of our self-identity and self-esteem. An attack on our group (in-group) is an attack on us and on our self-esteem. However, this bond allows other in-group members to become a viable source of information about social reality, thus making possible processes of mutual social influence and persuasion (Turner, 1991). This means that we can often pay more attention to our in-group than to our own values and ideas. The differences between the groups to stimulate the bias may be trivial, such as eye colour. Jane Eliot in 1968 did a classic study highlighting this point. She identified two groups in her primary school class based on eye colour (blue eyes or brown eyes). It was then suggested to the children that on a given day, one group such as the blue-eyed group were superior and, furthermore, the brown-eyed group were not to play or mix with them. The brown-eyed group had to wear labels. Within a very short time, differences in behaviour between the two groups became apparent. The blue-eyed group behaved arrogantly, while the brown-eyed group behaved in a helpless state. The next day, she reversed the situation with the brown-eyed group being told they were superior and the blue-eyed group wearing the labels. This showed how quickly behaviour could be modified on the basis of a stereotype based on a trivial difference between groups and the effects of stereotypes on self-esteem. This is where an in-group/out-group bias is created on a single trivial characteristic but still using human characteristics. The question is if a human encountered a non-human being, would this in-group/out-group bias still work? Gong (2008) carried out a study to try to answer that. The study looked at preferences for computer-synthesised white avatars, black avatars, and robot characters for virtual social roles, including virtual friend or tutor. He found that highly prejudiced whites who had minimal interest in robots (out-group) still preferred robot characters to black ones for all social roles and did not show any in-group bias towards humans. This highlights that the expected bias towards humans (albeit of a different ethnic group) was surpassed by the prejudice felt towards that ethnic group and the non-humans (the robots) were preferred for the social roles.

Effects of online ostracism and prejudice

The effects of online **ostracism** and prejudice are just as strong and real to the people who experience it and to their self-esteem. Williams *et al.* (2000) demonstrated that people can feel ostracised when playing an online game with competitors they visualise, even when what they see on the screen are simple coloured representations. Even when people are told that the game is controlled by a computer, the effects of ostracism are about as negative as when they are ostracised by actual others (Zadro *et al.*, 2004).

How can we reduce prejudice online?

One method of reducing prejudice (Allport, 1954) is the **contact hypothesis** which asserts that positive contact between an in-group and an out-group reduces the intergroup bias. This effect is enhanced if there is a common goal for both groups. Where there is a need to work cooperatively to achieve a common goal and there is a shift in thinking from 'us' and 'them' to 'we', then intergroup bias will also be reduced. Contact must also be between people of equal status, occur frequently and in a range of situations. There is some debate as to whether context (where) and depth of contact produce an effect, with results of studies being mixed. A study into gaming by Vang and Fox (2014) found that playing both cooperatively and competitively in a single session led to more positive evaluations of black avatars than white avatars from white participants. This shows that games and the virtual environment can be used effectively to foster positive intergroup attitudes and reduce prejudice and in-group bias. A study on the contact hypothesis and CMC by Walther, Hoter, Ganayem and Shonfeld (2014) using Muslim students and Jewish (religious and secular students) in the context of an online course in which they collaborated on educational technology doing assignments for a year showed that the students who participated in the virtual groups experience had significantly less prejudice towards these respective out-groups at the end of the course, compared to control subjects who did not participate. Tynes *et al.* (2008) have shown that the more time spent online interacting with out-groups by European American participants, the more open they were to diverse groups. So there are mixed results for the effectiveness of the contact hypothesis within online settings.

Positive perceptions of out-groups can be bolstered by emphasising a positive trait that is considered stereotypical of that group. This means that if people are encouraged to focus on the positive stereotypical characteristics of individual out-group members, they are likely to feel more positive about that out-group. This is positive stereotyping and the Internet is able to facilitate such positive encounters through chatrooms, gaming and in virtual worlds.

Another way of reducing prejudice is to enhance similarity between people. This is often done when we feel empathy – the experience of emotion congruent with another person's situation (Batson *et al.*, 2002). Empathy is linked with decreased prejudice. Someone who is high in trait empathy is likely to identify with someone who is victimised or ostracised and to experience concern for the victim. In terms of harassment, lower levels of empathy are associated with greater acceptance of sexual harassment and prejudice. Interventions using immersive virtual environments (IVEs) have shown successful reductions in ageism (Yee & Bailenson, 2006), but other studies

(Groom *et al.*, 2009) where participants viewed themselves in the IVE embodied as black avatars and others viewed themselves as white avatars indicate that automatic racial bias is not reduced by embodying a person of a disfavoured racial group. So it seems that using virtual reality technologies (IVEs) did not work as well in reducing racial prejudice.

Individual differences and prejudice

Are there certain personality types that are more prone to using stereotypes than others? Are there times when we are more likely to rely on a stereotype? The problems arise when people make decisions and judgements solely based on a shortcut due to stress or cognitive overload. They are not paying attention and just take the cognitive shortcut. Then there are certain personality traits which can make people prone to the effects of stereotyping and prejudice. These include the need for cognition (Cacioppo & Petty, 1982) which has been defined as the 'tendency for an individual to engage in and enjoy thinking'. Low-need for cognition individuals are more prone to following stereotypical information as well as other forms of social influence online like e-wom (e – Word of Mouth) recommendations. Another trait is the personal need for structure which operates when there are individual differences in the need to organise their world into simple cognitive structures. High-need individuals would have a need to organise their environments and structure their lives in a more rigid way than low-need individuals (Schaller *et al.*, 1995). These personality variables may influence group stereotype formation in certain social contexts (where there is little public accountability or in anonymous conditions) and make individuals more likely to follow the stereotype with little cognitive evaluation. This may mean that the Internet with its capacity for anonymity can render these personality types more likely to rely on stereotypes when online.

SEXUAL HARASSMENT ONLINE

Some online environments can be highly sexualised, and sometimes anyone with a female name may receive unwanted comments or approaches from strangers. The anonymity that the Internet provides can heighten the problem leading to sexual harassment. There are different forms of sexual harassment online, it can be from an environment where women can often be perceived as 'cyberbabes' with whom one can have cyber-sex (Doring, 2000) to more direct contact, which can range from obscene comments in chatrooms, to emails with lewd content/pictures.

The growth of female gamers has been accompanied with sexual harassment which has become an issue in the gaming community. Fox and Tang (2014) had online game players relate the last incident of harassment they had witnessed or experienced; 10 per cent of these incidents reported sexist remarks ranging from traditional sexism to sexual harassment. One of the reasons for this may be the stereotypical roles that female game characters play. It can be a very pretty-in-pink princess who needs to be saved or it could be a highly sexualised female warrior. A study by Yao *et al.* (2010) revealed that playing games with sexualised characters leads players to normalise sexual harassment, and men indicate a greater likelihood to harass women after play. Fox *et al.* (2013) found that women who were embodied in sexualised avatars that resembled the self demonstrated greater rape myth acceptance than women who were embodied in other avatars. This means that users of sexualised avatars may be at risk for developing negative attitudes towards women and the self, outside of the virtual environment. This is an effect of the *Proteus Effect* in this study.

Another factor that can contribute is that in some networked games, the atmosphere can be akin to a locker room in that bad language, derogatory comments and swearing may be common. The female gamer may feel like she is trespassing. Gaming may be perceived as a man's pursuit and this could explain the anti-normative behaviour that female gamers experience. In a field experiment, conducted by Kuznekoff and Rose (2013), they played a networked violent video game with other anonymous players and interacted with them using male or female pre-recorded voices. The female voice received three times the amount of negative comments than the male voice had received. Personality factors too can influence the amount of sexual harassment that female gamers receive. Fox and Tang (2014) have found that social dominance orientation and two forms of masculinity, the desire for power over women and the need for heterosexual self-presentation, predicted video game sexism. Many female gamers, aware of the hyper masculine environment in gaming, adopt a variety of strategies to avoid harassment; these include not using feminine names or characters/avatars or any method that could identify their gender.

CYBERSTALKING

This is just like physically stalking a person but using the Internet or other forms of technology such as mobile phones to pursue and harass another. It follows the same characteristics of stalking behaviour such as persistently sending unwanted gifts or presents, threatening to damage the victim's property, and causing the victim's reputation to suffer by either spreading rumours or sharing personal information. In cyberstalking, unsolicited contact is made by email, instant messenger, social networking or online chat rooms. The victim's inbox may be flooded with offensive messages or images. The stalker may have an obsessive interest in the victim's life and activities both online and offline. The stalker may even use spy software to track everything that happens on the victim's computer. In some cases, the stalker may assume the victim's identity and post material online which may or may not be false. The Internet can facilitate cyberstalking as it allows the stalker a perceived feeling of anonymity. The cyberstalker may threaten the victim by phone and can even approach the victim offline. There are many steps that a person can take to reduce the risk of being a victim of cyberstalking. It is important to check privacy settings on calendar and social media sites which may alert a person to your location. Using both good password management and updated security software will also help lessen your chance of being a victim. Reyns *et al.* (2012) found that 48 per cent of the 974 college students sampled had experienced cyberstalking. This study also found that females, non-whites, non-heterosexuals and non-singles all experienced greater overall cyberstalking victimisation than did males, whites, heterosexuals and singles. Furthermore, in 44 per cent of cases, the cyberstalker was a complete stranger. This could be down to the ease that the Internet allows people to interact with each other in anonymity.

GRIEFING

Griefing is a term used by online gaming communities to describe general aggressive behaviour. Warner and Raiter (2005, p. 47) have defined it as 'the intentional harassment of other players which utilizes aspects of the game structure or physics in unintended ways to cause distress for other players'.

It has been linked to cyberbullying as grief play is deliberate harassment aimed at another player. However Coyne *et al.* (2009) have made the distinction that griefing is aimed at an avatar whereas cyberbullying, although being carried out using technology, is aimed at a real person (see Chapter 17 for more details on cyberbullying). That is not to say that those who experience it aimed at their avatar don't suffer emotionally. According to Coyne *et al.* (2009), 41 per cent perceived griefing to have the same or more of an impact than cyberbullying. This could be particularly acute for those who strongly identify with their avatar (their avatar is part of their self-concept) or for those who see their avatar as being a part of them. One of the motivations linked to grief play is the desire to dominate or exert power. It is also seen as a chance to show off technical skills or expertise especially when aimed at a new player or resident in a virtual world. It is aimed at disrupting games and enjoyment of virtual worlds. In virtual worlds, it can disrupt the sense of security that residents can feel in these environments.

Foo and Koivisto (2004) categorised four overall motivations for grief play online. These are *game-influenced*, which occurs when anonymity afforded by the game gives protection to the person who believes that their behaviour is expected and thus tolerated by the other gamers. Next, *player-influenced*, which is due to personal traits such as spite and vindictiveness. Then, *griefer-influenced*, which is due to a desire to build up a reputation and to maintain/establish a group identity, and finally *self-influenced*, which is due to personal motivation of the griefer to exert power and get enjoyment from watching the effects. It can be difficult to control griefing in avatars, as often avatar names may not be tracked to an individual in real life. This means that the person cannot be held accountable for virtual behaviours.

CONCLUSION

This chapter set out to provide an overview of some of the negative and disruptive behaviours that people may encounter online. It identified some of the more common negative behaviours such as trolling, cyberstalking and flaming that one might encounter online. It also described some of the effects of these behaviours on the victims. Some guidelines on how to reduce negative behaviours such as online prejudice were given in the chapter.

> ## DISCUSSION QUESTIONS
>
> 1   What can we do as a society to reduce online prejudice?
> 2   What steps, if any, should social media and other online providers take to prevent trolling and online harassment?
> 3   Which in your opinion is more influential in online prejudice – the social group to which you belong or your own personality?
> 4   How does griefing differ from cyberbullying?

RECOMMENDED READING LIST

This book conveys good technical and legal terms and explanations. It provides research findings to support the claims made in the book and is a good read for anyone who wants more information on this topic.

Bocij, P. (2004). *Cyberstalking: Harassment in the Internet Age.* Praeger: London.

The following article is a very interesting one examining the personality traits of trolls with the dark tetrad of psychopathy, narcissism, Machiavellianism, psychopathy and sadistic personality.

Buckels, E. E., Trapnell, P. D. & Paulhaus, D. L. (2014). Trolls just want to have fun. *Personality and Individual Differences, 67*, 97–102.

GLOSSARY

Bite   This is what a troll wants a person to do, to rise to the bait and react to the bait.

Contact hypothesis   Allport's idea of how to reduce bias by encouraging contact as equals between two individuals or groups.

Deindividuation   The process by which you don't feel personally accountable for actions due to being part of a group.

Flaming   When personal insults are exchanged online.

Implicit Association Test (IAT)   Test which measures attitudes that the person is unaware of or unwilling to admit to having.

Online disinhibition   The online disinhibition effect was coined by Suler (2004). It refers to a loosing or removal of social inhibitions when interacting online that would normally be present in face-to-face communication.

Ostracism   When one is excluded or isolated from a group.

Prejudice   General term for any negative attitude towards a social group.

Social Categorisation Theory   Putting people into groups on the basis of some shared attribute.

Social Identity Theory   Theory which seeks to explain intergroup discrimination and how we form in-groups/out-groups.

Trolling   Negative behaviours in online environments (such as social media and gaming) designed to provoke a reaction such as inducing annoyance or disruption.

REFERENCES

Allport, G. (1954). *The Nature of Prejudice*. Reading, MA: Addison-Wesley.

Batson, C. D., Chang, J., Orr, R. & Rowland, J. (2002). Empathy, attitudes and action: Can feeling for a member of a stigmatized group motivate one to help the group. *Personality and Social Psychology Bulletin*, 28, 1656–1666.

Cacioppo, J. & Petty, R. (1982). The need for cognition. *Journal of Personality and Social Psychology*, 42, 116–131.

Coyne, I., Chesney, T, Logan, B. & Madden, N. (2009). Griefing in a virtual community: An exploratory survey of second life residents. *Journal of Psychology*, 217(4) 214–221.

Doring, N. (2000). Feminist views of cybersex, victimization, liberation and empowerment. *CyberPsychology & Behaviour*, 3(5), 863–883.

Dotsch, R. & Wigboldus, D. J. H. (2008). Virtual prejudice. *Journal of Experimental Social Psycholgoy*, 55(4), 1194–1198.

Foo, C. Y. & Koivisto, E. M. (2004, December). Grief Player Motivations. Paper presented at the Other Players Conference, Denmark.

Fox, J. & Tang, W. T. (2014). Sexism in online video games: The role of conformity to masculine norms and social dominance orientation. *Computers in Human Behavior*, 33, 314–320.

Fox, J., Bailenson, J. N. & Tricase, L. (2013). The embodiment of sexualized virtual selves: The Proteus effect and experiences of self-objectification via avatars. *Computers in Human Behavior*, 29, 930–938.

Gong, L. (2008). The boundary of racial prejudice: Comparing preferences for computer-synthesized white, black, and robot characters. *Computers in Human Behavior*, 24, 2074–2093.

Greenwald, A. G., McGhee, D. E. & Schwartz, J. L. K. (1998). Measuirng individual differences in implicit cognition: The implicit association test. *Journal of Personality and Social Psychology*, 74(6), 1464–1480.

Groom, V., Bailenson, J. N. & Nass, C. (2009). The influence of racial embodiment on racial bias in immersive virtual environments. *Social Influence*, 8, 1–18.

Hardaker, C. (2010). Trolling in asynchronous Computer Mediated communication: From user discussions to academic definitions. *Journal of Politeness Research*, 6, 215–242.

Herring, S. C. (2002). Slouching toward the ordinary: Current trends in computer-mediated communication. *New Media Society*, 6, 26–37.

Hopkins, C. (2013). Trolling in online discussions: From provocation to community–building. *Brno Studies in English*, 39(1), 4–26.

Kafai, Y. B., Fields, D. A. & Cook, M. S. (2010). Your second selves: Avatar designs and identity play. *Games and Culture* (special issue), 5(1), 23–42.

Kuznekoff, J. H. & Lindsey M. Rose, L. M. (2013). Communication in multiplayer gaming: Examining player responses to gender cues. *New Media & Society*, 15(4), 541–556.

Lange, P. G. (2005). Getting to know you: Using hostility to reduce anonymity in online communication. *Texas Linguistic Forum*, 49, 95–107.

Lea, M. & Spears, R. (1991). Computer mediated communication, de-individuation and group decision-making. *International Journal of Man-Machine Studies*, 34, 283–301.

Lee, J. R. & Park, S. W. (2011). 'Whose second life is this?' How avatar-based racial cues shape ethno-racial minorities' perception of virtual worlds. *Cyberpsychology, Behavior, and Social Networking*, 14(11), 637–642.

O' Sullivan, P. B. & Flanagin, A. J. (2003). Reconceptualizing 'flaming' and other problematic messages. *New Media Society*, 5(69), DOI: 10.1177/1461444803005001908.

Moor, P. J., Heuvelman, A. & Verleur, R. (2010). Flaming on YouTube. *Computers in Human Behavior*, 26, 1536–1546.

Reyns, B. W., Henson, B. & Fisher, B. S. (2012). Stalking in the twilight zone: Extent of cyberstalking victimization and offending among college students. *Deviant Behaviour*, 33(1), 1–25, DOI: 10.1080/01639625.2010.538364.

Schaller, M., Boyd, C. Yohannes, J. & O'Brien, M. (1995). The prejudiced personality revisited: Personal need for structure and formation of erroneous group stereotypes. *Journal of Personality and Social Psychology*, 68(3), 544–555.

Shachaf, P. & Hara, N. (2010). Beyond vandalism: Wikipedia trolls. *Journal of Information Science*, 35(3), 357–370.

Suler, J. (2004). The online disinhibition effect. *Cyberpsychology & Behavior*, 7(3), 321–326.

Turner, J. C. (1991). *Social Influence*. Milton Keynes: Open University Press.

Tynes, B. M., Giang, M. T. & Williams, D. (2008). Online racial discrimination and psychological adjustment among adolescents. *Journal of Adolescent Health*, 43, 565–569.

Vang, M. H. & Fox, J. (2014). Race in virtual environments: Competitive versus cooperative games with black or white avatars. *Cyberpsychology Behaviour and Social Networking*, 17(4), 235–240.

Walther, J. B., Hoter, E., Ganayen, A. & Shonfeld, M. (2014). Computer Mediated communication and the reduction of prejudice: A controlled longitudinal field experiment among Jews and Arabs in Israel. Retrieved from *Computers in Human Behavior*, at: http://dx.doi.org/10.1016/j.chb.2014.08.004.

Warner, D. E. & Raiter, M. (2005). Social context in massively-multiplayer online games (MMOGs): Ethical questions in shared space, *International Review of Information Ethics*, 4, 47–50.

Widyanto, L. and Griffiths, M.D. (2011) An empirical study of problematic internet use and self esteem. *International Journal of Cyber Behvavior, Psychology and Learning*, 1, 13–24.

Williams, K. D., Cheung, C. K. & Choi, W. (2000). Cyberostracism: Effects of being ignored over the Internet. *Journal of Personal and Social Psychology*, 79(5), 748–762.

Yao, M., Mahood, C. & Linz, D. (2010). Sexual priming, gender stereotyping , and likelihood to sexually harass: Examining the cognitive effect of playing sexually-explicit video games. *Sex Roles*, 62(1), 77–88.

Yee, N. & Bailenson, J. (2006). Walk a mile in digital shoes: The impact of embodied perspective taking on the reduction of negative stereotyping in immersive virtual environments. Paper presented at PRESENCE: The 9th Annual International Workshop on Presence, Cleveland, OH.

Zadro, L., Williams, K. D. & Richardson, R. (2004). How low can you go? Ostracism by a computer lowers belonging, control, self-esteem, and meaningful existence. *Journal of Experimental Social Psychology*, 40, 560–567.

6 Love and relationships online

Nicola Fox Hamilton

CHAPTER OVERVIEW

Technology has permeated every aspect of our lives, even to the core of our love lives. We expand our dating options and meet people we wouldn't otherwise know, we ask each other on dates, investigate in depth the lives of our potential mates, profess our love, reassure of our affection, say hurtful and healing things in the heat of an argument, end our relationships and observe our ex-partners in the aftermath of a break-up. We use technology to both support and to undermine our relationships, but there are few areas left untouched. This chapter will outline how we use technology in each of these areas, and help us understand the impact of Computer Mediated communication (CMC) on a topic close to our hearts.

KEY TERMS

Some of the key terms that will be addressed in this chapter are **self-presentation** in online dating. We will look at **uncertainty reduction** strategies, which are used at almost every stage in a relationship to reassure the dater about aspects of their partner or relationship. We will consider the effects of **Computer Mediated communication** (CMC), and **hyperpersonal communication** on the various ways in which couples communicate with each other during relationship initiation, maintenance and termination.

SEEKING LOVE ONLINE

Seeking help in finding a romantic partner is not a new phenomenon. Family, friends, matchmakers and personal advertisements in newspapers are just some of the ways in which people have been brought together through the years. More recently, looking for love online has become increasingly common and acceptable. More and more people form relationships in cyberspace and successfully transition those relationships into their offline world. The way in which we communicate online is different in a number of ways to our face-to-face interactions (see Chapter 3), and this impacts on many aspects of our relationships.

Meeting online: where, who and why?

Meeting a new partner online has grown exponentially, and has become the third most likely way for new heterosexual couples to meet since 2009 (Rosenfeld & Thomas, 2012). However, not everyone meets through online dating. Of those who meet online, about half meet through online dating, over a fifth meet through social networking sites, and a quarter through online communities such as discussion groups, virtual worlds and multiplayer games (Hall, 2014). The PEW Research Internet Project found that 20 per cent of people have asked someone out on a date online or by e-mail and 15 per cent of SNS users have asked someone on a date through one of the social networking sites (Smith & Duggan, 2013). The average age of couples that married after meeting through SNS increased from 2005 to 2012, and the overall

FIGURE 6.1 Technology has changed how we experience romance

proportion grew, indicating that as more people adopt SNS use, this will become a more common way to meet new partners (Hall, 2014).

It is interesting to note that CMC has shifted the gender dynamic of asking someone on a date. Men are still more likely to call someone to ask them out, but men and women are equally as likely to text someone to ask them on a date (Smith & Duggan, 2013). Men and women also experience online dating differently. Studies have found that men send significantly more messages than women do, between three and four times more. The gender of the person initiating contact also has an effect on how successful that connection will be, with messaging initiated by women twice as likely to result in a connection (Kreager *et al.*, 2014).

WHAT MOTIVATES PEOPLE TO FIND ROMANCE ONLINE?

One of the primary reasons for people to try online dating is to meet people who are similar to themselves (Hitsch *et al.*, 2010). Going online can open up a multitude of possibilities for those who share similar backgrounds, ethnicity, beliefs and values, and interests and hobbies. Online dating can also be a more discreet option than traditional avenues for those who may not feel safe dating offline. For example, it may be difficult for those seeking same-sex relationships to openly date offline in very conservative societies. The majority of online daters are looking for a long-term relationship, with a significant minority looking for short-term fun (Smith & Duggan, 2013; Whitty & Carr, 2006). There is a reduced fear of rejection online in four distinct ways. Online dating eliminates face-to-face solicitation, and the possibility that the person will be unavailable because of their relationship status, they are signalling their availability by their presence on the site. The general anonymity of online dating also reduces the social stigma of rejection, and a lack of response from a potential partner can be interpreted in a number of alternative ways, such as not having received the message (Rosenfeld & Thomas, 2012).

Experiences and outcomes

While the number of people trying dating online has increased, so too has the number of people who make a date to meet offline. Over 60 per cent of same-sex couples meeting in 2008–2009 met online, and a third of marriages in the US between 2005 and 2012 began online (Rosenfeld & Thomas, 2012).

People's experience of online dating is largely a good one; however, almost half of daters experienced someone misrepresenting themselves, and over a quarter, primarily women, felt harassed or uncomfortable while dating online (Smith & Duggan, 2013).

The stigma around meeting online has considerably reduced over time and it has become a more acceptable way for people to find a partner. However, there are still a significant minority who feel that those who use online dating sites are desperate – 21 per cent in 2013, down from 29 per cent in 2005. In addition, a third of respondents feel that online dating keeps people from settling down because of the array of options available to them on the sites (Smith & Duggan, 2013).

A number of studies have looked at the long-term effects of a relationship having started online. Hall (2014) found that the setting in which people met online predicted how satisfied they were with their relationship. Couples who met on social networking sites had similar levels of marital satisfaction to those that met offline or through online dating. However, couples who met in online communities had significantly lower levels of marital satisfaction.

Those who meet online have relationships that are slightly less likely to end in divorce or separation (Cacioppo *et al.*, 2013). Paul (2014) found that couples who meet online are less likely to marry, but instead tend to be involved in romantic relationships or dating. This study also found that couples who met online are more likely to break up than those who met offline. While the results of Cacioppo *et al.* (2013) and Paul (2014) contradict each other, it is worth bearing in mind that online dating only started to grow significantly as a means of meeting in the last decade or so, and long-term studies on the effect of meeting online are still a work in progress.

Online dating profiles

Dating profiles typically consist of one or more photographs, a number of fixed choice questions about surface characteristics such as height, body type, education or relationship status, and one or more open text sections where the dater describes themselves and possibly the kind of person they would like to meet. Levine (2000) said, 'the beauty of the virtual medium is that flirting is based on words, charm, and seduction, not physical attraction and cues', and the 'about me' text section of a profile is the second most important in determining the attractiveness and trustworthiness of a dater. However, physical attractiveness plays an important role in both offline and online dating, and somewhat more so for men than women (Cloyd, 1977; Fiore *et al.*, 2008). As such, the single most important element of a dating profile is the photograph or photographs. Photographs have what is known as a **halo effect** on the whole profile, where a photograph that is considered attractive influences the judgement of the profile in a positive way, or an unattractive photograph brings down the overall attractiveness rating of the whole profile (Fiore *et al.*, 2008). Photographs also play an important part in daters validating their claims to enjoy certain hobbies or interests by showing images of themselves engaged in those activities (Donath, 1999). Walther and Park's (2002) **warranting principle** posits that people are more likely to trust information online if it cannot be easily manipulated. Hence, photographic evidence of a person's body type, physical fitness or interest in a hobby is a better source of information than text. Multiple images in a profile will increase the levels of perceived intimacy, social orientation, informality, composure and other positive outcome values experienced by daters (Ramirez *et al.*, 2015). However, in contrast to this, Lo *et al.* (2013) found that very attractive photographs received lower ratings of authenticity than those pictures judged to be of lower attractiveness.

Computer Mediated Communication and its effect on online romance

Because so much is being communicated about a dater through the medium of text in the 'about me' section of the profile, and through initial messages exchanged with potential dates, it is important to look at how computer-mediated communication affects the way we share and perceive information in the context of online dating (see Chapter 3 for an overview of CMC research and theory, in particular hyperpersonal communication). For example, errors in spelling in a dating profile may be interpreted by different online daters in a number of ways, such as lack of education or not caring sufficiently about their profile, and even message length and the timing of a reply can be as important as the actual content of the message in forming impressions of the dater (Ellison *et al.*, 2006).

In online dating the speed at which communication becomes intimate can be a lot faster than offline. 'Online dating usually begins with a flurry of email messages, each more intimate than the last' (Rosen *et al.*, 2008). Social penetration theory posits that relationships move from less intimate to more intimate involvement over time, with people disclosing deeper information about themselves as the relationship progresses (Taylor & Altman, 1987). In the initial stages of a relationship people act with caution disclosing less intimate information, but gradually when they see signs of reciprocity, they begin to open up and admit to other aspects of themselves. In online dating this dynamic shifts, as dating profiles reveal a lot of the information that people would typically use for getting to know someone, removing the opportunity to gradually learn about each other. Additionally, because of the anonymity of online dating, the online environment can feel like a safer space in which to reveal core aspects of the self, and so communications can become intimate very quickly. On the other hand, the quantity of information in a dating profile can also halt communication before it has even begun, as decisions about attraction are often made before any interaction has taken place.

Self-presentation and deception in online dating

Self-presentation is 'a strategic negotiation of how one presents one's self to audiences' (Cunningham, 2013, p. 2). Online daters typically strive to present an image of themselves which is both accurate and positive, this is mediated by their fundamental wish to meet a potential partner face-to-face with the possibility of developing a relationship (Ellison *et al.*, 2006; Whitty, 2008). This results in a balance between the desire to self-market with truthful self-presentation, as they want to avoid disappointing a date with an exaggeratedly positive profile. Writing a profile is a dynamic process, often considered difficult, taking place over a period of time with quite a number of people, particularly women, seeking outside help in creating them (Whitty & Carr, 2006). Daters tend to be considered in how they present themselves, often analysing other profiles for suspicious or unattractive elements, and then carefully adapting their own profiles. For example, a female dater describes viewing the photographs of other female daters and realising that when they were sitting down in the images it appeared as though they were being deceptive about their weight by hiding their body. Her response was to ensure that she had a selection of photographs of herself standing full length on her profile to avoid that impression (Ellison *et al.*, 2006). However, daters must be careful not to create a profile that appears unrealistically good, as profiles considered to match an ideal self rather than a real self are liked less (Norton *et al.*, 2007).

A number of studies have shown that deception is widespread in online dating profiles. Daters prefer profiles that they consider to be genuine and honest, and are rarely forgiving of lies told by others; however, 51 per cent of them lie about some aspect of themselves (Whitty, 2008). Both men and women lie about many aspects of themselves, but men are more likely to lie about their height, their relationship status or children, women more about their age, looks or weight, particularly by using outdated photographs (Ellison *et al.*, 2006; Hancock & Toma, 2009; Toma *et al.*, 2008; Whitty, 2008). Women also use more deceptive self-presentation in general then men (Lo *et al.*, 2013). The amount by which people lie tends to be small, again mitigated by the desire to meet in real life, and most daters consider it to be exaggeration rather than blatant lying (Toma *et al.*, 2008; Whitty, 2008). However, in Hardie and Buzwell's study (2006), an equal number of single and partnered people admitted that they had experienced online romance, thus indicating that many people may be cheating online. One of the reasons that online daters seek to quickly meet face-to-face after striking up communication with another dater, is to ensure that the person matches the impression that they have created in their profile. Often this is not the case and the dater has misrepresented themselves in some way (Smith & Duggan, 2013). Interestingly, honesty is not necessarily a successful self-presentation strategy in online dating. Greater amounts of self-disclosure can lead to greater self-presentation success, but more honesty does not (Gibbs *et al.*, 2006). People believe that the more they know someone the more they will like them; however, this is not always the case. With the exception of rare cases where additional information confirms compatibility or similarity, additional information more often than not confirms dissimilarity and so in fact reduces liking (Norton *et al.*, 2007; Rosen *et al.*, 2008).

WHAT MAKES A DATING PROFILE ATTRACTIVE?

People tend to approach online dating as though shopping for a partner, complete with the requisite shopping list. Some of the most important qualities for daters include physical attributes, shared similar interests and values, socioeconomic status, personality, honesty, age and sense of humour. Shared similar interests and values are important, as 85 per cent of daters listed it as a quality they looked for when dating online (Whitty & Carr, 2006). It is called **homophily**, where people tend to like people who are similar to themselves. Online daters in particular seek this more than offline daters, perhaps because dating profiles highlight this information and make it more salient than it would be offline. Social penetration theory suggests that offline daters would gradually learn this information about each other as the relationship progresses, whereas online daters are presented with it from the initial point of contact. Thus, for online daters it is at the forefront of their minds as they seek a partner. Online daters in particular are more attracted to those who have similar demographic and life course characteristics such as marital history and desire for children. They also prefer others with similar physical build, attractiveness, ethnicity, occupation, education, socio-economic status and smoking habits (Fiore *et al.*, 2010; Hitsch *et al.*, 2010). It is particularly interesting that these preferences appear more in their actions (who they choose to contact and respond to) than in the stated preferences on their profile (Fiore & Donath, 2005). One area where daters prefer dissimilar others is attractiveness. Here there is a vertical preference, where all daters prefer others more attractive than themselves, within the limits of who they might realistically date (Kreager *et al.*, 2014). It is possible that online dating makes this possible because of the low risk in contacting someone online, and the reduced fear of rejection (Rosenfeld & Thomas, 2012), as well as the greater access to attractive daters.

What men and women find attractive in dating profiles differs a little. Women tend to prefer men who are older, more educated and have higher levels of self-reported attractiveness, possibly translated as having higher levels of self-esteem. Men tend to send more messages to women who have a photograph on their profile, and who have higher levels of self-reported attractiveness; again, this may be higher self-esteem (Fiore & Donath, 2005).

Shifting modalities: moving offline

Relationships that start online tend to move slowly, with the participants gradually developing trust by giving out an email address, then a phone number and then meeting face-to-face (Baker, 2002; Whitty & Gavin, 2001). However, online dating tends to moves more quickly through these stages to the face-to-face contact, as daters don't want to waste time getting to know someone online before they have established if there is any physical chemistry present. They also want to ensure that the online persona matches the real person and to be able to consider other profiles if a date doesn't work out (Baker, 2001; Whitty & Gavin, 2001). More recent research suggests that this is a successful strategy, as extended interactions result in more negative outcomes (Ramirez *et al.*, 2015). We know that hyperpersonal communication is common to online dating, and can result in idealised impressions being created in the minds of daters about their prospective dates. Extended online communication amplifies this, as distortions may increase over longer periods of interaction. As a result, when the daters meet and are presented with a different person from their idealised mental construct, it can be difficult for them to accept, and the relationship is less likely to succeed. However, by meeting after a shorter interaction, people are more able to accept the discrepancies between their fantasy, which has not had too long to form, and reality. It is suggested that there is a tipping point somewhere between 17 and 23 days where further communication online brings negative results on meeting in real life (Ramirez *et al.*, 2015).

MAINTAINING RELATIONSHIPS ONLINE

Technology has impacted the way that couples maintain their relationships in both positive and negative ways (Lenhart & Duggan, 2014). Some couples find that technology allows them to feel closer to their partner, while others feel that it introduces friction, and these experiences tend to be amplified for younger couples. The online disinhibition effect of CMC, particularly the effects of invisibility and asynchronicity, can make it easier for couples to open up and disclose intimate information that they may find it difficult to do face-to-face. For example, couples report finding it easier to resolve arguments through CMC because the asynchronicity of the communication allows them time to respond to their partner rather than responding immediately with heightened emotions. It can also allow them to feel closer to each other because of text or online exchanges that they engage in, and because

FIGURE 6.2 Technology can bring couples together or create distance between them

their phone or computer stores a history of their relationship in the form of conversations, images of their partner or themselves as a couple, which they can use to reaffirm their affection and love. Women tend to use various CMC channels more than men to maintain all of their relationships; however, both men and women use CMC to communicate openness and assurances to each other. Openness involves discussing the relationship and aspirations for it, and assurances are messages that convey the desire to continue the relationship (Houser *et al.*, 2012). Texting in particular is associated with positive relationship maintenance, particularly using texts to express affection. However, using technology to send hurtful messages can be particularly damaging to a relationship, particularly if men send those messages (Schade *et al.*, 2013).

Facebook is typically used more frequently as a means of communication for friends and relatives than for couples. However, couples use it at different stages of their relationship with a variety of outcomes. During the initial stages of getting to know someone, Facebook is used as the primary tool for uncertainty reduction, with daters delving deep into the profile of their romantic interest. Here photographs are again used to confirm behaviours, interests and other aspects of the person's identity. This is generally seen as a positive approach, being able to take the time to learn more about who the person is, check friends in common and look for information, such as a relationship status that is not set to single, or evidence of hard partying, that might be a deal breaker (Fox *et al.*, 2013).

However, beyond the initial stages of the relationship it can place pressure on a relationship in other ways. Going 'Facebook official', changing the relationship status of a profile to 'in a relationship with . . .' a named person, is an additional stage or milestone in a relationship after it has become exclusive and stable. This is a public broadcast of an exclusive, long-term commitment to a person, and as a result there can be significant social pressure, and pressure from one partner in the relationship, typically the female, to take this step. The very act of being on Facebook while in a relationship can become pressurised for many young adults, where they feel the relationship has the potential to be shaped by its audience (Fox *et al.*, 2013).

Jealousy, surveillance and infidelity

The lack of cues and the lack of context in social networks and online generally can sometimes lead to problems with misinterpretation of communications (Walther, 1996). This can result in jealousy flaring up in response to communications posted online. Levels of self-esteem mediate how people behave in social networks, and those with lower self-esteem experience more Facebook jealousy.

Surveillance

Managing private relationships in a public forum can be tricky to accomplish. There is much discussion of the idea of Facebook stalking in popular media, and indeed there is an element of truth to the idea. People commonly engage in surveillance of potential, current and ex-partners online, but few reach the point where they cause fear in their targets. Recently, the PEW Research Internet Project found that nearly a third of people had searched for information about a current or prospective partner, and a third of SNS users had searched for information about a past partner (Smith & Duggan, 2013). In fact, Joinson (2008) found that social surveillance is the second most likely thing to come to mind when thinking about social network sites. Partner surveillance through technology is not universally negative (Elphinston *et al.*, 2013). It may, in fact, be beneficial to those who are experiencing jealous thoughts, if it is done without rumination and with positive self-talk, and a positive association was found between surveillance and relationship satisfaction. Rumination appears to be the mediator between jealousy, surveillance and relationship satisfaction. Rumination is an unconstructive cognitive-emotional experience that is difficult to stop engaging in, and if people engage in surveillance while experiencing rumination, it leads to greater relationship dissatisfaction. Tokunaga (2011) found no connection between surveillance and previous infidelity, and posited that surveillance may be a benign information seeking strategy used in healthy relationships to reduce uncertainty.

Cyber-stalking

However, online surveillance is not always benign, and while much of what people engage in online does not meet the legally required standard of stalking, some cross the line into criminal behaviour. There are three types of harassment observed on Facebook: covert provocation involves actions that may not be overtly obvious or damaging, but provokes the target of the harassment none the less; public harassment; and venting on Facebook about the ex-partner. **Cyber obsessional pursuit (COP)** involves using technology-based stalking behaviours to harass someone or demand intimacy from them; this becomes cyber-stalking when the behaviour is repeated and severe, and likely to cause fear in a reasonable person. Those who engage in Facebook harassment both covert and overt, are more likely to commit COP, and this in turn is more likely to lead to offline stalking behaviour (Lyndon *et al.*, 2011).

Infidelity and cyber cheating

People who discover that their partners have engaged in online infidelity experience great emotional upset. Whitty and Quigley (2008) found that men and women view online infidelity differently, with men more upset by sexual and women by emotional infidelity, but both were more upset by offline acts of unfaithfulness than online. However, the feelings evoked are the same as offline infidelity, but tend to be less intense than offline (Dijkstra *et al.*, 2013). They may feel betrayal and anger where the infidelity has been explicitly sexual or has led to falling in love, and fear or threatened where it has resulted in a close emotional bond but not necessarily a sexual relationship.

Even when sexual behaviours are limited to online, partners can lose trust in the relationship and feel traumatised. Cyber infidelity can have serious negative consequences for relationships, even when they have never moved beyond the virtual domain. Of those affected by cyber infidelity, 35 per cent reported that it caused the end of their relationship (Schneider *et al.*, 2012)

BREAKING UP

It is not only in the development and maintenance of relationships that technology has had an impact; increasingly, relationships come to an end via CMC as well. A total of 17 per cent of people who have been dating recently have broken up with someone by text, email or online message, and equally, 17 per cent had it happen to them (Lenhart & Duggan, 2014). The **online disinhibition** that accompanies CMC use makes it easier for people to break up a relationship by these means. The invisibility of the communication means that a partner's negative reaction is not experienced face-to-face, and it is easier for people to open up about their thoughts and feelings.

Facebook can be used as a form of uncertainty reduction during relationship termination, with people who ended the relationship less likely to use it than those who were broken up with. A break-up initiated by the other person may result in higher levels of uncertainty, thus leading to increased surveillance on Facebook. There are a number of motivations at play including monitoring an ex-partner's social activity, new romantic partners and what the partner is saying to others (Tong, 2013). Facebook may have a negative impact on emotional recovery when used to stay in contact with an ex-partner after a break-up. Surveillance can result in a number of negative outcomes including more negative feelings, lower growth, longing for the ex, and sexual desire, and it can in fact obstruct healing (Marshall, 2012).

CONCLUSION

This chapter has looked at how we use technology to find new partners, initiate contact and begin to develop a relationship. CMC has been explored in the context of the impact that it has in our relationships, both to help people form connections, and to avoid situations they find stressful or unpleasant such as asking someone out, or breaking up with them. We have looked at how to utilise online tools to reduce uncertainty about situations, both in support of relationships, but also in unhealthy ways such as surveillance of ex-partners. Technology has touched upon almost every aspect of our personal lives, and will only continue to do so as its reach expands.

ACTIVITY

Form groups. Each person should create an online dating profile 'About me' text. It doesn't have to be truthful. Shuffle all the profiles and swap them with another group. Take one profile each and answer the following questions, then discuss them within your group:

a) Think about whether a man or woman wrote this profile. What is it about the text that makes you pick that particular gender?
b) Describe three different cues you notice that give you extra information about the dater. These may be impressions that you form that don't come directly from what is written about in the text itself. For example, expressions that the dater uses, or other techniques such as punctuation, emoticons or spelling and grammar.
c) Explain how you think that other people might interpret those cues differently.

DISCUSSION QUESTIONS

1 Would you be more comfortable asking someone out, or breaking up with a partner face-to-face or using CMC? Why? Would different channels of CMC make this more or less acceptable?
2 People have mentioned that technology can support or cause friction in relationships. Do you think that technology is destroying our ability to form close relationships or increasing our ability to create close connections?
3 Many people engage in surveillance of potential, current or ex-partners on Facebook and other social network sites. Think about your own experience. Do you think that this is socially acceptable or healthy behaviour? If you knew that someone was seeking information from your profile, would that raise concerns for you about your privacy?
4 If a person has an online relationship with someone other than his or her partner but never meets them offline, is it really cheating?

RECOMMENDED READING LIST

A look at all aspects of online romance, the positive and negative aspects of online relationships are presented.

> Whitty, M. T. & Carr, A. N. (2006). *Cyberspace Romance: The Psychology of Online Relationships.* Basingstoke: Palgrave Macmillan.

An exploration of relationships and interactions online from the perspective of deception and trust.

> Whitty, M. T. & Joinson, A. (2009). *Truth, Lies and Trust on the Internet.* London: Routledge.

An overview of the psychological literature on online dating.

> Finkel, E. J., Eastwick, P. W., Karney, B. R., Reis, H. T. & Sprecher, S. (2012). Online dating a critical analysis from the perspective of psychological science. *Psychological Science in the Public Interest, 13*(1), 3–66. Retrieved from: http://static1.goedgevoel.be/static/asset/2012/Online_dating_proof_101.pdf

Interesting and accessible articles about academic research on online dating. Retrieved from: www.psychologytoday.com/search/site/online%20dating

GLOSSARY

Computer Mediated Communication (CMC)   Human communication that relies on the medium of computer technology

Cyber obsessional pursuit (COP)   Using technology-based stalking behaviours to harass someone or demand intimacy from them.

Hyperpersonal communication   A model by Walther (1996) describing how computer-mediated communication can lead to enhanced feelings of intimacy.

Online disinhibition   The online disinhibition effect was coined by Suler (2004). It refers to a loosening or removal of social inhibitions when interacting online that would normally be present in face-to-face communication.

Halo effect   A cognitive bias that occurs when one element of the dating profile, usually the photograph, influences the observer's impressions of the profile as a whole.

Homophily   The tendency for people to like others similar to themselves.

Self-presentation   A strategic negotiation of how one presents one's self to audiences.

Uncertainty reduction   Strategies used at almost every stage in a relationship to reassure a person about aspects of their partner or relationship. This can include information seeking.

Warranting principle   People are more likely to trust information online if it cannot be easily manipulated.

REFERENCES

Baker, A. (2002). What makes an online relationship successful? Clues from couples who met in cyberspace. *CyberPsychology & Behavior, 5*(4), 363–375.

Cacioppo, J. T., Cacioppo, S., Gonzaga, G. C., Ogburn, E. L. & VanderWeele, T. J. (2013). Marital satisfaction and break-ups differ across on-line and off-line meeting venues. *Proceedings of the National Academy of Sciences, 110*(25), 10135–10140.

Cloyd, L. (1977). Effect of acquaintanceship on accuracy of person perception. *Perceptual and Motor Skills, 44*(3), 819–826.

Cunningham, C. (ed.). (2013). *Social Networking and Impression Management: Self-presentation in the Digital Age*. Lanham, MD: Rowman & Littlefield.

Dijkstra, P., Barelds, D. P. H. & Groothof, H. A. K. (2013). Jealousy in response to online and offline infidelity: The role of sex and sexual orientation. *Scandinavian Journal of Psychology, 54*, 328–336.

Donath, J. S. (1999). Identity and deception in the virtual community. *Communities in Cyberspace, 1996*, 29–59.

Ellison, N., Heino, R. & Gibbs, J. (2006). Managing impressions online: Self-presentation processes in the online dating environment. *Journal of Computer-Mediated Communication, 11*(2), 415–441.

Elphinston, R. A., Feeney, J. A., Noller, P., Connor, J. P. & Fitzgerald, J. (2013). Romantic jealousy and relationship satisfaction: The costs of rumination. *Western Journal of Communication, 77*(3), 293–304.

Fiore, A. T. & Donath, J. S. (2005). Homophily in online dating: When do you like someone like yourself? *Computer–Human Interaction 2005*, 1371–1374.

Fiore, A. T., Taylor, L. S., Mendelsohn, G. A. & Hearst, M. A. (2008). Assessing attractiveness in online dating profiles. *Computer–Human Interaction 2008, 797*. New York: ACM Press.

Fiore, A. T., Taylor, L. S., Zhong, X., Mendelsohn, G. A. & Cheshire, C. (2010). Who's right and who writes: People, profiles, contacts, and replies in online dating. In *Proceedings of Hawaii International Conference on System Sciences, 43*, Persistent Conversation minitrack.

Fox, J., Warber, K. M. & Makstaller, D. (2013). The role of Facebook in romantic relationship development: An exploration of Knapp's relational stage model. *Journal of Social & Personal Relationships, 30*, 771–794. doi:10.1177/0265407512468370.

Gibbs, J. L., Ellison, N. B. & Heino, R. D. (2006). Self-presentation in online personals: The role of anticipated future interaction, self-disclosure, and perceived success in Internet dating. *Communication Research, 33*(2), 1–26.

Hall, J. A. (2014). First comes social networking, then comes marriage? Characteristics of Americans married 2005–2012 who met through social networking sites. *Cyberpsychology, Behavior, and Social Networking, 17*(5), 322–326.

Hancock, J. T. & Toma, C. L. (2009). Putting your best face forward: The accuracy of online dating photographs. *Journal of Communication, 59*(2), 367–386.

Hardie, E. & Buzwell, S. (2006). Finding love online: The nature and frequency of Australian adults' Internet relationships. *Australian Journal of Emerging Technologies and Society, 4*(1), 1–14.

Hitsch, G. J., Hortaçsu, A. & Ariely, D. (2010). What makes you click? Mate preferences in online dating. *Quantitative Marketing and Economics*, *8*(4), 393–427. doi: 10.1007/s11129–010–9088–6.

Houser, M. L., Fleuriet, C. & Estrada, D. (2012). The cyber factor: An analysis of relational maintenance through the use of Computer Mediated communication. *Communication Research Reports*, *29*(1), 34–43.

Joinson, A. N. (2008, April). Looking at, looking up or keeping up with people?: Motives and use of Facebook. In *Proceedings of the SIGCHI Conference on Human Factors in Computing Systems* (pp. 1027–1036). ACM.

Kreager, D. A., Cavanagh, S. E., Yen, J. & Yu, M. (2014). Where have all the good men gone? Gendered interactions in online dating. *Journal of Marriage and Family*, *76*(2), 387–410.

Lenhart, A. & Duggan, M. (2014). Couples, the internet, and social media. *Pew Internet & American Life Project*.

Levine, D. (2000). Virtual attraction: What rocks your boat. *CyberPsychology & Behavior*, *3*(4), 565–573.

Lo, S. K., Hsieh, A. Y. & Chiu, Y. P. (2013). Contradictory deceptive behavior in online dating. *Computers in Human Behavior*, *29*(4), 1755–1762.

Lyndon, A., Bonds-Raacke, J. & Cratty, A. D. (2011). College students' Facebook stalking of ex-partners. *Cyberpsychology, Behavior, and Social Networking*, *14*(12), 711–716.

Marshall, T. C. (2012). Facebook surveillance of former romantic partners: Associations with postbreakup recovery and personal growth. *Cyberpsychology, Behavior, and Social Networking*, *15*(10), 521–526.

Norton, M., Frost, J. & Ariely, D. (2007). Less is more: The lure of ambiguity, or why familiarity breeds contempt. *Journal of Personality and Social Psychology*, *92*, 97–105.

Paul, A. (2014). Is online better than offline for meeting partners? Depends: are you looking to marry or to date? *Cyberpsychology, Behavior, and Social Networking*, *17*(10), 664–667.

Ramirez, A., (Bryant) Sumner, E. M., Fleuriet, C. & Cole, M. (2015). When online dating partners meet offline: The effect of modality switching on relational communication between online daters. *Journal of Computer Mediated Communication*, *20*, 99–114. doi: 10.1111/jcc4.12101.

Rosen, L., Cheever, N., Cummings, C. & Felt, J. (2008). The impact of emotionality and self-disclosure on online dating versus traditional dating. *Computers in Human Behavior*, *24*(5), 2124–2157.

Rosenfeld, M. J. & Thomas, R. J. (2012). Searching for a mate: The rise of the internet as a social intermediary. *American Sociological Review*, *77*(4), 523–547.

Schade, L. C., Sandberg, J., Bean, R., Busby, D. & Coyne, S. (2013). Using technology to connect in romantic relationships: Effects on attachment, relationship satisfaction, and stability in emerging adults. *Journal of Couple & Relationship Therapy*, *12*(4), 314–338.

Schneider, J. P., Weiss, R. & Samenow, C. (2012). Is it really cheating? Understanding the emotional reactions and clinical treatment of spouses and partners affected by cybersex infidelity. *Sexual Addiction & Compulsivity*, *19*(1–2), 123–139.

Smith, A. & Duggan, M. (2013). Online dating & relationships. *PEW Internet & American Life Project*. Washington, DC. Retrieved from: www.pewinternet.org/Reports/2013/Online-Dating.aspx.

Taylor, D. & Altman, I. (1987). Communication in interpersonal relationships: Social penetration processes. In M. E. Roloff & G. R. Miller (eds), *Interpersonal Processes: New Directions in Communication Research* (pp. 257–277). Thousand Oaks, CA: Sage.

Tokunaga, R. S. (2011). Social networking site or social surveillance site? Understanding the use of interpersonal electronic surveillance in romantic relationships. *Computers in Human Behavior*, 27(2), 705–713.

Toma, C. L., Hancock, J. T. & Ellison, N. B. (2008). Separating fact from fiction: An examination of deceptive self-presentation in online dating profiles. *Personality and Social Psychology Bulletin*, 34(8), 1023–1036.

Tong, S. T. (2013). Facebook use during relationship termination: Uncertainty reduction and surveillance. *Cyberpsychology, Behavior, and Social Networking*, 16(11), 788–793.

Walther, J. B. (1996). Computer Mediated communication impersonal, interpersonal, and hyperpersonal interaction. *Communication Research*, 23, 1, 3–43. doi:10.1177=0093650960 23001001.

Walther, J. B. (2007). Selective self-presentation in Computer Mediated communication: Hyperpersonal dimensions of technology, language, and cognition. *Computers in Human Behavior*, 23, 2538–2557.

Walther, J. B. & Parks, M. R. (2002). Cues filtered out, cues filtered in: Computer Mediated communication and relationships. In M. L. Knapp & J. A. Daly (eds), *Handbook of Interpersonal Communication* (3rd edn, pp. 529–563). Thousand Oaks, CA: Sage.

Whitty, M. T. (2008). Revealing the 'real' me, searching for the 'actual' you: Presentations of self on an internet dating site. *Computers in Human Behavior*, 24, 1707–1723. doi: 10.1016/j.chb.2007.07.002.

Whitty, M. T. & Carr, A. N. (2006). *Cyberspace Romance: The Psychology of Online Relationships*. Basingstoke: Palgrave Macmillan.

Whitty, M. & Gavin, J. (2001). Age/sex/location: Uncovering the social cues in the development of online relationships. *CyberPsychology & Behavior*, 4(5), 623–630.

Whitty, M. T. & Quigley, L. L. (2008). Emotional and sexual infidelity offline and in cyberspace. *Journal of Marital and Family Therapy*, 34(4), 461–468.

7 Attention and distraction online

John Greaney

CHAPTER OVERVIEW

Many students now study in a multitasking environment, where the goal of study is one option among many: listening to music, responding to texts, watching videos, talking online. This chapter examines the prevalence and effects of such media multitasking with regard to the influence on attention, learning and emotional states. The psychology of attention, multitasking and self-control are brought to bear on the issue. Finally, some strategies for effectively managing technological distractions while learning are introduced.

KEY TERMS

Attention means directing the mind to any object of sense or thought.
Multitasking involves doing more than one thing at once.

STUDYING IN A MULTITASKING ENVIRONMENT

Many individuals now have access to a range of media devices with streams of media input available at the touch at the button. Whether at home, work, school/college or travelling, there is choice about what we attend to and this raises the question of the overall effect of such choice on attention, learning and emotional well-being. In particular, if we want to study and concentrate, what are the effects of **multitasking** and what strategies can students employ to manage information overload? According to Clifford Nass (Nass, 2013), the top 25 per cent of Stanford students are using four or more media at one time whenever they're using media technology. 'So when they're writing a paper, they're also Facebooking, listening to music, texting, Twittering, et cetera' (Nass, 2013).

Using technology while studying at home

The question of how media multitasking influences learning or not has been the focus of recent research. Students working in their home environments were the focus of Rosen *et al.* (2013) research that looked at the impact of technological distractions on the learning of school and university students. They observed 263 students in their homes during 15-minute study periods. The average time on a task was less than six minutes before participants switched their focus, most often to a technological distraction such as social media or texting. The tendency to switch task was associated with having more distracters available. Finally, students who more consciously applied study strategies (such as self-testing to check their learning) were more likely to remain focused on-task than those who did not.

Using technology during class time

Technology also presents a distraction during lecture and class time. Kraushaar and Novak (2010) measured multitasking during a lecture using both self-reported and activity monitoring **spyware** running on students' laptops. Task switching was categorised into 'productive' multitasking (course-related) versus 'distractive' multitasking (non course-related). The results showed that students had applications unrelated to their course running about 42 per cent of the time. The researchers found that academic success was related to a greater proportion of time spend on 'productive' versus 'unproductive' multitasking. Furthermore, students under-reported their frequency of email and instant messaging use. This study is in line with the view that similar tasks do not add up to as high cognitive load as tasks that are very different (Rogers and Monsell, 1995).

> Our brains are built to receive many stimuli at one time, but they're related stimuli. The problem with multitasking is not that we're writing a report of Abraham Lincoln and hear, see pictures of Abraham Lincoln and read words of Abraham Lincoln and see photos of Abraham . . . The problem is we're doing a report on Abraham Lincoln and tweeting about last night and watching a YouTube video about cats playing the piano, et cetera.
>
> (Nass, 2013)

For the student, this statement can relate to the experience of sitting down to complete an assignment and finding their attention wandering to other sources of information (all available at the click of a button) online.

HOW DO HIGH MULTITASKERS COMPARE TO LIGHT MULTITASKERS?

As multitasking is very prevalent, researchers have looked at whether there are any advantages to this practice. Orphir *et al.* (2009) divided student participants into two groups: those who reported that they used several applications simultaneously 'most of the time' were designated as 'high media multitaskers' and these were compared to a group of students who were 'low multitaskers' in three computer-based tests.

Ability to ignore irrelevant information

The first study measured how well the participants were able to ignore irrelevant information. Participants viewed pairs of red rectangles on a screen that were surrounded by different numbers of blue rectangles. Each configuration was glimpsed twice, and the participants had to decide whether the red rectangles moved position between the first and second trial. The low multitaskers were able to ignore the blue rectangles to complete the task, but the heavy multitaskers were unable to ignore the distractions in the form of irrelevant blue shapes.

Working memory capacity

Working memory is the system for temporarily storing and managing the information required to carry out cognitive tasks such as learning and comprehension. The researchers wondered whether the high multitaskers had better memories due to their inability to ignore information. Thus, in a second study they measured participants' ability to organise items in their working memory. This task was to categorise a random string of words, although not to do this for words that were preceded by a beep. The results showed that high multitaskers performed badly compared to the light multitaskers. The high multitaskers kept seeing more letters and had difficulty keeping them sorted in working memory.

Skill in switching from one thing to another

The researchers questioned whether the high multitaskers had developed superior ability in switching from one thing to another. A third study tested this idea. Participants were shown letters and numbers simultaneously. They had to either pay attention to the letters or the numbers. A category judgement was required: whether the digits were even or odd; whether letters were vowels or consonants. The results showed the light multitaskers did better than the high multitaskers in this measure of ability to switch focus.

Effects of habitual multitasking

Students who habitually multitasked could not easily separate relevant from irrelevant information: they were always drawn to the information in front of them. In situations where there are multiple sources of information, the high multitaskers are slowed down by the irrelevant information because they are not able to filter out what is currently relevant. This information may be the external world or the requirement to be sorting in memory. The researchers were unable to pinpoint anything that the high multitaskers were better at although it is possible there are as yet unknown benefits. The essence of this study is clear – high media multitaskers fared worse on several measures of handling information. In essence they are worse at multitasking. Those who multitasked less often were better at ignoring irrelevant information, showed higher working memory capacity and a better ability to switch focus.

Impact on depth of learning

Multitasking may also influence the depth of learning and this was investigated by Foerde *et al.* (2006) who conducted an experiment in which students learned on a computer while carrying out a peripheral (additional) task. Students who did both tasks at once seemed to learn as much as those who did the first task alone. However, the group who multitasked were less able to apply their knowledge to new situations. They possessed less flexibility in applying their knowledge, which implies less depth of learning.

Why do people multitask?

Given the evidence from above that multitasking confers no benefit to performance, the question of why people multitask is relevant. To answer that question, Wang and Tchernev (2012) recruited 32 college students who agreed to report on media usage three times a day for a month. The students reported on whether they were multitasking (such as reading while watching TV) and also provided their motivations for each activity. Overall, multitasking occurred most often when students needed to study or work. Results showed that students who multitasked (e.g. watched TV while studying) reported feeling more emotionally satisfied when compared to those who studied without additional media (e.g. watching TV). While multitasking seemed to meet certain emotional needs (for fun/entertainment/relaxation), there was a negative impact on study so these students did not achieve their cognitive goals as well. The emotional boost from multitasking had not been something consciously sought by the students according to the research. However, this emotional lift may explain why multitasking is habit-forming. The results also showed that multitasking is a habit that strengthens over time so that if a student multitasks one day, it is more likely to happen the next.

It is easier to give into distraction than persist when difficulty or boredom arises. Digital distractions offer easy but variable rewards that can promote an almost addictive checking (e.g. of social media). The emotional satisfaction that comes from multitasking may be short-lived when compared with the satisfaction derived from completing a difficult project or mastering a challenge. For such achievement it is necessary to hone certain abilities. In particular, the faculties of attention and self-control are vital for managing awareness and persistence.

ATTENTION

To look more closely at what is going on when people attend to information online, we need to consider the psychology of attention. **Attention** is 'the taking possession by the mind, in clear and vivid form, of one out of what seem several simultaneously possible objects or trains of thought,' wrote psychologist and philosopher William James (James, 1890, pp. 403–404). 'It implies withdrawal from some things in order to deal effectively with others, and is a condition which has a real opposite in the confused, dazed, scatterbrained state which in French is called distraction.'

Attention capacity has limits. People may feel that they are taking in everything but large changes can happen without being noticed. In the 'invisible gorilla' experiment, participants watch a video that shows a group of people passing a basketball (Simons & Chabris, 1999). Participants have to count the number of passes made by people wearing white. Midway through the video a man wearing a gorilla suit walks past the throwers and does a dance. However, only half of those watching noticed the gorilla when watching the video for the first time. When it comes to technology, the word multitasking is a misnomer; it is more accurate to say that attention is switching back and forth.

According to neuroscientist Michael Posner (Posner & Petersen, 1990) attention consists of distinct but overlapping systems – alerting, orienting and the executive, a classification that was later supported by neuroimaging studies that probed what areas of the brain are active under different conditions.

Alerting

The alerting system activates and maintains a wakeful state. This is related to a feeling of 'readiness'. The alert state may wane leading to 'spacing out' and overlooking details. Coffee is one common way to maintain alertness.

Orienting

Orienting allows us to perceive something new and determine its importance. It focuses our senses on relevant information. In the case of looking at information online, we orient our attention by moving our eyes from place to place to take in details while ignoring distractions. Shifting focus to changes in our environment is an important skill in evolutionary terms since it allows us to become aware of potential dangers. So this offers one explanation for why technological distractions are so enticing – we have an attentional system that is tuned to respond to novel information.

Executive

The executive system can be compared to air traffic control when managing multiple planes arriving and departing. The executive allocates attention in a flexible manner to our present voluntary goals (monitoring conflict between different desires).

We may be presented with information such as advertisements that are often designed to attract attention (orienting) through colour and animation. As such, we have conflicting demands on our focus and in order to stay on-task, we need to apply effortful control despite distractions.

Attention Network Test

Posner and others have put forward the idea that attention is trainable. They developed the Attention Network Test, a computer-based measure of efficiency in each of these three networks. The development of a measure allows researchers to calibrate methods for improving attention.

Training attention using mindfulness meditation

Jha *et al.* (2007) investigated whether training in **mindfulness** had an impact on performance on the Attention Network Test (ANT; Fan *et al.*, 2002). Participants who received an eight-week mindfulness-based stress reduction (MBSR) course demonstrated significantly improved orienting when compared to a control group and participants who had gone on a one-month intensive mindfulness retreat. The retreat participants all had previous experience with meditation and showed better executive function than did control participants. Experienced meditators showed greater improvement in alerting after their retreat than controls. Taken together, the authors interpret the findings as evidence that mindfulness training can modify attention first by sharpening focus (orienting) and then promoting a broader wakeful awareness (alerting). A notable finding was a carry-over effect – the training in mindful breathing led to enhanced performance on computer-based tasks. This carry-over effect is a notable finding, as if learning to skip made you better at juggling.

It is possible to train attention skills even at a young age. Tang *et al.* (2007) looked at mindfulness meditation in undergraduates and found significant improvements in executive attention. Posner *et al.* (2013) developed exercises to help children enhance executive attention skills such as self-control, planning and observation. They found that after seven half-hour sessions, six-year-olds showed brainwave activity patterns similar to that of adults. They also had significant increases in executive attention.

These studies show the potential for training attention that may even be applied to young children.

DEVELOPING SELF-CONTROL

Students are faced with the challenge of having to regulate their emotions and impulses if they want to master certain disciplines. For example, sustained concentration is needed to solve equations. Students will need to persist rather than opting for a more immediately satisfying activity (such as videos and social networking sites, which are all available at the click of a button). These skills of persistence, self-control and delaying gratification can have far-reaching implications.

The marshmallow test: self-control and delayed gratification

In a well-known research study carried out in the late 1960s, Mischel *et al.* (1972) conducted an experiment with preschool children who were given the option of eating a marshmallow immediately or waiting 15 minutes to receive two marshmallows. When compared to those children who ate the first marshmallow straight away, children who delayed gratification went on to higher educational achievement and increased ability to cope with stress as adults. This marshmallow test has parallels with the online world that is replete with tempting distractions.

A digital marshmallow test: the Academic Diligence Task

A creative approach to studying online self-control led Galla *et al.* (2014) to devise a digital marshmallow test. They wanted to research the skill of self-control in a realistic scenario. The researchers were concerned to measure how people actually behave (rather than what they say or think they do as measured through self-report). The diligence task has a split screen which presents students with a choice: on the left side, participants can choose to do a series of maths problems; on the right side, they can watch short entertaining videos or play games.

Schoolchildren who participated were instructed to answer as many problems as they wanted, as fast as they could. They were told that the maths problems would enhance their problem-solving skills in the long term. The maths problems were presented in five sessions, each four minutes long. Students could take a break at any time to watch videos or play games.

The schoolchildren spent on average half the time on the maths skills. Scores on the maths skills were correlated with academic success and personality variables such as conscientiousness and grit. The scores on the maths imply a degree of success in ignoring the digital temptations on offer. Unlike IQ, the researchers believe that self-control in school work is a skill that can be nurtured and taught.

STRATEGIES FOR IMPROVING FOCUS AND HANDLING DISTRACTION

The research has uncovered the downsides to distraction, but what strategies can people employ to stay focused when faced with tempting options close at hand? There are several research-based approaches worth considering that will be discussed in turn.

Turning study into a game

When Galla *et al.* (2014) probed to see how the more focused students in their study had fared, they discovered that some students resisted the distractions by turning the maths problem-solving into a game – e.g. seeing how many problems they could solve in a set period of time. Other students worked on the maths problems and then switched to the videos/games for a break.

Technology breaks

Rosen *et al.* (2011) examined the strategy of using technology breaks'. These are designed to address the 'separation anxiety' that may be felt by someone who is used to routinely checking their smartphone or computer throughout the day. This procedure asks students to silence their smartphones for a study period, and an alert informs them when they can check in next. Rosen *et al.* (2012) tested the effects of alternating a technology break of one minute followed by a fifteen-minute study period. Students who participated in this research reported enhanced attention, focus and learning.

Listening to music

Listening to familiar music while studying is one option than may not have the downsides of other technology choices. Rosen *et al.* (2012) found that listening to music while studying was not associated with lower grades and did not influence time spent off-task. Music – especially familiar music – draws upon different sensory modalities from those involved in study. This means that there should be minimal interference between the study task and the listening to familiar music task.

Setting up an intention to wait to check technology

This strategy involves setting up an intention to wait until the end of a study period/lecture and ignore the marshmallow of incoming text messages. Rosen *et al.* (2011) found students who delayed replying to a text until the class was over did better than those who responded immediately. This intention to wait is an example of a metacognitive strategy or 'plan of action' that a student could adopt in advance of a study session.

Taking a break from media: walking outside in natural environment

A break that involves switching to another technology source (e.g. reading emails) may not provide as many benefits as getting outside. One study found that a walk in nature sharpens and refreshes the mind relative to a walk taken in a more urban stimulating environment. Berman *et al.* (2008) asked participants to walk through an urban centre, while a second group walked through an arboretum. The participants who walked in nature showed a 20 per cent improvement in measures of attention and memory, while those who walked in the urban centre did not. Working on a computer requires directed attention and leads to fatigue eventually. A walk in nature allows this directed attention to rest in comparison to an urban walk, where you need to remain alert to possible dangers such as traffic.

Using technology to block distractions

In recent years, several programs have been developed that allow a person to block the Internet (or certain sites) for set periods of time, although there has not been much research to determine their effectiveness. RescueTime (www.rescuetime.com) tracks the amount of time spent online and breaks this down by types of application and sites visited. Zhou *et al.* (2013) had student participants install RescueTime and later asked these participants, at random intervals, for retrospective estimates of social network usage over the previous 24 hours. Although there was no significant change in the amount of time participants spent on social networks, the use of RescueTime was associated with increased accuracy in estimates of social networks usage. Further, having accurate data about their social network usage led these students to feel an increase in their sense of control over time and to a reduction in perceived stress.

Value of time unplugged

A more general strategy can be to recognise the value of time 'unplugged', through getting outside, meditating or just daydreaming. Thomée *et al.* (2012) found that young adults who constantly use a computer or mobile phone can develop stress, sleeping disorders and depression.

Recent research has highlighted how the importance of taking breaks from online screen-based interaction may be more important than previously realised. In particular, researchers have started to probe the importance of the resting state of the brain and the value of free-form daydreaming and internal reflection. Yang-Immoldino *et al.* (2012) have highlighted the value of this resting state in terms of allowing space for internal reflection on memories and emotions. They further argue that pauses and rests from input are important for off-line consolation of thinking, and social and emotional learning.

CONCLUSION

The typical student now has access to a proliferation of devices for connecting with new media and the Web at the click of a finger. The research on the effects of attention, distraction and learning points to no discernible benefits for multitasking. Attention is a limited resource although it can be trained and some tasks fit together easier than others. Certain strategies can be applied to enhance focus and reduce distractions. Successful strategies often have an element of enjoyment, either through scheduling breaks for fun, or through transforming periods of focus into a game. Time unplugged from input can be important for learning and memory.

ACTIVITIES

1 Try one or more of the activities described in the Strategies section (such as technology breaks).
2 The diligence task demo is available here: http://174.129.19.201/~sdmello/DiligenceTaskDemo/DiligenceTaskDemo.html.

3   Experiment with software designed to block or track internet usage. For example: RescueTime [Computer software]. (2015). Available at: www.rescuetime.com/.
4   Watch the Invisible Gorilla selective awareness test from Daniel Simons and Christopher Chabris. Available at: www.youtube.com/watch?v=vJG698U2Mvo.
5   Headspace is a course of guided mindfulness meditations delivered via an app. Available at: www.headspace.com/.

DISCUSSION QUESTIONS

1   William James thought that attention could not be highly trained 'by any amount of drill or discipline'. Posner would disagree. Do you think attention can be trained?
2   We cannot always indulge our desire for doughnuts without accepting the negative consequences further down the line. In a similar vein, we can no longer afford to indulge our automatic desires for mental distraction. Discuss.
3   Share experiences of concentrating for quite a long time without distractions. Why do you think this was and what was the overall experience like? (e.g. to what extent was the experience enjoyable? Challenging? Boring? Satisfying?) How do these feelings compare to the emotional boost that participants say that they get from multitasking?
4   Of the strategies outlined in the chapter, which of these approaches do you think would be most effective and why?
5   Do you think that having grown up with the Internet gives individuals an ability to multitask?
6   'The bottom line is that our students are multitasking and we cannot stop them without placing them in a boring, unmotivating environment. The trick is to develop educational models that allow for appropriate multitasking and that improve learning' (Rosen et al., 2010, p. 95). Do you agree with the statement? What is meant by 'appropriate multitasking'? Is boredom necessary sometimes?

RECOMMENDED READING LIST

This paper by Bennett et al., tackles the simplistic division of people into digital natives (those who grew up with the Web) and digital immigrants (those who encountered the Web as adults).

Bennett, S., Maton, K. and Kervin, L. (2008). The 'digital natives' debate: A critical review of the evidence. British Journal of Educational Technology, 39, 775–786.

This book includes twelve chapters that focus on how technology may contribute to the development of different psychological disorders. These include narcissism, obsessive-compulsive disorder, addiction, attention-deficit disorder and social phobia.

Rosen, L. D., Cheever, N. A. & Carrier, L. M. (2012). *iDisorder: Understanding our Obsession with Technology and Overcoming its Hold on Us.* New York: Palgrave Macmillan.

This paper discusses how a motivation beyond self-interest may help overcome feelings of boredom and help in persisting on challenging academic tasks.

Yeager, D. S., Henderson, M., Paunesku, D., Walton, G., Spitzer, B., D'Mello, S. & Duckworth, A.L. (2014). Boring but important: A self-transcendent purpose for learning fosters academic self-regulation. *Journal of Personality and Social Psychology, 107,* 559–580.

GLOSSARY

Attention   Directing the mind to any object of sense or thought.
Mindfulness   Paying attention in the present moment, on purpose and non-judgementally.
Multitasking   Doing more than one thing at once.
Spyware   Software that enables a user to obtain covert information about another's computer activities.
Working memory   The system for temporarily storing and managing the information required to carry out cognitive tasks such as learning and comprehension.

REFERENCES

Bennett, S., Maton, K. & Kervin, L. (2008). The 'digital natives' debate: A critical review of the evidence. *British Journal of Educational Technology*, 39, 775–786.

Berman, M., Jonides, J. & Kaplan, S. (2008). The cognitive benefits of interacting with nature. *Psychological Science*, 19, 1207–1212.

Fan, J., McCandliss, B. D., Sommer. T., Raz, A., & Posner M. I. (2002). Testing the efficiency and independence of attentional networks. *Journal of Cognitive Neuroscience*, 14, 340–347.

Foerde, K., Knowlton, B. J. & Poldrack, R. A. (2006). Modulation of competing memory systems by distraction. *Proceedings of the National Academy of Sciences of United States of America*, 103, 11778–11783.

Galla, B. M., Plummer, B. D., White, R., Meketon, D., D'Mello, S. K., & Duckworth, A. L. (2014). The Academic Diligence Task (ADT): Assessing individual differences in effort on tedious but important schoolwork. *Contemporary Educational Psychology*, 39, 314–325.

HeadSpace (computer software). (2015). Retrieved from: www.headspace.com/.

James, W. (1890). *The Principles of Psychology*. New York: Holt.

Jha, A. P., Krompinger, J. & Baime, M. J. (2007). Mindfulness training modifies subsystems of attention. *Cognitive Affective and Behavioral Neuroscience*, 7, 109–119.

Kraushaar, J. M. & Novak, D. C. (2010). Examining the effects of student multitasking with laptops during the lecture. *Journal of Information Systems Education*, 21, 241–251.

Mischel, W., Ebbesen, E. B., & Zeiss, A. R. (1972). Cognitive and attentional mechanisms in delay of gratification. *Journal of Personality and Social Psychology*, 21, 204–218.

Nass, C. (2013). The myth of multitasking. Interview with Clifford Nass. Available at: www. npr.org/2013/05/10/182861382/the-myth-of-multitasking.

Orphir, E., Naas, C. & Wagner, A. D. (2009). Cognitive control in media multitaskers. *Proceedings of the National Academy of Sciences of the United States of America*, 106, 11583–11587.

Posner, M. I. & Petersen S. E. (1990). The attention system of the human brain. *Annual Review of Neuroscience*, 13, 25–42.

Posner, M. I., Rothbart, M. K. & Tang Y. (2013). Developing self-regulation in early childhood. *Trends in Neuroscience and Education*, 2, 107–110.

RescueTime (computer software). (2015). Retrieved from: www.rescuetime.com/.

Rogers, R. & Monsell, S. (1995). The costs of a predictable switch between simple cognitive tasks. *Journal of Experimental Psychology: General*, 124, 207–231.

Rosen, L. D., Carrier, L. M. & Cheever, N. A. (2010). *Rewired: Understanding the iGeneration and the Way They Learn*. New York: Palgrave Macmillan.

Rosen, L. D., Lim, A. F., Carrier, L. M. & Cheever, N. A. (2011). An empirical examination of the educational impact of text message-induced task switching in the classroom: Educational implications and strategies to enhance learning, Psicologia Educativa, 17(2), 163–177.

Rosen, L. D., Carrier, L. M. & Cheever, N. A. (2013). Facebook and texting made me do it: Media-induced task-switching while studying. *Computers in Human Behavior*, 29, 948–958.

Rosen, L. D., Cheever, N. A. & Carrier, L. M. (2012). *iDisorder: Understanding our Obsession with Technology and Overcoming its Hold on Us*. New York: Palgrave Macmillan.

Simons, D. J. & Chabris, C. F. (1999). Gorillas in our midst: Sustained inattentional blindness for dynamic events. *Perception*, 28, 1059–1074.

Tang, Y., Ma, Y., Wang, J., Fan, Y., Feng, S., Lu, Q., Yu, Q., Sui, D., Rothbart, M. K., Fan, M. & Posner, M. I. (2007). Short-term meditation training improves attention and self-regulation. *Proceedings of the National Academy of Sciences*, 104, 17152–17156.

Thomée, S., Harenstam, A. & Hagberg, M. (2012) Computer use and stress, sleep disturbances, and symptoms of depression among young adults – a prospective cohort study. *BMC Psychiatry*, 12, 176.

Wang, Z. & Tchernev, J. (2012). The 'myth' of media multitasking: Reciprocal dynamics of media multitasking, personal needs, and gratifications. *Journal of Communication*, 62, 493–513.

Yang-Immordino, M. H., Christodoulou, J. A. & Singh, V. (2012). Rest in not idleness: Implications of the brain's default mode for human development and education. *Perspectives on Psychological Science*, 7, 352–365.

Yeager, D. S., Henderson, M., Paunesku, D., Walton, G., Spitzer, B., D'Mello, S. & Duckworth, A. L. (2014). Boring but important: A self-transcendent purpose for learning fosters academic self-regulation. *Journal of Personality and Social Psychology*, 107, 559–580.

Zhou, Y., Bird, J., Cox, A. L. & Brumby, D. (2013) Estimating Usage Can Reduce the Stress of Social Networking. CHI 2013 Personal Informatics Workshop, Paris, France.

8 The dynamics of groups online

Olivia Hurley

CHAPTER OVERVIEW

This chapter outlines how online groups form and regulate themselves. It examines the dynamics of online groups compared to their offline counterparts, focusing on why online group membership is an attractive option for many people, especially in today's digital age. Specifically, the chapter addresses topics such as how roles, norms and group identity are expressed in online groups. Other recent research areas, such as the impact of an over-reliance on online social networks on individuals' mental well-being, and the phenomenon of groupthink related to online groups, are also presented.

KEY TERMS

Collective identity describes how people are similar to each other, when the psychological connection between the individual self and the social group the individual is a member of is considered. **Groupthink** refers to 'the tendency for cohesive groups to become so concerned about group consolidation that they fail to critically and realistically evaluate their decisions and antecedent assumptions' (Park, 1990, p. 229). **Group norms** are the rules individuals are expected to obey as members of a particular group, while **group roles** are the parts that individuals play within a group, or the positions they fill within a group, both formal and informal. **Social loafing** describes the reduction in effort exerted by some individuals when performing a task as part of a group, compared to completing the task alone.

INTRODUCTION

This chapter outlines how online groups form and regulate themselves. Some key questions one might be interested in posing when considering this topic of groups online could include: What is the psychological impact of being a member of an online group, such as a Facebook group, a Twitter group, or being a LinkedIn member, compared with being a member of an offline group – for example, in a physical work setting or a sports club setting? Are people more likely to join groups online than they would be to join a similar group offline? Are online groups more or less homogeneous – that is, do individuals in online groups share more common characteristics with other group members, when compared to similar offline groups? Are shy people really 'bolder' or 'braver' online? In order to answer such questions, one must first understand what a group is, how it is formed and why such groups form.

What is a group? How and why do groups form?

A group is any collection of people in a particular location or setting. Most people are considered members of many groups during their lifetime, such as their class group, their work group, or, more common in today's digital age, a member of an online group, such as an online social networking group (Kirwan & Power, 2014). The question of how and why groups form has been investigated for decades, perhaps most frequently by social psychologists, such as Maslow (1943), who, in his paper 'The theory of human motivation', described how human beings have 'needs', which are prioritised, with physical needs and safety needs positioned at the bottom levels of a hypothetical pyramid that he had suggested, followed by love and belonging needs. These love and belonging needs refer to the human 'need' to be cared for, to form social bonds, and to seek out contact with other human beings. Such needs are considered fundamental to what it means to be human. So, human beings are considered social creatures with a need to 'belong', to be accepted by their peers, to be valued, yet unique individuals, with common goals and interests compared to other group members (Baumeister & Leary, 1995). This social need to 'belong' appears to be a strong motivating factor for why many people join groups, including groups in the online world (Chiu et al., 2008). However, online group membership is determined by more than just social factors. It is also determined by users' access to the necessary technology to enable them to join and interact in such groups, and their usability skills for such technology (Daneback et al., 2012). So, having addressed some of the issues surrounding what groups are, and what motivates individuals to join groups, the reasons why individuals join online groups specifically, and group behaviours online will now be discussed.

Why do individuals join online groups?

According to researchers such as Code and Zaparyniuk (2009), and Kirwan and Power (2014), some of most common reasons for joining online groups include, first, the *need to alleviate loneliness* (whether that is temporary, such as moving to a new city, or chronic, such as being housebound for long periods of time due to ill health, for example), and second, the attraction of the *relative anonymity* that such online groups provide, which may be especially appealing for shy individuals, such as those struggling with social anxiety disorders (Kirwan & Power, 2014), or those who wish to control the *amount and type of self-disclosures* they provide to other members of their social groups. People with social anxiety disorders, for example, who find it difficult to interact in groups in everyday real life, may find the online community a more attractive option for them in which to interact with others because they may feel safer, and more at ease expressing themselves online as they are not required to be physically present for such interactions to take place. Similarly, individuals' anxieties regarding the reactions of others in their offline world, to *their 'different' or 'special' interests*, could result in such individuals being, or feeling, ostracised and isolated from their offline, real world, peer groups, thus accounting perhaps for their, and a third motivation, to seek out like-minded individuals online to converse with instead (Bargh & McKenna, 2004; Kirwan & Power, 2014; Walther, 2007).

A fourth attraction to joining online groups is their ability to allow individuals to *communicate remotely* with other members of a group they share perhaps a common predicament or problem with, or when time to meet in person is not possible due to time constraints, work/family commitments, or location difficulties – i.e. living in a remote place with little public transport services. There is no need to be in the same location or face to face with group members in order to communicate online in such situations. However, many visual cues – for example, body language – are often lost in such online interactions (i.e. those that are type-based communications, via email or message boards). Such non-verbal cues in face-to-face exchanges are considered to add to the richness of the discourse taking place between the group members (Riva, 2002). The loss of visual contact between online group members can mean a loss of understanding of the discourse, in its meaning and context, by individuals who only have written words, and perhaps emoticons, on which to base their interpretations of what is being communicated. However, such typed responses also afford group members the luxury of re-reading their responses before sending them on to other group members, meaning that such responses may be 'toned down' or rephrased in a way that is not truly reflective of what would be said if the group members were engaged in a face to face exchange (Murgado-Armenteros *et al.*, 2012).

Despite the above cited limitation, of typed online group interactions losing their non-verbal cues, such online social communities continue to grow in number and popularity (Kuss & Griffiths, 2011; Facebook, 2012; Van Belleghem *et al.*, 2012). Indeed, the growth of such online communities has resulted in researchers debating the previously held views of how social and psychological dynamics contribute to human relationships, communication and community formation. For example, some early research supported the view that the relative anonymity of Internet communication encourages self-expression and facilitates the formation of relationships outside of what might be considered 'normal' socially mediated communication (Wallace, 1999).

A fifth attraction of online group membership is that the Internet offers a way for individuals to *present a 'version' of themselves* to their group. Identities online are, therefore, sometimes described as 'fluid' or dynamic in nature – that is, they are subject to change, depending on the demands of the online group membership. Indeed, Code and Zaparyniuk (2009) described how individuals often join online groups because this affords them the capacity to experiment and develop their identities in their online groups. Such 'impression management' continues to be extensively researched by cyberpsychologists (Kirwan & Power, 2014).

A sixth attraction of online group membership is perhaps the possibility of forming *multinational groups* as again, cited above, physical contact is not needed to form such online relationships. This ability to communicate with individuals from other countries and cultures opens up a world of interesting exchanges between online group members. However, it is often the case that group members are less spontaneous and more guarded in what they communicate in such multicultural group settings online, as there is perhaps greater uncertainty about the way an exchange in such an environment might be interpreted (Murgado-Armenteros *et al.*, 2012).

The online environment also removes environmental variables, such as room temperature, seating types and arrangements, noise levels – that is, the physical personal space, from the interaction, which may be a favourable feature of online group interactions for individuals who like to control such variables as much as possible. The offline world often places great emphasis on the physical appearance of individuals also, which is removed from interactions in many online settings. This can result in individuals forming bonds with other individuals they share common views and goals with, rather than being related to physical attractiveness, for example. Such relationships may then have greater opportunities to grow in the online world, which could greatly benefit the social bonds of the individuals concerned. Indeed, some early research by Parks and Floyd (1995) reported that people felt the personal relationships they formed via the Internet were close, meaningful and rewarding. This view was supported by McKenna *et al.* (2002) in their two-year longitudinal study of randomly selected Internet newsgroup participants. McKenna *et al.* reported that 84 per cent of their participants claimed that their Internet relationships were as important and 'real' to them as were their non-Internet relationships.

OVER-RELIANCE ON ONLINE GROUP MEMBERSHIP

There are, however, implications for group members who display an over-reliance on their online social groups, such as their 'friends' on social media websites like Facebook, or their 'followers' on Twitter, for example. Melville (2010) reported that individuals may suffer symptoms of depression if they feel rejected by their online 'friends'. Such individuals then risked alienating themselves from their online groups, in a similar fashion to that which may occur with members of groups in their offline world. Also, Kalpidou *et al.* (2011) reported the longer such individuals spend with their online groups in the online world, the lower their self-esteem levels appeared to become offline. However, Kim *et al.* (2009) reported that individuals who scored low on their ability to function in offline social settings declared the beneficial use of online social groups in meeting their unfulfilled social offline group needs. These group members perceived their online groups existed in a 'safer' environment for them. Kim *et al.* did also comment, however, that the difficulties individuals reported having in their offline social interactions, and how they felt about them, were not enhanced, or solved, by participating in online social groups. Therefore, reliance on the online world for social support may result in individuals becoming more socially withdrawn from the offline world, thus facilitating their social anxiety to a greater degree.

Some researchers have specifically tested the psychological impact of denying individuals time to interact on their social networking websites. For example, in their study, Sheldon *et al.* (2011) denied students access to their Facebook accounts for a 48-hour period. These students actually displayed lower levels of aggression and procrastination, while also reporting greater levels of life-satisfaction, for the period they were denied access to their Facebook accounts. They did, however, display a rebound effect in their extended use of Facebook following their 48-hour period of absence from their sites in order, it would appear, to 'make up' for their reported feelings of being 'disconnected' from this online world during the 48-hour period of abstinence imposed during the study.

Gentzler *et al.* (2011) also reported that group members who spent more time interacting with their parents through social media groups displayed higher levels of loneliness and anxious attachment with their parents compared to those who interacted more with their parents in the offline world. The individuals who reported spending more time with their parents in an offline environment stated that their relationships with their parents were more intimate, supportive and satisfying for them, compared to the individuals who interacted more with their parents online.

As previously cited, the Internet and online social networks may provide socially shy individuals with a comfortable environment in which to communicate with others, while avoiding face-to-face interactions (Ebeling-Witte *et al.*, 2007). However, is it true that such individuals are more confident and less self-conscious online? Brunet and Schmidt (2008) attempted to answer this question. They reported that the behaviour and confidence exhibited by shy individuals, who reported being more self-conscious in social settings, was context dependent when they communicated online. For example, when there was a webcam operating, the self-conscious individuals provided less self-disclosure information compared to their less shy counterparts.

To conclude this section, perhaps online groups can provide a peer-supportive forum and a positive environment in which to interact, for some group members, such as those who are shy or self-conscious, or who have special interests. However, some online groups can also be a negative source of social support, especially if they result in feelings of 'disconnectedness', or if they lead to anxious attachments to significant others, such as family and friends in the real world. They can also be damaging, if their online groups encourage, and foster, negative health-related behaviours, such as disordered eating (Tierney, 2006). Such groups can also have a contagion-like effect on vulnerable group members (Lewis & Arbuthnott, 2012).

Having addressed some of the reasons why individuals are motivated to join online groups, and some key advantages and disadvantages of such online group memberships for individuals, the issues of how people behave in groups online, compared to offline, and how such online groups maintain their membership numbers will now be discussed, considering issues such as group identity, roles, norms and social loafing in online groups.

HOW DO PEOPLE BEHAVE IN ONLINE GROUPS?

So, how does group behaviour online differ from group behaviour offline, if indeed any differences do exist? In order to answer such a question, the term 'group dynamics' should first be explained. According to Moran (2012), group dynamics is a term used to describe the way individuals act in groups, the factors thought to influence group behaviour and the processes thought to change group behaviour. But first, what constitutes examples of online groups? In the online world, environments which constitute groups include social networks, such as Facebook, Twitter and Instagram, chat-rooms, email lists, discussion boards, bulletin boards, news and discussion groups, list servers, as well as Massively Multiple Online Role Playing Games (MMORPG; such large groups will be discussed in detail in Chapter 19). The main objective of such online groups is to provide members with a common cyberspace in which to share their experiences, to seek advice, and to communicate with others (Castelnuovo *et al.*, 2003). There are many similarities between such online groups and their offline equivalents (e.g. clubs, societies, gym groups, political groups), such as the need of members for social connections and social support, as outlined earlier in this chapter. However, there are also some key differences between such groups online, compared to similar offline groups (Howard, 2014). So, do online groups serve a different purpose in a person's life, compared to their offline groups? Do individuals fulfil different roles in online groups, when compared to their offline roles in their real-world lives? According to Chmiel *et al.* (2011), Internet communication patterns do appear to differ when compared to those displayed in traditional, face-to-face settings. Therefore, the influence of cohesion, roles and norms on online group functioning, the types of leadership structures that exist online, and some of the negative features of online group behaviour, such as groupthink and social loafing, will now be discussed.

Online group cohesion

Similar to the concept of team cohesion in sporting and work-related environments (Moran, 2012), group survival in the online world relies on groups sharing some form of task and social cohesion. This means that a group must help an individual to fulfil some objectives or goals (i.e. tasks), while also meeting some interpersonal (or social) needs of the individual, if that individual is to remain a member of the group. The extent to which the task, or social, element of this 'bond' between the group and its members remains a topic of interest for researchers, and similar to the sport, and organisational, psychology literature, the cyberpsychology literature seems to suggest that task needs are somewhat more important in maintaining the online group environment, than are social requirements. For example, Ren *et al.* (2012) specifically examined the impact of enhancing members' attachment to their online communities, by manipulating levels of group identity or interpersonal bonds. The results of their study revealed that increasing group identity was a more effective way to enhance members' attachment to their online communities, compared to increasing the interpersonal bonds between the members. This implies that members of groups seem to feel a stronger attachment to groups they can relate to more in terms of group objectives and characteristics, rather than those in which they have specifically close-knit social, or attraction-based bonds with other members of the group. Therefore, group identity in online groups appears to fulfil an important function in online group growth and development.

Group and collective identity, roles and norms

The term 'group identity' is a term used to describe the common characteristics and common goals, similar beliefs and standards that often exist between group members (Chen & Li, 2009). 'Collective identity' is a related term which refers to how people are similar to each other within a group, when the psychological connection between the individual self and the social group is considered (Abrams & Hogg, 2001). As with many groups, roles and norms emerge within online groups to allow them to function effectively. A role within any group refers to the 'position' a person may fill within that group, such as a 'leadership' role, similar to a 'captain's role' within a team perhaps. Roles within groups can, therefore, be described as formal or informal. An example of a formal role would be a managerial role or a captaincy role. Such roles are explicitly stated and clearly identified. An informal role could include the 'joker' role, or indeed, the 'peacemaker' role within the group. Norms differ from roles in groups as they typically refer to the rules a group puts in place in order to regulate the behaviour of the group members. Groups often develop their norms by observing the 'normal' or 'accepted' behaviours of other groups (Borsari & Carey, 2003). For example, a norm within a work setting might be that all employees are expected to arrive to work on time, with only special exceptions to this rule being tolerated. Penalties are often put in place to punish members of groups when they 'break' the rules, in order to motivate the members to conform to the group norms, and so that the group can exist in a harmonious way (Kirwan & Power, 2014).

'Depersonalisation' is a specific term within group dynamics used to describe the phenomenon where people conform to a group prototype and behave according to group norms (Code & Zaparyniuk, 2009). At times, in such groups, individuals relinquish their individual views, beliefs or needs, in order to accept the group's views. When individuals find themselves being influenced in such a way by the opinions of other group members, the term 'groupthink' may be used to describe the phenomenon.

Groupthink

As cited above, sometimes a kind of 'groupthink' can emerge in groups. Groupthink refers to changes in the cognitions of individuals in groups, especially when they are in contact with, or interacting with, other group members. The reasons why groupthink occurs has been examined extensively by many social psychologists (Bandura, 1986). Among young people who are likely to join online groups, peer pressure may be one reason why groupthink occurs. In 2008, boyd completed a qualitative study on American teenagers who joined online social networks. boyd reported that strong and direct peer pressure was placed on American teenagers to join online social networks, such as Facebook and Bebo. The teenagers interviewed in boyd's study reported that, in addition to pressure from peers to join these groups, they also experienced feelings of isolation and being 'left out' if they did not join such online communities.

Perhaps different types of online groups are also more, or less, susceptible to features such as groupthink? Researchers have attempted to characterise and generalise online group topographies (Bargh & McKenna, 2004). A limitation of this research has emerged, namely, whether different online groups communicate and interact in similar ways that makes them comparable, or is it possible that they differ significantly in the way they function? Howard (2014) attempted to address this limitation of some of the previous research examining online group formation and function (Bargh & McKenna, 2004), which had, overall, failed to examine the generalisability of online group features identified, such as group identity and social support issues. Howard (2014) specifically examined some of the overlapping qualities of online groups previously identified by researchers such as McKenna and colleagues (see Bargh & McKenna, 2004), qualities such as group identity, social support, self-presentation and well-being. Howard compared three types of online groups, namely a cancer support group (representing an online 'support group'), a Harry Potter fan group (representing an online 'avocation group') and a Lesbian Gay Bisexual Transgender (LGBT) group (representing a 'stigmatised group'). All three groups selected represented forum online groups only. The decision to include such groups alone was made in an attempt to maintain consistency in the comparisons made between the three types of online groups examined. Howard's results indicated that online groups do indeed appear to differ in their properties, especially in relation to their group members' group identity, social support and well-being features. Howard suggested that future research might attempt to uncover *why* group members vary in their characteristics across different types of online groups. Perhaps such research could also shed some light on the reasons why features, such as groupthink, emerge among some online groups more than others.

Of course, group formation and function is influenced by many other factors. One such factor could be the leadership structure within groups, which will now be discussed in relation to online groups.

Leadership roles in online groups

Formal leadership roles have often been examined in the offline world (Moran, 2012). Based on the social identity theory of leadership (Hogg & Reid, 2001), individuals who exhibit more prototypical characteristics of a group typically emerge as the group's leaders. Such individuals often exhibit a high degree of overlap between their own characteristics and the characteristics of the other group members (especially in relation to their goals, values and attitudes). While such incidences apply in the offline world, they could apply more strongly on the Internet where other influential factors for leadership are not as apparent, such as physical appearance and the degree of interpersonal dominance potential leaders might have over other group members (Hogg & Reid, 2001). Regarding specific leadership research in online groups, the question of who governs online chat-rooms, for example, has been examined (Bowker & Liu, 2001). However, overall, this area does not appear to have been researched in great depth in the past ten years and could now be considered in need of examination by current researchers.

Social loafing

Of course, some negative group interactions also exist in online groups, in the same way as they are present in offline groups, such as social loafing. This term refers to individuals' decreased efforts when they are working together as part of a group, compared to working alone on the task. In the offline world, such behaviour can have a significant negative effect on performance, especially within sporting, and work-based, groups (Moran, 2012). Online, social loafing in groups has been linked to variables such as increased group size (Blair *et al.*, 2005), a finding also reported as groups increased in size in the offline environment (Moran, 2012). Ways to minimise the occurrence of such behaviour while maximising the contributions of group members remains a challenge for online groups, as it does for their offline counterparts.

Having discussed matters related to online group cohesion, group identity and negative aspects of group behaviour, such as groupthink and social loafing, the debate surrounding the ability of the Internet either to strengthen the bonds of groups or diminish face-to-face interactions will now be considered.

There was some concern that online communication platforms would dilute traditional human relations (Arora, 2011). However, research findings from the early 2000s suggested that, rather than weakening social bonds between groups and communities, online communities have the ability to add to the offline relationships enjoyed by members of groups (see Wellman *et al.*, 2002). Such online networks may add new layers of activities to offline groups and can, therefore, enhance their positive group interactions. Later research has also shown that some individuals do prefer and form stronger social bonds with online support group members than they do with offline social group members, especially if they are left unsatisfied with the support they have or are receiving within their offline groups – for example, individuals not happy with health, or medically related, concerns or conditions (Eun Chung, 2013).

FUTURE DIRECTIONS FOR RESEARCH IN ONLINE GROUPS

Having reviewed some key issues related to online groups, their behaviours and advantages for group members, a number of exciting areas for future research have emerged. For example, more research on the characteristics of members attracted to different types of online groups is a potential area for future research, as advocated by Howard (2014). More specific research examining the characteristics of online leaders is also warranted, to follow up on research by the likes of Bowker and Liu (2001). Such research could help to increase the number of female leaders in the offline world also – for example, where female representation in power positions remains low, compared to their male counterparts (United Nations (UN) Women, 2014).

CONCLUSION

To conclude, this chapter has given an overview of groups online, what they are, why and how they exist, what their strengths and weaknesses are for group members, and how their continued study may contribute to the overall understanding of group dynamics, both in the online and offline world.

ACTIVITY

Create an online social support network group (on Facebook or Twitter) for young adolescents, focusing on a topical issue, such as cyberbullying or mental health issues (e.g. suicide prevention). Document in a final report all activity on the site, such as the material posted, the membership numbers, the volume of traffic to the site and an analysis of the comments posted on the site.

DISCUSSION QUESTIONS

1 Compare and contrast the behaviours of groups in online and offline environments.
2 Discuss the increasing use of the Internet as a source of social support for group members.
3 Outline the dangers of an over-reliance on social networks, such as Facebook, Twitter and chat-rooms, for primary social support.
4 Discuss the impact of individuals experimenting with their social identity online, both for the individual and the group as a whole.

RECOMMENDED READING LIST

Lina Eklund's study examined the link between online/offline group interactions, using social online gaming. The findings of the study demonstrate how on-and offline interactions are closely linked.

Eklund, L. (2014). Bridging the online/offline divide: The example of digital gaming. *Computers in Human Behaviour*. DOI: 10.1016/j.chb.2014.06.018.

Howard's study set out to examine the dynamics of three different online groups: a cancer support group, an LGBT forum and a Harry Potter fan forum. The results indicate that such groups do differ in their properties, such as their group members' group identity.

Howard, M.C. (2014). An epidemiological assessment of online groups and a test of a typology: What are the (dis)similarities of the online group types? *Computers in Human Behavior*, *31*, 123–133.

This textbook is a comprehensive source of information on social aspects of the Internet. It provides detail on both the positive and negative influences of the online world.

Amichai-Hamburger, Y. (2013). *The Social Net: Understanding Our Online Behaviour*. (2nd edn). Oxford: Oxford University Press.

GLOSSARY

Collective identity   Describes how people are similar to each other, when the psychological connection between the individual self and the social group the individual is a member of is considered.

Groupthink   'The tendency for cohesive groups to become so concerned about group consolidation that they fail to critically and realistically evaluate their decisions and antecedent assumptions' (Park, 1990, p. 229).

Group norms   The rules individuals are expected to obey as members of a particular group.

Group roles   The parts that individuals play within a group, or the positions they fill within a group (formal or informal).

Social loafing   Describes the reduction in effort exerted by some individuals when they are performing as part of groups.

REFERENCES

Abrams, D. & Hogg, M.A. (2001). Collective identity: Group membership and self-conception. In M.A. Hogg & S. Tinsdale (eds), *Blackwell Handbook of Social Psychology: Group Processes* (pp. 425–460). Malden, MA: Blackwell.

Arora, P. (2011). Online social sites as virtual parks: An investigation into leisure online and offline. *The Information Society, 27,* 113–120.

Bandura, A. (1986). *Social Foundations of Thought and Action.* Englewoods Cliffs, NJ: Prentice-Hall.

Bargh, J.A. & McKenna, K.Y.A. (2004). The Internet and social life. *Annual Review of Psychology, 55,* 573–590.

Baumeister, R.F. & Leary, M.R. (1995). The need to belong: Desire for interpersonal attachments as a fundamental human motivation. *Psychological Bulletin, 117*(3), 497–529.

Blair, C.A., Thompson, L.F. & Wuensch, K.L. (2005). Electronic helping behaviour: The virtual presence of others makes a difference. *Basic and Applied Social Psychology, 27,* 171–178.

Borsari, B. & Carey, K.B. (2003). Descriptive and injunctive norms in college drinking: A meta-analytic integration. *Journal of Studies on Alcohol and Drugs, 64*(3), 331–341.

Bowker, N.I. & Liu, J.L. (2001). Are women occupying positions of power online? Demographics of chat room operators. *CyberPsychology and Behavior, 4*(5), 631–644.

boyd, d. (2008). Taken out of context: American teen sociality in networked publics. Ph.D. dissertation. University of California-Berkeley, School of Information.

Brunet, P.M. & Schmidt, L.A. (2008). Are shy adults really bolder online? It depends on the context. *CyberPsychology & Behavior, 11*(6), 707–709.

Castelnuovo, G., Gaggioli, A., Mantovani, F. & Riva, G. (2003). From therapy to e-therapy: The integration of traditional techniques and new communication tools in clinical settings. *CyberPsychology & Behavior, 6*(4), 375–382.

Chen, Y. & Li, X. (2009). Group identity and social preferences. *American Economic Review, 99*(1), 431–457.

Chiu, P.Y., Cheung, C.M.K. & Lee, M.K.O. (2008). Online social networks: why do 'we' use Facebook? *Communications in Computer and Information Science, 19,* 67–74.

Chmiel, A., Sienkiewicz, J., Thelwall, M., Paltoglou, G., Buckley, K., Kappas, A. & Holyst, J.A. (2011). Collective emotions online and their influence on community life. *PLoSONE, 6*(7), e22207.DOI: 10.1371/journal.pone.0022207.

Code, J.R. & Zaparyniuk, N. (2009). Social identities, group formation, and the analysis of online communities. In S. Hatzipanagos & S. Warburton (eds), *Handbook of Research on Social Software and Developing Communities Ontologies* (pp. 86–101). Hershey, PA: Ideal Group.

Daneback, K., Månsson, S. & Ross, M.W. (2012). Technological advancements and Internet sexuality: Does private access to the Internet influence online sexual behaviour? *CyberPsychology, Behavior & Social Networking, 15*(8), 386–390.

Ebeling-Witte, S., Frank, M.L. & Lester, D. (2007). Shyness, Internet use, and personality. *CyberPsychology and Behavior, 10*(5), 713–716.

Eklund, L. (2014). Bridging the online/offline divide: The example of digital gaming. *Computers in Human Behaviour.* DOI: 10.1016/j.chb.2014.06.018.

Eun Chung, J. (2013). Social interaction in online support groups: Preference for online social interaction over offline social interaction. *Computers in Human Behaviour, 29,* 1408–1414.

Facebook. (2012). One billion people on Facebook. Retrieved from: http://newsroom.fb.com/News/One-Billion-People-on-Facebook-1c9.aspx.

Gentzler, A.L., Oberhauser, A.M., Westerman, D. & Nadorff, D.K. (2011). College students' use of electronic communication with parents: Links to loneliness, attachment, and relationship quality. *CyberPsychology, Behavior, and Social Networking, 14*(1–2), 71–74.

Hogg, M.A. & Reid, S.A. (2001). Social identity, leadership, and power. In A.Y. Lee-Chai & J.A. Bargh (eds), *The Use and Abuse of Power: Multiple Perspectives on the Causes of Corruption* (pp. 159–180). Philadelphia, PA: Psychology Press.

Howard, M.C. (2014). An epidemiological assessment of online groups and typology: What are the (dis)similarities of the online group types? *Computers in Human Behavior, 31,* 123–133.

Kalpidou, M., Costin, D. & Morris, J. (2011). The relationship between Facebook and the wellbeing of undergraduate college students. *CyberPsychology, Behavior, and Social Networking, 14*(4), 183–189.

Kim, J., LaRose, R. & Peng, W. (2009). Loneliness as the cause and the effect of problematic Internet use: The relationship between Internet use and psychological well-being. *CyberPsychology and Behavior, 12,* 451–455.

Kirwan, G. & Power, A. (2014). What is cyberpsychology? In A. Power & G. Kirwan (eds), *Cyberpsychology and New Media: A Thematic Reader* (pp. 3–14). Hove: Psychology Press.

Kuss, D.J. & Griffiths, M.D. (2011). Online social networking and addiction – a review of the psychological literature. *International Journal of Environmental Research & Public Health, 8,* 3528–3552.

Lewis, S.P. & Arbuthnott, A.E. (2012). Searching for thinspiration: The nature of Internet searches for pro-eating disorder website. *Cyberpsychology, Behavior and Social Networking, 15*(4), 200–204.

Maslow, A.M. (1943). A theory of motivation. *Psychological Review, 50,* 370–396.

McKenna, K.Y.A., Green, A.S. & Gleason, M.E.J. (2002). Relationship formation on the Internet: What's the big attraction? *Journal of Social Issues, 58,* 9–31.

Melville, K. (2010). Facebook use associated with depression. Retrieved from: www.science agogo.com/news/201001022311001data_trunc_sys.shtml.

Moran, A.P. (2012). *Sport and Exercise Psychology: A Critical Introduction*. Hove: Routledge.

Murgado-Armenteros, E.M., Torres-Ruiz, F.J. & Vega-Zamora, M. (2012). Differences between online and face to face focus groups, viewed through two approaches. *Journal of Journal of Theoretical and Applied Electronic Commerce Research*, 7, 73–86. DOI: 10.4067/S0718–18762012000200008

Park, W. (1990). A review of research on groupthink. *Journal of Behavioral Decision Making*, 3(3), 229–245.

Parks, M.R. & Floyd, K. (1995 May). Friends in cyberspace: Exploring personal relationships formed through the Internet. Paper presented at the annual meeting of the International Communication Association, Albuquerque, NM.

Ren, Y., Harper, F.M., Drenner, S., Terveen, L., Kiesler, S., Riedl, J. & Kraut, R.E. (2012). Building member attachment in online communities: Applying theories of group identity and interpersonal bonds. *MIS Quarterly*, 36(3), 841–864.

Riva, G. (2002). The sociocognitive psychology of computer-mediated communication: The present and future of technology-based interactions. *CyberPsychology and Behaviour*, 5(6), 581–598.

Sheldon, K.M., Abad, N. & Hinsch, C. (2011). A two-process view of Facebook use and relatedness need-satisfaction: Disconnection drives use and connection rewards it. *Journal of Personality and Social Psychology*, 100(4), 766–775. DOI:10.1037/a0022407.

Tierney, S. (2006). The dangers and draw of online communication: Pro-anorexia websites and their implications for users, practitioners, and researchers. *Eating Disorders*, *14*, 181–190.

United Nations (UN) Women. (2014). Progress for women in politics, but the glass ceiling remains firm. Retrieved from: www.unwomen.org/en/news/stories/2014/3/progress-for-women-in-politics-but-glass-ceiling-remains-firm.

Van Belleghem, S., Thys, D. & De Ruyck, T. (2012). Social media around the world 2012. Retrieved from: www.slideshare.net/InSitesConsulting/social-media-around-the-world-2012-by-insitesconsulting.

Wallace, P.M. (1999). *The Psychology of the Internet*. New York: Cambridge University Press.

Walther, J.B. (2007). Selective self-presentation in Computer Mediated communication: Hyperpersonal dimensions of technology, language and cognition. *Computers in Human Behaviour*, 23, 2538–2557.

Wellman, B., Boase, J. & Chen, W. (2002). The networked nature of community: Online and offline. *IT & Society*, 1(1), 151–165.

9 Persuasion and compliance in cyberspace

Hannah Barton

CHAPTER OVERVIEW

This chapter sets out to explain the concepts of compliance and conformity and will give examples of how social influence operates in the online environment. It will present how the models of persuasive communication are being used online. One example of how the principles of persuasion are being used through technology is in a field called **captology**. Examples of applications of social influence in advertising and online political campaigning will be described.

KEY TERMS

Social influence can be thought of as how we are affected by the real or imagined and even virtual presence of others. There are many types of social influence from **compliance** (public adherence to the requests of others) to **persuasion** (an attempt to bring about an attitude change). There is even a field of study called **captology** which looks at computers as persuasive technologies.

WHAT IS SOCIAL INFLUENCE?

Every day we face pressure to 'fit in' and to 'do the right thing'. We are social beings and so we want to be just like the others in our group, despite the fact that we also like to see ourselves as unique individuals. **Social influence** is the way we respond to the real or imagined presence of others.

Social influence can be activated by the experience of playing with the others in an online game, the number of likes in Facebook and even by the presence of lurkers in a chat room online. Lurkers are those who do not actively participate or engage with others online, but just watch what is happening.

Deutsch and Gerard (1955) describe two different types of social influence. Informational influence occurs when information is accepted from another as being right. It appeals to our reason. We are influenced because we agree with what they say. Normative influence on the other hand is when we accept it because we want to fit in and be accepted by the source of the information. We want approval from others or there is social pressure to conform. It appeals to our emotions. Some cues such as recommendations, reviews and ratings on online retail sites may influence our purchasing decisions through normative influence.

There are three different processes of social influence that we will discuss in this chapter. These include:

1 **Compliance**: This is an external or obvious change in behaviour in response to a direct request. It can also happen when under the influence of an external party like a group. There is no change in the person's actual attitude, but their behaviour is amended.
2 **Obedience**: This involves compliance with the wishes of an authority figure.
3 **Conformity**: This is a change in attitudes as a result of pressure. This pressure can come from friends (**peer pressure**) or from belonging to a group (group norms).

Every day we are bombarded with messages through a variety of media such as television, newspapers and the Internet (e.g. social media) telling us the best films to watch, the coolest music to listen to and the 'right' way to vote. These persuasive communications are deliberate attempts to influence our attitudes, thoughts and behaviours. **Persuasion** works by either appealing to our emotions or to our reason. We face it every day online with spam or junk mail in our email. Pop-up advertisements used to be common before the use of blockers. Nowadays it is in-app advertisements or banner advisements that fill our screen as we try to watch online videos which are more frequently encountered.

COMPLIANCE

Cialdini and Goldstein (2004, p. 592) have described compliance as a particular kind of response (agreement) to a request. The request may be as direct as a request for help or money, or it may be implicit, as in a political advertisement that touts the qualities of a candidate without directly asking for a vote.

Cialdini (2001) has identified six principles which make it more likely for us to comply with a request from an external source. Some of these include:

1 **Reciprocity**: As humans we like to pay back any debt that we feel we owe to another; in fact, we feel obligated to repay any favour, present, card or invite that we receive. This sense of indebtedness is universal in human culture. It is a powerful tool of social influence and so we will comply willingly with a request

from a person we feel indebted to. This works equally in online exchanges and has been shown to be a factor in why we treat computer agents the same as human agents as we often ' mindlessly' apply social rules to online avatars and computers (Nass & Moon, 2000). This has been triggered by the Ethopoeia concept, which states that automatic social reactions are triggered by situations as soon as they include social cues (Nass & Moon, 2000).

2   **Liking**: We are more willing to comply with the request of someone we like. Liking can be in the form of someone we trust or someone we feel similar to or familiar with.

3   **Scarcity**: Things are more appealing or attractive to us if their availability is limited. This can be seen in shops which tell us 'final offer' or ' last ones remaining'.

4   **Social proof**: This is how Cialdini (2001, p. 109) describes social proof: 'We view a behaviour as correct in a given situation to the degree that we see others performing it.' Basically, we look to others for guidance on how to behave in a given situation and take our cue on how to behave from them. We are more susceptible to this principle when we're feeling uncertain, and we're even more likely to be influenced if the people we see seem to be similar to us. This is one rationale for the power of online rating systems where you can see how many 'likes' or 'thumbs up' a video or film has received. It can also describe the retweeting of messages on Twitter which can take on greater influence if repeated frequently and spread widely to a large number of recipients (Kim *et al.*, 2014). Retweets are powerful sources of influence.

5   **Commitment and consistency**: We like to appear consistent. If we say we are going to carry out a behaviour, we try to follow through and do it. We feel under pressure to behave consistently with that commitment. This is the most powerful of the principles and is the focus of several influence techniques that Cialdini (2001) has described.

6   **Authority**: This will be dealt with later in the chapter.

The **foot in the door technique** (FITD) is a two-step technique in which a requester first presents a participant with an extremely small request that is almost certain to be agreed to, such as signing an online petition. Then a larger request such as joining an online group or making a donation is made of the participant; this request is more likely to be met with compliance than if it had been presented by the same person as the first request. This technique works by activating self-perception theory (Bem, 1972). If the initial small request enables us to see ourselves as being a helpful person, we are more likely to exhibit the helpful behaviour of complying with the second request.

Another two-step compliance technique is the **door in the face** (DITF) technique. This is a person who is presented with an extremely large request that is almost certain to be declined. Then a more modest request is made of the participant; this request is more likely to be met with compliance than if it had been presented in the absence of the extremely large request. Teenagers might use this effectively when asking for a large sum of pocket money and later 'backing down' to accept a more modest amount, which is the amount that they really wanted. It works on the norm of reciprocity (Cialdini & Goldstein, 2004). We are more likely to comply with the second request because we perceive that the requester has made a concession (backed down and made a lower request), and so we are more likely to make our own concession by moving to a position of compliance. The DITF technique is primarily an affiliative phenomenon (Cialdini & Goldstein, 2004). We agree to the second request because we feel some measure of obligation to help the requester.

Compliance online

The techniques above have been examined in online settings. For example, the FITD technique has been used in online studies such as that of Gueguen *et al.* (2002), where an email solicitation was used to ask for instructions on how to save a document in rich text format while a second request was made to fill out a 40-item survey on their diet habits. Some of the participants were only given the second request and their compliance rate was 44 per cent compared to 76 per cent of the participants who had been asked both requests.

The DITF technique has been examined in an online study using avatars in the virtual world of there.com by Eastwick and Gardner (2008). The experimenters' avatar approached other avatars and made requests. The large request was to ask the participant avatar to take a screenshot of someone in 50 different locations (a task which would take about two hours of teleporting and travelling within the game), while the smaller request was to be permitted to take a screen shot of the participant avatar (which required little effort on the participant's part). The DITF effect was less effective when the requesting avatar was dark-skinned, thus implying that reciprocity concerns took on greater importance when the requesting avatar was light-skinned. This means that the characteristics of the requester (such as attractiveness or race) can moderate the DITF effect.

There has also been research carried out using compliance without pressure. This is a set of techniques likely to encourage people to do what is expected of them of their own choice. This is known as the 'but you are free to . . .' technique, which gives the appearance of freedom of choice to the person. Gueguen *et al.* (2002) identified this technique in an online asynchronous situation. These authors sent an email to Internet users chosen at random in an electronic directory. The email proposed the visit of a website via an HTML link. The tab to click on to get to the site in question read variously 'enter', 'click here' or 'you are free to click here'. The results obtained indicated that when the 'you are free to click here' tab was available, there were significantly higher number of participants visiting the site (82 per cent), in comparison with the 'click here' tab (65.3 per cent) and the 'enter' tab (52.7 per cent).

OBEDIENCE

Another of Cialdini's (2001) principles is authority. This means that we are often influenced by the recommendations of those who we perceive to be an authority figure. As we are social beings, we have a tendency to categorise ourselves and others in terms of where we are in the social hierarchy. This can be done by using information such as social status. It can also be achieved using cues such as expertise (titles such as 'doctor' or 'professor') and authority (a position of power, such as a police officer) as part of the social evaluation. Sociometric popularity is another one of the social evaluations to determine position in the social hierarchy. It can be seen that sociometric popularity is associated with physical attractiveness – the more physically attractive one is, the more sociometrically popular they are perceived to be. This association takes place among both children and adults.

Research looking at the popularity and online contacts has shown that the number of Facebook friends of a profile owner generates positive impressions of that individual up to a point, but then it becomes a negative interaction (Tong *et al.*, 2008). So we are influenced by popularity, expertise and authority both offline and online.

Milgram's electric shock experiments offline and online

Stanley Milgram (1974) set out in a series of experiments to investigate just how much we are influenced by authority and authority figures. He was interested in the extent to which people would follow orders from authority figures even if it meant going against their own beliefs and values. These infamous experiments ran from 1960 to 1963 and took place primarily in Yale University. Participants were recruited via newspaper adverts and were told that the purpose of the study was to look at the effects of punishment on learning.

An actor was used to play the part of the learner and every time that a mistake was made, the real participant was to administer an electric shock. The learner was apparently hooked up to a machine which was used to give out the electric shocks. No shocks were actually given to the learner but the real participant did not know that. If the participant hesitated in administering the shock, the authority figure in the study would prompt them verbally (such as 'please continue'). Obedience rates following the order to go the maximum shock voltage of 450 volts were between 50 and 65 per cent depending on the variation of the study. There was less obedience the closer the participant was to the learner (being in the same room) and the lowest rates of obedience (30 per cent) was when the participants had to put the learner's hand on the machine to get the shock. There have been variations of the studies (for example, different locations, cultures and using different authority figures, such as nurses) and a recent partial replication by Burger (2009) has shown that obedience to authority figures remains high.

Would it happen online? An interesting variation of the study investigating how people would respond to such a dilemma in a virtual environment was conducted using avatars by Slater *et al.* in 2006. This study showed how participants reacted strongly and became stressed to an unknown female virtual person receiving electric shocks and displaying pain. Of the 34 participants, 23 saw and heard the virtual human, and 11 communicated with her only through a text interface. The results showed that in spite of the fact that all participants knew that neither the virtual person nor the shocks were real, the participants who saw and heard her tended to respond to the situation at the subjective, behavioural and physiological (heart rate) levels as if it were real. This shows that we may react to similar situations online just as we would in real life and that we might treat avatars in pain exactly as we would treat a real human. This has been shown

FIGURE 9.1 Examples of avatars

(subarashii21/Shutterstock)

even if the virtual human is a representation of a stranger, but we feel more empathy towards a known virtual human (Bouchard *et al.* 2013). These findings have interesting repercussions for online gaming, where many games require users to hurt or kill the avatars of other players in order to progress. The gamer is aware that they are harming the avatar and can often speak directly to the player controlling that avatar using the gaming headsets. However, there are notable differences between most gaming situations and that presented in the studies above – in most games the avatar does not demonstrate behaviours indicative of the pain which would be inflicted by the injuries inflicted. Second, most games allow the gamer's avatar to 'respawn' relatively quickly after its virtual demise, and so permanent damage rarely occurs. Finally, the avatar is normally in a position where they have the possibility to defend themselves – they are usually armed in a similar manner to the perpetrator of an attack. It may also be that the infliction of electric shocks is relatively rare in gaming scenarios, with firearm wounds being a far more frequent occurrence, and so the use of the electric shock in the studies may represent a departure from online behaviour perceived by gamers to be normal.

CONFORMITY

Conformity (or majority influence) refers to the change in opinions, perceptions, attitudes and behaviour that can be observed when we want to think in the same way as those around us, or when we want people to believe that we have formed similar conclusions that they have. Experiments, such as that by Asch (1951), have shown that most people sometimes deny their own perceptions and yield to the influence of others. Participants and confederates of the experimenter were asked to identify lines which matched other lines in length. Each person had to answer out loud and occasionally the confederates gave the wrong answer. Asch was interested in whether the real participants would conform and give the wrong answer or avoid conformity, giving the correct answer. The participants conformed by giving incorrect answers in 37 per cent of the trials where the majority answer in the group was incorrect (Asch, 1951). This demonstrates the strong pressure to fit in, and how we are motivated by normative influence to go along with the majority.

Asch's paradigm has been used to compare face-to-face conformity with 'cyber-conformity' (Cinnirella & Green 2007). The participants in the face to face condition were in a room with three confederates all sitting at computers. All answers to the task were given verbally. The Computer Mediated Communication (CMC) condition had no confederates but the computer that the participant sat at gave the same pre-determined answers as the confederates in the face-to-face condition. In both conditions participant judgements were influenced by confederate answers. This means that we are prone to being influenced by the answers of others, despite the medium in which we receive those answers. And so social conformity can occur in CMC such as email, chatrooms and on social networking sites.

Conformity is generally explained by the theory of normative influence – that is, we conform because we want to maintain harmony within the group. The simple fact of making the social norms prominent and obvious can influence the behaviour of individuals in the direction of these norms (Cialdini, 2001). This is done offline by group norms, by signs or through the rules of the group. Online norms are sometimes made explicit through 'Frequently Asked Questions' sections or pages. We also try to gauge the group opinion informally and this can affect us through social impact, a phenomenon in which people affect one another in social settings. This suggests that people will look at the collective opinion in social media environments such as Twitter (retweet button) and Facebook (number of likes as well as the sharing of photographs or items), and use this information to make judgements and decisions. People follow collective opinion because they see it as what is accepted as the norm. Under social impact theory (Latané, 1981) there are three factors that affect the degree of social impact: strength, immediacy and number of people. The online group that the person is a member of could be important to the individual, the group could feel close to the individual who is interested in the same information as the group, and the number of people in the group is often large (as represented by the number of likes or retweets that an item gets).

Some studies (e.g. Smilowitz et al., 1988) have shown that the media of communication, either CMC or face to face, can affect one's ability to resist majority pressure (conformity). Using an adapted version of the Asch Paradigm, Smilowitz et al. found that those who used CMC were better able to resist pressure from the majority then those who communicated face to face. A very interesting cross-cultural effect was noted by Cinnirella and Green (2007) – in general, those from collectivistic cultures are expected to have a higher tendency to conform than those from individualistic cultures. But Cinirella and Green (2007) noted that this behaviour was mediated by CMC, with cultural tendencies to conform evident in face-to-face interactions, but less so when using CMC. However, the tendency to avoid conformity online may have changed as CMC has risen in popularity. More recently, Rosander and Eriksson (2012) found that over half of participants exposed to information about other individuals' responses in a web-based questionnaire demonstrated conformity to incorrect alternatives, with the proportion increasing with question difficulty level. They proposed several reasons for such conformity online, including the protection of self-esteem and the avoidance of social isolation.

PERSUASION

So far we have looked at processes that have sought external agreement or change in behaviour rather than influence tactics that try to change private attitudes or beliefs. These influence tactics can be considered as **persuasion**. CMC can be used to persuade in two ways: through mass media persuasion (for example, by broadcasting online advertisements or highlighting the number of likes or stars that a person or product has been given), or through interpersonal persuasion. The same models of persuasion can be applied to both online and offline environments. There are several models of persuasion which we can refer to, including the Yale model of persuasive communication and the Elaboration Likelihood Model. Finally, we will examine the phenomenon of **captology.**

The Yale model of persuasive communication

The Yale model of persuasive communication focuses on three components (Hovland *et al.*, 1953), with the effectiveness of the persuasive communication depending on the combination of these. The three components are:

1 **Characteristics of the source or sender**: This can include many factors, including the personality and intelligence of the speaker and their attractiveness. In essence, this component asks if we trust the credibility of the source.
2 **Characteristics of the message itself**: This can include elements such as how factual it is, how strong the arguments are and if it appeals to our emotions, such as fear.
3 **Characteristics of the audience**: Who is the target audience? What are their needs and concerns? Do they identify with the speaker? What about their personality traits?

How can we adapt CMC messages to enhance interpersonal persuasion? Research by Wilson (2005) looking at CMC system features and persuasive ability has found that when senders are motivated to persuade or are concerned about their self-image, they are less likely to use visuals in their messages. Yet the study concluded that CMC system features that augment messages with images and graphics were found to increase message persuasiveness. So when we consciously want to persuade, we are less likely to use images, yet we find the visual input from CMC more persuasive.

The Elaboration Likelihood Model (ELM)

The Elaboration Likelihood Model (ELM) develops the Yale model further by looking at what and how we pay attention to persuasive communications. It was developed by Petty and Cacioppo (see, for example, Petty & Cacioppo, 1986). The ELM takes the same variables as the Yale model, but also looks at how they interact with emotions, motivation and cognition to determine how we will react to the communication.

There are two ways that a persuasive message can affect us – a central route and a peripheral route. Due to our personality, we may use one route more often than the other, but we are always able to access both of the routes. The central route is taken when people are motivated to examine in detail the content of the message – that is, we read the small print and are influenced by the quality of the argument or of the data being presented. We are motivated to pay attention to the content of the message. In the peripheral route, we pay attention to cues that are not important to the content of the message, such as the attractiveness of the source, the design of the website and the photos on the website.

Another factor that is a key peripheral cue is source credibility. A source is deemed credible and more worthy of our trust if they are seen to be an expert and unbiased (see Pornpitakpan, 2004 for a review of literature in this field). If we perceive that the source is like us in some way (similar to us) then we are also more likely to trust them and deem them as being a credible source. For example, Lu and Eysenbach (2013) completed an experiment using online health blogs, and found that health-related similarities were particularly persuasive.

There are also individual differences in terms of how we process information. This tendency to engage with information has been called the Need for Cognition (Cacioppo & Petty, 1982). While this is a stable trait, it can by influenced by situational factors. Low Need for Cognition individuals do not enjoy exerting cognitive effort and prefer to use heuristics (short cuts), such as the opinion of others (ideally experts) or the attractiveness of the speaker or source of the communication. High need for cognition (HFC) individuals, on the other hand, will actively seek out knowledge and will engage with it. They like facts and will attend to the content of a message. Research by Kaynar and Amichai-Hamburger (2008) has shown that these differences in dealing with information extend to online behaviour. High NFC individuals believe that it is the information on a website that is more important and use the web for seeking out information or professional services rather than for social or leisure purposes. So individual differences such as the Need for Cognition, mood and perceived similarity to us all can influence which route (central or peripheral) is taken. In addition, cognitive overload and stress can mean that we do not always have enough time or resources to attend to the message, and so even HFC individuals may use the peripheral route under those conditions (Petty & Cacioppo, 1979).

Captology

Captology (Computers As Persuasive Technologies) was first pioneered by the Stanford Persuasive Technology Lab, directed by B. J. Fogg. The focus is on software programs and smart products that encourage or change behaviour in the fields of health, safety, environment and personal management. There are numerous examples of captology described by Fogg (2009), including commerce sites, social networking, smartphone applications, commercial texting services, specialised consumer electronic devices such as 'talking' pedometers and personalised online recommendation systems found on some retail websites. Fogg also identified health-promoting video games as an example, and this has received some interest from researchers. For example, Khalil and Abdallah (2013) and Fialho *et al.* (2009) have examined the effectiveness of using personalised motivators and avatars to encourage people to exercise more, eat the right foods and engage in more healthy lifestyles. The use of such technologies can motivate behavioural change.

There are a number of persuasive technology tools identified by Fogg (2003) which are designed to change attitudes or behaviours by making the target behaviour easy to achieve. These include 'reduction' and 'tailoring'. 'Reduction' is when the target behaviour is made easy and effortless to do. 'One-click shopping', where the user can purchase an item with a single mouse-click, is one example of reduction in action. 'Tailoring' refers to personalising content. For example, when an email or message comes in and it is specifically addressed to you personally, rather than a generic message, this can be an effective strategy in changing attitudes or behaviours. While tailoring strategies may make us feel special and unique, the use of technology in this way can raise ethical concerns.

CONCLUSION

In this chapter we reviewed the concept of social influence and looked at some of the processes which underlie it such as compliance, conformity and obedience. We saw examples of these processes at work in the online environment. The models of persuasion were described including examples of how they work online. Individual factors and situational factors influencing which route to persuasion were also discussed.

ACTIVITY

Select a number (three to four) of advertisements from the press (newspapers, magazines), television and from the Internet (banner advertisements or pop-up advertisements) and compare them in terms of the content/ message of the advertisement, the target audience and the source. How are they similar? How do they differ? Which route (central or peripheral) are they trying to activate?

DISCUSSION QUESTIONS

1 How can politicians use the theories of persuasion when using online presence to persuade their audiences?
2 What individual factors make it more likely that a person will be susceptible to persuasive technologies such as tailoring and reduction?
3 Which of Cialdini's principles of compliance would be the most effective in an online environment?
4 Why do you think the participants became distressed when shocking an avatar? It is not a real person so does it matter then to hurt them?

RECOMMENDED READING LIST

A more detailed understanding of Cialdini's principles can be gathered by reading his book.

Cialdini. R. (2006). *Influence: The Psychology of Persuasion* (5th edn). New York: William Morrow Publications.

Fogg presents a comprehensive guide to captology, full of online examples of persuasive technology in action.

Fogg, B. J. (2003). *Persuasive Technology: Using Computers to Change What We Think and Do.* San Francisco, CA: Morgan Kaufmann Publishers.

Petty, Brinol and Priester's chapter provides a good historical account of persuasion in the media and applies the ELM model to media campaigns.

Petty, R. E., Brinol, P., & Priester, J. R. (2009). Mass media attitude change: Implications of the Elaboration Likelihood Model of persuasion. In J. Bryant & M. B. Oliver (2009). *Media Effects: Advances in Theory and Research* (3rd edn; pp. 125–164). New York: Routledge.

Rosander and Eriksson's study examines conformity in online communication, with particular focus on gender and the difficulty of tasks.

Rosander, M., & Eriksson, O. (2012). Conformity on the Internet – The role of task difficulty and gender differences. *Computers in Human Behaviour, 28* (5), 1587–1595.

GLOSSARY

Captology   Field of using computers as persuasive technologies.
Compliance   Public adherence to the requests of others.
Conformity   Change in our opinions, perceptions, attitudes and behaviour that can be observed when we want others to believe that we agree with others around us.

Door in the face technique (DITF)   Two-step compliance technique where the person is initially asked with a large request, which is then followed by a second, more modest, request.

Foot in the door technique (FITD)   Two-step compliance technique where the person is first asked a small request which is then followed up with a second, much larger, request.

Persuasion   An attempt to bring about a change in attitude or behaviour.

Peer pressure   Pressure to fit in with those we spend time with.

Social influence   How we are affected by the real or imagined presence of others.

REFERENCES

Asch, S. E. (1951). Effects of group pressure upon the modification and distortion of judgments. In H. Guetzkow (ed.), *Groups, Leadership and Men: Research in Human Relations* (pp. 177–190). Oxford: Carnegie Press.

Bem, D. J. (1972). Self-perception theory. In L. Berkowitz (ed.), *Advances in Experimental Social Psychology (Vol. 6,* pp. 1–62). New York: Academic Press.

Bouchard, S., Bernier, F., Boivin, E., Dumoulin, S., Laforest, M., Guitard, T., Robillard, G., Monthuy-Blanc, J. & Renaud, P. (2013). Empathy toward virtual humans depicting a known or unknown person expressing pain. *Cyberpsychology, Behaviour and Social Networking, 16* (1), 61–71.

Burger, J. (2009). Replicating milgram: Would people still obey today? *American Psychologist, 64* (1), 1–11.

Cacioppo, J. T. & Petty, R. E. (1982) The need for cognition. *Journal of Personality and Social Psychology, 42* (1),116–131.

Cialdini, R.B. (2001). *Influence: Science and Practice* (4th edn). Boston, MA: Allyn & Bacon.

Cialdini, R. B. & Goldstein, N. J. (2004). Social influence: Compliance and conformity. *Annual Review of Psychology, 55,* 591–621.

Cinnirella, M. & Green, B. (2007). Does 'cyber-conformity' vary cross-culturally? Exploring the effect of culture and communication medium on social conformity. *Computers in Human Behaviour, 23* (4), 2011–2025.

Deutsch, M. & Gerard, H. B. (1955). A study of normative and informational social influences upon individual judgment. *The Journal of Abnormal and Social* Psychology, *51* (3), 629–636.

Eastwick, P. W. & and Gardner, W. L. (2008). Is it a game? Evidence for social influence in the virtual world. *Social Influence, 4* (1), 18–32.

Fialho, A., van den Heuvel, H., Shahab, Q., Liu, Q., Li, L., Saini, P., Lacroix, J. & Markopoulos, P. (2009, April). Active share: Sharing challenges to increase physical activities. In *CHI'09 Extended Abstracts on Human Factors in Computing Systems* (pp. 4159–4164). ACM.

Fogg, B. J. (2003). *Persuasive Technology: Using Computers to Change What We Think and Do.* San Francisco, CA: Morgan Kaufmann Publishers.

Fogg, B. J. (2009, April). Creating persuasive technologies: An eight-step design process. In Persuasive '09: Proceedings of the 4th International Conference on Persuasive Technology (Article No. 44). ACM. Retrieved from: http://ejournal.narotama.ac.id/files/an%20eight-step%20design%20process.pdf.

Gueguen, N., Pascual, A., Jacob, C. & Morineau, T. (2002). Request solicitation and semantic evocation of freedom: An evaluation in a Computer Mediated communication context. *Perceptual and Motor Skills*, *95* (1), 208–212.

Hovland, C .I., Janis, I. L. & Kelley, H. H. (1953). *Communication and Persuasion: Psychological Studies of Opinion Change*. New Haven, CT: Yale University Press.

Khalil, A. & Abdallah, S. (2013). Harnessing social dynamics through persuasive technology to promote healthier lifestyle. *Computers in Human Behaviour*, *29* (6), 2674–2681.

Kaynar, O. & Amichai-Hamburger, Y. (2008). The effects of Need for Cognition on Internet use revisited. *Computers in Human Behaviour*, *24* (2), 361–371.

Kim, E., Sung, Y. & Kang, H. (2014). Brand followers' retweeting behaviour on Twitter: How brand relationships influence brand electronic word-of-mouth. *Computers in Human Behaviour*, *37*, 18–25.

Latané, B. (1981). The psychology of social impact. *American Psychologist*, *36* (4),343–356.

Lu, A. S. & Eysenbach, G. (2013). An experimental test of the persuasive effect of source similarity in narrative and nonnarrative health blogs. *Journal of Medical Internet Research*, *15* (7), 1–11.

Milgram, S. (1974). *Obedience to Authority: An Experimental View*. New York: Harper & Row.

Nass, C. & Moon, Y. (2000). Machines and mindlessness: Social responses to computers. *Journal of Social Issues*, *56*, 1, 81–103.

Petty, R. E. & Cacioppo, J. T. (1979). Issue-involvement can increase or decrease persuasion by enhancing message relevant cognitive responses. *Journal of Personality and Social Psychology*, *37*, 1915–1926.

Petty, R. E. & Cacioppo, J. T. (1986). The elaboration likelihood model of persuasion. *Advances in Experimental Social Psychology*, *19*, 123–205.

Pornpitakpan, C. (2004), The persuasiveness of source credibility: A critical review of five decades' evidence. *Journal of Applied Social Psychology*, *34* (2), 243–281.

Rosander, M. & Eriksson, O. (2012). Conformity on the Internet – The role of task difficulty and gender differences. *Computers in Human Behaviour*, *28* (5), 1587–1595.

Smilowitz, M., Compton, D. C. & Flint, L. (1988). The effects of computer mediated communication on an individual's judgement: A study based on the methods of Asch's social influence experiment. *Computers in Human Behaviour*, *4* (4), 311–321.

Slater, M., Antley, A., Davison, A., Swapp, D., Guger, C., Barker, C., Pistrang, N. & Sanchez-Vives, M. V. (2006). A virtual reprise of the Stanley Milgram obedience experiments. *PLoS ONE 1*(1): e39.

Tong, S. T., Van Der Heide, B., Langwell, L. & Walther, J. B. (2008). Too much of a good thing? The relationship between number of friends and interpersonal impressions on Facebook. *Journal of Computer Mediated Communication*, *13* (3), 531–549.

Wilson, E. V. (2005). Persuasive effects of system features in Computer Mediated communication. *Journal of Organizational Computing and Electronic Commerce*, *15* (2), 161–184.

10 Privacy and trust online

Gráinne Kirwan

CHAPTER OVERVIEW

In the earliest days of civilisation, humans lived in relatively small groups, often within the same room (or tent, or cave!) with very little privacy. Even today, in some small villages inhabitants note that their activities and actions are known throughout the community, with such information being spread from person to person. On the other hand, those living in larger communities such as cities might find that they do not even know the names of their next-door neighbours. Nevertheless, they may find that this privacy is negated by the impact of the Internet as they disclose large amounts of information online, and also have their information disclosed to others, sometimes without their consent. This chapter considers our concepts of online privacy and trust, the sacrifices we make to our privacy in order to make other perceived gains, and the important theories in the field that inform our understanding of privacy and security. It examines how we share information, what happens to our data online, how we decide what information to share, and how we go about reducing the available amount of online information about ourselves.

KEY TERMS

Research has long identified the tendencies of individuals to disclose considerable volumes of information online, particularly via online social networks (Gross & Acquisti, 2005). **Privacy** is a difficult concept to define clearly, to the extent that some researchers have suggested that the most effective definition instead involves the application of prototypes (Vasalou *et al.*, 2015). For the purposes of clarity in this chapter, it will be used to describe the state or condition of not having personal information disclosed in public or semi-public settings. While many people appear to value privacy, many do not engage in behaviours that secure their information, a phenomenon sometimes referred to as the **knowing-doing gap.**

SHARING INFORMATION ONLINE

Imagine living in a world where all of the inhabitants (including you) had telepathic abilities. Ambiguities and misunderstandings could be clearly resolved. But on the other hand, there would be no such thing as secrets and all information would be public knowledge. Many people would probably like to have telepathic abilities themselves – after all, it would give you an advantage in many business transactions and inter-personal relationships, but most individuals are also probably very grateful that everyone else does not have access to their most private thoughts. We like to have the ability to control what we share with others, and this is a core principle of privacy management.

If we had to choose a handful of individuals who could read our thoughts, who would they be? For some people these are likely to be their closest friends. But others might be happier if the potential telepaths were complete strangers who they would never meet. Perhaps we might be very comfortable with sharing the majority of our secrets with a small group of people who we know well, but when seeking advice about an embarrassing or deeply personal matter, we'd instead share our secrets with strangers who might be able to provide advice without being able to identify us by our face or name. The concept of privacy is complex, but we do share information online relatively readily. We will consider the concept of who we share what information with in more detail later in this chapter.

A considerable volume of research in cyberpsychology examines how we share our personal information online, and why we might choose to do so (or not to do so) depending on the circumstances. Some people carefully curate the information about themselves online, while others might find that they are of sufficient public interest that they cannot control what is said about them. Some eschew online contact with others entirely, or use the Internet solely to consume content, rather than sharing any of their own. However, this is not necessarily a reliable way of ensuring that our data is secure.

Think for a moment about how we share our personal and/or private information online. Some methods of doing so are easy to think of – we might post status messages or updates on social media, we might check in with our friends at a certain location, we might write blog posts about our lives or our opinions on current events. Thinking a little more, we might add our more private communications to that list – emails, instant messages and text messaging. But we share other aspects of our lives unwittingly – our mobile phones can easily imbed location data into photographs that are taken or messages that are sent. Data is accumulated about the websites that we visit, the information that we regularly type into online forms (including search engines), items that we browse in online stores, and where and when we access online information. Websites utilise **Internet cookies** to record information about user visits and compile information about user activity. En masse, this information provides a substantial overview of our lives, and reduces our privacy considerably.

In addition to the concerns that might be raised by the information that any individual online service might hold about us, it is also worth considering what the accumulated data about us amounts to. Say, for example, that our social media account is listed under our real name, but contains relatively little profile data. However, we also have an online dating account, which does not include our real name, but has a lot more information, some of it deeply personal. We might feel relatively secure that these online accounts are separate, but we may not be aware that they could potentially be linked through a variety of means, including our log-on locations, a single smartphone being used for both accounts, or even the use of facial recognition and search software which could link both accounts to the same individual. Indeed, the combination of face recognition from photographs and social media information has important implications not only for privacy but also for other purposes such as commercial strategies, for example developing targeted and personalised advertising to previously anonymous shoppers in offline contexts based on their online profiles (Acquisti *et al.*, 2014).

Another potential risk lies with the permanency of the information that we provide online. While a user might go to significant lengths to delete any posts and accounts that they have created in the past, sometimes this information is still held and can be accessed through applications as common as search engines. Situations such as this have led to individuals lodging complaints against agencies who store this information. One of the outcomes of complaints such as these is the clarification regarding the 'Right to be forgotten' in Europe (European Commission, 2014), as well as similar rulings in other jurisdictions, which help to reduce the permanency of online information. However, many users do not go to such lengths to remove such data, or they may be unaware of the existence of it at all.

Finally, users may not consider who has access to their information before sharing it. When posting a status update on social media we may not consider who may be able to read it. Even if we restrict the comment to a relatively small group of people, such as our close friends and family, it is easy to forget that those individuals can share the information with others. Or if we comment on a friend's photograph, we may not realise that it is our friend's contacts that can see our message, rather than our own contacts. It is also very easy to forget how many people we are sharing information with, particularly if many of our contacts are generally silent 'lurkers' who do not post themselves. As well as our contacts, others with potential access to our information include the company who provides the software (for example, the social media site), our Internet service provider, and anyone who they share the information with – potentially advertisers or government agencies. Finally, it is also possible that our information is divulged through other means, such as an intrusion into the data by cybercriminals.

With so many ways that our information can be shared, it might be expected that users take care with their data before divulging it online. The next section considers how users decide what information to share, and describes some theories which are relevant to our understanding of information sharing.

Deciding what information to share

Given the amount of information that we share, it may be tempting to think that Internet users are not concerned about their privacy. However, this is not the case. For example, Paine *et al.* (2007) noted that users are greatly concerned about privacy. It may simply be that users perceive more benefits in sharing such information than they perceive risks in such disclosure. However, there may be many other, more subtle factors which determine our sharing of information online. This section considers various factors which may affect our decision to share what would otherwise be relatively private information in online settings. In particular, the section examines the role of cognitive psychology and decision making, Petronio's Communication Privacy Management Theory, the concepts of social spheres and space, and the paradoxes and trade-offs that users might be susceptible to.

Cognitive psychology and decision making

Cognitive psychology has examined how humans make decisions in considerable depth, and much of this can be applied to our decision making regarding privacy. For example, Kirwan (in print) considers the work of Nobel Prize winner Daniel Kahneman and its application to online decision making, particularly with regard to security and privacy. Kahneman (2011) describes two different types of thinking, which he called System 1 and System 2. When we make fast, almost instinctive decisions then we engage System 1 – these tend to be decisions that we make quickly and without much thought. An example could be when we are instant messaging a friend online – we don't tend to put too much thought into each individual word that we use, otherwise the conversation would take a very long time and our friend would wonder what the delay is in our responses. On the other hand, System 2 is a 'slow' system, where we deliberate and consider a decision, expending a considerable amount of effort while doing so.

When we are thinking about purchasing a new mobile phone or laptop we are more likely to engage System 2, as it is an important and expensive decision. Applying this model to online privacy, it is easy to see how many of our decisions relating to online privacy might be managed under System 1, when really we should be considering the decision in more depth. For example, if we are installing a new game or other application onto our smartphone, we are likely to be excited by the prospect of using it, and we want to see what it can do. Therefore, when the application asks for access to information about us via social media or location based services, we might favour System 1 over System 2, as it allows us quicker access to the software, as well as use of more features of that software. A very common example of this occurs when the user is asked to confirm that they have read the terms and conditions of use when downloading new software or completing an online form. The documents outlining these terms and conditions are often extremely long, and a user may be tempted to avoid the complex task of reading and comprehending the legal points in the document, in favour of achieving their current goal more quickly. However, these terms and conditions often include the information regarding the sharing of user data, and so by agreeing to them without having read the document, users are often consenting to the sharing of their information without realising it. Another example of using the incorrect System occurs when posting status updates or other information online.

In these cases we may engage System 1 in our excitement of posting the message, especially if we are distracted by other factors such as being in an interesting environment. As we bypass System 2, we may make ourselves vulnerable by not considering the context of the information that we send or the potential recipients of this data.

Other aspects of cognitive psychology may also be relevant. For example, confirmation bias (Einhorn & Hogarth, 1978) describes how we tend to seek further information to support a tentatively held hypothesis, and we may avoid or ignore information that conflicts with this hypothesis. With regard to online privacy, we can consider an individual who has heard of the risks of online disclosure, but who has no direct evidence that their own information has ever been shared without their explicit consent. Without such explicit evidence they may believe that this has never happened to them, and they may feel that it is therefore safe to continue sharing information in the way that they have previously done without running the risk of their privacy being compromised.

On the other hand, if a person has recently experienced negative consequences of disclosure of personal information, either through personal experience or through witnessing it occur to someone else, then the potential negative effects of unwanted disclosure are likely higher in their mind – they can visualise the consequences more clearly and it comes to mind more frequently. Tversky and Kahneman (1973) refer to this phenomenon as the availability heuristic, as the scenario is readily 'available' to the individual and can be easily visualised. In this case, the individual may be more conscious of the potential risks of disclosure and may change their behaviours accordingly. However, if they have not experienced such events, then the risks are less available to them, and they may engage in riskier behaviours.

The theories and biases outlined above are a small subset of the vast literature in cognitive psychology, and particularly decision making, which is relevant to our choice whether or not to disclose information, or to share it with third parties. As making decisions regarding privacy are subject to the same cognitive processes, biases and heuristics as making decisions regarding many other matters, their relevance to online privacy cannot be overstated. However, we will now consider several other theories which can help to inform our understanding of online disclosure of information.

Communication Privacy Management

Sandra Petronio (Petronio, 2002, 2013; Petronio & Durham, 2015) has developed a theory regarding the sharing of private information, and this theory can be applied to online contexts. Her **Communication Privacy Management** (CPM) theory includes several principles describing how individuals and groups view their information. One of these is that the individual or group believes that they own their private information and that they have the right to control the dissemination of the information. This includes the determination of how much information is shared and how it is shared. The individual or group also presumes that others who might hold this information will follow these rules. Turbulence will occur if another individual or group shares the information without permission. As is evident, trust is a vital factor in choosing who an individual might disclose information to – the discloser is trusting their confidante to follow their rules when considering disclosure.

It is easy to see the applications of CPM theory in our offline communications – it is especially evident when the trust in a person is broken after the realisation that a secret has been shared. Confidantes may also face conflicts if someone discloses a secret to them, but the confidante feels that they must share that information with another party (for example, in a case where a child admits that they have been abused, but asks their confidante not to share this information with anyone).

Petronio's theory can also be applied to online settings. Users tend to hold beliefs about how a company or organisation will use their data, often expecting privacy and confidentiality. They may not realise the business model of companies who provide services to users without fee but instead gain income by selling user data to third parties. In many of these cases users will have given the organisation the right to share their information by indicating their acceptance of the organisation's terms and conditions, but they are unaware of this as they may not have read that documentation in advance of accepting it (see the section regarding cognitive psychology on pp. 127–128 for why this might occur). Users may also be surprised by the obligations of some organisations to share their information with government agencies without consulting the user in advance. Or the user may have unrealistic expectations regarding the ability of the organisation to protect their data from online intruders such as malicious hackers.

CPM theory is a very useful theory in understanding online disclosures by users, and its application to various online settings have been examined, including blogs (Child et al., 2012), online health (Smith & Brunner, 2015), social media (Kisekka et al., 2013), and academic communications (Thompson et al., 2012), among others.

Social spheres and space

As mentioned above, who we are comfortable disclosing private information to can vary greatly. It may be that we are only comfortable talking about our problems with close friends or family, or we may only trust one highly regarded other with our secret. But sometimes, if we feel that we are anonymous, we may be comfortable sharing our situation with a wider group of people, and perhaps even posting our experience and situation publicly. A brief perusal of online boards relating to pregnancy can quickly uncover many women who have recently discovered that they are pregnant, but who are not yet ready to disclose this to their family or friends as their pregnancy is in an early stage. Nevertheless, they may wish to compare their symptoms and situations with others in similar circumstances, and so groups of anonymous soon-to-be mothers form online to aid each other with their condition.

Such anonymous sharing of private information is only one of many examples of online sharing. The presence of privacy settings in social media results in circumstances where users may be selective about which of their acquaintances receive which information about them. Indeed, this selective inclusion of others into their social media circles can be an important method of enhancing privacy (Ellison et al., 2011). Problems may arise when there are 'conflicting social spheres' (Marder et al., 2012, p. 859) as some communications may be perceived by some social spheres as negative, while to other spheres they are positive or neutral, depending on the members' social norms and standards. These multiple audiences can result in dilemmas for the user, and online self-presentation may veer towards the 'ought self' – who the user feels that they ought to be, rather than who they actually are (Marder *et al.*, 2015).

Such curated presentation of the self can sometimes be exhausting, to the extent that we may feel a need for some space from even those closest to us. We might feel 'crowded' and seek privacy from those around us, at least for a while. However, social media may mean that we experience a new phenomenon – 'digital crowding' (Joinson *et al.*, 2011). Joinson *et al.* (2011) outline that as social media relies on disclosure, and as privacy settings can be complex, 'excessive social contact prompts users to search for coping mechanisms or to withdraw' (p. 42). This may be another mechanism for dealing with actual or perceived invasions of privacy.

Paradoxes, trade-offs and gaps

As previously mentioned, individuals are often aware of the risks of privacy disclosure, and they may even feel a sense of exposure or invasion when they feel that their privacy has not been sufficiently cared for (boyd, 2008). Even with the awareness of the vulnerability of our data online, we may still choose to engage in behaviours that increase the risk of unwanted disclosure. Such behaviours are examples of a phenomenon known as the **knowing–doing gap** (Cox, 2012; Workman *et al.*, 2008). This describes a situation where the user knows what the most secure behaviour is, but fails to behave in a way which promotes such security. Similarly, Barnes (2006) described the privacy paradox, where users seemed concerned about their data but their behaviour seemed to conflict with this concern.

A possibility is that individuals utilise a variety of techniques to maintain privacy – these include privacy settings, but also the use of selective disclosures and selective inclusion of others into their social media circles (Ellison *et al.*, 2011). It may be that users maintain a balance between these three techniques when disclosing information. But it is also possible that many users do not take such care.

Here, the overlap between privacy and security must also be emphasised – one of the easiest ways in which a user can unwittingly disclose information is by failing to secure it effectively. As we accumulate highly personal data on portable devices such as smartphones, we increasingly put ourselves at risk of such data falling into the wrong hands through theft or misplacement of such devices. The risks of disclosure can be minimised by including adequate security measures, such as complex passwords and passcodes for the device and each account on it, and not leaving these accounts logged in. However, such behaviours make accessing our accounts a relatively lengthy process, and the more secure the behaviours (for example, using different, complex passwords for each account), the more difficult they become for the user to complete. There are obvious rewards for the user in choosing less safe behaviours – including quicker access to the applications and less likelihood of forgetting the passwords. Tam, *et al.* (2009) noted this phenomenon, referring to it as the convenience–security trade-off. For many users, unless a complex log-in process is a mandatory element of the interaction (such as, for example, online banking), then they will tend towards choosing the more convenient, and less secure, option.

In the light of all of the above, it is possible that users' propensity to engage in secure behaviours is triggered by a complex collection of criteria. Rogers (1975, 1983) proposed **Protection Motivation Theory**, which identified several factors which might trigger engagement in more secure behaviours. These include how severe the user perceives the threatened event to be, how likely they perceive the event to be, how effective the preventative measure is, what are the potential rewards if the threat is avoided, what are the potential costs of implementing the preventative measure, and if the user believes that they can successfully implement the preventative measures (self-efficacy). It may be that it is a combination of these elements which results in a user taking or avoiding precautions with their privacy. However, with regard to online security, many studies have found that perceived self-efficacy is particularly important (e.g. Johnston & Warkentin, 2010; Lee *et al.*, 2008; Ng *et al.*, 2009). Unfortunately, given the role of various organisations in maintaining privacy and the potential for government agencies to request user data, it is possible that individuals may feel a lack of self-efficacy in protecting their own data as so many aspects of this task are beyond their control (Power & Kirwan, 2015).

REMOVING OUR DATA ONLINE

Once our data has appeared online it is difficult to remove all traces of it. While the clarification of legislation regarding the right to be forgotten has resulted in easier removal of data, including the deletion of online profiles, it is still difficult to erase all evidence of our online lives, once created. Partially, this is because of the easy replicability of digital information – should a person wish to make, keep or distribute copies of an image or file it is extremely easy for them to complete this.

Nevertheless, it is important to consider why an individual might decide to remove information online. This may occur as a result of many factors, perhaps a user notices unwanted attention on their profile and fears cyberstalking activity. Or perhaps they change their mind regarding a message which was posted during an emotional time, or desire to remove a post which attracted negative comments or criticism. In other cases, a user may have been tagged in a photograph or post which they feel presents them in an unflattering light, and they may wish to remove evidence of this. The potential success of each of these can vary – for example, if a user wishes to distance themselves from undesirable photos on social media they have a variety of methods of managing such a situation, including untagging, which is often the preferred method (Lang & Barton, 2015). However, untagging does not remove the photo from the social media website entirely, and it may remain visible to other users.

A similar range of motivations, including 'impression management triggers, personal safety identity triggers, relational trigger and legal/disciplinary triggers' (Child *et al.*, 2011, p. 2017) can result in bloggers 'scrubbing' their entries and altering protective behaviours. Other motives for the deletion of information by bloggers can include employment security, fear of retribution and relational cleansing (Child *et al.*, 2012). Privacy concerns may even result in the complete removal of an online social networking profile, a phenomenon referred to as **virtual identity suicide** by Stieger *et al.* (2013).

Despite the behaviours above, many users do not engage in removal behaviours, instead leaving their information online and available. As social media platforms wax and wane in popularity, it is possible that individuals will leave a legacy of abandoned profiles, photographs and posts in their wake. As mentioned earlier in this chapter, the accumulation of information across platforms may also be a risk factor in online privacy, and it is only as our online lives progress that we will become fully aware of the consequences of multiple online profiles.

CONCLUSION

There are many ways in which we share our information online, potentially threatening our privacy. The reasons why we share this information and how we decide who we share the information with are complex, involving aspects of cognitive psychology, social spheres and communication theories. However, they are also vulnerable to paradoxes and trade-offs, and users may be unaware of the quantity and type of information that they are sharing. While it is becoming easier for users to remove their data from online settings, it is unknown how widespread such activities are, or what the consequences will be as private information accumulates across a variety of online settings.

ACTIVITY

Take a look at the profile set-up forms for one example of each of the following types of online accounts. What data do they ask users for? Is it essential or optional for users to provide each of these items of data? In your opinion, are there practical reasons for the company or organisation to ask for this information? Is it acceptable for certain organisations to require more information, and different types of information, than others?

a   An online banking account.
b   A social media account.
c   An airline membership programme for accumulation of airmiles.
d   An online retailer selling groceries /electrical items /books /clothing / other small items.
e   A mobile phone operator.
f   An email service provider.

DISCUSSION QUESTIONS

1   Do we give away our privacy too easily? Consider what sources we give information too, and what information they require of us.
2   Are users generally aware of how their data is shared? Would they act differently if they had a greater level of awareness of this?

3   Do you think that Petronio's CPM theory accurately explains how individuals think about their communications?

4   Do users take adequate security measures when using online services? How could their behaviours be changed to increase their security?

RECOMMENDED READING LIST

Bruce Schneier has published widely in the areas of security and privacy. While all of his books are highly insightful readings in these areas, two of the most recent specifically consider data privacy and trust.

Schneier, B. (2015). *Data and Goliath: The Hidden Battles to Collect Your Data and Control your World.* New York: W.W. Norton & Company.

Schneier, B. (2012). *Liars and Outliers: Enabling the Trust that Society Needs to Thrive.* Indianapolis, IN: John Wiley & Sons.

This paper by Vasalou, Joinson and Houghton examines the complexity of the concept of privacy, describing new methods of conceptualising it which may aid in both research and practice.

Vasalou, A., Joinson, A.N. & Houghton, D. (2015). Privacy as a fuzzy concept: a new conceptualization of privacy for practitioners. *Journal of the American Society for Information Science and Technology, 66*(5), 918–929.

Some complaints against organisations that share or organise data online have resulted in increased clarity regarding the rights of users to control their online data. Some of the background and information about European rights are provided by the European Commission in the factsheet below.

European Commission (2014). Factsheet on the 'Right to be Forgotten' ruling (C-131/12). Retrieved from: http://ec.europa.eu/justice/data-protection/files/factsheets/factsheet_data_protection_en.pdf.

Trepte and Reinecke (2011) are the editors of a collection of papers concerning online privacy, particularly in relation to social aspects of online life.

Trepte, S. & Reinecke, L. (eds) (2011). *Privacy Online: Perspectives on Privacy and Self-disclosure in the Social Web.* Heidelberg: Springer.

Sandra Petronio considers why individuals share or conceal private information generally and what decision-making processes they might go through during this practice. It is useful to consider her theory in light of how users share information online.

Petronio, S. (2002). *Boundaries of Privacy: Dialectics of Disclosure.* Albany, NY: SUNY Press.

GLOSSARY

Communication Privacy Management (CPM)   A theory developed by Sandra Petronio (2002) describing how individuals view and share their private information.

Internet cookies   Data used by websites to record user activity.

Knowing–doing gap   A situation where the user knows what the most secure behaviour is, but fails to behave in a way which promotes such security.

Privacy   The state or condition of not having personal information disclosed in public or semi-public settings.

Protection Motivation Theory   A theory proposed by Rogers (1975, 1983) which identified several factors which might trigger engagement in protective behaviours.

Virtual identity suicide   The removal of an online profile, sometimes to increase privacy.

REFERENCES

Acquisti, A., Gross, R. & Stutzman, F. (2014). Face recognition and privacy in the age of augmented reality. *Journal of Privacy and Confidentiality, 6*(2), 1–20.

Barnes, S. (2006, September). A privacy paradox: Social networking in the United States. *First Monday, 11*(9). Retrieved from: http://firstmonday.org/htbin/cgiwrap/bin/ojs/index.php/fm/article/viewArticle/1394/1312%23note4.

boyd, d. (2008). Facebook's privacy trainwreck. *Convergence: The International Journal of Research into New Media Technologies, 14*(1), 13–20.

Child, J.T., Haridakis, P.M. & Petronio, S. (2012). Blogging privacy rule orientations, privacy management and content deletion practices: The variability of online privacy management activity at different stages of social media use. *Computers in Human Behavior, 28*, 1859–1872.

Child, J.T., Petronio, S, Agyeman-Budu, E.A. & Westermann, D.A. (2011). Blog scrubbing: Exploring triggers that change privacy rules. *Computers in Human Behavior, 27*, 2017–2027.

Cox, J. (2012). Information systems user security: A structured model of the knowing-doing gap. *Computers in Human Behavior, 28*, 1849–1858.

Einhorn, H.J. & Hogarth, R.M. (1978). Confidence in judgement: Persistence of the illusion of validity. *Psychological Review, 85*, 395–416.

Ellison, N.B., Vitak, J., Steinfield, C., Gray, R. & Lampe, C. (2011). Negotiating privacy concerns and social capital needs in a social media environment. In S. Trepte and L. Reinecke (eds) *Privacy Online: Perspectives on Privacy and Self-disclosure in the Social Web* (pp. 19–32). New York: Springer.

European Commission (2014). Factsheet on the 'Right to be Forgotten' ruling (C-131/12). Retrieved from: http://ec.europa.eu/justice/data-protection/files/factsheets/factsheet_data_protection_en.pdf.

Gross, R. & Acquisti, A. (2005) Information revelation and privacy in online social networks. In *Proceedings of the workshop on privacy in the electronic society*, ACM, Alexandria, pp. 71–80.

Johnston, A.C. and Warkentin, M. (2010). Fear appeals and information security behaviours: An empirical study. *MIS Quarterly, 34*(3), 549–566.

Joinson, A.N., Houghton, D.J., Vasalou, A. & Marder, B.L. (2011). Digital crowding: Privacy, self-disclosure, and technology. In S. Trepte and L. Reinecke (eds) *Privacy Online: Perspectives on Privacy and Self-disclosure in the Social Web* (pp. 33–45). New York: Springer.

Kahneman, D. (2011). *Thinking, Fast and Slow.* London: Penguin.

Kirwan, G. (in print). Psychology and Security: Utilising psychological and communication theories to promote safer cloud security behaviours. In R. Ko and K-K. R. Choo (eds) *The Cloud Security Ecosystem: Technical, Legal, Business and Management Issues.* Waltham, MA: Elsevier.

Kisekka, V., Bagchi-Sen, S. & Rao, H.R. (2013). Extent of private information disclosure on online social networks: An exploration of Facebook mobile phone users. *Computers in Human Behavior, 29*, 2722–2729.

Lang, C. & Barton, H. (2015). Just untag it: Exploring the management of undesirable Facebook photos. *Computers in Human Behavior, 43*, 147–155.

Lee, D., Larose, R. & Rifon, N. (2008). Keeping our network safe: A model of online protection behaviour. *Behaviour & Information Technology, 27*, 445–454.

Marder, B., Joinson, A. & Shankar, A. (2012, January). Every post you make, every pic you take, I'll be watching you: Behind social spheres on Facebook. In Proceedings of the 45th Hawaii International Conference on System Sciences (pp. 859–868). IEEE.

Marder, B., Joinson, A., Shankar, A. & Archer-Brown (2015). Any user can be any self that they want so long as it is what they 'ought' to be: Exploring self-presentation in the presence of multiple audiences on social network sites. In L. Robinson Jr (ed.) *Marketing Dynamism & Sustainability: Things Change, Things Stay the Same . . . Developments in Marketing Science.* Proceedings of the Academy of Marketing Science (pp. 621–626). Academy of Marketing Science, Springer International Publishing.

Ng, B.Y., Kankanhalli, A. & Xu, Y.C. (2009). Studying users' computer security behaviour: A health belief perspective. *Decision Support Systems, 46*, 815–825.

Paine, C., Reips, U.-D., Stieger, S., Joinson, A., & Buchanan, T. (2007). Internet users' perceptions of 'privacy concerns' and 'privacy actions'. *International Journal of Human-Computer Studies, 65*(6), 526–536.

Petronio, S. (2002). *Boundaries of Privacy: Dialectics of Disclosure.* Albany, NY: SUNY Press.

Petronio, S. (2013). Brief status report on Communication Privacy Management theory. *Journal of Family Communication, 13*(1), 6–14.

Petrionio, S. & Durham, W.T. (2015). Communication privacy management theory: Significance for interpersonal communication. In D.O. Braithwaite & P. Schrodt (eds) *Engaging Theories in Interpersonal Communication: Multiple Perspectives* (2nd edn; pp. 335–347). Thousand Oaks, CA: Sage Publications.

Power, A. & Kirwan, G. (2015). Privacy and security risks online. In A. Attrill (ed.) *Cyberpsychology* (pp. 233–248). Oxford: Oxford University Press.

Rogers, R.W. (1975). A protection motivation theory of fear appeals and attitude change. *The Journal of Psychology, 91*, 93–114.

Rogers, R.W. (1983). Cognitive and physiological processes in fear appeals and attitude change: A revised theory of protection motivation. In J.Cacioppo and R. Petty (eds) *Social Psychophysiology* (pp. 153–176). New York: Guilford Press.

Smith, S.A. & Brunner, S.R. (2015). The great whoosh: Connecting an online personal health narrative and Communication Privacy Management. *Health Communication*. Published online ahead of print at: www.tandfonline.com/doi/abs/10.1080/10410236. 2014.930551#.VTMoti7-TEY.

Stieger, S., Burger, C., Bohn, M. & Voracek, M. (2013). Who commits virtual identity suicide? Differences in privacy concerns, internet addiction and personality between Facebook users and quitters. *Cyberpsychology, Behavior and Social Networking, 16*(9), 629–634.

Tam, L., Glassman, M. & Vandenwauver, M. (2009). The psychology of password management: A tradeoff between security and convenience. *Behaviour & Information Technology, 29*, 233–244. DOI: 10.1080/01449290903121386.

Thompson, J., Petronio, S. & Braithwaite, D.O. (2012). An examination of privacy rules for academic advisors and college student-athletes: A Communication Privacy Management perspective. *Communication Studies, 63*(1), 54–76.

Tversky, A. and Kahneman, D. (1973). Availability: A heuristic for judging frequency and probability. *Cognitive Psychology, 5*(1), 207–232.

Vasalou, A., Joinson, A.N. & Houghton, D. (2015) Privacy as a fuzzy concept: A new conceptualization of privacy for practitioners. *Journal of the American Society for Information Science and Technology, 66*(5), 918–929.

Workman, M., Bommer, W.H. & Straub, D. (2008). Security lapses and the omission of information security measures: A threat control model and empirical test. *Computers in Human Behavior, 24*, 2799–2816.

3 | Applied cyberpsychology

11 Forensic cyberpsychology

Gráinne Kirwan

CHAPTER OVERVIEW

Forensic psychology holds huge potential in cybercriminal cases, including in work such as offender rehabilitation, victimology, offender profiling and crime reduction strategies. It may also be used to help juries and police officers serving in cybercrime cases. This chapter begins with an introduction to the various types of cybercrime and proposed methods of classifying cybercrime. It then provides an overview of forensic psychology and how it can be applied to online crime. Key criminological and forensic psychological theories will be described and their application to cybercrime will be assessed. Finally, the difficulties in completing research in forensic cyberpsychology will be described.

KEY TERMS

Forensic psychology is often a popular module in undergraduate psychology courses. According to Davies and Beech (2012), most aspects of forensic psychology can be classified as either **legal psychology** (which deals with the process of law, and particularly focuses on areas such as evidence, eyewitness memory, policing and the courts) and **criminological psychology** (which deals mostly with understanding and reducing criminal behaviour). While **offender profiling** of suspects by forensic psychologists is a popular media portrayal of the field, relatively few forensic psychologists actually work within this area.

Cybercrime encompasses a wide variety of different criminal behaviours and can broadly be considered as any unlawful act which is conducted using computing technologies. Most cybercrimes can be described as either **Internet-specific** or

Internet-enabled, depending on whether or not the crime is specific to the Internet (and technology as a whole), or whether it can also occur in offline settings, but is enabled by advances in technology (Kirwan & Power, 2013).

CYBERCRIME

Cybercrime can refer to any criminal activity that is carried out using computers and computer networks. The term encompasses a wide variety of offences, and although much of the criminal act might occur online, in many cases the actions have offline consequences or implications. For example, consider the circumstances surrounding use of Internet technologies to enable human trafficking or trade in illegal substances. In some other types of cybercrime there are fewer offline aspects, and sometimes the entirety of the offence is contained within computer networks.

One of the types of cybercrime which may be entirely contained online is malicious hacking. For many people, this is the first type of activity which springs to mind when the word 'cybercrime' is mentioned, possibly due to the frequent portrayal of this activity in film and the interest the news media shows in high-profile cases. It should be remembered that the term 'hacking' has varied usage in language – in popular media usage it regularly refers to illegal infiltration of a computer network, but it originally had a much more positive connotation, referring to pushing the limits of a computer (or other device) so that it can achieve more or be used for a positive, and legal, goal. It should be remembered that many modern hackers use the term with this definition in mind, and that 'hacking' does not even have to refer to computing technologies. Over the years, various attempts have been made to generate an alternative term which could be used to describe those involved in illegal or malicious hacking activities, with examples of such terms including 'black-hat hackers' and 'crackers'. However, such alternatives are rarely employed in popular media, so many people only associate the term with illegal and/or malicious activities. Hacking is often associated and/or confused with 'hacktivism' – the use of hacking techniques in activism, especially involving online agencies. As with hacking for other goals, this behaviour may be legal and indeed beneficial to society as a whole, although again the term has frequently been used in purely negative connotations. Because of the confusion regarding this nomenclature, the term 'malicious hacking' is used in this chapter to refer to incidences when hacking is conducted with the intent to cause harm or detriment.

Malware is a catch-all term for 'malicious software' – including viruses, worms, Trojan horses, spyware, and many other types of code which may cause harm to our computers or networks. Early malware often specifically attacked the computer that it infiltrated, damaging files or corrupting data (see Kirwan & Power, 2013, pp. 79–86 for examples of different types of malware). More recent malware more commonly has the goal of spying on user activity (perhaps with the intent of identity theft or impersonation), or of gaining control of the computer to use it as part of a 'botnet' – a network of infiltrated systems which can be used for a variety of purposes, but which are controlled by the cybercriminal.

Both malware and hacking have been associated with cyberterrorism. Researchers have varied in their definitions of cyberterrorism, mainly because of the wide variety of ways that terrorists can use the Internet in furthering their activities – such as recruitment, fundraising, operations, networking, communication and the dissemination of propaganda. But many researchers (e.g. Conway, 2007; Denning, 2007) suggest that the term 'cyberterrorism' should refer to use of the Internet to carry out an attack which results in severe violence and/or significant economic damage. This suggests that even high-profile website defacements or 'Denial of Service' attacks would be unlikely to be classified as cyberterrorism.

Many parents are concerned about the risks of technology for their children, with the greatest fear likely to be the presence of sexual predators who may be communicating with young people online. Considerable research has examined not only these offenders, but the risk factors for young people online, and there are many excellent resources for individuals who may be concerned by these risks. While such predators may also create and distribute explicit images of children being abused, these are frequently separate activities to predation. The literature regarding the former activity may refer to it as 'child pornography', but many authors and researchers prefer the term 'child exploitation material' as there are concerns that the term 'pornography' implies consent. Individuals such as David Finkelhor and Ethel Quayle have been particularly prominent in psychological and criminological research regarding child related offending online (see, for example, Mitchell et al., 2014; Quayle et al., 2014).

Children, and adults, may also be at risk of cyberbullying and cyberstalking. While these are certainly disruptive online behaviours, they are not always criminal in nature. In many jurisdictions, unless there is a threat to the physical well-being of the victim, these are not considered as illegal actions. That is not to say that these behaviours are not hurtful and do not have serious consequences, including suicides by victims. Other instances where cyberbullying and cyberstalking might be considered illegal can occur if hate speech forms part of the online communication, or if a 'revenge porn' image of an underage victim is circulated.

Thankfully, the most frequent cybercrimes have much less severe consequences. Most Internet users have at some point received an email promising significant financial reward should they agree to what appear to be very minor requests (this is often an example of **advance fee fraud**). Similarly, most users have also received emails which appear to be from banks, revenue agencies or online retailers asking them to click on a link embedded in the email so as to prevent a scam or confirm their details. Such **phishing** emails are attempts to engage in identity theft, where a cybercriminal seeks to obtain the user's login details in order to gain access to their financial affairs. Susceptibility to these emails can often be explained by many of the decision-making biases uncovered in research on cognitive psychology.

Many otherwise law-abiding Internet users engage in cybercrime through copyright infringement or digital piracy. The temptation to watch a film or television series without paying for the experience can be too much for many to resist, especially if that content would otherwise be unavailable for several days or weeks if it is legally available earlier in some countries than others. Films and television series are not the only media downloaded – software and music are also frequently illegally copied and distributed online. It should be remembered that copyright infringement occurred long before Internet technologies became popular, but the copying of analogue media such

FIGURE 11.1 While copyright infringement is not a recent development, analogue media such as video cassettes, audio cassettes and vinyl records were more difficult to copy than modern digital files

(photograph by Liam Kirwan)

as that depicted in Figure 11.1 was more difficult to do, and remained a more geographically localised problem than what is evident today. There have been many proposed psychological factors which may increase a user's tendency to download copyrighted media, and in particular peer influence and low self-control appear to be especially relevant (see, for example, Higgins *et al.*, 2012).

Finally, it should also be remembered that crime may occur in online virtual worlds, such as those used for socialising and gaming. There have been several reported incidents of assaults on **avatars** within these worlds, with an early, and very famous, case being that of assaults conducted by an avatar called 'Mr Bungle' on some of the other users of the text-based virtual world 'LambdaMoo' (Dibbell, 1993). Similar to cyberbullying and cyberstalking, many incidences of attacks within virtual worlds are not illegal acts, and indeed it would be extremely difficult to classify them as such as many online games require the killing and assault of other players' avatars to progress gameplay, and it is considered an acceptable part of the experience. Similarly, in some online virtual worlds conducting property crimes against other players, through theft or piracy, is also part of normal gameplay. But in virtual worlds where such activities are not the norm, an assault on a person's avatar or a theft of their property might result in strong psychological responses in the victim (Kirwan, 2009).

Categorising cybercrime

Many attempts have been made to categorise the types of cybercrime above in order to provide a mechanism by which we can more carefully evaluate, understand and combat them. Two of these taxonomies will be briefly described here – specifically those suggested by Wall (2001, 2007) and Kirwan and Power (2013).

David Wall (2001) suggested four areas of harmful activity online, specifically 'cyber-trespass' (unauthorised passing of virtual boundaries); 'cyber-deceptions/thefts' (such as identity theft and fraud); 'cyber-pornography/obscenity' (such as publishing explicit materials) and 'cyber-violence' (such as cyberstalking or hate speech). Later, Wall (2007) suggests that cybercrime has three main criminologies – computer integrity crimes (which attack network security, such as malicious hacking), computer-assisted crimes (which use networks to commit crimes, such as phishing scams) and computer-content crimes (considering illegal content on networks, such as the distribution of certain types of obscene materials).

In contrast, Kirwan and Power (2013) differentiate between three types of cybercrime. One type consists of crimes against the virtual person, including those which occur in online virtual worlds as described above. A second type identified by Kirwan and Power, Internet-enabled offences, includes types of crime which can and have occurred without the use of the Internet, but which are made easier or intensified because of Internet technologies. Examples of such offences include child predation and fraud. Much cybercrime literature utilises the term 'old wine in new bottles' to describe this phenomenon. Internet-enabled offences are contrasted with Internet-specific offences, which require Internet technologies during their conduction and did not exist before these technologies were developed. An example of such an Internet-specific offence is malicious hacking. This distinction between Internet-enabled and Internet-specific offences is useful when considering the psychological aspects of

FIGURE 11.2 Internet offences which have pre-existing offline equivalents have sometimes been referred to as 'old wine in new bottles'

(photograph by Liam Kirwan)

cybercrime – previous research regarding the offline equivalents of Internet-enabled offences may be useful in understanding online offenders, while it may be that those who engage in Internet-specific offences would not otherwise conduct criminal activity, and therefore these might demonstrate psychological traits and mechanisms which are not usually found in other offenders. Because of this it is important that researchers of cybercriminal psychology also hold expertise in the broader field of forensic psychology as a whole. A brief synopsis of research and practice in this field is provided below.

FORENSIC PSYCHOLOGY: AN OVERVIEW

Forensic psychology incorporates two subjects that many of the general public find fascinating – psychology and crime. Adding technology, such as the Internet, into this mix, creates a combination that is difficult for television and movie producers to ignore. Unfortunately, as with the depictions of many professions online, the portrayal of the work forensic psychologists in fictional media is often highly misleading (Kirwan, 2014). This is somewhat regrettable, as the actual work conducted by forensic psychologists and cybercrime investigators often involves much more scientific rigour and intricate consideration of minutiae than is seen in the media, and so a false impression of the professions involved may be formed in the minds of viewers. Forensic psychology is also much broader than media portrayals suggest – almost exclusively the psychologists depicted in such shows work with detectives in criminal cases, but the majority of forensic psychologists instead work in other settings, such as prisons, probation centres, hospitals and universities. This section will continue by providing a very brief outline of some of the key research areas in forensic psychology with examples of how these are applicable to cybercrime.

Research topics in forensic psychology

Many lay people have come across the term 'offender profiling', primarily because of the fictional portrayals mentioned above. In reality, there are several different approaches to offender profiling, such as clinical, typological and statistical methodologies. Some researchers have attempted to investigate if profiling can be used to uncover the characteristics of cybercriminals, such as the Hackers Profiling Project (Chiesa et al., 2009). Offender profiling can be considered an aspect of investigative psychology (see Canter & Youngs, 2009), which incorporates other ways in which psychologists can be of assistance to police investigations (such as linking cases, interviewing suspects and advising on deception). For example, psychologists can advise on the accuracy of lie detection methods (see, for example, Granhag et al., 2014), the potential of a suspect to give a false confession (Gudjonsson & Pearse, 2011) or the probable accuracy of eyewitness testimony (Loftus, 2013).

As mentioned, criminal psychology is an important aspect of forensic psychology. Much research attempts to determine what the risk factors of criminality are (see, for example, Farrington, 2005; Loeber et al., 2015) or to develop a greater understanding of specific types of offenders, such as psychopathic offenders (Neumann et al., 2014) or sex offenders (see, for example, Marshall & Hollin, 2014; Wilcox et al., 2014).

Similarly, research has attempted to identify the characteristics of various cybercriminal types (e.g. Babchishin *et al.*, 2011; Bachmann, 2010; Rogers *et al.*, 2006). When conducting research regarding criminality and criminal psychology, attempts are often made to predict offending, to enhance understanding of the offender, and also to determine the most appropriate assessment and rehabilitation of these offenders. Forensic psychology also attempts to determine the most effective punishments for different types of offenders (for example, if a financial penalty is as much of a deterrent for an action as a prison sentence is, then it is a much more socially acceptable and economically viable alternative). Forensic psychologists working in prisons will frequently assess offenders to determine if the attempts at rehabilitation and punishment have resulted in a decreased likelihood of reoffending. The psychologist may also develop new rehabilitation programmes and psychological measures to determine if these are more effective than previously existing ones. For example, Middleton *et al.* (2009) evaluate the effectiveness of a treatment programme specifically designed for Internet sex offenders.

Forensic psychology also has a role to play within the courtroom, as it considers the decision-making strategies of jurors and judges (Bornstein & Greene, 2011). It considers the role of victims – in terms of their experiences within the criminal justice system, the effects of the crime on them, and the impact that they can have on other individuals and groups (e.g. Landström *et al.*, 2015; Loughnan *et al.*, 2013). Research in forensic psychology also examines how efforts can be made to reduce and prevent crime, through prevention and educational programmes, and also through less obvious methods, such as environmental design (for example, planning effective street layouts and lighting). It considers who is most fearful of cybercrime victimisation, while considering why others are not as afraid (Davinson & Sillence, 2010). It also attempts to find methods by which such individuals can still live life to its fullest without substantially increasing their risk of victimisation (Tynes, 2007).

As is evident from this section, forensic psychology is an extremely broad area, with conclusions based on a substantial body of empirical research. The interested reader should consider initially reviewing a forensic psychology textbook, such as that by Davies and Beech (2012), before delving further into the plethora of excellent research articles in the field. Students interested in pursuing a career in forensic psychology should visit the website of their local psychological society (such as the British Psychological Society or the American Psychological Association) to identify the training and experience requirements in their region.

Theories of crime

A society without crime would seem extremely strange, no matter how utopian it might be. Researchers and theorists from many different fields have attempted to form theories of crime that describe why crime occurs and who is most likely to become an offender. Some of these theories have a criminological focus, some psychological, some sociological, but most can give us some valuable insights. Here we will briefly consider a small selection of such theories of crime and their applicability to cybercrime.

It is tempting to want to identify a single factor which differentiates criminals from non-criminals, and many attempts have been made to do this. Researchers have searched for consistent differences between offenders and non-offenders in moral development, intelligence, empathy, social skills, cognitive skills, aggressiveness, extraversion and many other traits. However, given the wide variety of types of offenders that there are, it is difficult to reliably find a single trait that provides a differentiating factor. For example, while some types of offenders might, on average, display a lower level of intelligence than the general population, this is frequently not the case for white-collar offenders or psychopaths. Similarly, there appears to be no personality structure indicative of terrorism (Horgan, 2003). There have also been attempts to uncover a genetic factor in offending, which does show some promise, but many who have the at-risk genetic structures never develop criminal tendencies.

Attempts have been made to apply learning theories to criminology, and the realisation that individuals often learn criminal behaviour by watching parents, siblings or peers engage in criminal acts has led to the suggestion that Bandura's social learning theory (Bandura, 1962) might allow partial explanation of such trends. As mentioned above, Morris and Higgins (2010) have applied social learning theory to digital piracy. It has also been thought that other learning theories, such as classical and operant conditioning, also have a role to play in criminality, with theories such as Rational Choice Theory (RCT) attempting to explain crime in terms of criminal decision making given the possibilities of reward and punishment (see the edited book by Cornish and Clarke, 2014, for further information).

A popular theory which provides some explanation of crime is Robert Agnew's General Strain Theory (Agnew, 1992), which suggests that when individuals are placed under strain criminality may occur (for example, if a person desires a certain goal, they may resort to criminal means to achieve it). Agnew has developed his theory significantly and adapted it to explain why certain individuals, such as younger males, are more likely to become offenders. Strain theory may provide insights into malicious hacking and malware, where cybercriminals may see themselves as having an advantage that they are lacking in other aspects of their lives.

Other researchers have suggested that many offenders do not subscribe directly to deviant norms, but develop ways of rationalising their behaviour to reduce feelings of guilt. Sykes and Matza (1957) termed such techniques 'neutralisations' – and these include various strategies such as denying any injury to the victim or denial of responsibility for their own offending. Other neutralisations have been identified by other researchers, such as 'everybody's doing it', identified by Coleman (1987, p. 413). The presence of such neutralisations may mean that the offender does not actually consider themselves to be a 'criminal', but rather is conducting a deviant behaviour for a specific purpose at a specific time, possibly because they do not perceive themselves as having an alternative. For example, much research in the area of child predators and collectors of explicit materials depicting children considers these offenders' use of 'cognitive distortions' – distorted ways of thinking that are similar to the neutralisations proposed by Sykes and Matza (1957) as they provide the offender with the perceived ability to justify their actions. The use of such cognitive distortions have been considered by many researchers, such as Taylor and Quayle (2003) and Howitt and Sheldon (2007). Neutralisations have also been applied to other types of cybercrime, such as digital piracy (e.g. Ingram & Hinduja, 2008; Morris & Higgins, 2009).

This relationship to identity perception is linked to 'labelling theory', which considers how individuals label themselves and others, and the behaviours that this may result in. A risk with a juvenile who has begun to offend is that they perceive that society has labelled them as a 'criminal', and they then begin to follow patterns of behaviour which they think is consistent with such a term. This may lead to an escalation of offending behaviour. Thankfully, many law-enforcement agencies make significant efforts to avoid the introduction of such a label for first-time offenders with the intention of avoiding such a situation. Labelling theory is of particular interest when we consider the nomenclature issues regarding hacking outlined above – many individuals involved in various hacking activities appear to be highly concerned regarding the use of the term in the media.

Another popular theory of crime known as Routine Activity Theory (RAT) considers how most criminal acts requires the co-presence of three elements – a motivated offender, a suitable target and an absence of guardians (Cohen & Felson, 1979). This theory allows us to consider how actions taken by offenders and potential victims might change the likelihood of a crime occurring, and provides insights into how to reduce crime rates. In cybercrime, the co-presence element is much easier to fulfil than for offline crimes, as geographical distance and boundaries are no longer a barrier to criminal activity. Almost any computer is a suitable target, as it either contains information which would be of use to a cybercriminal, or can be used as part of a 'botnet' in other cybercriminal activity. So, the only element of RAT which remains, the absence of guardians, becomes particularly important. This theory provides insights into the importance of protective behaviours online, especially the use of antivirus and firewall technologies. However, it should be remembered that 'no matter how well designed, security methods rely on individuals to implement and use them' (Huang *et al.*, 2010, p. 221).

Finally, it should also be remembered that crime itself tends to be socially constructed – in other words, an action is a crime because society creates laws and regulations regarding it. Because laws tend to be created by those with the most power or control in a society, they tend to reflect the values of those individuals, and in some regrettable circumstances, may be intentionally or unintentionally used by those individuals to ensure that other groups are marginalised. Some types of cybercrime were easily identified as criminal because of their similarity and overlaps with pre-existing offline offences (this is especially true of the Internet-enabled offences). However, for Internet-specific offences, it has been necessary to alter existing law, or create new laws, in order to ensure that they were reflected within criminal justice systems.

It should be noted that explanations of crime do not have to be considered as separate and discrete. Ideally, multiple theories can be integrated to provide a more cohesive model of offending. This has been attempted by some researchers, including Hans Eysenck (Eysenck & Eysenck, 1970), who have integrated various aspects into a single theory, although such models have not been without critique. Such composite theories may also be applied to cybercriminal cases, but the validity of these models is difficult to verify, partially because of the problematic nature of cybercriminal research.

Researching cybercrime

It is tempting to say that cybercrime is fast-paced, and that waiting for empirical evidence to support a hypothesis is not feasible. But speculation in cybercrime can be as dangerous as speculation in other types of crime, and all crime is a serious issue that requires suitable research. Of course, technical solutions, such as software patches and updated malware lists, are extremely time-sensitive, but many of the psychological components of cybercrime have similar underlying aspects as are seen in offline crime, or in other aspects of psychology, such as cognitive or social theories.

Responding to cybercrime does require a certain amount of thinking on our feet, but this thinking needs to be based on existing literature and empirically supported theories. Thankfully, psychologists working in this area do not need to generate their advice on pure speculation. However, it should also be remembered that any hypotheses proffered need to be empirically tested at the first opportunity. For this reason, empirically sound research with real cases and cybercriminals needs to be conducted.

There are problems with such research – for example, how can we contact such offenders? If an individual does respond to a call for research participants, how can we be sure that they are indeed the offender that they claim to be, as asking them to demonstrate their actions is at best an inconvenience and may potentially be a criminal act in itself. Even if they are a cybercriminal, it is possible that those who volunteer as research participants are fundamentally and qualitatively different from those offenders who do not, so it may not be possible to ensure that our findings can be applied to the wider community. It is difficult to overcome these problems, and research in this field must be careful to consider such limitations when presenting findings and suggestions for policy.

CONCLUSION

Forensic psychology is an established field, with a significant quantity of high quality research. The study of cybercrime can draw from this pre-existing knowledge and further it as it examines areas of crime and types of criminals which did not exist before recent advances in technology. There are many types of cybercrime, with a wide variety of offender types, but research in forensic psychology and theories of crime provide insights into how and why these offences occur, as well as how offenders might be rehabilitated and how future cybercrimes might be prevented.

ACTIVITY

Keep a log of any emails that you receive which include attempts at identity theft or fraud. For example, these might be emails that pretend to be from banks, online auction sites, other online retailers, or officials from other countries. What is it about these emails that makes you think that they are fraudulent? What tactics do they use to try to persuade victims to provide information or click on links?

DISCUSSION QUESTIONS

1   Consider any fictional film or television programme that portrays cybercrime. How does the reality of cybercrime differ from that portrayed in the media? Why are they different?

2   Does it surprise you that forensic psychology is so much broader than offender profiling? Compare your perceptions of the field before and after reading this chapter.

3   Are some types of cybercrime really 'old wine in new bottles', or are they fundamentally different types of offences?

4   Considering the online disinhibition effect and other aspects of online behaviour, would some people commit crime online who would never contemplate offending in offline environments?

RECOMMENDED READING LIST

Readers who are interested in gaining a fuller insight into the complexity and breadth of forensic psychology will find this textbook by Davies and Beech helpful. The text is approved by the British Psychological Society.

Davies, G. & Beech, A. (2012). *Forensic Psychology: Crime, Justice, Law, Interventions* (2nd edn). Chichester: BPS Blackwell.

This chapter, by necessity, provides only a very brief overview of the various types of cybercrime and the psychological research which furthers our understanding of it. Further detail can be found in this textbook by Kirwan and Power.

Kirwan, G. & Power, A. (2013). *Cybercrime: The Psychology of Online Offenders*. Cambridge: Cambridge University Press.

Brenda Wiederhold considers how psychology can aid in the enhancement of cybersecurity in her 2014 editorial in the journal *Cyberpsychology, Behavior and Social Networking*.

Wiederhold, B.K. (2014). The role of psychology in enhancing cybersecurity. *Cyberpsychology, Behavior and Social Networking*, *17*(3), 131–132.

The second edition of Yar's *Cybercrime and Society* considers the problem of cybercrime from a criminological and sociological approach, and is a useful text with some excellent pedagogical features.

Yar, M. (2013). *Cybercrime and Society* (2nd edn). London: Sage Publications.

GLOSSARY

Advance fee fraud   A type of online fraud where a user is promised a significant financial reward should they meet what initially appear to be minor demands and fees.

Avatar   An online representation of a user, especially in three-dimensional virtual worlds.

Criminological psychology   A branch of psychology which deals mostly with understanding and reducing criminal behaviour.

Cybercrime   Any unlawful act which is conducted using computing technologies.

Forensic psychology   A branch of psychology which encompasses legal and criminological psychology.

Internet-specific cybercrime   Cybercrimes for which offline equivalents do not exist.

Internet-enabled cybercrime   Crimes for which offline equivalents exist, but which Internet technologies enable or extend.

Legal psychology   A branch of psychology which deals with the process of law.

Offender profiling   The creation of profiles of criminal suspects, sometimes by forensic psychologists.

Phishing   Emails which appear to be from a reputable source which are designed to elicit sensitive information from a user, leaving them vulnerable to identity theft.

REFERENCES

Agnew, R. (1992). Foundation for a general strain theory of crime and delinquency. *Criminology*, *30*(1), 47–88.

Babchishin, K.M., Hanson, R.K. & Hermann, C.A. (2011). The characteristics of online sex offenders: A meta-analysis. *Sex Abuse*, *23*, 92–123.

Bachmann, M. (2010). The risk propensity and rationality of computer hackers. *International Journal of Cyber Criminology*, *4*(1–2), 643–656.

Bandura, A. (1962). Social learning through imitation. In M.R. Jones (ed.) *Nebraska Symposium on Motivation* (pp. 211–274). Oxford: University of Nebraska Press.

Bornstein, B.H. & Greene, E. (2011). Jury decision making: Implications for and from psychology. *Current Directions in Psychological Science*, *20*, 63–67.

Canter, D. & Youngs, D. (2009). *Investigative Psychology: Offender Profiling and the Analysis of Criminal Action*. Chichester: John Wiley & Sons.

Chiesa, R., Ducci, S. & Ciappi, S. (2009). *Profiling Hackers: The Science of Criminal Profiling as Applied to the World of Hacking*. Boca Raton, FL: CRC Press.

Cohen, L.E. & Felson, M. (1979). Social change and crime rate trends: A routine activity approach. *American Sociological Review*, *44*, 588–608.

Coleman, J.W. (1987). Toward an integrated theory of white-collar crime. *The American Journal of Sociology*, *93*(2), 406–439.

Conway, M. (2007). Cyberterrorism: Hype and reality. In L. Armistead (ed.) *Information Warfare: Separating Hype from Reality* (pp. 73–93). Potomac Books.

Cornish, D.B. & Clarke, R.V. (eds) (2014). *The Reasoning Criminal: Rational Choice Perspectives on Offending.* New Brunswick, NJ: Transaction Publishers.

Davies, G. & Beech, A. (2012). *Forensic Psychology: Crime, Justice, Law, Interventions* (2nd edn). Chichester: BPS Blackwell.

Davinson, N. & Sillence, E. (2010). It won't happen to me: Promoting secure behaviour among internet users. *Computers in Human Behaviour, 26,* 1739–1747.

Denning, D.E. (2007). Cyberterrorism – Testimony before the special oversight panel on terrorism committee on armed services US House of Representatives. In E.V. Linden (ed.) *Focus on Terrorism, Volume 9* (pp. 71–76). New York: Nova Science Publishers.

Dibbell, J. (1993). *A Rape in Cyberspace.* Retrieved from: http://loki.stockton.edu/~kinsellt/stuff/dibbelrapeincyberspace.html.

Eysenck, S.B.G. & Eysenck, H.J. (1970). Crime and personality: An empirical study of the three-factor theory. *The British Journal of Criminology,* 10(3), 225–239.

Farrington, D.P. (2005). *Integrated Developmental and Life-Course Theories of Offending.* New Brunswick, NJ: Transaction Publishers.

Granhag, P.A., Vrij, A. & Verschuere, B. (2014). *Detecting Deception: Current Challenges and Cognitive Approaches.* Chichester: John Wiley & Sons.

Gudjonsson, G.H. & Pearse, J. (2011). Suspect interviews and false confessions. *Current Directions in Psychological Science,* 20(1), 33–37.

Higgins, G.E., Marcum, C.D., Freiburger, T.L. & Ricketts, M.L. (2012). Examining the role of peer influence and self-control on downloading behaviour. *Deviant Behaviour, 33,* 412–423.

Horgan, J. (2003). The search for the terrorist personality. In A. Silke (ed.) *Terrorists, Victims and Society: Psychological Perspectives on Terrorism and its Consequences.* Chichester: John Wiley & Sons.

Howitt, D. & Sheldon, K. (2007). The role of cognitive distortions in paedophilic offending: Internet and contact offenders compared. *Psychology, Crime & Law, 13*(5), 469–486.

Huang, D., Rau, P.P. & Salvendy, G. (2010). Perception of information security. *Behaviour & Information Technology, 29,* 221–232.

Ingram, J.R. & Hinduja, S. (2008). Neutralizing music piracy: An empirical examination. *Deviant Behaviour, 29*(4), 334–366.

Kirwan, G. (2009). Presence and the victims of crime in online virtual worlds. Proceedings of Presence 2009 – the 12th Annual International Workshop on Presence, International Society for Presence Research, 11–13 November, Los Angeles, CA.

Kirwan, G. (2014). Scripts and sensationalism: The depiction of forensic psychology in fictional media. *The Irish Psychologist, June 2014, 40*(8), 224–225.

Kirwan, G. & Power, A. (2013). *Cybercrime: The Psychology of Online Offenders.* Cambridge: Cambridge University Press.

Landström, S., Ask, K. & Sommar, C. (2015). The emotional male victim: Effects of presentation mode on judged credibility. *Scandinavian Journal of Psychology, 56*(1), 99–104.

Loeber, R., Byrd, A.L. & Farrington, D.P. (2015). Why developmental criminology is still coming of age: The influence of biological factors on within-individual change. In J. Morizot & L. Kazemian (eds) *The Development of Criminal and Antisocial Behaviour* (pp. 65–73). New York: Springer International Publishing.

Loftus, E.F. (2013). 25 years of eyewitness science . . . Finally pays off. *Perspectives on Psychological Science, 8*(5), 556–557.

Loughnan, S., Pina, A., Vasquez, E.A. & Puvia, E. (2013). Sexual objectification increases rape victim blame and decreases perceived suffering. *Psychology of Women Quarterly, 37*(4), 455–461.

Marshall, W.L. & Hollin, C. (2014). Historical developments in sex offender treatment. *Journal of Sexual Aggression.* Published online ahead of print. DOI: 10.1080/13552600.2014.980339.

Middleton, D., Mandeville-Norden, R. & Hayes, E. (2009). Does treatment work with internet sex offenders? Emerging findings from the internet sex offender treatment programme (i-SOTP). *Journal of Sexual Aggression, 15*, 5–19.

Mitchell, K.J., Jones, L., Finkelhor, D. & Wolak, J. (2014). Trends in unwanted online experiences and sexting: Final report. *Crimes Against Children Research Centre, University of New Hampshire.* Retrieved from: www.unh.edu/ccrc/pdf/Full%20Trends%20Report%20Feb%202014%20with%20tables.pdf.

Morris, R.G. & Higgins, G.E. (2009). Neutralizing potential and self-reported digital piracy: A multitheoretical exploration among college undergraduates. *Criminal Justice Review, 34*(2), 173–195.

Morris, R.G. & Higgins, G.E. (2010). Criminological theory in the digital age: The case of social learning theory and digital piracy. *Journal of Criminal Justice, 38*(4), 470–480.

Neumann, C.S., Hare, R.D. & Pardini, D.A. (2014). Antisociality and the construct of psychopathy: Data from across the globe. *Journal of Personality.* Published online ahead of print DOI: 10.1111/jopy.12127.

Quayle, E., Allegro, S., Hutton, L., Sheath, M. & Lööf, L. (2014). Rapid skill acquisition and online sexual grooming of children. *Computers in Human Behavior, 39*, 368–375.

Rogers, M.K., Smoak, N. and Liu, J. (2006). Self-reported criminal computer behaviour: A big-5, moral choice and manipulative exploitive behaviour analysis. *Deviant Behaviour, 27*, 1–24.

Sykes, G.M. & Matza, D. (1957). Techniques of neutralization: A theory of delinquency. *American Sociological Review, 22*(6), 664–670.

Taylor, M. & Quayle, E. (2003). *Child Pornography: An Internet Crime.* Hove: Brunner-Routledge.

Tynes, B.M. (2007). Internet safety gone wild? Sacrificing the educational and psychosocial benefits of online social environments. *Journal of Adolescent Research, 22*, 575–584.

Wall, D.S. (ed.) (2001). *Crime and the Internet: Cybercrimes and Cyberfears.* London: Routledge.

Wall, D.S. (2007). *Cybercrime: The Transformation of Crime in the Information Age.* Cambridge: Polity Press.

Wilcox, D.T., Garrett, T. & Harkins, L. (2014). *Sex Offender Treatment.* Oxford: John Wiley & Sons.

12 Abnormal cyberpsychology and cybertherapy

Cliona Flood

CHAPTER OVERVIEW

Technology is a really important part of today's world and how we live our lives, enabling instant communication with friends and family. However, for some people, the Internet can be problematic. This chapter will look at how the Internet impacts on mental health, particularly in the arena of pathological Internet usage. It will also explore the topics of **Internet Addiction Disorder**, **social networking**, **online gaming** and mobile phone dependency, and will look at therapeutic options.

KEY TERMS

Abnormal psychology is the study of mental health. This chapter will look at some of the mental health issues that relate to the overuse of technology. It considers **psychopathology**, which is the scientific study of **mental disorders**. One of the problems with overuse of the Internet is that some people may become addicted to it. Internet addiction or problematic Internet use can be considered a **behavioural addiction** similar to problematic gambling. Excessive time **online gaming**, online gambling or using **social media** can be considered problematic. Some people suffer anxiety when they are separated from their mobile phones or technologies. One word used to describe problems relating to mobile phones is **nomophobia**. This is a term that refers to the fear of being out of mobile phone contact, having a run- down battery or losing the phone itself. Different forms of technology-enhanced **cognitive behavioural therapy** and treatment in **virtual environments** have been found useful in the treatment of mental health problems, especially in children. **Online counselling** is another useful treatment for mental health sufferers.

WHAT IS ABNORMAL PSYCHOLOGY?

Pinning down a finite definition of what abnormal psychology is can be an elusive task. There is some agreement that there are certain shared features. Comer (2013) argues that these are often called 'the four Ds' – *deviance* (being different, displaying extreme, bizarre or extreme behaviours), *distress* (upsetting or unpleasant to the person or to those around them), *dysfunction* (an inability to perform daily life tasks in a constructive way) and *danger* (a danger to oneself, others or society). It is also important to consider the cultural context in which the behaviour takes place. For example, the extreme behaviours of entertainers may be tolerated as a performance but not in society in general. **Abnormal psychology** is considered the scientific study of abnormal behaviour aiming to describe, predict, explain and change abnormal patterns of functioning (Comer, 2013). The term 'abnormal psychology', or **psychopathology**, is a strange one, for after all what is normal psychology? But in psychological terms, abnormal psychology refers to the issues that surround mental health.

The study of **mental health** embraces a broad field of psychological problems that may occur in people's lives. The scope of the issues covered in abnormal psychology range from problems relating to stress and anxiety, problems of mood, mind and body. It also studies psychosis and life-span problems. As a scientific subject relating to clinical practice, it embraces strict research methods, explores different models of abnormality and looks at clinical assessment, diagnosis and treatment options.

DSM-5 and how it views the Internet

The *Diagnostic and Statistical Manual of Mental Disorders* (DSM), is published by the American Psychiatric Association and is considered to be the standard tool used to classify mental disorders. It uses a common language and standard criteria for the diagnosis of mental illness. The current edition, the DSM-5 was published in 2013 and is used by researchers, clinicians, policy makers, the legal system and insurance companies as a benchmark. An alternative diagnostic tool is the International Statistical Classification of Diseases and Related Health Problems (ICD), which is published by the World Health Organization (WHO, 2004).

The DSM-5 has identified **Internet gamers** as an at-risk population, who may develop dependence or an addiction to online gaming. The DSM-5 outlines the proposed criteria for the inclusion of Internet Gaming Disorder in the manual: 'Persistent and recurrent use of the Internet to engage in games, often with other players, leading to clinically significant impairment or distress' (DSM-5, p. 795). The criteria includes preoccupation with Internet games, withdrawal symptoms when not playing, tolerance, unsuccessful attempts to control usage, loss of interest in previous hobbies, continued excessive use of Internet games despite knowing that it is causing problems, deception, escapism and the loss or jeopardisaton of a significant relationship, job, education or career. Internet gaming may be similar to gambling as the reward systems of the brain are activated and can be considered **behavioural addictions** (DSM-5). The main body of research comes from Asian countries and looks mainly at young males (see Wan & Chiou, 2006; Young, 1998a; Yee, 2006). These studies suggest that persistent use of the Internet can lead to the pathways in the brain being triggered in the same way as a drug addict's brain. The neurological responses are feelings of pleasure and reward, which is manifested as addictive behaviour. Internet Gaming Disorder is listed in Section III of the manual and it is envisaged that further research will determine whether the condition should actually be included in the manual as a disorder. Interestingly, Problematic Internet Use (PIU) wasn't included in the DSM-5, although it was considered. More evidence and research is required in order for inclusion in future publications. However, it does raise some interesting questions. For example, if somebody becomes overly anxious without the constant availability of their mobile phone, if a person's sole source of friendships and relationships is online, or if online health-seeking behaviour leads to a perceived escalation in illness symptoms, then we need to consider the possibility that something problematic is happening and needs to be addressed.

WHAT IS THE RANGE OF INTERNET-BASED DISORDERS?

There are many terms used when referring to problematic usage, these consist of PIU, problematic computer use, Internet addiction, Internet dependency and pathological Internet use (Morahan-Martin, 2007). Addiction relating to the Internet draws on much of the addiction literature and the classic models of addiction – for example, Jellinek's classic model (Jellinek, 1960). In the classical models, addiction came to signify a 'state' that limits voluntary control over a substance or behaviour. The issues of tolerance to the substance or behaviour, denial and withdrawal symptoms were all part of the addiction (Clark, 2011). Early models of addiction were inclined to restrict the definition to dependence on substances.

Today, this has expanded to included exercise, sex, gambling, gaming, relationships, shopping and general Internet usage (Griffiths, 1997); many of these activities have now migrated online. Holmes (1997, cited in Morahan–Martin, 2007) warns that people can develop problems with certain online activities. He makes the distinction between being addicted to being online and being addicted to what is online, and considers that the content is the problem. Another issue that needs careful consideration is that there can be other underlying mental health issues, such as depression, anxiety or loneliness that may contribute to a person's overuse of the Internet.

Internet gaming

Internet gaming has attracted media and academic attention. Wan and Chiou (2006) investigated the conscious and unconscious psychological motivations of ten Taiwanese teenaged gamers who were considered by the researchers to be addicted to online gaming. They found that the gamers identified four main reasons for playing games. These included entertainment and leisure, emotional coping, excitement and challenge seeking, and escaping from reality. The virtual worlds hosting the games can be interesting and engaging places that can be manipulated by the gamers. Players can create and manipulate themselves and their fantasies (Young, 2009). Gamers can gain status from other players, create resources and gain power within the game. However, there can be a downside to excessive gaming. Many hard-core players may suffer from emotional problems and low self-esteem and self-worth (Yee, 2006).

We also need to consider the context in which the gaming activity takes place. Griffiths (2010) outlines two case studies, in which the two participants claimed to spend up to 14 hours per day playing Massively Multiplayer Online Role-Playing Games (MMORPGs) and, on the face of it, their behaviour was identical in terms of their game playing. However, they had very different psychological motivations and the meaning that the gaming had for their lives. One player, although unemployed, reported that gaming was a positive influence in his life as his social life revolved around the game, and gaming boosted his self-esteem and gave a structure to his day. When he started a new job and formed a relationship with a woman he met in-game, his excessive gaming decreased significantly. The other player had experienced family and relationship breakdown due to his excessive gaming, and his low mood and craving for the game increased his anxiety levels. Gaming was used to escape the reality of everyday life and, although he tried, he was not successful in abstaining from the game.

The cultural context of Internet gaming needs to be considered and the reported addiction rates vary considerably. Kuss (2013) reports that German addiction rates are as low as 0.2 per cent but as high as 50 per cent in Korea. The differences could well be to do with the measurement instruments and the range of constructs that are used when discussing PIU – for example, 'Internet gaming', 'addiction', 'dependence' or 'excessive play'. Nevertheless, the Asian countries consider the negative impact of Internet gaming addiction very seriously and have developed initiatives to limit the impact (Kuss, 2013). In South Korea, gaming addiction is considered as a real concern for public health and up to 24 per cent of children who have been diagnosed have been hospitalised (as described in Kuss, 2013).

Apart from Internet gaming, PIU has been researched quite extensively since the late 1990s (O'Reilly, 1996; Young, 1998a; Griffiths, 2000). The framework that was adopted could be more linked to substance abuse and pathological gambling than the addictive nature of the Web. More recently, subtypes of PIU have emerged and attention is now being paid to a broader range of Internet-based problems – for example, Internet gambling, online gaming and problematic instant messaging (Lee & Cheung, 2014).

Social networking

What is it about the Internet that attracts users? Is it the content or the social connections? Chen and Kim (2013) looked beyond general Internet use and extended the scope to social networking sites (SNSs – sometimes called **social media**). They sought to understand what factors enhance or reduce users' compulsive behaviours and overuse of SNSs. Social networking is very much part of everyday life for many people.

Therefore, if PIU is a concern, then this is an area that should be investigated to explore the reasons why people spend excessive amounts of time online. Chen and Kim (2013) investigated the types of gratifications that SNS offers users and suggested that three types of gratifications were evident – diversion, self-presentation and relationship building. The social-orientated features of social networking platforms create pleasant social interactions for their users (Lee & Cheung, 2014). Due to the pleasant interactions and feedback, users are encouraged to use social networking. This can lead to overuse and even problematic behaviours.

Valkenburg *et al.* (2006) saw the need to investigate the consequences of teenagers' use of SNSs. The reason behind their research was the concern that social networking could have a negative impact on the developing sense of self of adolescents and the impact on self-worth and self-esteem. They found that adolescents' self-esteem was impacted by the tone of the feed received and the young people who received more negative feedback on their profiles had more adverse effects on their self-esteem. As one of the initial pieces of research in this area, it raises a flag for the possible negative consequences for young people's mental health. Byrn *et al.* (2009) considered the capacity of the Internet for socialisation one of the main reasons for excessive time spent on the Internet. Activities such as e-mail, discussion forums, chat rooms and gaming absorbs not only personal time but professional time as well. These networking capabilities can cause social isolation and daily living problems. A negative impact can be felt in the workplace and Internet addiction can impact negatively on work performance and engagement with co-workers. This in turn can lead to a reduction in job satisfaction and loss of efficiency (Byrn *et al.*, 2009).

Social isolation and low self-esteem are not the only negative impacts that can impact on the lives of adolescents. Jelenchick *et al.* (2013) investigated depression and social networking in a population of older teenagers and were unable to establish a link. Banjanin *et al.* (2015) also investigated the potential relationship between depression and Internet usage, specifically relate to social networking in Serbia. Their findings indicate that Internet use and level of Internet addiction showed a positive correlation with depression. However, no relationship was shown between social networking use and depression.

MOBILE PHONE SEPARATION ANXIETY AND THE INTERNET

Mobile phone addiction is a relatively new form of dependency, particularly among adolescents (Chóliz, 2012). According to Chóliz, a mobile phone is one of the most used and desired devices of teenagers. He argues that the mobile phone is particularly relevant to adolescent development as it can help to reinforce personal autonomy and provides identity and prestige among the peer group. The innovative nature of the technology is particularly attractive to the age group and the phone provides a source of fun and entertainment, and establishes and maintains relationships. As a tool, it is really useful and allows a number of functions to be used, but it can be problematic for some users. What is particularly interesting about Chóliz's research is that he argues that mobile phone dependence in teenagers is important for a number of reasons. He outlines that although technology is extremely useful and a necessary part of society, these technologies are susceptible to abuse and can lead to addiction. These addictions are different from other addictions – for example, drug addiction, because no social consensus currently exists regarding the risk factors of technological addiction. Chóliz considers the population most at risk to be teenagers due to cortical development and their fascination with developing technologies.

What happens if people are separated from their mobile technology? Siggins and Flood (2014) found no significant difference in anxiety levels in an experiment of planned mobile phone separation. However, what was evident was that 60 per cent of the participants were unwilling to separate from their phones. Indeed, participants failed to complete questionnaires when it was mentioned that there was a possibility of separation from their mobile phones. So it is quite possible that technological dependency is becoming more apparent and anxiety around separation from technological devices is on the increase. Indeed, by 2008 a new word had entered into our vocabulary – **nomophobia**. The term refers to the fear of being out of mobile phone contact, having a run-down battery or losing the phone itself. The popular media no doubt promoted the term (Wrenn, 2012; Elmore, 2014). However, there was a call to include the term as a disorder in the DSM-5 by Bragazzi and Puente (2014) suggesting that much more attention needs to be paid to the psychopathological effects of new media. King *et al.* (2013) used the term and defined nomophobia as 'the discomfort caused by the non-availability of a mobile phone, PC or any other virtual communication device' (p. 140). According to these researchers, there seems to be a close link between the term 'nomophobia' and Internet dependency. They caution that nomophobic behaviour can produce changes in daily habits and caution, and that it is necessary to investigate the possibility of comorbid mental health issues.

PATHOLOGICAL INTERNET USAGE

The possibility of Internet addiction

Psychiatrist Ivan Goldberg introduced the concept of **Internet Addiction Disorder** in 1995 as a satirical hoax in an attempt to parody how the American Psychiatric Association *Diagnostic and Statistical Manual* (DSM) attempts to create medical explanations for excessive behaviours (Beato, 2010). Today, there are numerous clinical detox programmes worldwide which attempt to regulate the use of the Internet for problematic Internet users.

One of the first papers on Internet addiction linked it to impulse control disorder, and viewed it nearest to pathological gambling of all the diagnosis referred to in the DSM-IV (Young, 1998a). The problems that Young identified included dependents versus non-dependents, time distortion, personal and work related, academic problems (despite the fact that the Internet is a great place to do research). Relationship issues were also evident – issues such as denial, hiding usage and distrust. Users found that online friendships and relationships were viewed as more exciting than face-to-face relationships. Dependents considered cybersex and romantic chat as harmless, yet neglected spouses over online 'dates'. Work-related issues were also evident, using employee access for personal use. Physical symptoms such as disrupted sleep patterns were identified and a sedentary lifestyle, carpal tunnel syndrome, eye strain and back strain were often the physical consequences of overuse. Users had no desire to cut down or restrict their usage and were unable to live without the Internet. Cravings, just like those a smoker feels, were also reported.

Griffiths (2000) identified a number of components that indicate issues with addiction relating to deviant Internet use. These included salience, mood modification, tolerance, withdrawal symptoms, conflict and relapse. In addressing the issue of addiction, he stated that there was little empirical evidence that computer-based activities were addictive. He used a number of case studies to explore the issue and he considered that all the participants in the study used the Internet excessively. However, this didn't necessarily indicate addiction, but could in fact have been masking other issues in their lives. Griffiths (2000) argues that technological addictions are a subset of behavioural addictions and the common view of an Internet addict was usually a male teenager who had little confidence and a poor social life. This, of course, is a stereotype and this has changed somewhat in the new millennium. Watson (2005) identified a number of subtypes of addiction: Internet overload or the compulsion to search the Web; online gambling; shopping compulsions; cyber relationships and cyber-sexual addictions through relationships, websites and graphic images.

Is it possible to be addicted to the Internet?

Ghassemzadeh *et al.* (2008) used Young's Internet Addiction Test (IAT), along with a number of other measures, UCLA Loneliness Scale, Rosenberg Self Esteem Scale (1965) and Matson Evaluation of Social Skills (Young, 1998b; Russell, 1996; Matson, 1983 cited in Ghassemzadeh *et al.*, 2008) on a sample of 977 students, all Internet users, in Iran. They found that 37 were Internet addicts and 304 were possible addicts. They suggested that the Internet addicts were lonelier, had lower self-esteem and had poorer social skills than moderate users and non-users. In a meta-analysis of 31 countries, Cheng and Li (2014) found that there appears to be about 6 per cent of the world addicted to the Internet. This varies across cultures, with Middle Eastern countries showing a higher prevalence than Western European and Northern European countries. Lopez-Fernandez *et al.* (2013) estimated that 5 per cent of Spanish adolescents had displayed problematic behaviour. Other areas of health have also been investigated, such as the link between Internet use and body mass index (BMI). In a Turkish sample of over 1,900 students, Canan *et al.* (2014) found that 12.4 per cent of their sample was considered to be addicted to the Internet and there was a strong relationship with Internet usage and increased BMI.

TREATMENT OPTIONS

By 2011, Kimberly Young was firmly convinced that Internet addiction was a new clinical disorder that had a major impact on relationships, work and social issues (Young, 2011). She outlined that this form of addiction has been documented in Italy, Pakistan and in the Czech Republic. Young also pointed out that the issue is a major concern in China, Taiwan and Korea, where it appears to be considered at epidemic proportions. How widespread the problem is can be difficult to estimate given the reach of the Internet and its use in everyday commercial and social transactions.

In order to treat Internet addictions, it is important that counsellors recognise this as a disease of contemporary society, due to its affordability, anonymity and accessibility (Didelot *et al.*, 2012). **Cognitive behavioural therapy** (CBT) may be useful; however, it is the long-term maintenance of the condition that needs addressing. Didelot *et al.* (2012) suggest that the culture of the Internet has a powerful role to play, particularly in two components of human relationships – that of communication and socialisation. The Internet offers a place for the lonely and this impacts on relationships.

Treatment options for many addictions suggest abstinence. However, this isn't an option for Internet addiction due to the prevalence of the Web in our lives. Therefore, the treatment options available consist of some of the traditional treatments, such as CBT. CBT was considered by Young (2011) to be effective as it helps clients to monitor their maladaptive thoughts and identify the triggers of addictive feelings. Clients can be taught coping skills to deal with their addiction. Young (2011) developed a new form of CBT called cognitive behavioural therapy – Internet addiction (CBT-IA) along with harm reduction therapy (HRT). The treatment plan consists of three phases. The first phase is behaviour modification, which is aimed at gradually decreasing the amount of time the person spends online. The next phase is cognitive restructuring, and identifies the thoughts that lead to the addiction and looks into the issues of why the addict spends so much time online. Finally, HRT is used to identify and treat any other issues, such as social isolation or depression that could also be involved in the development of compulsive Internet use.

Using technology to support recovery

Technology can be used to help recovery and treatment of poor mental health. **Virtual reality** (VR) has been identified as a potentially useful treatment option in the field of clinical psychology. VR is an emerging technology and can generate simulations of real or imagined environments where a patient can interact using their own movements. Both physical and cognitive functioning can be improved (Weiss *et al.*, 2004). It is useful as a rehabilitative tool because it provides feedback in a controlled but motivating environment, which can enhance motor learning. This is particularly beneficial for patients with brain injuries, and therapists showed positive attitudes towards VR as useful, and were positive towards using it more in the future (Glegg *et al.*, 2013). Gega *et al.* (2013) support the notion that **virtual environments** (VE) can support CBT interventions. In a study they conducted, a group of six men, recovering from early psychosis, severe social anxiety and moderate paranoia, used a VE with video capture for a one-hour session midway through their 12-week CBC treatment. By replaying the video capture the patients could discuss how the different situations made them feel and what thoughts were triggered. There was a significant improvement in outcomes. The VE helped patients to understand the role of avoidance and safety behaviours in the maintenance of their social anxiety and paranoia. VR and its role in psychological therapy is considered in more detail in Chapter 20.

Granic *et al.* (2014) explored the mental health benefits of gaming, including improved mood. McGonigal (2011) suggested that intense positive emotional experiences are triggered when playing video games. Gaming offers the potential for reducing depression due to the natural benefits that the game elements afford (Li *et al.*,

2014). In conducting a meta-analysis of the research conducted to date, Li *et al.* (2014) found that self-help interventions were more effective than supported interventions and psycho-education. However, research into the effectiveness of gaming as a treatment for depression is still fairly new.

CBT, based on Aaron Beck's work (1991), has a long history as a psychological intervention for a range of mental health issues. In a literature review of how this transfers to a computer-based therapeutic tool, Twomey *et al.* (2013) outlined that in the United Kingdom, technology has been used to increase access to psychological therapies. CBT was particularly evident and this was given the term 'computerised CBT' (cCBT). They outline that cCBT has many advantages, as it can be either self-help or therapist based, it can be relatively inexpensive and covers a wide range of health difficulties, such as depression, anxiety, stress and alcoholism. They found 25 programmes that met the inclusion criteria. These include online access to cCBT programmes such as 'Beating the Blues' and 'MoodGym', which are designed to treat more than one difficulty at a time. The real value of cCBT programmes is that they are relatively low-cost and low-intensity interventions, which cover a wide range of psychological issues and are particularly useful in supporting primary care mental health services.

Computer gaming as a therapeutic tool is particularly successful in treating children suffering from anxiety disorders (Coyle *et al.*, 2011). O'Reilly and his team at University College Dublin have developed a CBT intervention called Pesky gNATS. This computer-based treatment is an excellent example of a user-friendly, destigmatising form of therapy in which young people engage and have a positive experience. The game was developed in support of face-to-face CBT interventions for young people who were experiencing medium to severe mental health problems. This computer-based game teaches children about the concept of **negative automatic thoughts** (NATS). O'Reilly calls these thoughts gNATs and they have the potential to sting humans and produce these negative thought patterns. The child-friendly gNAT trap game was devised so that children can address their negative thoughts, such as 'The Over-Generalising gNAT', 'The Jumping to Conclusions gNAT' and the 'Predicting the Future gNAT'. Using an engaging computer game or App, children 'swot' the gNATS and with their therapist explore alterative approaches to situations.

Although gaming is a relatively new treatment intervention, **online counselling** has been an effective means of offering counselling to clients for a number of years. Psychological interventions can be provided over the Internet and this can be either synchronously, either by chat or webcam or asynchronously by e-mail. Text-based counselling is by no means new; Freud conducted many of his analysis by letter – for example, the case study of 'Little Hans' (Freud, 2001). However, it has taken some time for this mode of therapy to gain in popularity in the online arena and face-to-face counselling remains the favoured option as outlined in Dowling and Rickwood (2014).

How do therapists feel about the online environment? Osborn and Flood (2014) investigated the potential attitudes of counsellors towards an online counselling service and this was measured and compared to the levels of stress that could be associated with the introduction of new technologies. A positive correlation between levels of stress and attitudes towards online counselling was found. At the time of the study, neutral to slightly positive attitudes were recorded towards the use of such a method of therapy.

In a study that explored the attitudes of psychotherapists to computerised psycho-therapy, McDonnell *et al.* (2014) found that overall there was a positive attitude to the use of computerised therapy, particularly for younger therapists. There was also a belief that artificially intelligent therapy systems would work, but synchronous forms of computer support communication received less support and a preference was found for face-to-face therapy. Although online counselling is relatively new, it may be particularly useful for young people and works particularly well as a blend between online and face-to-face therapy (Dowling & Rickwood, 2014). In Dowling and Rickwood's study they found that young people would contact the service for immediate support, but would only access the service once or twice. An interpretation of this could be that their problems were addressed during the brief therapy or that there was dissatisfaction with the service. However, another interpretation would be that the help received was enough to terminate the counselling.

CONCLUSION

This chapter has discussed how the Internet impacts mental health. It identified a number of possible Internet addictions, such as gaming, social networking and mobile phone addictions. The chapter has also identified treatment options for Internet overuse and how useful Internet applications such as gaming can be in the treatment of mental health issues.

ACTIVITY

Describe an approach you might choose if you were trying to change a friend's maladaptive social networking or online game usage.

DISCUSSION QUESTIONS

1 Evaluate the mental health information and treatments that are available online for sufferers and their families.
2 Social networking is how we communicate today; therefore, using the Internet is a way of life not an addiction. Discuss.
3 How would you feel and behave if you were without access to the Internet for 48 hours?
4 Discuss the benefits of gaming. Do these outweigh the problems?

RECOMMENDED READING LIST

The fundamentals of mental health can be found in a range of Abnormal Psychology books. Ronald Comer's textbook is an example.

Comer, R.J. (2013). *Abnormal Psychology* (8th edn). New York: Worth Publishers.

Larry Rosen's book covers many aspects of digital technologies and addresses how they can enhance or harm our mental health. There are many helpful suggestions to deal with the issues that technology poses on our lives.

Rosen, L.D. (2012). *iDisorder: Understanding our Obsession with Technology and Overcoming its Hold On Us*. New York: Palgrave Macmillan.

GLOSSARY

Abnormal psychology   The scientific study of abnormal behaviour.

Addiction   The state of being enslaved to a habit or practice or to something that is psychologically or physically habit-forming.

Behavioural addictions   Involve a repeated compulsion to perform a particular behaviour.

Cognitive behavioural therapy (CBT)   A short-term psychotherapy developed by Aaron Beck and Albert Ellis.

Internet Addiction Disorder   A disorder associated with the overuse of the Internet.

Internet gamers   Gamers who play online video games.

Mental disorders   Cover a wide range of mental health issues, which include anxiety, stress, mood disordersand addiction.

Mental health   'Mental health is defined as a state of well-being in which every individual realises his or her own potential, can cope with the normal stresses of life, can work productively and fruitfully, and is able to make a contribution to his or her community' (WHO, 2014).

Negative automatic thoughts (NATS)   Thoughts that are unhelpful and negative.

Nomophobia   The term refers to the fear of being out of mobile phone contact, having a run-down battery or losing the phone itself.

Online counselling   Delivery of therapeutic interventions over the Internet.

Online gaming   Playing video games over a computer network, often with other players.

Psychopathology   The scientific study of mental disorders.

Social media   Websites, applications and online social networks which individuals use to make contact with others, and to communicate and share information online.

Social networking   The use of social media.

Virtual environments (VE)   A computer-generated three-dimensional representation of a setting or situation.

Virtual reality (VR)   The use of computer technologies to create three-dimensional virtual worlds or objects which users can interact with.

REFERENCES

American Psychiatric Association (2013). *Diagnostic and Statistical Manual of Mental Disorders (DSM-5)*. American Psychiatric Publishing.

Banjanin, N., Banjanin N. Dimitrijevic, I. & Pantic, I. (2015). Relationship between internet use and depression: Focus on psysiological mood oscillations, social networking and online addictive behavior. *Computers in Human Behavior, 43*, 308–312.

Beato, G. (2010, Aug./Sept.). *Internet Addiction*. Retrieved from: Reason.com:http://reason.com/archives/2010/07/26/internet-addiction.

Beck, A.T. (1991). *Cognitive Therapy and the Emotional Disorders*. London: Penguin Books.

Bragazzi, N.L. & Del Puente, G.D. (2014). A proposal for including nomophobia in the new DSM-V. *Psychology Research and Behaviour Management*, 155–160.

Byrn, S., Ruffini, C., Mills, J., Douglas, A., Niang, M., Stepchenkova, S. & Blanton, M. (2009). Internet addiction: Metasynthesis of 1996–2006 quantitative research. *CyberPsychology & Behaviour, 12*(2), 203–207.

Canan, F., Yildirim, O., Ustunel, T.Y., Sinani, G., Kaleli, A. H., Gunes, C. & Ataoglu, A. (2014). The relationship between Internet addiction and body mass index in Turkish adolescents. *Cyberpsychology, Behaviour, and Social Networking, 17*(1), 40–45.

Chen, H. &. Kim, Y. (2013). Problematic use of social network sites. The interactive relationship between gratifications sought and privacy concerns. *Cyberpsychology, Behaviour, and Social Networking, 16*(11), 802–812.

Cheng, C. & Li, A.Y.L. (2014). Internet additiction prevalence and quality of (real) life: a meta-analysis of 31 nations across seven world regions. *Cyberpsychology, Behavior, and Social Networking, 17*(12), 755–760.

Chóliz, M. (2012). Mobile-phone addiction in adolescence: The test of mobile phone dependence (TMD). *Progressin Health Sciences, 2*(1), 33–44.

Clark, M. (2011). Conceptualising addiction: How useful is the construct? *International Journal of Humanities and Social Science, 1*(13), 55–64.

Comer, R.J. (2013). *Abnormal Psychology* (8th edn). Basingstoke: Palgrave Macmillan.

Coyle, D., McGlade, N., Doherty, G. & O'Reilly, G. (2011). Exploratory evaluations of a computer game supporting cognitive behavioural therapy for adolescents. In *Proceedings of the SIGCHI Conference on Human Factors in Computing Systems* (pp. 2937–2946). ACM.

Didelot, M.J., Hollingsworth, L. & Buckenmeyer, J. A. (2012). Internet addiction: A logotherapeutic approach. *Journal of Addictions & Offender Counseling, 33*(1), 18–33.

Dowling, M.J. & Rickwood, D.J. (2014). Experiences of counsellors providing online chat counselling to young people. *Australian Journal of Guidance and Counselling, 24*(2), 183–196.

Elmore, T. (2014, 26 August). Curing students of nomophobia. Retrieved from: Huff Post Parents: www.huffingtonpost.com/tim-elmore/curing-students-of-nomoph_b_5710427.html.

Freud, S. (2001). The standard edition of the *Complete Psychological Works of Sigmund Freud. Two Case Histories: 'Little Hans' and the 'Rat Man'*. (Vol. X). London: Hogarth Press.

Gega, L.W., White, R., Clarke, T., Turner, R. & Fowler, D. (2013). Virtual environments using video capture for social phobia and psychosis. *Cyberpsychology, Behavior, and Social Networking, 16*(6), 473–479.

Ghassemzadeh, L., Shahraray, M. & Moradi, A. (2008). Prevalence of Internet addiction and comparison of Internet addicts and non-addicts in Iranian high school. *CyberPsychology & Behaviour, 11*(6), 731–733.

Glegg, S.M.N., Holsti, L., Velikonja, D., Ansley, B., Brum, C. & Sartor, D. (2013). Factors influencing therapists' adopting of virtual reality for brain injury rehabiliation. *Cyberpsychology, Behaviour, and Social Networking, 16*(5), 385–401.

Granic, I., Lobel, A. & Engels, R.C. (2014). The benefits of playing video games. *American Psychologist, 69*(1), 66.

Griffiths, M.D. (2000). Does Internet and computer 'addiction' exist? Some case study evidence. *CyberPsychology & Behavior, 3*(2), 212–218.

Griffiths, M.D. (2010). The role of context in online gaming excess and addiction: Some case study evidence. *Intentional Journal Mental Health Addiction, 8*, 119–125.

Griffiths, P.E. (1997). *What Emotions Really Are: The Problem of Psychological Categories* (p. 114). Chicago: University of Chicago Press.

Jelenchick, L.A., Eickhoff, J.C. & Moreno, M.A. (2013). 'Facebook Depression?' Social networking site use and depression in older adolescents. *Journal of Adolescent Health, 5*(1), 128–130.

Jellinek, E. (1960). *The Disease Concept of Alcholism*. New Haven, NJ: Hillhouse.

King, A.L.S., Valença, A.M., Silva, A.C.O., Baczynski, T., Carvalho, M.R. & Nardi, A.E. (2013). Nomophobia: Dependency on virtual environments or social phobia? *Computers in Human Behavior, 29*(1), 140–144.

Kuss, D.J. (2013). Internet gaming addiction: Current perspectives. *Psychology Research and Behaviour Management, 3*(6), 125–137.

Lee, Z.W. & Cheung, C.M.(2014). Problematic use of social networking sites: The role of self-esteem. *International Journal of Business and Information, 9*(2), 143–159.

Li, J. Theng, Y. & Foo, S. (2014). Game-based digital interventions for depression therapy: A systematic review and meta-analysis. *Cyberpsychology, Behavior, and Social Networking, 17*(8), 519–527.

Lopez-Fernandez, O., Freixa-Blanxart, M. & Honrubia-Serrano, M.L. (2013). The problematic Internet entertainment use scale for adolescents: Prevalence of problem Internet use in Spanish high school students. *Cyberpsychology, Behavior, and Social Networking, 16*(2), 108–118.

Matson, J.L., Rotatori, A.F. & Helsel,W.J. (1983). Development of a rating scale to measure social skills in children: The Matson Evaluation of Social Skills with Youngsters (MESSY). *Behaviour Research and Therapy, 21*(4), 335–340.

McDonnell, D., Rooney, B. & Flood, C. (2014). Attitudes to computerised psychotherapy. In A. Power &. G. Kirwan (eds). *Cyberpsychology and New Media: A Thematic Reader* (pp. 170–182). Hove: Psychology Press.

McGonigal, J. (2011). *Reality is Broken: Why Games Make Us Better and How They Can Change the world*. New York: Penguin Press.

Morahan-Martin, J. (2007). Internet use and abuse and psychological problems. In A.M. Joinson & A.M. Joinson (ed.), *The Oxford Handbook of Internet Psychology* (pp. 331–345). New York: Oxford University Press.

O'Reilly, M. (1996). Internet addiction: A new disorder enters the medical lexicon. *Canadian Medical Association Journal*, *154*(12), 1882–1883.

Osborn, A. & Flood, C. (2014). Establishing an online counselling service for substance use: An exploratory study. In A. Power & G. Kirwan (eds), *Cyberpsychology and New Media: A Thematic Reader* (pp.149–157). Hove: Psychology Press.

Rosenberg, M. (1965). *Society and the Adolescent Self-image*. Princeton, NJ: Princeton University Press.

Russell, D.W. (1996). UCLA Loneliness Scale (Version 3): Reliability, validity, and factor structure. *Journal of Personality Assessment*, *6*(1), 20–40.

Siggins, M. & Flood, C. (2014). Mobile phone separation and anxiety. In A. Power &. G. Kirwan (eds), *Cyberpsychology and New Media: A Thematic Reader* (pp. 38–48). Hove: Psychology Press.

Twomey, C., O'Reilly, G. & Byrne, M. (2013). Computerised cognitive behavioural therapy: Helping Ireland log on. *Irish Journal of Psychological Medicine*, *30*(1), 29–56.

Wan, C.S. & Chiou, W.B. (2006) Why are adolescents addicted to online gaming? An interview study in Taiwan. *CyberPsychology & Behavior*, *9*(6), 762–766.

Watson, J.(2005). Internet addiction diagnosis and assessment: Implications for counselors. *Journal of Professional Counseling: Practice, Theory, & Research*, *33*(2), 17–30.

Weiss, P.L., Rand, D., Katz, N. & Kizony, R. (2004). Video capture virtual reality as a flexible and effective rehabilitation tool. *Journal of NeuroEngineering and Rehabilitation*, *1*, 1–12.

World Health Organization (2004). *International Statistical Classification of Diseases and Related Health Problems* (Vol. 1). World Health Organization.

Wrenn, E. (2012). The biggest phobia in the world? 'Nomophobia', *The Mail Online*. Retrieved from: www.dailymail.co.uk/sciencetech/article-2141169/The-biggest-phobia-world-Nomophobia–fear-mobile–affects-66-cent-us.html.

Valkenburg, P.M., Peter, J. & Schouten, A.P. (2006). Friend networking sites and their relationship to adolescents' well-being and social self-esteem. *CyberPsychology & Behavior*, *9*(5), 584–590.

World Health Organization (WHO). 2014. Retrieved from: www.who.inst/features/factfiles/mental_health/en/.

Yee, N. (2006). Motivations of play in online games. *CyberPsychology & Behavior*, *9*(6) 772–775.

Young, K.S. (1998a). The emergence of a new clinical disorder. *CyberPsychology & Behaviour*, *1*(3), 237–244.

Young, K.S. (1998b). *Caught in the Net: How to Recognize the Signs of Internet Addiction – and a Winning Strategy for Recovery*. New York: John Wiley & Sons.

Young, K.S. (2009). Understanding online gaming addiction and treatment issues for adolescents. *The American Journal of Family Therapy*, *37*, 355–377.

Young, K.S. (2011). CBT-IA: The first treatment model for Internet addiction. *Journal of Cognitive Psychotherapy: An International Quarterly*, *25*(4), 304–312.

13 Sport and health cyberpsychology

Olivia Hurley

CHAPTER OVERVIEW

This chapter introduces readers to the potential impact of technology on the sporting lives and health behaviours of individuals. The first part of the chapter presents information related to athletes' use of technology to prepare, mentally and physically, for their sport, as well as the use of technology to help athletes cope with rehabilitation from sports injuries. The use of technology to assist in the athlete–sport psychologist-consulting process is discussed, along with topical issues, such as the influence of social media (e.g. Twitter and Facebook) on individuals' involvement in sport. The second part of the chapter addresses issues related to the impact of technology in promoting health-related behaviours online. Topics such as the sharing of health-related information online, the benefits and dangers of online support groups, and the debate surrounding the existence of the condition, cyberchondriasis, are also addressed.

KEY TERMS

Mental preparation is a broad term used to describe the ways in which athletes 'ready' themselves, mentally, to participate in their sport. Such preparation could be influenced by **social media,** which refers to websites and online social networks that individuals use to communicate and share information online. **Twitter** is an example of such an online social network, and involves individuals posting short messages that their 'followers' can read, favour and retweet. While social media use has 'boomed' in recent years, the emergence of **exergaming** has also risen.

It is the term used to describe the activity of playing interactive games consoles, such as the Wii and WiiFit. Such games have been devised in part to increase the activity levels of the individual players, given the increasing sedentary lifestyles that many now lead. The use of technology to address such health-related issues has also led to other problems, such as **cyberchondriasis.** This term refers to the condition where individuals misinterpret common symptoms of often minor illnesses as serious, lifethreatening signs of disease, having researched their symptoms on the Internet.

INTRODUCTION

As already explained in earlier chapters in this text, cyberpsychology is the study of the human mind and behaviour with regard to human–technology interaction. It encompasses all psychological phenomena associated with, or impacted upon by, emerging technology (Power & Kirwan, 2013). Sport and health cyberpsychology can then be considered the study of human interaction with such emerging technologies, including the Internet, mobile phones, games consoles and **virtual reality** – indeed, any technology that has the ability to alter human behaviour within sport and health domains.

SPORT CYBERPSYCHOLOGY

A number of key areas for research have emerged in recent times within sport cyber-psychology, such as the impact of the Internet, games consoles and virtual reality on sport, from the competitors', spectators', coaches' and support teams' points of reference. Exciting developments are also being made in helping athletes to rehabilitate from, or indeed, prevent injury. For example, the world of virtual reality is becoming popular as an avenue worth exploring for such purposes (Independent Pictures, 2013). Athletes' use of technology to interact with their public has also increased dramatically in the past number of years, with many high-profile teams and athletes embracing social media, especially Twitter and Facebook, to communicate directly with, and provide information to, their public about their daily sporting and non-sporting lives (Browning & Sanderson, 2012). In the following section, athletes' use of technology to assist in their physical, and mental, preparation for their sport will be examined.

Athletes' use of technology to prepare for their sport

The use of technology to prepare athletes in professional and semi-professional sport has greatly increased in recent years, with the introduction of sophisticated equipment to monitor the performances of athletes, and the impact of such performances on their bodies. In a recent documentary, Irish rugby player Tommy Bowe was shown using various pieces of apparatus to prepare for his sport and also to recover from a number of serious injuries he sustained during the making of the programme (Independent Pictures, 2013). An Alter-G-Anti-Gravity Treadmill and pressure pads were used to analyse the running and jumping technique of the player respectively. An Alter-G-Anti-Gravity Treadmill allows injured athletes to train at a reduced body weight while recovering from injury (Hickie, 2014). The use of equipment to measure the force of collisions and tackles made within many sports, such as Rugby Union, has also become popular, with elite teams frequently using **Global Positioning System** (GPS) devices, for example, to allow coaches to measure the work rate of their players during training and in matches (Hartwig *et al.*, 2011). This has, however, a potentially significant psychological, as well as a physical, impact on players, as they can be informed of their own, as well as their teammates', performance statistics, which, in an environment where competition for places in a starting team is high, means they cannot afford to have lapses in concentration, because such errors are being recorded and shared with the whole team. However, empirical research to determine the impact of such GPS devices on the mental well-being of the athletes is lacking and is a potential avenue for future research in the sport cyberpsychology arena.

Gaming in sport

The popularity of computer games has risen significantly in recent years also (Goh *et al.*, 2008) and as such, a number of companies have developed products to help athletes prepare mentally and physically for their sport. Perry *et al.* (2011) examined the potential of a biofeedback technology tool called FlexComp Infiniti on athletes' performances and reported that the athletes' ability to control their emotions using this technology did indeed assist and enhance their sporting performances. Developers have also specifically created virtual worlds to help prepare athletes for their sporting competitions. Some gaming companies have developed products that mimic the environ-ments of major sporting events such as the recent FIFA World Cup, the Rugby World Cup and Formula One motor racing. Research on the benefits of individuals playing video games in order to benefit mentally from them, for example, in their sporting events, has produced some positive results, with improvements recorded for reaction times (Ramsey *et al.*, 2009), mental imagery skills and spatial awareness skills (Spence & Feng, 2010).

Computer-generated games have also been devised to teach various desirable on-field behaviours during sport. For example, 'Alert Hockey' was designed specifically to train ice-hockey players to engage in less aggressive behaviours (Ciavarro *et al.*, 2008). Such behaviours had led to players sustaining concussions in the past. The game, Alert Hockey, rewards safe plays aimed at winning, rather than attempting to teach such behaviours in training sessions through explicit learning drills, for example. Ciavarro *et al.* (2008) indicated that their experimental group who played Alert Hockey showed a significant increase in desired 'safe' behaviours in their real playing behaviour on the ice, compared to those who did not play the game. This finding indicates a potential use for such video games in changing real-time game-play behaviours.

Virtual reality and gaming for injury rehabilitation

Virtual reality is also an exciting avenue for potentially preparing athletes, both physically and mentally, for their sport. One of the most appealing uses of virtual reality technology, to date, has been its use to help athletes maintain or improve their mental skills, such as their reaction times and spatial awareness skills, especially when returning from long periods of time spent away from their sport (e.g. when they are injured or are preparing to return to playing following a period of illness or suspension). In one such example, the Nintendo Wii game, described as a video gaming system that employs virtual reality technology, was employed to determine its usefulness in helping an adolescent with cerebral palsy (Deutsch *et al.*, 2008). The researchers concluded that the Wii is a potentially useful therapeutic tool to assist in the rehabilitation of such individuals, and also for those who have suffered other injuries or neurological episodes, such as strokes (Pessoa *et al.*, 2014). Thus, the potential benefits of new technologies to help athletes prepare to perform in their sport is apparent, with some exciting avenues for future empirical research in this area identified. However, what impact could such new technologies have for the athlete–sport psychologist consultancy relationship? The following section will look at this question.

Technology use by sport psychology consultants

Cotterill and Symes (2014) examined the benefits and dangers of using a wide range of new social media and technologies in the context of consulting as sport psychologists with athletes. They explored the potential of Twitter, Facebook and LinkedIn, along with the use of communicating with their athletes via **Skype**, text and podcasts. A major advantage of Skype and Facetime sessions with athletes appears to be that they help all individuals involved in the process to overcome the obstacle of being in different physical locations. This is often the case for athletes who must travel to locations to access specialised training facilities, or to compete in various competitions. Knowing their sport science support team, their family and their friends are accessible via their mobile devices may be a source of comfort for the athlete. Such easy access to their social support network may help the athletes to remain calm and relaxed, thus assisting in their ability to perform at their best while they are away from home competing and training. However, such easy access by athletes to their consultants at any time of the day or night could result in an erosion of the work–life balance for the consultant. It could also result in ethical issues for the consultant regarding professional boundaries being overstepped, and security issues regarding online data protection. However, Cotterill and Symes (2014) concluded that while technology and social media are potentially beneficial to the consulting process, they should be used, but with ethical and security principles in mind. Indeed, they remarked that use of Skype and Facetime to consult with athletes has become so popular that, in many cases, it has replaced traditional face-to-face meetings, historically considered the only way, apart from by telephone, to communicate with clients. However, this new approach to the delivery of consulting services is in need of empirical evaluation, in order to determine the specific advantages and disadvantages of such uses of new technologies when consulting with athletes. However, the dangers of **social media** use by athletes has been investigated somewhat in recent years and will now be outlined.

Athletes' use of social media

According to a 2013 Global WebIndex study, over 1.15 billion individuals are Facebook users, while Twitter boasts over 500 million registered users. These figures indicate large increases in global use of social media. Public interest in professional athletes also appears to have grown in recent years, and the invention of the social media tools, Twitter and Facebook especially, has allowed spectators and fans of many sports to 'follow' and communicate with their sporting heroes. Indeed, in 2012, Campbell stated that 'over 70 million people worldwide follow pro (professional) athletes and teams on Twitter, while another 400 million Facebook users have clicked the "like" button on pages dedicated to sports stars and squads' (p. 1). It appears that Twitter has become the most popular form of social media communication for athletes and their supporters, perhaps because it provides users with a way to immediately and directly interact with each other (Sanderson & Kassing, 2011). Athletes, and the media who report on sporting events, appeared to 'on mass' embrace the use of such social media for the first time during the London 2012 Olympic Games. Indeed, these Games were referred to as the 'Twitterlympics' (Adebayo, 2013), and the 'Social Media Olympics' (Androich, 2012). Interesting questions such as why do athletes use social media such as Twitter and how do they present themselves on this media should be posed. How athletes react to criticism posted in tweets sent to them, for example, is also an interesting psychological research question to address, most importantly because such posts may impact negatively on the athletes' sporting performances.

In an attempt to answer some of the questions posed above, researchers have begun to examine the impact of social media interactions between athletes and their public, first, on the athletes' performances, and second, on their relationship with spectators, and their own fans (Browning & Sanderson, 2012). A number of reasons athletes use social media, such as Twitter, have been proposed. The instant contact and information it provides is perhaps the primary reason most individuals report using it (Browning & Sanderson, 2012). For fans and spectators of sport, it can also narrow the 'gap' between them and their sporting idols. It allows both groups to interact and converse with each other (Clavio & Kian, 2010), as was evident during the 2014 FIFA World Cup recently (Dredge, 2014). In a case study of athletes' use of Twitter, Pegoraro (2010) commented that athletes used Twitter to share aspects of their daily lives with their supporters, and to answer fans questions about their lives.

With sponsorship and investment opportunities also more prevalent in modern sport, many athletes are also 'business' men and women. Social media such as Facebook, Twitter and LinkedIn can provide such athletes with a means to connect with their customers and business partners. It also provides them with a vehicle to brand themselves and to sell their business products (Atencio, 2010; Feil, 2012). Some sports teams have even placed their Twitter handles on their jerseys in place of their names as a marketing strategy (Knapp, 2011).

However, athletes, like any other individuals using social media, are not immune to the negative aspects of such social media use. Athletes have frequently been the target of cyberbullying. For example, Team GB diver, Tom Daley, was the subject of some unkind comments from an individual on Twitter, following Tom's, and his teammate, Pete Waterfield's performance in the paired diving event at the London 2012 Olympic

Games (British Broadcasting Corporation; BBC, 2012). Such behaviour resulted in the individual who posted the comments being arrested. This example illustrates the misconception many individuals have of social media – that is, that their computers provide them with a veil of anonymity and that they are untraceable because they are operating from behind a machine, rather than physically saying the comments directly to the targeted person (Kirwan & Power, 2013).

Examples of athletes sending controversial tweets are also well documented. Indeed, some posts have resulted in athletes facing serious consequences, such as fines and bans from their clubs and sporting organisations, as a result of their misuse of social media. In severe cases, criminal charges have been brought against athletes (Poeter, 2012). Such negative consequences for, and of, athletes using social media has prompted many teams, clubs and sports governing bodies to devise social media use codes of practice for their athletes and all those associated with the athletes (e.g. coaches, medical staff, agents and parents). Therefore, the 'Twitter-bans', or 'black-outs', for certain periods of time around matches that some clubs place upon their players may be justified (Hauer, 2012).

Given its potential to be a source of aggravation for athletes, one might then wonder if it would perhaps be better for athletes not to use social media networks at all. However, in a survey by the football fan website, Fourfourtwo.com, when asked whether they thought Twitter should be banned, 70 per cent of the players who responded to the survey 'disagreed' that its use by players should be banned (Fourfourtwo.com, 2012). Thus, while athletes do appear to acknowledge the negative side of social media use, they seem unprepared to remove themselves from the cyber world, and it could indeed be argued that they should continue to employ it, given its advantages, as cited above. Therefore, those involved in managing such athletes should support and advise them on how best to use this media to their advantage, while helping them to minimise the negative impact of such technology on their athletic careers.

Having discussed the potential of new technologies to (1) help athletes remain 'connected' with their social networks, (2) assist them in their mental preparation for their sport and (3) help their recovery from injury, let us now examine the potential of such technologies to assist other individuals, with health-related issues in their daily lives.

HEALTH CYBERPSYCHOLOGY

A number of key areas for research have emerged in recent times within the discipline of health cyberpsychology, such as the impact of the Internet, games consoles and virtual reality on the health behaviours of the general population. Technological developments have also been made in helping individuals to cope with illnesses and to recover from various medical conditions. The following section will start by specifically addressing the potential benefits and risks of the Internet, and social media, when searching for, and sharing, health-related information.

Technology and the promotion of healthy behaviours

Perhaps a good starting point for this section is to outline why individuals do, or should, engage in exercise, or indeed, any kind of physical activity. Statistics on diseases associated with obesity and inactivity, especially among young children and teenagers, have alarmingly indicated that conditions, such as various cancers, diabetes and heart disease, currently on the rise in such groups, will continue to do so into the future unless some drastic measures are taken (Park, 2014). The strain on healthcare systems around Europe have reached critical levels, with the cost of diseases linked to obesity and inactivity estimated to be between 2 per cent and 8 per cent of the total health-care costs (World Health Organization; WHO, 2010). Recommended levels of physical activity, including walking, housework and gardening, are currently set at one hour each day. Many individuals, however, are not reaching such levels of activity, on a consistent basis, leading to weight gain and increased risk of disease in such individuals.

The specific health benefits of exercise, both physical and mental, are well docu-mented (Moran, 2012). They include, but are not limited to, positive effects on blood pressure, body weight and cognitive functioning. Many social benefits are also derived from engaging in exercise, for fitness, or indeed, within a competitive context. Research findings have repeatedly shown that social reasons such as 'I get to hang out with my friends' as some of the most frequently cited reasons why children and young adults engage in sport (LeUnes, 2008; Weinberg & Gould, 2011).

Given the many well-supported reasons why people should exercise or take part in structured sport, the question then arises, why do so many people stop exercising or playing sport, and how can technology be used to encourage more people to return to exercise or participating in sport? The most common reason cited for not engaging in exercise is a lack of time, as well as a lack of resources and/or facilities (Moran, 2012). Many inactive individuals have also been found to lack confidence and motivation to participate in exercise, while some cite fear of injury and embarrassment as the reasons for not completing any form of formal or informal exercise (Grieser et al., 2006).

With this information in mind, how have psychologists and technologists worked, often together, to address these issues, and specifically, to encourage more people to engage in some form of exercise? Research on the benefits of new gaming devices, known as Exergames (e.g. the WiiFit and Kinect games), to promote higher levels of activity among populations of various ages, has provided evidence of the potential benefits of such new technologies (Wollersheim et al., 2010). These technologies can offer individuals a way to combine their interests in gaming, which has traditionally been a sedentary activity, with more physical activity and exercise, and this develop-ment should be welcomed.

In conjunction with reductions in activity levels among many populations, diets have also changed in recent times, with more processed and convenience fast foods now available to meet the demands of increasingly busy lifestyles. Unhealthy eating habits have become the norm and have added to the risks of various diseases such as diabetes, heart disease and various cancers. A number of applications for mobile devices (i.e. apps) have been devised in an attempt to combat these unhealthy practices (Ho, 2013). Their goal is often to help individuals eat more healthy foods, maintain a balanced diet and lose excess body weight by exercising. A large number of these apps are designed to record the food eaten by individuals on a daily basis, along with the calorific and nutritional values of these foods – for example, Calorie Counter and Diet Tracker by MyFitnessPal, and GO-Meal and Fitness Tracker. Many apps, which are often free to download, also have tools included to enable users to monitor their activity levels, such as trackers for calculating distances walked or run – for example, Nike+ Running, CycleNav, Zombies, Run! 5K Tracker and Couch to 5K by RunDouble. They may also provide demonstrations to allow users to watch and then repeat exercises completed by a trainer on their digital screen in the comfort of their own homes (Endomondo Sports Tracker Pro and Daily Workouts), thus removing the need for the person to journey to a gym or club to engage in exercise, something which many individuals do not have the time, finances, motivation or confidence to do (Grieser et al., 2006).

Technologies as therapeutic tools for mental health issues

Due to the popularity of computer game-playing, especially among the computer-native generation, researchers have also begun to examine the effectiveness of using computer games and mobile devices, such as mobile phones, as therapeutic tools for treating mental health disorders in children and young adults (Seko et al., 2014). However, the Internet can also be a negative source of support for such vulnerable individuals, such as individuals suffering from general health anxiety conditions. Thus, the dangers for such individuals, of online health-related searches will now be discussed.

The benefits and risks of online searches for health information

While computing and gaming can assist in changing behaviours towards exercise, the Internet although also beneficial for information gathering on health-related issues, can pose risks and dangers for some individuals sourcing information online. Research has shown that large numbers of individuals searching for information online often accept such information as accurate, and from reliable sources, when the reality is that much of the information available online is inaccurate and from unreliable sources (Human Factors and Ergonomics Society, 2014). There is evidence of patients refusing or failing to adhere to the treatment advice of medical health professionals as a result of reading alternative information on the Internet, despite discontinuing treatment prescribed by expert professionals being detrimental to their health (Weaver et al., 2009). Some individuals may also resort to self-medicating by purchasing, for example, unregulated drugs/medication online. This behaviour may be very dangerous, even life-threatening, as there is no medical expert, such as a doctor or healthcare professional, overseeing such drug-taking behaviour (Ardito, 2013). Searching for medical information online can also lead to increased levels of stress for individuals as the information is often unregulated (Sillence et al., 2004).

The Internet can, however, provide positive sources of support for various properly diagnosed conditions, such as online support groups for individuals suffering from or recovering from various forms of cancers, chronic, incurable, progressive or terminal diseases, such as inflammatory bowel disease, coeliac disease, Chron's disease, diabetes, muscular sclerosis, and degenerative neurological diseases, such as Huntington's disease (Coulson *et al.*, 2007). Computer Mediated social support groups, such as those provided by 'friends' on the social media site, Facebook, can also be effective when individuals are experiencing stress due to life transitions, derived from experiences such as recovering from illness, coping with the birth of a child, moving home, changing jobs or separating from a spouse or partner (Mikal *et al.*, 2013). However, when searching for information on health-related conditions becomes obsessive, this may be a sign that an individual is suffering from a particular cyber-related mental illness, sometimes referred to as cyberchondria (Fergus, 2013). So, what is cyberchondria?

The specific case of hypochondriasis and cyberchondriasis

The term 'cyberchondriasis', derived from the term 'hypochondriasis', has been coined to describe the condition where individuals misinterpret common symptoms of often minor illnesses as serious, life-threatening signs of disease, having researched their symptoms on the Internet (American Psychiatric Association, 2013). In recent times, however, the term hypochondriasis, as a specific term used to describe a particular psychological condition, has been questioned. Many medical and mental health professionals have reverted to using terms such as 'health anxiety' or 'illness anxiety disorder' to describe individuals who exhibit symptoms of being overly fearful for the condition of their health due to experiencing what are often minor ailments. The term 'hypochondriasis' is now reserved for extreme cases of the condition (Hart & Björgvinsson, 2010) and, according to Muse *et al.* (2012), the prevalence of cyberchondriasis, also relatively rare, is considered to be greater in individuals who experience higher levels of general health anxiety.

CONCLUSION

This chapter has aimed to present readers with an overview of some topics being researched by sport and health psychologists interested in the impact of technology on the sporting and general health lives of individuals. As is evident from the research cited above, many developers are creating novel and useful technologies to help athletes train, and prepare, more effectively for their sport, while also encouraging the general population to engage in more health-conscious practices related to exercise and diet. The risks and dangers associated with using the Internet as a sole source of health-related information has also been highlighted.

Some exciting areas for future research in this area of sport and health cyberpsychology have been also been suggested, and could include (1) empirical explorations of the potential impact of GPS monitoring on the psychological well-being of athletes, which, to date, has been anecdotal in nature, (2) more research on the possible uses of biofeedback tools in Exergames and (3) further development of the uses for virtual reality and social media, to assist athletes in their preparations for their sport, and to assist the normal population to lead healthier and more active lives.

ACTIVITY

Start by discussing the impact of some health-related conditions with your class – e.g. the physical and psychological impact of being diagnosed with asthma, diabetes or coeliac disease. Then, perhaps in groups, ask your students to design an 'app' that might help to make life easier for a person with any one of the above cited ailments.

DISCUSSION QUESTIONS

1   What role can new technologies play in helping athletes to cope with the physical and psychological difficulties they often experience when injured?
2   'The Internet can be used for good or evil in the fight to combat growing health-related issues.' Discuss this statement in the light of the growing global impact of the digital age in everyday life.
3   How has the consulting role of many sport psychologists changed in recent times, due to the development of new communication technologies?
4   'Virtual reality (VR) can contribute in a positive way in many sport, health and medical settings.' Discuss this statement in the light of recent advances in VR technology.

RECOMMENDED READING LIST

A number of psychology journals have been published in recent years devoted to studies on cyberpsychology, sport psychology and related topics. Students wishing to read more in-depth research studies about the areas discussed in this chapter would be encouraged to consult the following peer-reviewed journals *Cyberpsychology, Behaviour and Social Networking, Cyberpsychology: Journal of Psychosocial Research on Cyberspace* and the *International Sport and Exercise Psychology Review*.

In this peer-reviewed article, Simon Cotterill and Rebecca Symes provide one of the first detailed reviews of the potential uses, and impact, of social media and new technologies (e.g. Twitter, Skype and Facebook) on the consulting work of sport psychologists. They highlight issues surrounding the ethical and security considerations for practitioners who opt to deliver their consulting services using such new methods of communication.

Cotterill, S.T. & Symes, R. (2014). Integrating social media and new technologies into your practice as a sport psychology consultant. *Sport & Exercise Psychology Review, 10*(1), 55–64.

Andrew Power and Gráinne Kirwan have written extensively on the topic of cyberpsychology. This text presents a number of chapters written by Power, Kirwan and a number of their colleagues, on topics in areas such as Internet interventions and therapies, and the Internet's role in education.

Power, A. & Kirwan, G. (eds) (2013). *Cyberpsychology and New Media*. East Sussex: Psychology Press.

GLOSSARY

Cyberchondriasis   The condition where individuals misinterpret common symptoms of often minor illnesses as serious, life-threatening signs of disease, having researched their symptoms on the Internet.

Exergaming   The activity of playing interactive games consoles, such as the Wii and WiiFit.

Global Positioning System (GPS)   A system that involves satellite tracking to plot the movement patterns of objects. GPS devices used in sport are typically smaller than a mobile phone and are positioned in a pouch within the training gear of the athletes, usually on the back, between the shoulder blades.

Mental preparation   A broad term used to describe the ways in which athletes 'ready' themselves, mentally, to participate in their sport.

Skype   A software application and online service that enables voice and video phone calls over the Internet.

Social media   Websites, applications and online social networks which individuals use to make contact with others, and to communicate and share information online.

Social networking   The use of social media.

Twitter   A microblogging tool and online social network, where individuals post short messages (tweets) of up to 140 characters that their 'followers' can read, favour and retweet.

Virtual reality   The use of computer technologies to create three-dimensional virtual worlds or objects which users can interact with.

REFERENCES

Adebayo, D. (2013). Eye on the stars: Twitter and the sporting hero. *Index on Censorship, 42*(1), 62–65.

American Psychiatric Association (2013). *Diagnostic and Statistical Manual of Mental Disorders* (5th edn). Washington, DC: American Psychiatric Association.

Androich, A. (2012). Demanding their share. *Marketing Magazine, 117*(12), 8–10.

Ardito, S.C. (2013). Seeking consumer health information on the internet. *Online Searcher, 37*, 45–48.

Atencio, J. (2010). New sponsored athletes can perform through social media. *Bicycle Retailer & Industry News, 19*(13), 46.

British Broadcasting Corporation (BBC; 2012). Tom Daley Twitter abuse: Boy arrested in Weymouth. Retrieved from: www.bbc.co.uk/news/uk-england-19059127.

Browning, B. & Sanderson, J. (2012). The positives and negatives of twitter: exploring how student-athletes use Twitter and respond to critical tweets. *International Journal of Sport Communication, 5*, 503–521.

Campbell, M. (May, 2012). Niche networks getting into the social media game. *Toronto Star.*

Ciavarro, C., Dobson, M. & Goodman. D. (2008). Implicit learning as a design strategy for learning games: Alert Hockey. *Computers in Human Behaviour, 24*, 2862–2872.

Clavio, G. & Kian, T.M. (2010). Uses and gratifications of a retired female athlete's Twitter followers. *International Journal of Sports Communication, 3*(4), 485–500.

Cotterill, S.T. & Symes, R. (2014). Integrating social media and new technologies into your practice as a sport psychology consultant. *Sport & Exercise Psychology Review, 10*, 55–64.

Coulson, N.S., Buchanan, H. & Aubeeluck, A. (2007). Social support in cyberspace: A content analysis of communication within a Huntington's disease online support group. *Patient Education and Counselling, 68*(2), 173–178.

Deutsch, J.E., Borbely, M., Filler, J., Huhn, K. & Guarrera-Bowlby, P. (2008). Use of a low-cost, commercially available gaming console (Wii) for rehabilitation of an adolescent with cerebral palsy. *Physical Therapy, 88*(10), 1196–1207. doi: 10.2522/ptj.20080062.

Dredge, S. (2014). *World Cup was biggest event for Twitter yet with 672m tweets.* Retrieved from: www.theguardian.com/technology/2014/jul/15/twitter-world-cup-tweets-germany-brazil.

Feil, S. (2012). The social side of sponsorship. *Adweek, 53*(4), S1–S4.

Fergus, T.A. (2013). Cyberchondria and intolerance of uncertainty: Examining when individuals experience health anxiety in response to internet searches for medical information. *Cyberpsychology, Behaviour and Social Networking, 16*, 735–739.

Fourfourtwo.com (February, 2012). The players' poll, 46–57.

Global WebIndex (2013). Global WebIndex Stram Social Report-Q2. Retrieved from: www.globalwebindex.net/product/stream–social–global–report–q2–2013–withembedded-data/.

Goh, D.H., Ang, R.P. & Tan H.C. (2008). Strategies for designing effective therapeutic gaming interventions for children and adolescents. *Computers in Human Behaviour, 24*, 2217–2235.

Grieser, M., Vu, M.B., Bedimo-Rung, A.L., Neumark-Sztainer, D., Moody, J., Rohm Young, D. & Moe, S.G. (2006). Physical activity attitudes, preferences and practices in African-American, Hispanic and Caucasian girls. *Health Education and Behaviour, 33*(1), 40–51.

Hart, J. & Björgvinsson, T. (2010). Health anxiety and hypochondriasis: Description and treatment issues highlighted through a case illustration. *Bulletin of the Menninger Clinic, 74*, 122–140.

Hartwig, T.B., Naughton, G. & Searl, J. (2011). Motion analyses of adolescent rugby union players: A comparison of training and game demands. *Journal of Strength & Conditioning Research, 25*(4), 966–972.

Hauer, M. (2012). The constitutionality of public university bans of student-athlete speech through social media. *Vermont Law Review, 37*, 413–436.

Hickie, G. (2014). LineoutCoach: Learn from the pros: Leinster's use of technology in rugby. Retrieved from: www.lineoutcoach.com/2014/07/28/learn-from-the-pros-leinsters-use-of-technology-in-rugby/.

Ho, K. (2013). Health-e-Apps: A project to encourage the effective use of mobile health applications. *British Colombia Medical Journal*, *55*(10), 458–460.

Human Factors and Ergonomics Society (2014). Younger, college-educated consumers more likely to use potentially unreliable online healthcare information. Retrieved from: www.hfes.org/WEB/DetailNews.aspx?ID=349. Accessed: 20 September 2015.

Independent Pictures (2013). Tommy Bowe's BodyCheck. Dublin, Ireland.

Kirwan, G. & Power, A. (2013). *Cybercrime: The Psychology of Online Offenders*. Cambridge: Cambridge University Press.

Knapp, A. (December, 2011). *Pro lacrosse team replaces names with Twitter handles on jerseys.* Retrieved from: www.forbes.com. Accessed: 20 September 2015.

LeUnes, A. (2008). *Sport Psychology*. Hove: Psychology Press.

Mikal, J.P., Rice, R.E., Abeyta, A. & deVilbiss, J. (2013). Transiton, stress and Computer Mediated social support. *Computers in Human Behaviour*, *29*, A40–A53.

Moran. A.P. (2012). *Sport and Exercise Psychology: A Critical Introduction*. East Sussex: Routledge.

Muse, K., McManus, F., Leung, C., Megreblian, B. & Williams, J.M.G (2012). Cyberchondriasis: Fact or fiction? A preliminary examination of the relationship between health anxiety and searching for health information on the internet. *Journal of Anxiety Disorders*, *26*, 189–196.

Park, A. (2014). Young kids, old bodies. *Time* (3 March).

Pegoraro, A. (2010). Look who's talking: athletes on Twitter: A case study. *International Journal of Sport Communication*, *3*, 501–514.

Perry, F.D., Shaw, L. & Zaichkowsky, L. (2011). Biofeedback and neurofeedback in sports. *Biofeedback*, *39*, 95–100.

Pessoa, T.M., Coutinho, D.S., Pereira, V.M., Pinho de Oliveira Ribeiro, N., Nardi, A.E. & Cardoso deOliveira e Silva, A. (2014). The Nintendo Wii as a tool for neurocognitive rehabilitation, training and health promotion. *Computers in Human Behaviour*, *31*, 384–392.

Poeter, D. (April, 2012). Inforgraphics: Athletes tweeting up a storm. *PC Magazine*.

Power, A. & Kirwan, G. (2013). *Cyberpsychology and New Media*. Hove: Psychology Press.

Ramsey, L., Tangermann, M., Haufe, S. & Blankertz, B. (2009). Predicting fast decision BCI using a goal-keeper paradigm. *BMC Neuroscience*, *10*(Suppl. 17)*(69)* doi: 10.1186/1471-2202-10-SI-P69.

Roberts, S. (2009). Pod casting feedback to students: Students' perceptions of effectiveness. *Innovations in Practice*, *1*, 44–47.

Sanderson. J. & Kassing, J.W. (2011). Tweets and blogs: Transformative, adversarial, and integrative developments in sports media. In A.C. Billings (ed.), *Sports Media: Transformation, Integration, Consumption* (pp. 114–127). New York: Routledge.

Seko, Y., Kidd, S., Wiljer, D. & McKenzie, K. (2014). Youth mental health interventions via mobile phones: A scoping review. *Cyberpsychology, Behaviour and Social Networking*, *17*(9), 591–602.

Sillence, E., Briggs, P., Fishwick, L. & Harris, P. (2004). Trust and mistrust of online health sites. In Proceeding of CHI' 2004, pp. 663–670.

Spence, I. & Feng, J. (2010). Video games and spatial cognition. *Review of General Psychology*, *14*, 92–104.

Weaver III, J.B., Thompson, N.J., Sargent Weaver, S. & Hopkins, G.L. (2009). Healthcare non-adherence decisions and internet health information. *Computers in Human Behaviour, 25,* 1373–1380.

Weinberg, S. & Gould, D. (2011). *Foundations in Sport and Exercise Psychology.* Leeds: Human Kinetics.

Wollersheim, D., Merkes, M., Shields, N., Liamputtong, P., Wallis, L., Reynolds, F. & Koh, L. (2010). Physical and psychosocial effects of Wii video game use among older women. *International Journal of Emerging Technologies and Society, 8*(2), 85–98.

World Health Organization (WHO; 2010). Global status report on non-communicable disease 2010. Retrieved from: www.who.int/nmh/publications/ncd_report_full_en.pdf.

14 The online workplace

Cliona Flood

CHAPTER OVERVIEW

In the Thompson Reuters Report (2014) the futuristic predictions for the year 2025 seem far-fetched by today's standards. They predict that everything will be digitally connected and responsive to our wants and likes. Today's workplaces are likely to be considered relatively simplistic by the interconnected and automated world of the future. The only thing that we can be sure of today is that the way we work and the places we work in tomorrow will be radically different. Our future will be constantly changing and technology is driving the change. All manner of commercial and human transactions can now be conducted online. There is no need to speak to an individual or interact with a traditional organisation such as a shop, a bank or an agency. It is even possible to raise substantial amounts of money through crowd-funding without the need of a financial institution (see www.wethinq.com for examples). Yet these websites, powered by technology, are designed and operated by people. It is the way they earn their living. Websites work in a different manner to the high-street shop but serve a similar purpose. Work today is different where workers and workplaces have had to adapt to the constant challenge of change.

This chapter will outline the emerging challenges that technology poses to organisations, particularly in the workplace. It will address the transition to new working environments that embrace new technologies. The aim is to explore issues of working in a virtual environment, working with virtual teams and team dynamics. The challenges and opportunities that technology poses will be explored and the future scope of work will be looked at.

KEY TERMS

In the evolution of an online-working environment certain new organisational structures have emerged. Today, many of us work in **boundaryless organisations**, where the walls of the institution do not end at the factory gate. The boundaryless organisation has a wide scope, often global. Because the boundaries of the organisation are now open and porous this gives rise to the **virtual organisation** (VO) and **virtual teams** (VT). As a result of technology, VOs have emerged. These organisations have a new type of organisational relationship (Priego-Roche *et al.*, 2012). The VO is an organisation that is a flexible network of independent groups, which can be linked together by information technology (Pang, 2001). The VO gives rise to the virtual team.

Virtual team members are drawn from diverse geographical backgrounds and may have different skill-sets to contribute to a project. This in turn gives rise to people working for an organisation in one location and living in another and bringing diversity to the workplace. Workers can develop a **boundaryless mindset** (Arthur & Rousseau, 1996) and are liberated from traditional organisational boundaries, working virtually, leading to flexible life-styles, enhanced work satisfaction and work–life balance. Individuals have the opportunity to constantly develop skills and have a greater adaptability within their careers and many workers no longer work in a specific workspace or building, but can be considered **telecommuters** who work independently from the 'hub' and touch base only when necessary.

Technology in the workplace can also have a downside and management may fear that workers may spend company time on the Internet pursuing their own interests. This phenomenon has been termed as **cyberslacking**. Other **cyberdeviant** behaviours (O'Neill *et al.*, 2014), such as **cyberbullying** can also be an issue. **Constant connectedness** is a fact of twenty-first-century life and being available 24 hours a day can lead to difficulties for some workers.

ORGANISATIONS TODAY: THE ONLINE WORKPLACE

Where we have come from

Think of a traditional department store on the high street, say fifty years ago. This store probably occupied an enormous amount of real estate, employed hundreds of people and supplied a myriad of goods and services to its loyal customers. In fact, Drucker (1988) argued that the businesses of the 1960s resembled a hospital or a symphony orchestra more than a manufacturing company. Consider another industry, for example, a car manufacturing plant, a pharmaceutical factory, a brewery, a clothing factory, a farm, or the publishing and a media company. In the past, these industries employed hundreds of thousands of skilled workers. Goods were mass-produced. The process demanded a heavy human input in order that the products were made, distributed and sold. These industries were the life-blood of towns and cities, offering secure and permanent employment to their populations. Work was mainly predictable, often seasonal, and many companies were autocratic in their management style. Work locations were fixed in time and space. The bosses ruled and the workers obeyed.

Traditional organisations had clear boundaries, with layers of management and a 'chain of command' mentality (Pang, 2001). Clear boundaries lay between functional units, where each department had a responsibility for a particular operation and functions were clearly defined. They often lacked flexibility and were unable to adapt quickly enough to rapid change. In the past, this model worked as change was gentle and predictable. However, this is not the case today.

What about today?

Today, the organisational and commercial landscapes are very different. Smaller, flatter organisations can reduce the management layers and achieve greater organisational efficiency and effectiveness. The high street still has the department stores. In many cases there is a virtual and a real presence, as customers will search online and in the shops for the best value and ideas. People buy products directly from store websites and sell on through websites such as e-Bay and Amazon. Some stores only have a Web presence now. The manufacturing industry has mostly given way to the service industry. Heavy manufacturing takes place mainly in Eastern countries rather than in the West. The publishing industry has also changed radically. People are still reading books and newspapers; however, they have much more choice as to how they connect to information and e-readers, Web-based information is consumed more than paper products. Rainie *et al.* (2012) estimated that 21 per cent of Americans have used an e-reader to access reading material in 2012. This has obvious implications for the publishing industry as to how it distributes material and how the public purchase and interact with it. There are also implications for how this work is now conducted.

Advances in technology have transformed organisations and the places people work in. Publishing is not alone in a radical overhaul in how business is conducted. A call centre is an example of a service or a place where technical enquiries can be handled in one location but serve an international audience. Not only have the work processes and protocols changed, the speed of how things are done and how we communicate has also changed. The expectation that the Internet and technology can give us instant answers prevails. The everyday dynamics of our working lives have changed. Technology is leading this change.

All this change offers challenge and excitement for twenty-first century organisations. Today's workplace is a fluid and adaptable place. It has to be adaptable to whatever economic trends are to the fore if the organisation is to survive and thrive. Staff can be drawn from different countries and cultures and may not be domiciled in the home location of the organisation. Workers are no longer tied to one location or indeed one career throughout their working lives. Today's workers develop flexible job portfolios and bring the skills from one organisation and sector to another. Skills today are transferrable. Technology keeps workers and management constantly connected to their markets and clients enabling diversity in job options and career development.

Over the last fifty years, but in particular in the last twenty years, technology has radically changed how people work, relate to each other and how organisations operate. The types of information technologies used in workplaces today range from e-mail, websites, instant messaging, blogging and social networks. Companies use Facebook and Twitter to communicate with their clients. Other platforms and tools, such as Yammer, a social network specially designed for enterprise, can be used to communicate internally and with virtual teams. Technology enables the continual connectedness with staff, who can now work from any location and are not tied to base. Regardless of the size of a company, they no longer have a local but a global focus. This global focus and instant communications result in the rise of VOs and VTs. The operation of these virtual entities give rise to some of the new and emerging challenges for today's workplace.

The Elance Global Business Survey (Elance, 2012) predicts that 54 per cent of the world's workforce will be online in 2017. Websites such as Elance recruit online for IT professionals in a global market. Of companies who are hiring staff by using online recruitment, 84 per cent argue that this method gives them advantages over their competitors. Hiring online is also advantageous because it offers cost savings, faster 'time-to-hire' and access to a wide range of talent that may not be tapped by local hiring. So being online gives companies the competitive edge and from this we can see that attractive and user-friendly websites are essential components of any modern business, whether they are hiring IT professionals or selling airline tickets. One of the interesting aspects of the market that Elance is targeting is the freelance staffing market. Indeed, their philosophy appears to indicate that the quality of talent online is better or equal to local talent.

THE CHALLENGES TECHNOLOGY POSES FOR TODAY'S WORKPLACES

The challenge of change

Today's fast-paced technological environments demand that companies are inter-connected and respond to environmental changes quickly. Many manufacturing processes are automated and Gore and Vitthal (2013) point out that this has a profound influence on our lives. Today, the traditional organisation would be hampered by the fact that they would be slow to react to change. The structural managerial layers would slow down effective communication. Slow responses to customer feedback would mean a loss in profitability. The modern organisation is flatter, has fewer management layers, it out-sources services as required, and is more effective as it responds to market trends immediately in order to evolve and stay viable. Companies today are willing to make mistakes and learn from them quickly. Google Wave is a good example of this. This application was a collaborative tool offering a real-time messaging platform. It used e-mail, instant messaging, videos and photos. The aim was to update and reinvent e-mail which was forty years old at that point. It enabled online synchronous and asynchronous collaboration. It was launched in May 2009 with Google razzmatazz but was discontinued by 2012. The lessons learned, such as the invite-only exclusivity, poor marketing, lack of speed and notifications are useful for future designers, and the real-time collaborative nature of the platform will inform future applications (Tan, 2010).

There is no doubt that the management of the virtual workplace has certain challenges that older organisations have not had to face before. As far back as 2000, Cascio posed the question 'How can I manage them if I can't see them?' (Cascio, 2000, p. 81). Managing multiple teams, who are physically separate, diverse in nature and culture and working remotely, will no doubt give rise to problems. A different set of supervisory skills is called for. Indeed, not all jobs can translate into the virtual workspace; however, those that do – for example, people in sales, design, marketing project management and consultancy – will have a competitive edge. Coscia (2000) suggests that motivated self-starters with a good working knowledge of their job and technology will be successful. He also suggests that not all managers are suited to the management of virtual workplaces and that a special skill set is required. Managers need to have an open, positive attitude that is solution focused. They need to have a results-orientated management style and possess good communication skills. Finally, they need to be able to delegate effectively, take risks, learn quickly from mistakes and then ensure that work has been completed.

IT'S A NEW WORLD: THE VIRTUAL ENVIRONMENT

The virtual organisation

Let's now look at what a **VOs** is today. Pang (2001) outlined the aspects of a VO. He argued that it is a flexible network of independent entities linked together by information technology in order to share skills, knowledge and expertise. VOs are collaborative entities where people do not have to be located in the same place or time zone. Rather than having an office, a network exists. Skills and people can be geographically dispersed and the virtual organisation can access a wider range of skills and only use, and indeed pay, for these skills when they are needed. Within the VO, **VTs** exist (further development in the next section). These can yield considerable savings, in time, money and expertise to an organisation (Cascio, 2000). The personal lives of staff can be accommodated and this will add positively to their work–life balance. Staff working in different time zones can access each other's work and keep a project moving. Digital technology facilitates asynchronous and synchronous communication, thus saving time and money. Working online also keeps a digital record of what has been done and the work yet to be completed. Some caution is needed when considering the value of VOs. Priego-Roche et al. (2012) outlined that this interorganisational relationship presents new challenges. As the VO can be considered as an alliance which integrates competencies from different sources and is often geographically spread, integration needs to be supported with the relevant technology and consideration given to streamlining discussions, analysis of the environment and stakeholder requirements.

Graf (2009) argues that we may have developed work practices and processes to get work done, but do we know if we are working efficiently with our virtual workmates? There is considerable management and technological change involved in this change and training for virtual leadership can be lacking. He argues that VOs are complex and constantly changing and often difficult to predict. He cites Kruger *et al.* (2005) who outlined that nearly 40 per cent of emails sent daily are misunderstood. Taking this into consideration, it is essential that social and cultural aspects of human communication be considered carefully so that the VO can be as effective as possible.

Technology enables the VO to exist. What are needed are well-designed websites, appropriate collaborative tools, a stable Internet connection and tech-savvy individuals. Technologies will be constantly evolving. Today, we use all forms of telecommunications to communicate and collaborate. Examples include social networking, Google Hangouts and Skype. VOs use these technological powered collaborative tools to work on projects together using a virtual team. Social networks such as Facebook and Twitter are used to advertise products and to keep in touch and respond instantly to a client base. Today, the boundaries between organisations have gone – we have **boundaryless** organisations (Hirschhorn & Gilmore, 1992). The challenges are for management to create more flexible organisations with horizontal networks rather than managerial hierarchies. These organisations will link functions and create strategic alliances with their clients and competitors. It was Jack Welch, CEO of General Electric in the 1990s, who envisioned such organisations where the walls of companies no longer exist and companies can interconnect for a variety of projects and purposes. Although geographical boundaries can disappear, new boundaries are evident. These are more psychological than organisational and reflect the company's structure and culture. The move from a clear-cut management structure to one of independent entities contributing to a project is challenging and often ambiguous. Traditional teams are giving way to VTs.

Virtual teams

Team working is by no means a new phenomenon. Work teams have been around for a very long time. Today's teams still keep the essence of the traditional team, which are goal and performance focused. Man would never have landed on the moon without teamwork. The National Aeronautics and Space Administration (NASA) is an excellent example of an organisation that responded to challenges and solved many of the challenges of the space race through teamwork (Keeton *et al.*, 2012). Salas *et al.* (1992) defined a team as 'a distinguishable set of two or more people who interact, dynamically, interdependently, and adaptively towards a common and valued goal/objective/ mission, who have each been assigned specific roles or functions to perform and who have a limited life-span of membership' (p. 4). Tannenbaum *et al.* (2012) maintain that most teams share some common characteristics. These are that team membership is reasonably stable over time, people are assigned to a team, and members have common and defined goals. Team members work mainly on well-defined tasks and usually exist in a common location.

However, how teams operate has changed in today's world. Teams are more fluid and dynamic today. Today, many organisations operate VTs. VTs are also operating in a more complex environment. Team working is a norm in the modern organisation and it is often taken for granted that they will work. The continual striving for competitive advantage and profit has put pressure on organisations to adapt quickly to a continually changing economic environment. This results in teams being formed, re-formed and disbanded quickly. People can be members of multiple teams simultaneously. The advantage is that multiple skills and talent can be drawn into teams regardless of location. VTs can be drawn from different time zones and different countries or continents. This diversity also leads to challenge. Tannenbaum *et al.* (2012) outline that VTs are different to face-to-face teams. They argue that the environment in which teams operate is more dynamic than here-to-fore, they operate using technology and work from a distance and VTs may have less managerial layers and may be more powerful.

Returning to our NASA example of a team putting a man on the moon (Keeton *et al.*, 2012) we can also see astronauts and cosmonauts as the ultimate **telecommuters**. Not only do they communicate with earth from space, they are also highly trained scientists and are experts in technology. Their missions are global co-operative enterprises, co-ordinated via technology. Today, the International Space Station Programme cooperates transglobally in order to advance our knowledge of space. Only relatively few people will get the opportunity to go into space, however most of us will work as part of a VT and communicate virtually with our organisation at some point in our lives.

Cascio (2000) pointed out some of the potential pitfalls of online working. These include the lack of physical interaction and the lack of non-verbal cues or body language. Setting up a virtual team needs careful construction. Some form of social activity at the initial stages is necessary for people to get to know each other. The first team meeting is vital, as this will establish how the team will work together. Team roles and responsibilities need to be clarified and each team member needs to know how to use the required technology. If team members are drawn from a broad geographical spread, some work needs to be undertaken so that cultural and language issues are clearly understood by members. Another consideration that must be taken into account when working in an online group is the fact that people may behave differently online. Suler (2004) coined the term the '**online disinhibition** effect' and argued that this interaction can either be toxic or benign. This effect is probably more noticeable in online groups that quite possibly interact with each other in a social context rather than a work context. However, this needs to be considered as a possibility in team working contexts.

THE CHALLENGES THAT TECHNOLOGY POSES FOR MODERN MEN AND WOMEN

Career planning

The workforce of today and tomorrow has many opportunities that were not open to previous generations. Today, the world appears smaller, travel is cheaper, education and health are greatly improved and these open new avenues for flexible career choices. However, Stoltz *et al.* (2013) tell us that workers now have to take on the responsibility for managing their own careers. They point out that there is an expectation that workers will be continually developing their skills which can be applied in different working environments. They draw on the work of Arthur and Rousseau (1996), which called for workers to develop a '**boundaryless mindset**'. In other words, workers must be psychologically and environmentally responsive to change and learning that breaks free from traditional organisational boundaries. Workers must not only create their own careers and constantly be updating their skills, but they must also be able to adapt to constant change that is at the core of today's workplace. This constant change can lead to stress and that high feelings of belongingness are associated with high coping resources (Stoltz *et al.*, 2013). So we can argue that one of the challenges of tomorrow's world will be to ensure that the social aspects of work are maintained, even if these are done virtually.

The darker side of technology

Modern companies that use the Internet to carry on their business may be faced with some slightly unwelcome challenges. The constant Web presence may mean that employees spend some of their working time on the Web for non-work activities. Employees may spend different amounts of time checking their social networking pages, shopping, checking personal emails. However, more serious activities may also be engaged in such as gambling and viewing pornography (Weatherbee, 2010). Garrett and Danziger (2008) explored the concept of personal Internet use at work and looked in particular at this form of behaviour in terms of workplace disaffection. They found mixed results and their analysis showed that workplace disaffection factors, such as stress and dissatisfaction didn't have a significant influence on Internet surfing or personal e-mail usage during work. They did find that workers' positive perception of the Web and its capabilities, routine use of computers, job commitment and organisational restrictions on computer use were a greater predictor of personal Internet usage. The fears that management have are that this **cyberslacking** will cause a loss in productivity and ultimately cost the organisation money. Garrett and Danziger (2008) say that the term 'cyberslacking' can have different meanings and they outline that some of the literature defines it as fairly neutral; however, it can also be seen as purposeful misconduct and 'computer abuse' (Lim, 2002). The counterproductive use of technology in the workplace appears to be on the increase (Weatherbee, 2010); however, given that most workplaces are heavily invested in Internet technologies it is difficult to tease out this issue.

The presence of the Web at work gives people the opportunity to pursue goals that are counter to the organisation that they work for. Banning personal Internet use may not work as many people have access to the net on their smartphones and other mobile devices. **Cyberdeviant** behaviour may also be present among teleworkers and remote workers and it may be increased due to the lack of supervision (O'Neill *et al.*, 2014). As the Web allows more people to work from home the issue needs to be addressed. O'Neill *et al.* (2014) investigated the role of the personality traits as predictors of cyberslacking. They found that cyberslacking was positively related to procrastination and negatively related to honesty, agreeableness and conscientiousness. They also found that cyberslacking was negatively related to satisfaction and perceived performance while working from a distance to the main organisation. They suggest that workers could be screened for such traits if working remotely. Organisations need to come to a considered agreement with their staff as to the acceptable use of the net at work.

Another cyberdeviant behaviour is an evolution of poor workplace relationships. In the past this took the form of bullying. Today, bullying still exists and along side it, is the issue of **cyberbullying**. The topic of cyberbullying has been explored in depth with child and adolescent populations (see Chapter 17). However, there is evidence that this phenomenon is also experienced in the workplace, although less research has been conducted on the topic (Privitera & Campbell, 2009; Piotrowski, 2012). Lutgen-Sandvic (2006) defines workplace bullying as 'persistent, verbal and nonverbal aggression at work that include personal attacks, social ostracism and a multitude of other painful messages and hostile interactions' (Lutgen-Sandvik, 2006, p. 406). In a world where it is possible to be connected via e-mail, and social networking sites, a cyberbully has an extended period of time in which to make his or her victim miserable. Constant connectedness is a fact of modern society and many people are contactable 24 hours a day. D'Cruz and Noronha (2013) explored what they called 'the extended reach' of the bully. They uncovered a number of core themes of 'being pursued', feeling 'haunted and hemmed in', 'receiving a settled score' and 'drawing advantage'. Piotrowski's (2012) research argues that administrators and organisational leaders do not appreciate the full impact of cyber abuse. There is a need for robust policies and social and organisational support in order to support the victim of cyberbullying and to prevent it from happening in the first place.

THE CHALLENGES FOR THE FUTURE OF WORK

Future scope

Disruptive technological innovations are creating new industries and ways of conducting business and are leaving older models behind them. Tomorrow's workplaces will need to consider continuously changing technologies, social networking and data analytics in order to be effective. Traditional career models are defunct as people work longer and have portfolio careers. Many of tomorrow's jobs have not even been imaged yet. The PCW report (2014) predicts that by 2017, assembly workers in Hanoi will start wearing sensors to gauge concentration, work rate and mood. They predict that by 2019 a doctor in China will carry out 'remote' surgery. By 2021, licences will be granted for driverless cars and in 2022 the first fully automated and robot-served hotel will open. There is no doubt that the speed of change will be accelerated faster than ever before in history. Some of the factors driving this change will be a scarcity of natural resources and climate change, shifts in global economic power, demographic shifts and continuing urbanisation.

A number of different organisational cultures and structures are already emerging. In the 'small is beautiful' organisation, for example, companies work in small independent units, in collaborative networks enhanced by technology. These small units can be specialists in what they do. The next type of emerging organisation is the 'organisation that cares'. These organisations take social responsibility seriously and are concerned with sustainability and being kind to the planet. The final type of emerging organisation possibly resembles the traditional organisation. These are large multinational and global corporations where the rules of capitalism still run through the veins of the individuals that run them. They are possibly more concerned with individualism than social responsibility. Yet these organisations will also be driven by new technologies and will rapidly adapt to the changing and dynamic environment.

Back to the future?

Before the Industrial Revolution, the workforce was made up of artisans and agri-cultural workers. The Industrial Revolution was the period that saw a transition from hand-made goods to machine manufacturing. Large factories and mills produced chemicals, iron, steel and textiles. This major turning point in history was powered by harnessing the power of steam, improved transportation, and the move from wood and biofuels to coal. The impact on society was enormous. The populations in towns and cities grew exponentially as industry and jobs were located near ports and transport lines. Is the mobile phone and smart technologies the catalyst for a revolution today? Quite possibly! The first mass-produced personal computer became available in the early 1980s (Knight, 2014) and this was the start of an informational and technological revolution. Industrial and social process has changed radically since the introduction of this type of technology. This change has been rapid and unrelenting. Technologies have been enhanced, miniaturised, computer capacity and memory enhanced. Electronics have become affordable to a wide audience and devices have become mobile and less dependent on distances. All these changes have altered how people work, socialise, communicate and learn. Rather than work in large organisations, factories and corporations, it is possible for small, specialised companies, entrepreneurs, sole traders and artists to work in a networked society powered by technology. Have we 'gone back to the future'? Who knows? It has possibly taken us three hundred years to rediscover that 'small is beautiful'. Roll on the future.

CONCLUSION

This chapter has considered the online workplace. We have looked at how traditional organisations have evolved, driven by the power of technology. We have considered the challenges that this change brings to organisations. We considered the VO that is 'boundaryless' and the VTs that make up these organisations. We looked at the challenges that technology brings to twenty-first-century workplaces and the people who work in them. Finally, we tried to predict the shape of future organisations and although the future predictions may not be quite right (only time will tell), one thing is certain – in the words of the Greek philosopher, Heraclitus (500 BC), 'The only thing that is constant is change.'

ACTIVITY

This activity can be done individually, in small groups or as a class activity:

Consider the jobs and professions of your grandparents. What types of work were they involved in? What technological aspects were involved in their work? How are these jobs and professions conducted today?

DISCUSSION QUESTIONS

1 Outline your technological predictions for the next 25 years. How will these changes impact on organisational life and the people who work within these new organisations?
2 What are the issues involved with staff using the Internet at work?
3 Discuss the advantages and disadvantages of working in a VO.
4 How can the challenges of working in a VT be addressed?

RECOMMENDED READING LIST

Anna Sutton's publication outlines the main issues in organisational psychology today. It is an excellent introduction to topics in work and organisational psychology.

Sutton, A. (2015). *Work Psychology in Action*, Basingstoke: Palgrave MacMillian.

In the focal article, 'Teams are changing: Are research and practice evolving fast enough?' you will find an overview of how teams have changed and are managed in the online world.

Tannenbaum, S.I., Mathieu, J.E., Salas, E. & Cohen, D. (2012). Teams are changing: Are research and practice evolving fast enough? *Industrial and Organizational Psychology, 5*, 2–24.

GLOSSARY

Boundaryless mindset   The mindset of staff who are not restrained by traditional organisational boundaries. They may work collaboratively across teams and as part of multidisciplinary teams.

Boundaryless organisations   Organisations that the barriers between internal and external functions have been reduced. Organisational layers are reduced in the hope of achieving greater organisational efficiency and effectiveness.

Constant connectedness   A consequence of twenty-first-century technology. Often there is an expectation of fast responses to requests and being available 24 hours a day.

Cyberbullying   Various types of bullying that occur using technology.

Cyberdeviant   A form of maladjusted Internet use at work that may be perpetuated by the lack of supervision in staff that work virtually.

Cyberslacking   Use of the Internet at work for personal reasons; for example, social networking, shopping, surfing the net, gambling, etc. Managers often fear that this can lead to loss of productivity and ultimately cost the organisation money.

Online disinhibition   The online disinhibition effect was coined by Suler (2004). It refers to a loosing or removal of social inhibitions when interacting online that would normally be present in face-to-face communication.

Telecommuters They work independently from the 'hub' and touch base only when necessary. Telecommuters stay connected to the workplace by using a variety of digital technologies.

Virtual organisation (VO) Members work for the same company but are geographically distant from each other and communicate by information technology.

Virtual teams (VT) These are made up of a number of different people who work together collaboratively using web-based technologies. They may never meet in person.

REFERENCES

Arthur, M.B. & Rousseau, D.M. (1996). A career lexicon for the 21st century. *Academy of Management Executive, 10*, 28–39. In Stoltz, K.B., Wolff, L.A., Monroe, A.E., Farris, H.R. & Mazahrea, L.G. (2013). Adlerian lifestyle, stress coping, and career adaptability: Relationships and dimensions. *The Career Development Quarterly, 61*(3), 194–209.

Cascio, W.F. (2000). Managing a virtual workplace. *Academy of Management Executive, 14*(3), 81–90.

D'Cruz, P. & Noronha, E. (2013). Navigating the extended reach: Target experiences of cyberbullying at work. *Information and Organization, 23*(4), 324–343.

Drucker, P.F. (1988). The coming of the new organization. *Harvard Business Review*, January–February, 4–11.

Elance (2012). Elance global business survey. Retrieved from: www.elance.com/q/global-business-survey?mpid=cj_10777892_6155871.

Garrett, R.K. & Danziger, J.N. (2008). Disaffection or expected outcomes: Understanding personal Internet use during work. *Journal of Computer Mediated Communication, 13*(4), 937–958.

Gore, V. & Vithal G. (2013). 21st century skills and prospective job challenges. *The IUP Journal of Soft Skills, VII*(4), 7–13.

Graf, T. (2009). The future of OD: Developing an effective virtual organization for the OD network. *OD Practitioner, 41*(3), 30–36.

Heraclitus (500 BC) *Internet Encyclopaedia of Philosophy*. Retrieved from: www.iep.utm.edu/heraclit/.

Hirschhorn, L. & Gilmore, T. (1992). The new boundaries of the "boundaryless" company. *Harvard Business Review* (May edition), *70*(3), 104–115. Retrieved from: http://hbr.org/1992/05/the-new-boundaries-of-the-boundaryless-company/ar/.

Keeton, K.E., Schmidt L.L., Slack, K.J. & Malka, A.A. (2012). The rocket science of teams. *Industrial and Organizational Psychology, 5*(1), 32–35.

Knight, D. (2014). Personal computer history: the first 25 years. *Low End Mac*. Retrieved from: http://lowendmac.com/2014/personal-computer-history-the-first-25-years/.

Kruger, J., Epley, N., Parker, J. & Ng, Z.W. (2005). Egocentrism over e-mail: Can we communicate as well as we think? *Journal of Personality and Social Psychology, 89*(6), 925.

Lim, V.K.G. (2002). The IT way of loafing on the job: Cyberloafing, neutralizing and organizational justice. *Journal of Organizational Behaviour, 23*(5), 675–694.

Lutgen-Sandvik, P. (2006). Take this job and . . . : Quitting and other forms of resistance to workplace bullying. *Communications Monographs*, *73*(4), 406–433.

National Aeronautics and Space Administration (NASA). Retrieved from: www.nasa.gov.

O'Neill, T.A., Hambley, L.A. & Bercovich, A. (2014). Prediction of cyberslacking when employees are working away from the office. *Computers in Human Behaviour*, *34*, 291–298.

Pang, L. (2001). Understanding virtual organizations. *Information Systems Control Journal*, *6*, 42–47.

PCW Report (2014). *The future of work. A journey to 2022*. Retrieved from: www.pwc.com/gx/en/managing-tomorrows-people/future-of-work/journey-to-2022.jhtml.

Piotrowski, C. (2012). From workplace bullying to cyberbullying: The enigma of e-harassment in modern organizations. *Organization Development Journal*, *30*(4), 44–53.

Priego-Roche, L.M., Thom, L.H., Rieu, D. & Mendling, J. (2012). Business process design from virtual organization intentional models. In *Advanced Information Systems Engineering* (pp. 549–564). Berlin, Heidelberg: Springer.

Privitera, C. & Campbell, M.A. (2009). Cyberbullying: The new face of workplace bullying? *Cyberpsychology and Behaviour*, *12*(4), 395–400.

Rainie, L., Zickuhr, K., Purcell, K., Madden, M. & Brenner, J. (2012). The rise of e-reading. *Pew Internet, Pew Internet & American Life Project*. Retrieved from: http://libraries.pew internet.org/2012/04/04/the-rise-of-e-reading/.

Salas, E., Dickinson, T.L., Converse, S.A. & Tannenbaum, S.I. (1992). Toward an understanding of team performance and training. In Tannenbaum, S.I., Mathieu, J.E., Salas, E. & Cohen, D. (2012). Teams are changing: Are research and practice evolving fast enough? *Industrial and Organizational Psychology*, *5*(1), 2–24.

Stoltz, K.B., Wolff, L.A., Monroe, A.E., Farris, H.R. & Mazahrea, L.G. (2013). Adlerian lifestyle, stress coping, and career adaptability: Relationships and dimensions. *The Career Development Quarterly*, *61*(3), 194–209.

Suler, J. (2004). The online disinhibition effect. *CyberPsychology & Behaviour*, *7*(3), 321–326.

Tan, P. (2010). RIP Google Wave – the lessons we learnt.Hyper office collaboration made simple. Retrieved from: www.hyperoffice.com/blog/2010/08/16/rip-google-wave-the-lessons-we-learnt/.

Tannenbaum, S.I., Mathieu, J.E., Salas, E. & Cohen, D. (2012). Teams are changing: Are research and Practice evolving fast enough? *Industrial and Organizational Psychology*, *5*(1), 2–24.

Thomson Reuters Report (2014). The World in 2025: 10 predictions of innovation. Retrieved from: http://sciencewatch.com/sites/sw/files/m/pdf/World-2025.pdf.

Weatherbee, T.G. (2010). Counterproductive use of technology at work: Information & communications technologies and cyberdeviancy. *Human Resource Management Review*, *20*(1), 35–44.

Wethinq.com (2014). Retrieved from: www.wethinq.com/en/blog/2014/08/12/39-Great-Crowdsourcing-Examples.html.

Yammer.com (2015). The enterprise social network. Retrieved from: www.yammer.com./

15 The Internet as an educational space

Marion Palmer

CHAPTER OVERVIEW

The Internet is a significant educational space. It has content and many tools that engage and support learners. This chapter presents an overview of learning enabled by the Internet. It discusses informal and formal learning as well as the developments in open, online and distance learning. It considers learning tools such as Twitter as well as **virtual learning environments (VLEs)** and **Massive Open Online Courses (MOOCs)**. The interaction of learning and technology is explored and learning theories considered. This chapter argues that at long last learning is being transformed by the access to technology and the ability of learners to create and develop in the online world.

KEY TERMS

Learning is the focus of this chapter as it considers the Internet as an educational space. Learning is considered a change in behaviour (Gagné *et al.*, 1992). **Informal learning** is learning that people do as and when it suits them. **Formal learning** occurs when students take courses at schools, colleges or at the workplace (Selwyn, 2011). **Experiential learning** occurs when learners learn through and from their experiences.

Learning is enabled by **instruction.** Gagné *et al.* (1992) consider this to be all the events that effect learning. **Teaching** is a key part of instruction where teachers (also called instructors) organise and plan the instruction for students and classes. **Assessment** is any process by which the learning is judged (Freeman & Lewis, 1998).

Educational technology can be the artefacts and devices – i.e. the technologies themselves, how the technologies are used in education and learning and the context for their use (Selwyn, 2011).

Learning using technology and electronic media has led to many associated terms often with similar meanings (Moore *et al.*, 2011). One of the first of these terms was **elearning,** meaning learning with electronic technology. **Online learning** is generally taken to mean learning using the Web (Harasim, 2012). **Technology-enhanced learning** tends to emphasise the use of technology to support learning, often complementing face-to-face classes. **mLearning** is learning using mobile devices such as phones and tablets. **Distance learning,** where the teachers and learners are in different physical spaces, has been transformed by the Internet.

Multimedia is any material that contains words and graphics. Words are **text** printed on a screen or spoken. **Graphics** are both static items such as illustrations, drawings, charts, maps, photographs and dynamic items such as animation and video (Clark & Mayer, 2003). One of the key features of the Internet as an educational space is the access it provides to many multimedia resources.

The Internet has led to the development of a range of learning environments and courses. Many colleges and schools have VLEs, Web-based electronic courses for students enrolled on specific courses or programmes. They are closed – i.e. restricted to specific students. Recently, **MOOCs** have been developed. These are courses accessible to all at little or no charge and taken by many students (Littlejohn, 2013).

THE INTERNET AND ITS IMPACT ON LEARNING

Learning is a key activity of human beings. It is a 'process that enables human beings to change behaviours and their capabilities' (Gagné *et al.*, 1992). It takes place at all times and in all places. Learning can be informal or unofficial. You can decide to learn something new and just look it up yourself or ask someone about it or you can learn formally by taking part in a course, do assessment and possibly aim for accreditation such as a degree or a certificate of achievement. Teachers, lecturers and trainers take part in formal learning and design the instruction, teach and manage the assessment. External and internal factors influence learning, the conditions of learning (Gagné *et al.*, 1992) and **mastery** is achieved when learners are successful at learning tasks.

Before the Internet

Thinking back 25 years (Hart, 2014a) to before the Internet, any kind of learning required movement. Looking something up required going to a library; talking to someone required a phone call or meeting them. Keeping up with an interest group required attending meetings and checking newsletters. Formal learning meant going to school or college, attending class, going to the library and meeting fellow students and teachers/lecturers, essentially **face-to-face learning (f2f)**. There was technology in education but it had little impact on formal learning and some impact on informal learning.

The Internet

The Internet was developed to network computers and enable communication around the world. Content could be uploaded to Web pages and shared via the World Wide Web (the Web) and files transferred between computers. Different kinds of media, memory and storage were developed and sharing media files both audio and video became much easier. YouTube, social media developed and social networking sites became commonplace.

Harasim (2012) argues that the Internet is the fourth major paradigm of communication following speech, writing and printing. She notes how quickly the Internet has had an impact on society and that the 'Internet represents a worldwide knowledge transformation on a global scale' (p. 23).

Tools and content on the Internet

We now have a range of digital technologies (Bower, 2015) and access to them has become routine through devices such as mobile phones and tablets as well as traditional desktop and laptop computers. Many tools are available for us to use and lots of content for us to access. We have the tools for designing, editing and content creation (McWilliam and Haukka, 2008). It can now be argued that the Internet is an enabler of learning.

Informal and formal learning

The impact on informal learning has been considerable. Harasim (2012) considers online learning as the use of communication networks for educational purposes mediated by the Web. Hart (2014a) argues that the Web enables 'learning the new' – i.e. keeping up-to-date with what is happening in a discipline, in a profession as well as finding out what is new to an individual. She argues that 'Learning the new involves being in the flow of new ideas and "joining the dots" between unstructured pieces of knowledge that are encountered' (Hart, 2014a). This informal learning takes place at an individual, group or indeed system level. What is clear is that as new technology is developed, how it is used for educational purposes and what contexts it is used in will be a surprise to us all. It depends on people and how they behave, and emerges through their experiences of the Internet, which can be considered a classic site of experiential learning.

The impact on formal learning is more difficult to discern. Hart (2014a) notes the little change in workplace learning over the 25 years of the Web as does Selwyn (2011) in schools and colleges. This is now considered.

Learning in schools, colleges and the workplace

Workplaces have changed, as have schools and colleges. In terms of workplace learning Hart (2014a) notes a shift from f2f learning to elearning but argues that it is 'still about designing and pushing-down content-centric materials'.

Workplace technologies such as word-processing, presentation graphics, electronic mail and the World Wide Web have moved to higher education and schools (Gilbert, 2011). These have become part of the taken-for-granted tools for both staff and students.

The role of the Internet in learning is becoming both more accepted and more explicit, as shown in Table 15.1. However, key issues for formal learning such as the curriculum, the role of the teacher and the role of the student and the control of the process, particularly assessment, are still contentious.

TABLE 15.1 Types of elearning

Type of learning	Features
Traditional	Classroom based, no course content online and no technology used.
Web-facilitated	Classroom based, up to 30 per cent of content online. Materials may include module outline, lecture/class notes and links to resources. There may be use of e-mail and a VLE.
Blended/hybrid	Course combines classroom and online delivery. Between 30 and 80 per cent of content online. Use of the Internet for online discussions and assessment, possibly online project work. Some reduction in classroom time.
Online	Online work using the Internet only. Over 80 per cent of the content online and few or no face-to-face meeting.

(Allen and Seaman, 2015, p. 7)

LEARNING USING THE INTERNET

In this section learning using the Internet is considered starting with learning resources available on the Internet. Then we move to formal learning and the classroom, followed by closed Internet systems and open networks. **Twitter** and **wikis** are reviewed, and this section concludes with a review of MOOCs. There is a shift from individual to group learning, and then learner networks and a parallel shift from formal to informal learning.

Learning resources on the Internet

The range of learning resources on the Internet is vast. There is a lot of information. There are many tools. Khan Academy provides practical exercises and instructional videos free to learners, teachers and parents on a range of subjects including maths, science and history (Khan Academy, 2014). TED talks and online videos provide learning about ideas and TED-Ed supports teachers to use these videos to create lessons and to share them for others to use. Lynda.com provides online videos and tutorial for a fee in technical and business disciplines and ALISON (2014) provides free certified training for workplace skills. YouTube provides videos on almost any topic. They can be used by individuals, groups or by teachers in classrooms. Using these resources is often experiential learning; learners use the resource (doing), reflect on how they use it and develop their understanding through their experience of the resource.

Parallel to the courses and content pages the Internet provides access to many tools. There is a technology tool for many educational tasks (Educational Technology Media, 2014). Jane Hart (2014b) defines a learning tool as 'any software or online tool or service that you use either for your own personal or professional learning, for teaching or training, or for creating e-learning' (Hart, 2014b). Each year since 2007 she has consulted learning development professionals to identify the Top 100 Tools for Learning. In 2007 the number one tool was Firefox, the Web browser; by 2009 it was Twitter and it remains at number one in 2014 (Hart, 2014c).

Twitter and wikis

Twitter (2015) is a microblogging tool. Each tweet can contain an idea, or a photo all in 140 characters. The tweeter decides what to tweet and decides who to follow or read but cannot decide who reads them. It is public and open to the world. This is a learning tool (Hart, 2014b) as it enables an individual to access ideas and thoughts from around the world. It is an example of 'learning the new' (Hart, 2014a) a way of keeping up-to-date with the leaders in a field or a discipline and of sharing such ideas with a personal network and it uses the Internet – the main network in the world – to do so. The author uses Twitter in this way becoming part of a range of networks who share ideas, concepts and information.

However, Twitter is not just a tool for individual or group informal learning, it can also be a resource for formal learning. Blessing *et al.*, (2012) used Twitter to reinforce classroom concepts in an undergraduate psychology course and noted that students who received psychology-related tweets from the teachers outperformed students who did not. This intervention is one way of using Twitter in formal learning.

Wikis are Internet tools that enable online collaboration (Tierney and Palmer, 2014). Online collaboration is a way of enabling professionals to share resources. It relies on developing a community that interacts and develops a resource. Tierney and Palmer (2014) explored the use of a wiki for continuous professional development for teachers on dyslexia – a matter of considerable professional concern. They noted that while the participants had the technical skills to use the wiki that the interaction between them was low until towards the end of the study. The study suggests that online learning such as through a wiki has the potential to be a useful tool for professional development.

The availability of resources and tools for learning on the Internet makes much of the argument for it as an educational space; however, it is how these resources are used that makes the impact on education and learning – i.e. formal learning. This is now considered.

Formal learning using the Internet

Classrooms are key sites of formal learning. They are places that teachers control; they decide the content and activities for any particular session. It may be a lecture, a tutorial or a seminar. The use of the Internet in the classroom is controlled by the teacher. Mobile phones and laptops may be permitted or banned. Classes may take place in computer labs. Data projectors and computers for teachers' use are provided in many classrooms and training rooms. These enable the use of **multimedia** by teachers for presentation of material. Once classrooms are connected to the Internet, teachers and learners have access to a wide range of tools and resources for learning; however, it is often the teacher/trainer who determines what is used.

Lecture capture is an example of using the Internet as an educational space. Multimedia lectures in classrooms can be created as audio/video recordings and made available to students as a supplement to the lectures or for distance learners as the lectures. In a study of lecture capture Dalton *et al.* (2014) noted that multimedia lecture capture appears useful as a supplementary learning aid rather than as a replacement for traditional learning materials such as textbooks.

One technology developed specifically for education is the VLE. These provide a closed Web-based system where teachers and students have access to a course. Students can access notes, contribute work, do assignments and assessments depending on the design of the relevant course. These have been part of Gilbert's (2011) revolution in education. Cosgrave *et al.* (2011) note that students depend on VLEs for access to course materials and that teachers use them for course notes and reading materials and assignments. Teachers may use VLEs to host presentations, and then give the presentations in class but student access is probably outside of class time. There may be labs that use the Internet for experiments or research. VLEs tend to support Web-facilitated learning (Allen & Seaman, 2015) although they can be used for both blended/hybrid and online learning.

It seems clear that there has been a shift from traditional learning with no technology use to Web-facilitated learning, but it can be hard to see where some of the class time is replaced by online work by students. Time in schools or colleges is often set and the use of online activities such as discussions or blogs reflect additions rather than replacements. Furthermore, students may also set up course Facebook pages, where Vivian *et al.* (2014) suggest that personal social networking sites may play an important role in a students' academic experience.

What are widely available are online courses (Harasim, 2012). They can be non-profit, commercial or run by academic institutions. They can be closed – the learner has to register and possibly pay. They can be open – where the learner decides what to do and how to use the learning resource. What distinguishes a course from a resource can be called **instructional design**. This means that a teacher/instructor has planned the learning resource, set the learning goals/objectives, it has a beginning, middle and an end, and throughout the course there may be readings, videos to watch, discussion questions to answer and posts to be made. It has a pathway designed by the instructor and assessments. It may lead to accreditation.

Massive open online courses (MOOCs)

Massive open online courses or MOOCs are a relatively new phenomenon enabled by the Internet. The first MOOC was run in 2008 (Littlejohn, 2013). MOOCs aim to enable large numbers of students to participate in learning and to work together to learn (Littlejohn, 2013) for free. Since the first MOOC two types of MOOCs have developed: the xMOOC and the cMOOC. In xMOOCs learners follow a traditional instructionally designed course working through learning activities set by the instructor. Completion of the course earns a certificate of completion (Littlejohn, 2013). Udacity and Coursera provide such online MOOCs. The second type of MOOC, the cMOOC takes a different approach; the goals are set by the learner, the learner decides the pathway through the learning activity and learner participation is expected to be initiated by the learner (Littlejohn, 2013). Digital Storytelling is an example of a cMOOC. MOOCs have been characterised by large number of students with varied backgrounds but there is little empirical evidence about the learning achieved and the learner experience (Littlejohn, 2013). Littlejohn (2013) outlines three types of participant in a cMOOC: active participants who interact with others through microblogging or similar; lurkers who follow the course but do not engage with other learners; and passive participants who did not enjoy the learning approach.

All the examples cited show that the Internet is being used as an educational space. However, there seems to be a clear difference between using it as an educational resource – i.e. a source of learning content and skills and using it as a learning environment – i.e. as a space to connect with and work with other learners. Learning using the Internet poses challenges to our conceptions of learning and how we learn. This is explored in the next section.

INTERROGATING LEARNING AND THE INTERNET

There are two ways to interrogate learning and the Internet. One approach is to start with the technology and see how it can support and enable learning. The second is to start with what learning is and explore how learning is enabled by the Internet.

The impact of technology

Technology, such as mobile phones or tablets, is now available to many. It can be used to access the Internet; it is interactive and meets the needs of individuals. This means that technology can be used in range of contexts, educational settings and for different educational purposes (Selwyn, 2011). Littlejohn (2013) identifies four learning behaviours in open networks: *consume* – using knowledge; *connect* – with relevant knowledge, people, resources; *create* – make new knowledge through using it; *contribute* back the new knowledge to the collective. These suggest ways that an individual learner can work within a network (Littlejohn, 2013) both formally and informally.

The substitution, augmentation, modification, redefinition (SAMR) model developed by Puentedura (2014) provides a framework for technology-enhanced learning. Where digital technologies are used to substitute or augment tools/learning activities, this is seen as enhancement of the learning and where technologies enable task redesign and new learning task development they are seen to transform learning. Romrell *et al.* (2014) reviewed literature on mobile learning (mlearning) and identified examples of learning that fell within each of the classifications of the SAMR model.

Churches (2012) argues that digital technologies can enable learning activities. He developed Bloom's Digital Taxonomy (Churches, 2012) as shown in Figure 15.1. He argues that for each hierarchical step in the cognitive domain of the taxonomy there

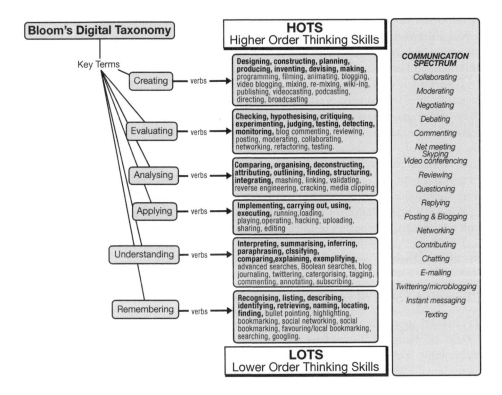

FIGURE 15.1 Bloom's Digital Taxonomy

(Churches, 2012)

are digital activities that can be used for learning. These are commonly expressed as verbs to focus on the activity link to the stage in the domain. Learner activity is changed by access to the Internet and different learning activities are possible.

Learning theories

There are many different views about how we learn with technology and they are informed by beliefs about 'the psychological basis of learning and cognition' (Selwyn, 2011, p. 87). Traditional learning theories focus on the individual and on the design of the instruction with the setting of goals and objectives (Gagné *et al.*, 1992) starting with behaviourism and developing into more cognitive approaches. Mayer (2005) developed his cognitive theory of multimedia learning when learning with **text** and graphics. He argues that learning with multimedia makes specific cognitive demands on learners and that 'Multimedia messages that are designed in light of how the human mind works are more likely to lead to meaningful learning than those that do not' (Mayer, 2005, pp. 46–47).

Constructivist learning theories present at different view of how people learn (Harasim, 2012) by considering how learners make meaning. More recent theories try to account for learning in a networked world such as the Internet. Downes (2012) developed a learning theory, connectivism, 'the thesis that knowledge is distributed across a network of connections, and therefore that learning consists of the ability to construct and traverse those networks' (Downes, 2012) to reflect the network of the Internet and how it enables learning.

Bransford *et al.* (2000) summarise research into learning theories. It is clear that learners come with preconceptions and this initial understanding has to be engaged if they are to grasp new concepts and information. Second, to develop competence learners need the basic facts; they have to be able to understand the facts and ideas in the context of a conceptual framework, and they have to gain the knowledge in ways that facilitate retrieval and application. They argue that effective learning requires thoughtful activity, collaboration for learning with learners taking responsibility for learning and that learners need to learn about learning (Bransford *et al.*, 2000). Watkins *et al.* (2002) echo Bransford *et al.* (2000) in their summary of effective learning and link experiential approaches to learning to the co-construction of learning by teachers and students. Although the paper does not mention the Internet, it argues clearly for the kind of learning opportunities that the Internet provides.

Changing roles of teachers and learners

Traditional approaches to teaching outlined by McWilliam (2007) and Watkins *et al.* (2002) are being challenged by the availability of technology, particularly mobile technology. Yet researchers observe that 'lecturers tend to make, on average, only incremental changes to their practice when faced with new technology' (Cosgrave *et al.*, 2011).

McWilliam (2007) argues that we need to 'unlearn pedagogy' if we are take advantage of the digital world. Reviewing the role of the teacher and reflecting learning theories she argues that educators/teachers should move from providers of knowledge to co-creators of knowledge with students, from the 'sage-on-the-stage and guide-on-the-side to meddler-in-the-middle' (McWilliam, 2007).

The Internet has changed learning. It has changed the source of information, the tools we use. This has required a rethink about how people learn and how to design learning. This linking of the opportunities for learning provided by the Internet with changing pedagogy is important and it means that learning can take advantage of the paradigm shift that Harasim (2012) argues it is. It enables individuals to achieve mastery through changed external conditions of learning (Gagné *et al.*, 1992).

FUTURE TRENDS

The Internet is now part of learning as much as mobile phones are part of our personal stuff. We all use it when we want an answer to a question, to find out how to do something and to talk to experts. It is part of our personal learning space and tools as much if not more so than a traditional library. It prompts and supports a wide range of informal learning both individually and in groups. Learning is being transformed by the access to technology and the ability of learners to create and develop in the online world. Some strengths and weaknesses of the Internet as educational space are identified.

The challenge of the Internet as an educational space is for formal learning. Johnson *et al.* (2014) in the 2014 New Media consortium (NMC) review identify some key trends for higher education such as the ubiquity of social media and the integration of online, hybrid learning and collaboration. Another trend noted is a shift of learners from consumers to creators. This reflects Churches's (2012) argument that the digital world enables students to make and create as well as consume. The impact of these trends on pedagogy is considered as is the evidence.

Sharples *et al.* (2014) examine innovative pedagogy enabled by the Internet and access to it using mobile devices. They see the **flipped classroom** and **bring your own devices (BYOD)** as among the innovating pedagogies that will change classrooms and formal learning. In the flipped classroom, learners have access to the content in their own time and the classroom space becomes space and time for discussion, collaboration and argument. With their own devices students can own their learning and their work. Both these models challenge teachers to become managers of learning much as McWilliam (2007) argues.

Strengths and weaknesses of the Internet as an educational space

The strengths and weaknesses of the Internet are many. The strength is the access to knowledge, tools and people. There is no doubt that it is an amazing resource for learning. This means that access to knowledge for all is possible and that teachers are no longer the gatekeepers.

The challenge and indeed the weakness is the volume of information and ideas. Evaluating the information available and identifying its quality is a key issue for all. Teachers effectively are becoming curators of learning resources. Learners have to know where they get information and referencing and attribution is a key issue for all.

A second challenge is using the tools and apps for learning. Bower (2015) notes the use of a narrow subset of tools in teaching. This is in part due the need for teachers to learn them; this low level of digital fluency is also noted by Johnson *et al.* (2014).

CONCLUSION

How the Internet as an educational space will develop is beyond our speculation. It now plays a role in all our learning. It is a key element of our personal informal learning, enabling us to find out, keeping us to date. In many ways it is part of our formal learning. Teachers and learners use it to access information, create and develop solutions to problems.

The Internet has changed access to knowledge and skills, and this is changing the role of the teacher and how learning is organised; the external **conditions of learning** (Gagné *et al.*, 1992). Access to technology enables learners to create and develop in the online world. Most of all it supports learners to achieve mastery in whatever they wish to learn. This makes learning available to all provided they have Internet access.

ACTIVITIES

1   Consider how you use technology in your everyday life. Take a day and over the day note what you do. How do you communicate, get information, do your work? What technology do you use? What is essential? What is useful?
2   Audit your approach to learning. How do you find out information? How do you learn a new skill? Where do you learn? What tools do you use? How do you know that you have learned?
3   Explore the Top 100 Tools for Learning at http://c4lpt.co.uk/top100tools/. Select an application or tool from the list. Find out what it is, what it does. Do you use it? Would you use it?
4   Select something you might like to learn. Find an online resource/course. Learn from the resource and then assess your learning and evaluate the online course/resource.

DISCUSSION QUESTIONS

1   There are many learning theories. What learning theories explain learning using the Internet and why?
2   What are the strengths and weaknesses of the Internet as an educational space? Is it a paradigm shift (Harasim, 2012)? Has it changed the external conditions of learning (Gagné et al., 1992)?
3   How can learners navigate the educational space of the Internet?
4   How can teachers support learning using the educational space of the Internet? Does Bloom's Digital Taxonomy help?

RECOMMENDED READING LIST

Linda Harasim provides a coherent overview of learning theory and online technologies.
   Harasim, L. (2012). *Learning Theories and Online Technologies*. New York and London: Routledge.

Multimedia is a key element of tools and content on the Web. Richard Mayer edits this handbook of research on how people learn from text and images in computer-based environments.
   Mayer, R. E. (ed). (2005). *The Cambridge Handbook of Multimedia Learning*. Cambridge: Cambridge University Press.

Selwyn takes a critical, reflective view of how technology is used in formal education and challenges the reader to think critically about educational technology.

Selwyn, N. (2011). *Education and Technology: Key Issues and Debates*. London and New York: Continuum International Publishing Group.

MOOCs have become part of learning using the Internet. Littlejohn's paper provides a coherent framework for understanding the MOOC phenomenon.

Littlejohn, A. (2013). *Understanding Massive Open Online Courses*. New Delhi: CEMCA EdTech Notes. Retrieved from: http://cemca.org.in/resources/edtech-notes#.VLumySyFmxt.

GLOSSARY

Assessment   Any process by which learning is judged. It may lead to accreditation.

Blended (hybrid) learning   Learning through a combination of classroom-based (face-to-face) learning and online learning.

Bring your own devices (BYOD)   Learners bring their own devices to the learning space.

Conditions of learning   The set of internal and external conditions that influence learning (Gagné *et al.*, 1992).

Distance learning   Learning with teachers and learners are in different physical spaces.

Educational technology   The technological artefacts and devices used in education, how the technologies are used in education and learning and the context for their use (Selwyn, 2011).

eLearning   Learning with electronic technology.

Experiential learning   Learning through a cyclical process of doing, reflecting on action, identifying learning and applying the new learning (Watkins *et al.*, 2002).

Face-to-face learning (f2f)   Teachers and learners are in the same physical space in classrooms, lecture theatres, labs and studios.

Flipped classroom   Learners' access concepts and ideas in their own time using video lectures, readings and the classroom (f2f) becomes a space for discussion and analysis enabling critical thinking and creativity.

Formal learning   Learning that takes place in formal settings such as schools and colleges or through courses. It often leads to accreditation.

Graphics (pictures)   Static items such as illustrations, drawings, charts, maps, photographs and dynamic items such as animation and video.

Informal learning   Learning that takes place when someone decides to learn something from a book, a video or from another person generally from interest or need.

Instruction   All the events that affect learning.

Instructional design   The systematic design of instruction to support learning (Gagné *et al.*, 1992).

Learning   A change in behaviour.

Lecture capture   Multimedia lectures in classrooms can be created as audio/video recordings.

Massive open online courses (MOOCs) These courses are available on the Internet and open to all who register at little or no charge and often taken by large numbers of students.

Mastery of learning   Achieved when learners are successful at learning tasks (Gagné *et al.*, 1992).

mLearning   Mobile learning using mobile devices such as phones and tablets.

Multimedia   Any material that contains words and graphics.

Online learning   Use of communication networks for educational purposes mediated by the Web.

Teaching   A key part of instruction where teachers (also called instructors) organise and plan the instruction for students and classes.

Technology-enhanced learning   The use of technology to support learning.

Text   Words printed on a screen or spoken.

Twitter   A microblogging tool and online social network, where individuals post short messages (tweets) of up to 140 characters that their 'followers' can read, favour and retweet.

Virtual learning environments (VLEs)   Also called learning management systems (LMS) or course management systems (CMS) (Moore *et al.*, 2011) are web-based courses that support formal learning in schools and colleges.

Web facilitated   Where learning is supported by online course materials and activities.

Wikis   Collaborative websites.

REFERENCES

ALISON. (2014). About ALISON. Retrieved from: http://alison.com/subsection/?section= about.

Allen, I. E. & Seaman, J. (2015). Grade level: Tracking online education in the United States 2014. Oakland, CA: Babson Survey Research Group and Quahog Research Group, LLC. Retrieved from: http://onlinelearningconsortium.org/read/survey-reports-2014/.

Blessing, S. B., Blessing, J. S. & Fleck, B. K. (2012). Using Twitter to reinforce classroom concepts. *Teaching of Psychology*, *39*(4), 268–271.

Bower, M. (2015). A typology of web 2.0 learning technologies. Retrieved from: www.educause.edu/library/resources/typology-web-20-learning-technologies.

Bransford, J. D., Brown, A. L. & Cocking, R. R. (2000). *How People Learn, Brain, Mind, Experience, and School*. Washington, DC: National Academy Press. Retrieved from: www.nap.edu/openbook.php?isbn=0309070368.

Churches, A. (2012). Bloom's digital taxonomy. Retrieved from: http://edorigami.wikispaces.com/Bloom%27s+Digital+Taxonomy.

Clark, R. C. and Mayer, R. E. (2003). *e-Learning and the Science of Instruction*. San Francisco, CA: Pfeiffer.

Cosgrave, R., Risquez, A., Logan-Phelan, T., Farrelly, T., Costello, E., Palmer, M., McAvinia, C., Harding, N. & Vaughan, N. (2011). Usage and uptake of virtual learning environments in Ireland: Findings from a multi institutional study, *AISHE-J The All-Ireland Journal of Teaching and Learning in Higher Education*, 3(1). Retrieved from: http://ojs.aishe.org/index.php/aishe-j/article/view/30.

Dalton, G., Connolly, I. & Palmer, M. (2014). Capturing lecturers: Using multimedia lecture captures to promote learning. In A. Power & G. Kirwan (eds), *Cyberpsychology and New Media: A Thematic Reader* (pp. 185–194). Hove: Psychology Press.

Downes, S. (2012). Connectivism and connected knowledge: Essays on meaning and learning networks. Downes: Canada. Retrieved from: www.downes.ca/me/mybooks.htm.

Educational Technology and Mobile Learning. (2014). A wonderful chart of educational web tools for use in class. Retrieved from: www.educatorstechnology.com/2014/09/a-wonderful-chart-of-educational-web.html.

Freeman, R. & Lewis, R. (1998). *Planning and Implementing Assessment.* London: Kogan Page.

Gagné, R. M., Briggs, L. J. & Wager, W. W. (1992). *Principles of Instructional Design* (4th edn). Belmont, CA: Wadsworth Thomson Learning.

Gilbert, S. (2011). [STILL] Unrecognized revolution in higher education. Retrieved from: http://tlt-swg.blogspot.com/2011/06/still-unrecognized-revolution-in-higher.html.

Harasim, L. (2012). *Learning Theories and Online Technologies.* New York and London: Routledge.

Hart, J. (2014a). The web is 25 years old today – so how has it changed the way we learn? Retrieved from: www.c4lpt.co.uk/blog/2014/03/12/the-web-is-25-years-old-today/.

Hart, J. (2014b). Top 100 tools for learning. Retrieved from: http://c4lpt.co.uk/top100tools/.

Hart, J. (2014c). Top 100 tools 2007–2014. Retrieved from: http://c4lpt.co.uk/top100tools/history/top-100-tools-2007-2013/.

Johnson, L., Adams Becker, S., Estrada, V. & Freeman, A. (2014). NMC horizon report: 2014 higher education edition. Austin, TX: The New Media Consortium. Retrieved from: www.nmc.org/publication/nmc-horizon-report-2014-higher-education-edition/.

Khan Academy. (2014). Khan academy about. Retrieved from: www.khanacademy.org/about.

Littlejohn, A. (2013). Understanding massive open online courses. New Delhi: CEMCA EdTech Notes. Retrieved from: http://cemca.org.in/resources/edtech-notes#.VLumySyFmxt.

McWilliam, E. (2007). Unlearning how to teach. Paper presented at Creativity or conformity? Building cultures of creativity in higher education. Retrieved from: www.creativityconference07.org/presented_papers/McWilliam_Unlearning.doc.

McWilliam, E. & Haukka, S. (2008). Educating the creative workforce: New direction for twenty-first century schooling. *British Educational Research Journal*, 34(5), 651–666.

Mayer, R. E. (2005). Cognitive theory of multimedia learning. In Mayer, R. E. (ed), (2005). *The Cambridge Handbook of Multimedia Learning* (pp. 31–48). Cambridge University Press: Cambridge University Press.

Moore, J. L., Dickson-Deane, C. & Galyen, K. (2011). e-Learning, online learning and distance learning environments: Are they the same? *Internet and Higher Education*, 14, 129–135.

Puentedura, R. R. (2014, 12 November). SAMR: First steps. Retrieved from: www.hippasus.com/rrpweblog/.

Romrell, D., Kidder, L. C. & Wood, E. (2014). The SAMR model as a framework for evaluating mLearning. *Journal of Asynchronous Learning Networks, 18*(2). Retrieved from: http://olj.onlinelearningconsortium.org/index.php/jaln/article/view/435/105.

Selwyn. N. (2011). *Education and Technology: Key Issues and Debates.* London and New York: Continuum International Publishing Group.

Sharples, M., Adams, A., Ferguson, R., Gaved, M., McAndrew, P., Rienties, B., Weller, M. & Whitelock, D. (2014). *Innovating Pedagogy 2014: Open University Innovation Report 3.* Milton Keynes: The Open University.

TED Conferences. (n.d.). TED Ideas worth spreading. Retrieved from: www.ted.com/.

TED Conferences. (n.d.). TEDEd Lessons worth sharing. Retrieved from: http://ed.ted.com/.

Tierney, R. & Palmer, M. (2014). Participation, interaction and learner satisfaction in a professional practice wiki for teachers. In A. Power & G. Kirwan (eds), *Cyberpsychology and New Media: A Thematic Reader* (pp. 196–214). Hove: Psychology Press.

Twitter. (2015). The story of a tweet. Retrieved from: https://about.twitter.com/what-is-twitter/story-of-a-tweet.

Vivian, R., Barnes, A., Geer, R. & Wood, D. (2014). The academic journey of university students on Facebook: An analysis of informal academic-related activity over a semester. *Research in Learning Technology, 22.* Retrieved from: http://dx.doi.org/10.3402/rlt.v22.24681.

Watkins, C., Carnell, E., Lodge, C., Wagner, P. and Whalley, C. (2002). Effective learning. NSIN Research Matters No. 17. London: Institute of Education. Retrieved from: www.ioe.ac.uk/about/documents/Watkins_02_Effective_Lng%281%29.pdf.

16 Consumer cyberpsychology and online marketing

Nicola Fox Hamilton

CHAPTER OVERVIEW

This chapter will provide an introduction to the psychology of online consumer behaviour. The types of customer who shop online and their characteristics will be explored, as well as the motivations and beliefs that influence their choice to engage in ecommerce. The consumer–brand relationship will be examined in the context of how the Internet has profoundly changed the interaction between business and customers, and the costs and benefits of increased choice and information will be discussed. Finally, the methods and effects of online persuasion and viral marketing will be explored.

KEY TERMS

Some of the key terms that will be addressed in this chapter are **customer segmentation**, dividing a customer base into groups of individuals that are similar in specific ways useful to marketing. The **technology acceptance model** (TAM) and **theory of reasoned action** (TRA) are designed to explain why people do or do not use technology, and their intention to adopt certain behaviours. We will consider the effect of social media on the **consumer–brand relationship** and **brand awareness,** particularly in relation to **eLoyalty,** the likelihood of the customer returning to purchase. **Persuasion** and **viral content** will also be examined.

THE RISE OF ONLINE SHOPPING

For both consumer facing and business-to-business retail, ecommerce has fundamentally changed the way in which they do business. New ways of engaging customers, new business practices which are often less costly, new payment methods such as in-app purchasing and micro-payment, and the opening up of the global market have all combined to shift retail and marketing online. Customers around the world are increasingly both adopting online shopping and utilising the Internet to assist with offline shopping (Centre for Retail Research, n.d.). It can be argued that the Internet has ushered in an age of consumer empowerment through increased access to products at a global level, and to vast quantities of information about products and services. Consumers also now have the ability to communicate with and about businesses and brands through social media and other platforms online. However, this level of access can also have its downside, particularly where the excess of options available can lead to decision-making difficulties and to poorer purchasing choices (Broniarczyk & Griffin, 2014). From a business perspective, the access to customers, and particularly to information about customers harvested through tracking online behaviour, is immensely valuable in enabling them to customise and personalise the online shopping experience of their customers. Social media allows businesses to develop brand relationships in a way that was more difficult offline, and in a way that has a great impact on customer awareness and loyalty (Park & Kim, 2014; Valvi & Fragkos, 2012).

It is important to know who is driving or resisting the adoption of online shopping and what are the characteristics that describe them, what are the motivations for shopping online, what makes an online shopping experience a satisfying one which leads the customer to return to purchase again, and what kind of marketing do people best respond to online. This chapter will explore the current knowledge in each of these areas.

Who shops online?

A number of studies have attempted to profile or segment online shoppers according to their characteristics in order to understand different shopping behaviours, which can be then targeted by businesses seeking their custom. A typology of the global online consumer market that aims to describe consumers based on their online activity was developed by Aljukhadar and Senecal (2011), and it segments consumers into three types – basic communicators, lurking shoppers and social thrivers. They found that it was not effective to use psychological and dispositional characteristics such as trust and need for cognition in predicting the consumer segments, but instead consumers from each of the three segments exhibit different behaviours online, also differing in demographic profiles and by their intensity of Internet use. Basic communicators are mostly highly educated women from a variety of income brackets, who use the internet less frequently and mainly to communicate via email. Lurking shoppers have the highest income, are frequently online navigating for information and are heavy online shoppers. Social thrivers have the heaviest intensity of Internet use and exploit the social features to engage in chat, blogging, streaming and downloading. They are more likely to be female, have the lowest education and income of all the groups, and are also the youngest.

These consumer segments not only exhibit different patterns of behaviour online, but also frequent distinctive types of website, which helps indicate to business where best to target their advertising. For example, lurking shoppers are more likely to visit news portal or search sites, and thus advertising to convince them to shop may be best focused in these areas. Alternatively, targeting social thrivers would best be achieved by placing ads on social media or interactive sites, while basic communicators can be best reached via promotional email (Aljukhadar & Senecal, 2011). Online window shoppers are a unique set of consumers who spend a considerable amount of time online without purchasing. Liu *et al.*'(2012) study found that these can be divided into four distinct groups: promotion finders who seek out sales discounts, recommendations and advertisments; social and hedonic experience seekers who don't linger on product details but instead spend time using social tools, reading product news and looking at product images; information gatherers; and learners and novices who may be seeking knowledge and reassurance before purchasing.

THE FACTORS AFFECTING ONLINE SHOPPING ACCEPTANCE

Increasing numbers of people are shifting to ecommerce for at least a portion of their purchases, but a sizeable proportion of the population are still not comfortable in doing so. There are a number of psychological reasons explaining why people accept this use of technology or not. The TRA (Fishbein & Ajzen, 2011) and the TAM (Bagozzi *et al.*, 1992) have been examined by many researchers as a way to explain this resistance to or acceptance of ecommerce, which can in turn help to attract consumers to shop online and to retain them as customers. The TRA examines people's intention to adopt certain behaviours, and that intention is determined by their attitude towards the behaviour and by subjective norms about the behaviour. TAM was designed to explain why people do or do not use technology in the context of the workplace. However, because online shoppers are also technology users, it has also been used to explain people's inclination to adopt technology in online shopping. There are two main beliefs shaping attitudes towards online shopping technology that TAM examines: perceived usefulness and ease of use. In addition to these, the other most common beliefs and variables examined in relation to online shopping adoption are trust, perceived risk, enjoyment and social influence.

Many studies have been conducted using these variables in a variety of contexts with differing results (see Ingham *et al.*, 2015 for a full review of the literature). Trust is typically measured in relation to the website, retailer or the online transaction process itself. Perceived risk examines the potential losses or negative outcomes that are present in all transactions, but are particularly salient in online shopping because of security and privacy issues. Enjoyment is the extent to which the activity itself is enjoyable, and is sometimes connected to the experience of flow, where the user becomes fully immersed in the task and experiences a deep sense of enjoyment in it (Csikszentmihalyi, 1990). Social influence examines the perception of an individual regarding the amount of online shopping that significant or important others believe that they should engage in.

Ingham *et al.* (2015) conducted a meta-analysis of all of the relevant studies undertaken to examine the influence of these beliefs, and created a strong model which explains 52 per cent of the intention to use online shopping. They found that attitude towards shopping online was the most influential variable in predicting whether people intended to shop online or not. The beliefs that helped to shape people's attitude towards ecommerce were perceived usefulness, enjoyment, perceived risk, ease of use and social intention. They also found that enjoyment, perceived risk, perceived usefulness and trust were all significant and direct predictors of intention to shop online.

Higher perceived risk creates more complex decisions for consumers, and greater likelihood of the transaction failing (Featherman & Pavlou, 2003). Despite the development of more secure payment methods and websites over time, many consumers still have a pervasive perception of risk in online shopping, leading to less intention to participate. Cognitive absorption, a concept closely related to Flow Theory and incorporating enjoyment, has been found to have a direct impact on behaviour intent online (Agarwal & Karahanna, 2000), and indeed Ingham et al.'s (2015) meta-analysis found that enjoyment has a direct positive effect on attitudes about online shopping and on intention to shop online. Designers of ecommerce websites should aim to create enjoyable shopping experiences through the usability and content of ecommerce sites to fully activate the enjoyment factor of shopping online. Social interaction has a small impact on attitudes towards ecommerce and a more significant impact on intention to shop online. In the light of the popularity of social networking sites for learning about brands and products, developing a strong social presence to encourage positive word of mouth could exploit the effect of social interaction on purchasing behaviour (Ingham et al., 2015).

Personality and online shopping

Individual differences in personality traits such as the Big Five (McCrae & Costa, 1999) also affect online shopping behaviour. Bosnjak et al. (2007) found that three of the Big Five traits have a small but significant influence on people's willingness to shop online. Neuroticism and agreeableness both had a negative effect, and openness to experience had a direct positive effect on willingness. Higher neuroticism is characterised by anxiety, fear and worry, and as such it is not surprising that it has a negative association with the desire to shop online, when online shopping is still considered a security and privacy risk by many (Ingham et al., 2015). Higher openness to experience on the other hand makes an individual more likely to seek variety or to be curious, explaining why this personality trait might influence an individual to try online shopping. Bosnjak et al. (2007) also found that affective involvement is a strongly significant predictor of shopping intention, indicating that the decision to shop online is an emotional rather than a cognitive one. They found that the need for cognition has a negative effect, and they suggest that perhaps online shoppers are cognitive misers seeking to minimise their efforts using shortcuts. The model arrived at in the study, incorporating these traits, was strongly predictive of willingness to shop online. It is possible that the actual product being shopped for will mediate the effects of personality on shopping behaviour. For example, Svendsen et al. (2013) found that extroversion significantly and positively affected buying intention of a piece of software. They suggest that because the software was a social computing and mobile technology, participants who were more social would be more positively oriented towards it, affecting the findings.

Motivation for shopping online

Rohm and Swaminathan (2004) created a typology of online shoppers based on their motivations to shop. Their findings suggest four different motivations of online shoppers: convenience shoppers who are a key driver of online shopping; variety seekers who are motivated by the choice of retail outlets, brands and products; balanced buyers who shop online because of convenience and the choices available; and store-oriented shoppers who are motivated by both the desire to possess the purchased product immediately and by the social aspects of shopping. The researchers also looked at who was more likely to purchase within several product classes including books, computer hardware and software, travel services and flowers. Convenience shoppers were the most frequent shoppers across all product types except computer software, which was purchased most by variety seekers. Store-oriented shoppers were the least frequent purchasers across all categories of product. While the convenience and social aspects of shopping are motivators in both online and offline contexts, there are some differences between other motivations in the two contexts. Variety seeking in particular is not cited as an offline shopping motivation and illustrates that the access to a wide choice of products is an important element of ecommerce. Contrary to expectations, time savings, and recreation and enjoyment were not found to be motivating factors online, but are cited as factors offline (Rohm & Swaminathan, 2004).

Parsons (2002) delved deeper in the non-functional, psychosocial motivations of online shoppers using qualitative analysis of participant responses. Some 71 per cent of online consumers felt that the anonymity of the Internet allowed them freedom to expand outside of their traditional shopping role. For example, fathers felt they could shop for clothes for their children. Online shopping offers a diversion from everyday life for 95 per cent of people. Learning about new trends was an important theme, with 93 per cent of people feeling this was an important motivator. Only 6 per cent of consumers felt that online shopping was cognitively taxing. Communication with others who have similar interests was a motivator for 96 per cent of participants, and they felt that online was more conducive to this than offline. Recommendations from friends or colleagues are very helpful for 57 per cent of people in the face of overwhelming choice online. This indicates that communities of consumers are important in online ecommerce behaviours.

There is a complex web of factors affecting online shopping acceptance including demographics, motivations to shop, personality, and attitudes and beliefs about the technology involved, but the research thus far has illuminated several areas that the designers of the shopping experience and marketers seeking customers can focus on to reduce risk, increase trust and build community.

CONSUMER–BRAND RELATIONSHIPS

The Internet has fundamentally changed the way that brands and customers interact. Where once brands almost exclusively communicated information to consumers, now the process has become a two-way channel where customers can express their excitement, satisfaction, apathy, frustration or anger, as well as communicate their feedback, ideas and knowledge to the business and other customers. This can benefit companies who build strong brand social network (BSN) pages on social platforms as it can lead to greater brand awareness, stronger consumer–brand relationships and greater transmission of positive **word of mouth** (WOM) traffic, which in turn can have a significant effect on consumer choices (Barreda *et al.*, 2015).

Building WOM traffic is vitally important to ensure the success of a retail business online. A meta-analysis of research looking at the effect of product reviews on retail sales confirms that online product reviews have a significant effect on sales elasticity (Floyd *et al.*, 2014). The most impactful variable is critic reviews, in which credible expert opinions are significantly more likely to sway opinion than that of another customer. Reviews from third-party sites also have a significant effect, appearing more credible to the consumer than those hosted on the brands' own sites. The valence of the review, whether they are positive or negative, also has an effect, with other research finding that negative reviews are perceived as more credible and influential than positive ones (Lee & Koo, 2012).

One way in which WOM traffic can be increased is by effectively presenting a brand on social media as this is likely to increase brand awareness, in turn leading to greater WOM traffic among the brand community (Barreda *et al.*, 2015). Brand awareness is the ability to recognise and recall the brand from a relevant cue. High levels can affect vitally important aspects of a business such as market share, and help to build brand equity, image and loyalty (Bilgihan *et al.*, 2014). A significantly important factor for increasing brand awareness is creating a virtually interactive environment in the BSN. This platform should allow users to exchange rich, reliable and up-to-date information in a timely manner, and is the interface that connects an individual to a brand. The quality of the system, the content, and the ability of consumers to engage in rewarding activities are all significant precursors of brand awareness (Barreda *et al.*, 2015).

The perceived benefits of a BSN page influence the consumers' relationship with the BSN, and a positive relationship leads to increased brand loyalty behaviour. Both experiential benefits such as social interaction with others and enjoyment, and functional benefits such as access to information and promotional deals, give a positive impression of the investment that the brand has made in the relationship with the customer. This leads to brand relationship quality and willingness to spread positive WOM about the brand by the consumer (Barreda *et al.*, 2015). Fans of BSN pages can contribute to the brand community in numerous ways, such as being brand advocates, answering other customer questions, sharing positive experiences, or working out problems together, creating an interactive social experience that illustrates their commitment to the community. Active participation in the BSN rather than passively lurking is important in generating brand trust and commitment, and strengthens the consumer–brand relationship. BSN pages are an effective means of attracting customers and emotionally connecting them to the brand, leading to benefits for the business.

eLoyalty and retention of customers

Building and maintaining brand loyalty is essential to both online and offline businesses. Long-lasting customer relationships are considerably more valuable than once-off transactions. Reichheld and Sasser (1990) calculated that by retaining just 5 per cent more of their customers, businesses could increase their profits by almost 100 per cent, meaning that building customer relationships is an investment worth making. The definition of eLoyalty varies across studies, but is generally conceived to be a favourable attitude towards an online business influencing the intention of the consumer to repurchase from a company, and the likelihood of them recommending the brand to someone else.

Online shopping has changed the landscape of the relationship between customers and brands in significant ways, such as the ease of switching brands and the access to information about available products from other retailers online. These changes affect the way in which businesses can encourage loyalty in their customers. Valvi and Fragkos (2012) conducted a literature review of the eLoyalty research and broke down the factors involved in online retail loyalty into a conceptual framework with three broad categories centred on purchase: pre-purchase, during-purchase and after-purchase. Pre-purchase involves the consumer recognising that they have a need to be satisfied and their search for alternative solutions to meet their need. This category divides into two subcategories: competitor attitudes and reputation, and customer characteristics. The competitive attitudes category consists of variables such as switching costs and barriers to the consumer, where higher costs and barriers make it more likely that the customer will remain loyal. Price and the reputation of the company also play a part in the competitive attitudes category. A strong reputation leads to loyalty through the development of trust. The second subcategory contains the characteristics of the customer profile such as demographics and the level of knowledge that the customer has. These are not characteristics that the business can change, but they can take them into account in their communications and actions involving the customer. The during-purchase process includes evaluating the alternatives available and choosing the best fit, purchasing the chosen product or service, and finally using it to satisfy the need. The factors involved here are the quality of the web service, including the efficiency of the website itself, the purchase process, delivery and service; and the enjoyment or entertainment of the customer during the process. Enjoyment is closely related to service, where poor service reduces enjoyment, and both high quality of service and high levels of enjoyment encourage customer repurchase intention. After-purchase involves evaluating how well the need was met, feeding back that evaluation to others, and ending the purchase process. After-purchase factors include satisfaction, where contentment with the purchase translates into greater loyalty towards the brand; trust, which has a direct and positive relationship with loyalty; and perceived value, which is the overall appraisal of the benefit of the product. Consumers who feel that they are not getting value from a transaction are more likely to look elsewhere for their purchases (see Valvi & Fragkos, 2012 for a full review of the loyalty literature).

Decision-making and purchase satisfaction

Consumers have been empowered by the Internet in two distinct ways: expansion of freedom of choice and expansion of information. There are now an unprecedented number of products and services available to consumers regardless of their location, often with the possibility of customisation or personalisation, and they have unparalleled access to information about those products through review sites, social media and user-generated content in order to decide which fits their needs best. However, despite the benefits of this empowerment and the opportunities it offers for optimal decision-making, it is not without cost. The difficulty of decision-making has been increased by mounting task complexity, trade-off difficulty and preference uncertainty (see Broniarczyk & Griffin, 2014 for a full review of the consumer decision-making literature).

Decision difficulty can develop from a multiplicity of variables, and these can be grouped into a framework of six concepts. Task complexity arises in the face of an excessive number of product alternatives or attributes, or in response to increasing uncertainty about product attributes. Information overload occurs when choice alternatives and attributes increase, and the decision becomes more demanding than our limited capacity to store and process information. The greater the information load the greater the cognitive resources required to process the task, and WOM in particular is known to increase the cognitive burden on decision makers because of its abundance alongside the additional need to evaluate the credibility of the source of information (Gershoff et al., 2001). Customers experience information uncertainty when the quality of information available is low, incomplete or contradictory. Trade-off difficulty occurs when a consumer must sacrifice one goal for another – for example, price for quality – and is cognitively taxing. Trade-offs can evoke emotional difficulty as well as cognitive demand, from anticipatory emotions such as anxiety and despair, to loss at having to relinquish a desired product or attribute when choosing another. Preference uncertainty arises when the preference for a product is not clearly defined or is unstable. Constructing preferences while shopping further increases the burden of choice (Broniarczyk & Griffin, 2014). Consumers are faced with a number of outcomes in the event of decision difficulty online, and most of those outcomes involve poor choice making. Many seek to avoid making the decision at all, or engage in choice simplification where they only engage with easily comparable attributes or choose the product that has been best described, and all of these decisions may lead to suboptimal purchases. There are also consequences after the decision has been made, when the effect of excessive choice can lead to decision regret and diminished satisfaction.

Decision difficulty can lead to reduced satisfaction after the purchase process is complete. As discussed previously, dissatisfaction can lead the consumer to shop elsewhere, so businesses need to ensure that they assist the consumer in the decision-making process in a way that reduces the cognitive load and simplifies the process. While on the one hand the Internet creates the sources of difficulty, it can also provide decision-making aids which can help towards resolving them. For example, a simple star rating system, with no further detailed information on each alternative, can reduce perceived task difficulty and increase decision satisfaction among consumers with low knowledge of the product (Morrin et al., 2012). Other useful tools include product filtering, comparison tools and product recommendations. It is important to test the efficacy of the tools chosen for a task, as they have the potential to increase rather than decrease task complexity if improperly used (Senecal et al., 2005).

One area where decision-making has an impact on the spending patterns of consumers is in-app purchases. Soroush, Hancock and Bonns (2014) found that frustration with being unable to progress within a game (Candy Crush Saga), and decision difficulty about whether to puchase something within the game to make progression easier, leads to ego depletion, in particular for those with low self-control.

This in turn led to higher in-app purchasing behaviour. This is an area, along with micro-transactions, which has not had significant research focus, particularly from a psychological point of view. As adoption of smartphones has increased, consumers are increasingly willing to use mobile payment methods because of their simplicity and convenience (Smith *et al.*, 2012). Soman (2003) found that payments via cash, rather than credit or pre-paid cards, were more immediate and transparent, increasing the pain felt in payment. As a result, people paying by card were more likely to spend more than those paying with cash. Due to the rise in these models of payment, it will be important for researchers to look at the effects of psychology on consumer behaviours with these payment methods.

PERSUASION

The Internet is permeated with persuasion across areas such as education, fitness, healthcare and activism, but it is particularly salient in the area of online marketing and online shopping. Fogg, Cuellar and Danielson (2007), members of the Persuasive Technology Lab at Stanford University, posit that creating successful human computer interactions requires skills in the motivation and persuasion of people through the design of the interfaces people use. The persuasion may occur at a macro level in technology specifically designed to persuade users to behave in a certain way, such as an online shopping website where everything on the website contributes to the goal of persuading a consumer to purchase; or at a micro level in technology not specifically designed to persuade, but containing persuasive elements, such as productivity software that creates experiences that build product loyalty.

There are four ways in which computers or technology are used as tools for persuasion. First, increasing self-efficacy, which helps people feel more efficient, productive and in control, contributes in an important way to the behaviour change process. Second, providing tailored information relevant to the specific needs of the consumer can help achieve a persuasive outcome, and with the level of data tracking that businesses can now access to monitor their customers' preferences, this is a common persuasive tactic in ecommerce. Third, interfaces can be used to trigger decision-making, tools such as product recommenders and comparison tools encourage consumers to engage in choice making in online shopping. Finally, simplifying or guiding people through a process can remove barriers to a desired behaviour. For example, an online store may have a facility to remember customer details such as delivery and billing address, as well as credit card details, thus speeding up and simplifying the checkout process. Additionally, computers can be used as persuasive media – for example, by providing simulated experiences that demonstrate the benefits of a particular choice. In online shopping, for example, this has been implemented with tools such as a virtual body model where the consumer enters their body dimensions and can preview desired clothing on their own body shape. Technology can also be used as a persuasive social actor, modelling desired attitudes or behaviours, such as video demonstrations from people considered attractive within the context of the product type – for example, for technological items, having respected technology reviewers demonstrating a new piece of equipment via video (Fogg *et al.*, 2007).

The impact of design on persuasion

There is also a direct relationship between the credibility of a website and its ability to persuade users to adopt a specific attitude or behaviour (Fogg *et al.*, 2003). The most important elements of a website for influencing credibility are the design look and the information structure. Fogg and colleagues (2003) found that 46.1 per cent of people assessing the credibility of websites commented on the design of the site, including the visual design, layout, white space, images and colour scheme; and 28.5 per cent commented on the structure of the information and ease of navigation. Diverse sites bring a diversity of elements to the fore when being assessed for credibility. In ecommerce in particular people commented on name recognition and reputation of the brand nearly twice as much as other types of website.

As such, it is important to understand how the design of online advertisements affects their persuasive influence. Few people actually click on banner advertisements, but they do however have an impact on brand awareness and can help foster favourable attitudes towards products (Yoo, 2008). Flores *et al.* (2014) conducted a study looking at the effect of different styles of banner advertisements (image display advertisements or text only); the website context in which it was displayed (congruent or not); and different product groups (high or low involvement products). Display advertisements containing imagery are significantly more appealing for high-involvement products (a smart phone in this case), while low involvement products (a global news magazine) are a little more appealing with text-only advertisements. Products were considered more appealing when advertised on a highly congruent website where the theme of the website matched the type of product being advertised, in this case a video site or newspaper. However, the shape of the banner advertisement (horizontal or vertical) made no difference to the appeal of it. Homepage design is just as affected by design as advertising. Yoo and Kim (2014) found that image-oriented homepage designs increased visual fluency, the ease with which visual stimuli can be processed. Given that first impressions of a website are instantaneous and that those impressions last (Lindgaard *et al.*, 2006), it is important that the storefront of an ecommerce site gives users a visually fluent first response, and this is even more the case for people who value aesthetics highly. Visually fluent homepages also lead to a greater preference for the site, and importantly, higher browsing and revisit intentions. The design of the page is more important for visual fluency than even brand familiarity (Yoo & Kim, 2014).

What makes content viral?

Many advertisers attempt to harness the power of **viral** advertising, as it can be a very cost-effective and successful way to exploit the power of WOM to communicate about a brand. The decision by the consumer to spread the viral advertisement is entirely voluntary, so understanding the motivations and reasons for passing along the ads are important. Berger and Milkman (2012) observed how the emotionality of content shapes the virality of it. Positively emotional content is more likely to be shared than negative, and they discovered that virality is driven by arousing emotions such as awe, anger and anxiety. Conversely, deactivating emotions such as sadness lead to significantly less sharing of content, even when accounting for surprising, useful or interesting content (all of which are also linked to virality). External factors (such as how prominently a piece of content is featured on a site) also have an impact on what gets shared online, but emotionality is the overall primary driver.

Ho and Dempsey (2010) also looked at people's motivations to pass on viral content, and found that people who are more individualistic and seek affection are more likely to spread viral content. They posit that opinion leaders are willing to individuate themselves by sharing their opinions with others, and this motivates the desire to share. Those who are altruistic have a need for affection or are concerned about the needs of others are also more likely to share, where sharing is an expression of love or friendship. There is also a significant link between the time a person spends consuming content and their likelihood of sharing viral content.

CONCLUSION

This chapter has provided an overview of consumer cyberpsychology and online marketing, looking at who shops online, how they can be grouped according to behaviour or motivations, and the beliefs and attitudes that influence their enthusiastic adoption of online shopping or resistance to it. The Internet has fundamentally changed the consumer–brand relationship, and the results of that have been increased consumer empowerment, changes in how loyalty is gained by brands, and also decision difficulty for consumers in the face of expansive choice and information. Finally, the means of persuading online customers have been explored, along with consumers' contribution to persuading others through WOM and spreading viral content.

ACTIVITY

Choose a product (for example, a smartphone, a book, or an item of clothing). Find three online retail websites which sell this item and identify the techniques used by each website to encourage sales.

Which techniques do you think are the most effective? Which website do you think will have the lowest number of sales? Is this because of the marketing techniques used, or is it because of a different reason? Which types of shoppers would be most likely to purchase this product online?

DISCUSSION QUESTIONS

1   Think about your own online shopping experiences. Do you often buy more online than your intended purchase? What are the tactics employed by online retailers that encourage you to do this?
2   What persuasion strategies do you think are most and least effective in convincing consumers to purchase online?
3   Which online shopping companies do you trust or not trust? In your own experience, what were the factors that gained or lost your trust.
4   Have you ever engaged in positive or negative word of mouth about a company, through reviews, feedback, complaints, spreading viral content, etc.? What were your motivations for engaging with the company publically in this way?

RECOMMENDED READING LIST

The advent of social media has changed the way consumers and advertisers behave. This book presents scholarly theory and research to help explain and predict online consumer behaviour.

Close, A. G. (ed.). (2012). *Online Consumer Behavior: Theory and Research in Social Media, Advertising and E-tail*. New York: Routledge.

Researchers have identified many different determinants of online loyalty and impacts on business relationships. This review summarises the literature dealing with loyalty to a commercial website.

Toufaily, E., Ricard, L. & Perrien, J. (2013). Customer loyalty to a commercial website: Descriptive meta-analysis of the empirical literature and proposal of an integrative model. *Journal of Business Research, 66*(9), 1436–1447.

This book by two of the leading experts in the field presents cutting-edge academic research on virtual social identity, explores consumer behavior in virtual worlds, and offers important implications for marketers interested in working in these environments.

Wood, N. T. & Solomon, M. R. (2009). *Virtual Social Identity and Consumer Behavior*. Armonk, NY: ME Sharpe.

The complex nature of consumer behaviour is one of the reasons why successfully managing a business is difficult. This book explores areas such as marketing, design and consumer word of mouth.

Posavac, S. S. (ed.). (2015). *Cracking the Code: Leveraging Consumer Psychology to Drive Profitability*. New York: Routledge.

GLOSSARY

Brand awareness   The ability to recognise and recall the brand from a relevant cue.

Consumer–brand relationship   What consumers think and feel about a brand and experience with a brand.

Customer segmentation   Dividing a customer base into groups of individuals who are similar in specific ways such as by demographics, lifestyle and values, or by psychological factors such as personality and motivations.

eLoyalty   A favourable attitude towards an online business influencing the intention of the consumer to repurchase from a company and the likelihood of them recommending the brand to someone else.

Persuasion   An attempt to bring about a change in attitude or behaviour.

Technology acceptance model (TAM)   Designed to explain why people do or do not use technology in the context of the workplace; however, because online shoppers are also technology users, it has also been used to explain people's inclination to adopt technology in online shopping.

Theory of reasoned action (TRA)   The TRA examines people's intention to adopt certain behaviours, and that intention is determined by their attitude towards the behaviour and by subjective norms about the behaviour.

Viral   A marketing technique where consumers voluntarily pass a marketing message about a company to others.

Viral content   Word-of-mouth endorsement or marketing , where customers pass on the business message to other potential customers. Viral marketin typically exploits existing resources such as social networking sites in order to do this.

Word of mouth (WOM)   Communication by a consumer to others actively influenced or encouraged by an organisation.

REFERENCES

Agarwal, R. & Karahanna, E. (2000). Time flies when you're having fun: Cognitive absorption and beliefs about information technology usage. *MIS Quarterly*, 665–694.

Aljukhadar, M. & Senecal, S. (2011). Segmenting the online consumer market. *Marketing Intelligence & Planning*, *29*(4), 421–435.

Bagozzi, R. P., Davis, F. D. & Warshaw, P. R. (1992). Development and test of a theory of technological learning and usage. *Human Relations*, *45*(7), 659–686.

Barreda, A. A., Bilgihan, A., Nusair, K. & Okumus, F. (2015). Generating brand awareness in Online Social Networks. *Computers in Human Behavior*. Advance online publication. doi:10.1016/j.chb.2015.03.023.

Berger, J. & Milkman, K. L. (2012). What makes online content viral? *Journal of Marketing Research*, *49*(2), 192–205.

Bilgihan, A., Peng, C. & Kandampully, J. (2014). Generation Y's dining information seeking and sharing behavior on social networking sites: An exploratory study. *International Journal of Contemporary Hospitality Management*, *26*(3), 349–366.

Bosnjak, M., Galesic, M. & Tuten, T. (2007). Personality determinants of online shopping: Explaining online purchase intentions using a hierarchical approach. *Journal of Business Research*, *60*(6), 597–605.

Broniarczyk, S. M. & Griffin, J. (2014). Decision difficulty in the age of consumer empowerment. *Journal of Consumer Psychology*. Retrieved from http://ssrn.com/abstract=2446095.

Centre for Retail Research. (n.d.). Online retailing: Britain, Europe, US and Canada 2015. Retrieved from www.retailresearch.org/onlineretailing.php.

Csikszentmihalyi, M. (1990). *Flow: The psychology of optimal performance*. New York: Cambridge University Press.

Featherman, M. S. & Pavlou, P. A. (2003). Predicting e-services adoption: A perceived risk facets perspective. *International Journal of Human-Computer Studies*, *59*(4), 451–474.

Fishbein, M. & Ajzen, I. (2011). *Predicting and Changing Behavior: The reasoned action approach*. New York: Psychology Press.

Flores, W., Chen, J. C. V. & Ross, W. H. (2014). The effect of variations in banner ad, type of product, website context, and language of advertising on Internet users' attitudes. *Computers in Human Behavior*, *31*, 37–47.

Floyd, K., Freling, R., Alhoqail, S., Cho, H. Y. & Freling, T. (2014). How Online Product Reviews Affect Retail Sales: A Meta-analysis. *Journal of Retailing*, *90*(2), 217–232.

Fogg, B. J., Cuellar, G. & Danielson, D. (2007). Motivating, influencing, and persuading users: An introduction to captology. In A. Sears & J. Jacko (eds), *Human Computer Interaction Fundamentals* (pp. 109–122). Boca Raton, FL: CRC Press.

Fogg, B. J., Soohoo, C., Danielson, D. R., Marable, L., Stanford, J. & Tauber, E. R. (2003, June). How do users evaluate the credibility of Web sites? A study with over 2,500 participants. In Proceedings of the 2003 Conference on Designing for User Experiences (pp. 1–15). ACM.

Gershoff, A. D., Broniarczyk, S. M. & West, P. M. (2001). Recommendation or evaluation? Task sensitivity in information source selection. *Journal of Consumer Research*, *28*(3), 418–438.

Ho, J. Y. & Dempsey, M. (2010). Viral marketing: Motivations to forward online content. *Journal of Business Research*, *63*(9), 1000–1006.

Ingham, J., Cadieux, J. & Berrada, A. M. (2015). e-Shopping acceptance: A qualitative and meta-analytic review. *Information & Management*, *52*(1), 44–60.

Lee, K. T. & Koo, D. M. (2012). Effects of attribute and valence of e-WOM on message adoption: Moderating roles of subjective knowledge and regulatory focus. *Computers in Human Behavior*, *28*(5), 1974–1984.

Lindgaard, G., Fernandes, G., Dudek, C. & Brown, J. (2006). Attention web designers: You have 50 milliseconds to make a good first impression! *Behaviour & Information Technology*, *25*(2), 115–126.

Liu, F., Wang, R., Zhang, P. & Zuo, M. (2012). A typology of online window shopping consumers. Proceedings of the Pacific Asia Conference on Information Systems 2012 (paper 128). Retrieved from: http://aisel.aisnet.org/pacis2012/128.

McCrae, R. R. & Costa, P. T., Jr. (1999). A five-factor theory of personality. In L. A. Pervin & O. P. John (eds), *Handbook of Personality: Theory and Research* (2nd edn, pp. 139–153). New York: Guilford.

Morrin, M., Broniarczyk, S. M. & Inman, J. J. (2012). Plan format and participation in 401 (k) plans: The moderating role of investor knowledge. *Journal of Public Policy & Marketing, 31*(2), 254–268.

Park, H. & Kim, Y. K. (2014). The role of social network websites in the consumer–brand relationship. *Journal of Retailing and Consumer Services, 21*(4), 460–467.

Parsons, A. G. (2002). Non-functional motives for online shoppers: Why we click. *Journal of Consumer Marketing, 19*(5), 380–392.

Reichheld, F. & Sasser, W. (1990). Zero defections: Quality comes to service. *Harvard Business Review, 68*(5), 105–111.

Rohm, A. J. & Swaminathan, V. (2004). A typology of online shoppers based on shopping motivations. *Journal of Business Research, 57*(7), 748–757.

Senecal, S., Kalczynski, P. J. & Nantel, J. (2005). Consumers' decision-making process and their online shopping behavior: A clickstream analysis. *Journal of Business Research, 58*(11), 1599–1608.

Smith, A., Anderson, J. & Rainie, L. (2012). The future of money in a mobile age. *PEW Internet & American Life Project*. Washington, DC. Retrieved from: www.pewinternet.org/2012/04/17/the-future-of-money-in-a-mobile-age.

Soman, D. (2003). The effect of payment transparency on consumption: Quasi-experiments from the field. *Marketing Letters, 14*(3), 173–183.

Soroush, M., Hancock, M. & Bonns, V. K. (2014, October). Self-control in casual games: The relationship between Candy Crush Saga(tm) players' in-app purchases and self-control. In *Games Media Entertainment (GEM), 2014 IEEE* (pp. 1–6). IEEE.

Svendsen, G. B., Johnsen, J. A. K., Almås-Sørensen, L. & Vittersø, J. (2013). Personality and technology acceptance: The influence of personality factors on the core constructs of the Technology Acceptance Model. *Behaviour & Information Technology, 32*(4), 323–334.

Yoo, C. Y. (2008). Unconscious processing of Web advertising: Effects on implicit memory, attitude toward the brand, and consideration set. *Journal of Interactive Marketing, 22*(2), 2–18.

Yoo, J. & Kim, M. (2014). The effects of home page design on consumer responses: Moderating role of centrality of visual product aesthetics. *Computers in Human Behavior, 38*, 240–247.

Valvi, A. C. & Fragkos, K. C. (2012). Critical review of the e-loyalty literature: A purchase-centred framework. *Electronic Commerce Research, 12*(3), 331–378.

17 Young people and the Internet

Irene Connolly

CHAPTER OVERVIEW

Developmental psychology examines the areas of cognitive, physical and language development, alongside social and emotional development in young people. This chapter presents these developmental areas in relation to a young person's interaction with the Internet. Research on social development demonstrates that the Internet offers entertainment and communication while cognitively providing an outlet for critical thinking and creativity. Online communication on social media provides a forum for social growth but also exposes young people to the risk of cyberbullying. An examination of the emotional and psychological effect of being a cybervictim as well as the role of anonymity, disinhibition and the bystander in cyberbullying will be presented.

KEY TERMS

Young people today are technologically savvy, embracing technology as part of their lives both from a social and learning perspective. The debate focuses on whether technology plays a positive or negative role in young people's lives. This chapter will focus on the **social and emotional development** of young people through the use of technology and also the risks they may encounter such as cyberbullying. Research has shown the average ages of first technological usage, with the owning of a mobile phone in Europe at 9 years of age and receiving a smartphone at 10 years old. Both are higher than the age of starting to use the Internet at 8 years of age. The Net Children Go Mobile study (2014) found that one third of 9–10 year olds have a Social Networking Site (SNS), with this percentage increasing to 90 per cent for older teenagers (Mascheroni & Ólafsson, 2014). In developed countries, pre-schoolers are also going online and most babies under the age of two have an **online presence**. The technology being used by young people today varies tremendously, including instant messaging (IM), blogs, SNSs, video or photo sharing and online computer games and virtual worlds, mobile phones and smart phones. Hence, the term **digital natives** (Prensky, 2001) in reference to young people's ease with technology, and **bedroom culture** where a great deal of this technological use occurs (Livingstone & Bovill, 2001) are now commonplace.

FIGURE 17.1 Young people use mobile phones

(Thomas Purcell)

THE POSITIVE ROLE OF TECHNOLOGY

From a positive perspective, young people use technology as an educational aid, for social interaction, play and creativity. The use of technology in the classroom is recognised as a fundamental learning tool which stimulates the language, cognitive and social development of young children (Couse & Chen, 2010). Digital technology allows children to easily apply concepts in an assortment of circumstances (Uden & Dix, 2000). It exposes them to an environment of activities and information that would be impossible without computers. According to Haugland and Wright (1997), it is the active participation of developmentally suitable computer practices for young children which provides knowledge through active participation, while simultaneously promoting intrinsic motivation through challenge and inquisitiveness. Furthermore, it is used by adolescents as an educational tool in seeking information about health and sex. Young people are more likely to seek this information online if it is not available from personal face-to-face sources like friends or family (Ngo *et al.*, 2008). Technology connects children to the world, by providing access to people and resources throughout the world.

The educational experience is one part of the draw towards technology for young people. Adolescents, in comparison to younger children, spend more time interacting with their friends than they do with their parents (Rubin *et al.*, 2006). Socialising with their peers and developing their own identities within the online world increases during the adolescent years. Adolescents are predominantly using the Internet to bolster offline relationships (Subrahmanyam & Greenfield, 2008). Communication of offline relationships and online relationships are strongly correlated, with adolescents interacting with people with whom they are familiar. Facebook 'friends' are usually offline friends also (boyd, 2008). Usually, young people use social networking environments to preserve current friendships rather than initiating new friendships (Subrahmanyam & Greenfield, 2008). Furthermore, self-disclosure through online communication can enhance the quality of youths' friendships (Valkenburg & Peter, 2009). Valkenburg and Peter's (2007, 2009) studies of Dutch adolescents found positive relationships between frequent IM communication and friendship quality. The researchers reported that the friendship quality increased when friendships had originated offline and IM supplemented offline interactions through self-disclosure. This was also supported by Blais *et al.* (2008) who found over a one-year longitudinal study of 884 adolescents and emerging adults in Canada that frequent instant messaging (IM) communication was positively associated with the quality of best friendships.

Identity

During adolescence identity formation is paramount, where young people reassess their childhood identifications as their awareness of societal values increases (Erikson, 1968). Changes to one's identity during this period are influenced dually by societal practices and cognitive changes. Now operating within the formal operations level of cognitive development (Piaget, 1981) permits the young person to begin to form an identity of themselves, encapsulating their role within society. The ability to adopt new and varied social roles magnifies the possibilities available to them as they form their self-theory. Today, the Internet provides individuals with even more options for identity experimentation. The increase in online communication for young people appears to encapsulate an appreciated image of oneself, which supports and is supported by one's peers (Livingstone, 2008a). Friends' replies are often strongly affirming, contributing reciprocated acknowledgment in the peer network (Valkenburg *et al.*, 2006). For example, receiving positive feedback from your friends online can boost self-confidence and, conversely, a negative comment can badly affect your self-image.

Social networking provides them with an opportunity to overcome the awkwardness related to face-to-face communication. This may be due to the fact that social networking provides asynchronous, evasive or playful communication where misinterpretation and insinuation is more manageable (Livingstone, 2008a).

Some research suggests that the online identity expressed by young people is congruent with their offline identity (boyd, 2007, 2008). Young people use their blogs to record and reflect on their daily practices, personal relationships and attitudes (Scheidt, 2006). As in offline contexts, young people's online self-expressions are affected by the nature of their peer relations. However, in relation to younger and older adolescents Livingstone (2008) found differences in the methods by which they represented themselves online. While the younger adolescents developed and frequently revamped intricate layout designs, where they concentrated on the visual appearance and content of their profile page, the older adolescents adopted a discreet profile which focused on peer connections, emphasising links and messages within friendship groups. Furthermore, research by Schmitt et al. (2008) in an examination of online identity expressions of 8- to 17-year-olds who kept a personal homepage. Within the pre-adolescents' age group, new identities were explored more frequently on their homepages than older adolescents. With the older adolescents, exploring their existing identities online. This was also found in a survey of Dutch youth aged 9–18 who participated in IM and online chat rooms (Valkenburg et al., 2005) that younger adolescents tended to experiment with their identities more than older adolescents. In addition, the topic that pre-adolescents concentrated on were their personal skills and accomplishments, with the older adolescents concentrating on expression of values and personality traits and their relationships (Schmitt et al. 2008). Increases of complexity on the homepage from age 8 to 17 were ascribed to specific skills such as abstract reasoning and the increased language complexity of adolescence.

GAMING

Alongside the developmental changes which occur through playing games, the fun involved plays an important role in a young person's development and is highly motivating. Much experimentation occurs through game playing and affords opportunities for language and cognitive development. This occurs when young people experiment with areas such as problem solving, the formation of thought constructs or providing cultural understanding (Fromberg, 1992; Vygotsky, 1976). A vital component to game playing is the element of fun. Gaming, whether video or computer based, provides all the elements which constitute play. Parents and professionals continue to monitor whether the violence children see in video and computer games may manifest in the real world, in the form of aggressive acts and desensitisation to aggression (Funk, 2005). While some research suggests a sizeable and reliable effect of violent games on aggressive beliefs and behaviours (Anderson, 2004), there exists contradicting research which suggests that any detrimental effects of interactive games are minor or the evidence is mixed (Browne & Hamilton-Giachritsis, 2005). Older children and adolescents may understand that violent video game play is simply a form of play; they distinguish fantasy aggression and violence from real-world behaviour that includes intent to harm a real victim (Malliet, 2006). According to catharsis theory, playing violent video games could provide a safe outlet for aggressive and angry feelings (Griffiths, 2000). It is possible that adolescent boys can explore aggression without causing harm through their video game play (Pellegrini, 2003; Pellegrini & Smith, 1998). Ferguson & Olson (2014) examined whether children with pre-existing mental health problems may be influenced adversely by exposure to violent games; even if other children are not, they found no evidence for increased bullying or delinquent behaviours among youth with clinically elevated mental health symptoms who also played violent video games.

Many games require social and emotional skills to play the game at the maximum level; these skills are also necessary to succeed in the workplace and adult life (Hromek & Roffey, 2009). Prosocial skills include controlling negative emotions, taking turns and sharing, and also support orientations to others that are reasonable and respectful. Furthermore, Massively Multiplayer Online Games encourage social links among players, creating a community constructed on cooperation (Cole and Griffiths, 2007). The positive effect of gaming is further reinforced by research. Colwell & Kato (2003) found links between interactive game play and social and emotional well-being of adolescents. Others have theorised that video games, including those with violent content, can potentially benefit adolescents (Gelfond & Salonius-Pasternak, 2005; Kirsh, 2003). In the real world, young people experiment with various roles in relation to social situations with both peers and parents. Through the use of gaming they can experience situations where they create, break and negotiate rules. The world of gaming can provide these young people with situations not typically experienced in the real world, where video game play may expedite examination of rules and their aftermath (Scarlett et al., 2004). Continuing with this theme of providing a safe haven for role and identity exploration, even violent games provide a safe place to experiment with emotions and roles that may be unacceptable in daily life (Jansz, 2005).

Malliet (2006) through the use of interviews on the perceptions of video/computer game realism of 32 Belgian older teens and young adults found that players made nuanced distinctions between the context of the game world and the context of reality. This finding is also confirmed by the work of Olson et al. (2008) where young people clearly differentiated between antisocial or violent behaviours that were unlikely to occur in their lives such as using guns or killing someone and those that were likely to occur such as verbal abuse. The results are suggestive of the 'third person effect' where the belief exists that other people are more susceptible to the influence of media messages. Violent video games incorporate realistic situations and consequences, with older children and adolescents understanding that violent video game play is simply a form of play. They have the ability to differentiate between fantasy aggression and violence from real world behaviour that involves intent to injure a real target. Earlier research by Olson et al. (2007) of children aged 12–14 suggested that both boys and girls who frequently played mature-rated games (age 17 and up) were more likely to use games as a medium in which they expressed their anger and a method to relax (Olson et al., 2007). In addition, a telephone survey of 11–13 year olds revealed that they felt that same-age peers and younger children were more likely to be affected by violent video games (Scharrer & Leone, 2006). Boys felt that violent video games may have a destructive effect on younger siblings, as they may not be able to differentiate between fictional and real life. As a result, they may carry over attitudes or behaviours from the game into real life. This concern is in line with research showing that children

FIGURE 17.2 Playing computer games

(Thomas Purcell)

under 9 years of age may indeed confuse media images with reality (Villani *et al.*, 2005). A concern regarding the types or amounts of video game play could affect emotions, cognition, perceptions and behaviours in ways that promote bullying and victimisation (Olson, 2004). Mascheroni & Ólafsson (2014) in the Net Children Go Mobile research reported that the youngest children (ages 9–10) are more likely to report being cyberbullied on a gaming website.

CYBERBULLYING

Cyberbullying has been defined as 'an aggressive, intentional act carried out by a group or individual, using electronic forms of contact, repeatedly and over time against a victim who cannot easily defend him or herself' (Smith *et al.*, 2008, p. 376). Research suggests that it is increasingly placing pressure on the psychological welfare of adolescents (Mason, 2008). Studies carried out provide the prevalence rates of cyberbullying for young people and also its effect both physically and psychologically (Corcoran *et al.*, 2012). Research has indicated that cyberbullying is more common in European countries that have pre-existing high levels of traditional bullying, rather than in countries where the Internet is more established (Livingstone *et al.*, 2010). This suggests that cyberbullying is another aspect of traditional bullying rather than something completely separate to it (Cassidy *et al.*, 2013; Hinduja & Patchin, 2012; O'Moore, 2012). It would appear that technological advancement is in effect providing another podium for bullies to target victims.

Unlike traditional bullying, cyberbullying does not involve face-to-face or physical confrontation. It does not require any close proximity to the cybervictim and can be conducted from any location. There is little escape from it: the cyberbullying can occur at any time as long as the cybervictim is accessing technology. Slonje *et al.* (2012) have suggested that, as with traditional bullying, cyberbullying represents an imbalance of power. In the case of cyberbullying, two possible factors in the power imbalance are the role of anonymity and technological prowess. Anonymity seems to embolden the cyberbully; the belief that they cannot be identified seems to remove social inhibition and norms (Hinduja & Patchin, 2006), resulting in **online disinhibition** (Suler, 2004) where young people say and do things online that they might never do face to face. Vandebosch and Van Cleemput (2008) argued that technological ability also contributes to the cyberbullying power imbalance as their research found that those who displayed deviant behaviour online and through mobile phones were more technically capable. Furthermore, students who were classed as cyberbullies categorised themselves as Internet experts compared to those who were not involved in cyberbullying episodes (Ybarra & Mitchell, 2004). Dooley *et al.* (2009) put forward an argument that a further power imbalance exists within cyberbullying which is the permanency of materials in the cyber world and the difficulties associated with attempting to remove it, hence contributing to the powerlessness of the cybervictim.

Under closer examination, it becomes apparent that many of the online behaviours may be variations of real-life behaviour now being carried out online. The following are methods used by cyberbullies in the execution of cyberbullying. First, *flaming*, an online fight with one person or a group, where the exchange is usually vulgar and explicit. This is similar to a real-world argument. *Denigration* involves sending or posting gossip or rumours about a person to damage his or her reputation or friendships. The equivalent real-world action is gossiping. *Social exclusion* is similar to the traditional form of exclusionary bullying, where one person is left out of the social group. In the cyberbullying context this occurs by being deleted from social network sites (Willard, 2004) or no longer involved in IM. In addition, there are also cyberbullying methods that are solely technologically based, such as *outing and trickery*: tricking someone into giving embarrassing information and either posting it online, or sending it on to others. *Masquerading/impersonation/fraping* is pretending to be someone else by obtaining access to their social media page/mobile phone so they can alter information about that person's status or send damaging messages to other people. *Cyberstalking* is repeated, intense harassment that includes threats or creates significant fear. An example of this is a young person receiving a multitude of e-mails/posts from the same person with whom they don't wish to have a conversation. It may continue despite a lack of response from the cybervictim. *Happy slapping* involves videotaping events and uploading these to a website. This form of bullying has progressed from being inoffensive to a serious type of cyberviolence. It involves the digital recording of an act of violence, followed by its uploading to the Internet (Willard, 2004). A further complication to these methods outlined above is the emergence of new technological apps/software to the market which allows young people to send photos/videos or texts to others but which can be deleted from the recipient's device after 10 seconds. Therefore, no evidence of the material sent to the cybervictim can retrieve it, if a cybervictimisation event has occurred.

Psychological effects of cybervictimisation

Research has begun to investigate the consequences of cybervictimisation where the magnitude of the effect on the cybervictims could be related to the potential audience to their harassment (Slonje, 2011; Slonje & Smith, 2008). Early research by Beran and Li (2005) of 432 Canadian students in grades 7–9 found the following psycho-social outcomes of being the victim of cyberbullying. The cybervictims reported anger, anxiety and feeling sad, but the cybervictims also reported that they found it difficult to concentrate in school, affecting both their learning ability and their consequential success at school. In addition, Hinduja and Patchin (2009) in a study of almost 2,000 middle-school students in the US also found that the cybervictims reported similar effects of anger and sadness, but also being frustrated and even scared following a cyberbullying episode. In addition, this research revealed that the self-esteem of both the cyberbullies and cybervictims were lower than their counterparts who were not involved in bullying.

Leading on from the psycho-social consequences of cybervictimisation is the negative effect that cyberbullying can have on a young person's mental health. Some of the earliest research on the psychological damage of cyberbullying by Ybarra (2004) reported a link between cybervictimisation and depressive symptoms. Within traditional bullying, the term 'bullycide', or suicide as a consequence of bullying, has been reported extensively (Bender, 2008; Marr & Field, 2001) with Hinduja and Patchin (2010) coining the term 'cyberbullicide' to describe suicide that occurs indirectly or directly through experiences of online aggression. In a study of 20,000 young people, Kessel Schneider et al. (2012) highlighted the connection between victimisation and psycho-logical stress, and as with Beran and Li (2005) found that cybervictimisation had a negative effect on school success. Their research found that one-third of students who were cyberbullied in the past 12 months reported symptoms of depression, a figure which rose to nearly one-half for those who experienced both cyber and traditional bullying. Suicide attempts for cybervictims were 9.4 per cent compared to 2 per cent for those not involved in cyberbullying as either a victim or bully. Higher percentage of suicide attempts was reported for those who were victims to both traditional and cyberbullying combined (15.2 per cent). Kessel Schneider et al. (2012) reported that cyberbullying in this study was assessed as part of a larger study on adolescent health rather than a specific study on cyberbullying. The researchers found a definition of cyberbullying was difficult to ascertain due to the constant emergence of new technology. They further stressed that as a result of the cross-sectional nature of the analysis neither causality nor temporality to the relation between bullying and distress could be offered. However, the distribution of the questionnaires as paper versions rather than online did not favour more technically able participants.

A survey in 2007 by Hinduja and Patchin of 1,963 middle-school students in the US of Internet use and experiences (Hinduja & Patchin, 2010) similarly found that young people who experienced cyberbullying, as either the bully or victim, had more suicidal thoughts and were more likely to attempt suicide than controls. Victimisation was more strongly related to suicidal thoughts and behaviours than offending. Cyberbullying victims were 1.9 times more likely and cyberbullying offenders were 1.5 times more likely to have attempted suicide than those who were not cyber-bullying at all. Again this research provides evidence of the potential damage that being cyber-victimised can produce. There is also evidence that victims of bullying in online environments report increased school truancy (Katzer *et al.*, 2009), diminished academic performance (Beran & Li, 2007), and feelings that school is no longer a safe place (Varjas *et al.*, 2009). Suicidal thoughts also appear to be directly correlated with both real-world (Kim *et al.*, 2005) and cyberbullying experiences (Klomek *et al.*, 2009).

CONCLUSION

Technology has become part of young people's lives. Parents and teachers need to guide them from a very early age, with regard to acceptable online behaviour and also of the dangers that exist there. The positive aspects of technological use are vast and increasing steadily. Cognitive development, social and emotional development, alongside linguistic development all occur through the use of technology. Further enhancement can occur through increased student motivation to learn, exploration of one's identity and of dangerous situations within the safe confines of the online world. While some risks do still exist, in particular with reference to the risks that anonymity and disinhibition play in cyberbullying and also the violence within video games. Specific attention for 'at risk' children is required as a result of increasing evidence that those low in self-esteem, or without satisfying friendships or relations with parents, are at risk through online social networking communication (Livingstone & Helsper, 2007; Ybarra & Mitchell, 2004) and that those at risk may also be those who then perpetrate harm towards others. Finally, a lack of distinction must also be made between how a young person behaves in the online world and their behaviour in the real world. One way to assist this would be the removal of anonymity in the online world. This would contribute to making the online world a more pleasurable place for all.

ACTIVITY

Technology offers wonderful opportunities for learning, working, sharing and having fun. It is a big part of young people's lives and their future. Design a board game (old-fashioned approach) highlighting the positives and negatives of technology. Then explore how this game could be implemented online, highlighting safety and responsibility online.

DISCUSSION QUESTIONS

1 If a young person reports a bullying incidence, what steps should be taken to resolve the issues?
2 Technology is part of a young person's social development. Do you think it is possible to live without technology in our society today? Support your answer.

3 Why do children and young people enjoy online gaming? Give examples using games that you play.

4 Should parents have access to a young person's online world? Or is this a breach of their privacy?

RECOMMENDED READING LIST

Sonia Livingstone and Moira Bovill have written extensively in the area. This book focuses on the meanings, uses and impacts of new media in childhood, family life, peer culture, and the relation between home and school.

Livingstone, S. & Bovill, M. (eds). (2013). *Children and their Changing Media Environment: A European Comparative Study.* London: Routledge.

The Net Children Go Mobile research gathers data from seven European countries on the use of technology by young people. It can also be compared to previous research carried out by the EU Kids Online research. Retrieved from: www.lse.ac.uk/media@lse/research/EUKidsOnline/Home.aspx.

Mascheroni, G. & Ólafsson, K. (2014). Net children go mobile: risks and opportunities. Educatt. Available at: www.netchildrengomobile.eu/.

Cheryl Olson writes about whether children should play video games and how to maximise potential benefits and to identify and minimise potential harms.

Olson, C.K. (2010). Children's motivations for video game play in the context of normal development. *Review of General Psychology, 14*(2), 180.

Justin Patchin and Sameer Hinduja have produced a great deal of research on cyberbullying in the United States. This book provides an amalgamation of their work to date.

Patchin, J.W. & Hinduja, S. (2012). An update and synthesis of the research. *Cyberbullying Prevention and Response: Expert Perspectives*, 13.

GLOSSARY

Anonymity   Nobody can identify you online.

Bedroom culture   Where young people spend large amounts of time using technology in their bedroom, away from the family unit.

Cyberbullying   Various types of bullying that occur using technology.

Digital natives   Native speakers of the digital language of computers, video games and the Internet.

Identity formation   Where young people reassess their childhood identifications as their awareness of societal values increases.

Online disinhibition The online disinhibition effect was coined by Suler (2004). It refers to a loosing or removal of social inhibitions when interacting online that would normally be present in face-to-face communication.

Online gaming Playing video games over a computer network, often with other players.

Online presence Any existence of an individual or business that can be found via an online search.

Social and emotional development Experience, expression and management of emotions, and the ability to establish positive and rewarding relationships with others.

REFERENCES

Anderson C.A. (2004). An update on the effects of playing violent video games. *Journal of Adolescence, 27,* 113–22.

Bender, J. (2008). Bullycide: The only escape for some brutalized children with disabilities. *The Cutting Edge.* Retrieved from: www.thecuttingedgenews.com/index.php?article=460.

Beran, T. & Li, Q. (2005). Cyber-harassment: A study of a new method for an old behaviour. *Journal of Educational Computing Research, 32*(3), 265–277. Doi: 10.2190/8YQM-BO4H-PG4D-BLLH.

Beran, T. & Li, Q. (2007). The relationship between cyber bullying and school bullying. *Journal of Student Wellbeing, 1,* 15–33.

Blais, J.J., Craig, W.M., Pepler, D. & Connolly, J. (2008). Adolescents online: The importance of internet activity choices to salient relationships. *Journal of Youth and Adolescence, 37*(5), 522–536.

boyd, d. (2007). The significance of social software. In T.N. Burg & J. Schmidt (eds), *Blog Talks Reloaded: Social Software Research & Cases* (pp. 15–30). Books on Demand: Norderstedt, Germany.

boyd, d. (2008). Facebook's privacy train wreck: Exposure, invasion, and social convergence. *Convergence, 14*(1), 13–20.

Browne, K.D. & Hamilton-Giachritsis, C. (2005). The influence of violent media on children and adolescents: A public-health approach. *Lancet, 365,* 702–710.

Cassidy, W., Faucher, C. & Jackson, M. (2013). Cyberbullying among youth: A comprehensive review of current international research and its implications and application to policy and practice. *School Psychology International: Special Issue on Cyberbullying, 34*(6), 575–612.

Cole, H. & Griffiths, M. (2007). Social interaction in massively multiplayer online role-playing games. *CyberPsychology & Behavior, 10,* 575–583.

Colwell, J. & Kato, M. (2003). Investigation of the relationship between social isolation, self-esteem, aggression and computer game play in Japanese adolescents. *Asian Journal of Social Psychology, 6,* 149–158.

Corcoran, L., Connolly, I. & O'Moore, M. (2012). Cyberbullying in Irish schools: An investigation of personality and self-concept. *Irish Journal of Psychology, 33*(1–4), 153–165.

Couse, L. J. & Chen, D.W. (2010). A tablet computer for young children? Exploring its viability for early childhood education. *Journal of Research on Technology in Education, 43*(1), 75–89.

Dooley, J.J., Pyzalksi, J. & Cross, D. (2009). Cyberbullying versus face to face bullying: A theoretical and conceptual review. *Journal of Psychology, 217*(4), 182–188. doi: 10.1027/0044-3409.217.4.182.

Erikson, E. (1968). *Identity: Youth and Crisis.* W.W. Norton & Company: New York.

Ferguson, C.J. & Olson, C.K. (2014). Video game violence use among 'vulnerable' populations: The impact of violent games on delinquency and bullying among children with clinically elevated depression or attention deficit symptoms. *Journal of Youth and Adolescence, 43*(1), 127–136.

Fromberg, D.P. (1992). A review of research on play. In Seefeldt, C. (ed.), *The Early Childhood Curriculum: A Review of Current Research* (2nd edn). New York: Teachers College Press.

Funk, J.B. (2005). Children's exposure to violent video games and desensitization to violence. *Child and Adolescent Psychiatric Clinics of North America, 14*(3), 387–404.

Gelfond, H.S. & Salonius-Pasternak, D.E. (2005). The play's the thing: A clinical-developmental perspective on video games. *Child and Adolescent Psychiatric Clinics of North America, 14*, 491–508.

Griffiths, M.D. (2000). Does internet and computer 'addiction' exist? Some case study evidence. *CyberPsychology and Behavior, 3*, 211–218.

Haugland, S. & Wright, J. (1997). *Young Children and Technology: A World of Discovery.* New York: Allyn & Bacon.

Hinduja, S. & Patchin, J.W. (2006). Bullies move beyond the schoolyard: A preliminary look at cyberbullying. *Youth Violence and Juvenile Justice, 4*(2), 148–169.

Hinduja, S. & Patchin, J.W. (2009). *Bullying Beyond the Schoolyard: Preventing and Responding to Cyberbullying.* Thousand Oaks, CA: Sage Publications.

Hinduja, S. & Patchin, J. (2010). Bullying, cyberbullying and suicide. *Archives of Suicide Research, 14*(3), 206–221.

Hinduja, S. & Patchin, J. (2012). Cyberbullying: Neither an epidemic nor a rarity. *European of Journal Developmental Psychology, 9*, 520–538. doi: 10.1080/17405629.2012.706448.

Hromek, R. & Roffey, S. (2009). Promoting social and emotional learning with games. "its fun and we learn things". *Simulat Gaming – Simulation & Gaming, 40*(5), 626–644.

Jansz, J. (2005). The emotional appeal of violent video games for adolescent males. *Communication Theory, 15*, 219–241.

Katzer, C., Fetchenhauer, D. & Belschak, F. (2009). Cyberbullying: Who are the victims? A comparison of victimization in internet chatrooms and victimization in school. *Journal of Media Psychology: Theories, Methods, and Applications, 21*(1), 25–36. doi: 10.1027/1864-1105.21.1.25.

Kessel Schneider, S., O'Donnell, L., Stueve, A. & Coulter, R.W.S. (2012). Cyberbullying, school bullying, and psychological distress: A regional census of high school students. *American Journal of Public Health, 102*(1), 171–177.

Kim, Y.S., Koh, Y.J. & Leventhal, B. (2005). School bullying and suicidal risk in Korean middle school students. *Pediatrics, 115*(2), 357–63.

Kirsh S.J. (2003). The effects of violent video games on adolescents: The overlooked influence of development. *Aggressive Violent Behaviour*, 8, 377–89.

Klomek, A.B., Sourander, A., Niemela, S., Kumpulainen, K., Piha, J., Tamminen, T., Almgvist, F. & Gould, M.S. (2009). Childhood bullying behaviours as a risk for suicide attempts and completed suicides: A population-based birth cohort study. *Journal of the American Academy of Child and Adolescent Psychiatry*, 48(3), 254–61. doi: 10.1097/CHI.0b013e3181 96b91f.

Livingstone, S. (2008). Engaging with media – a matter of literacy? *Communication, Culture and Critique*, 1(1), 51–62.

Livingstone, S. (2008a). Internet literacy: Young people's negotiation of new online opportunities. In T. McPherson (ed.), *Digital Youth, Innovation, and the Unexpected* (pp. 101–122). Cambridge, MA: The MIT Press.

Livingstone, S. & Bovill, M. (2001). *Children and their Changing Media Environment*. Abingdon: Routledge.

Livingstone, S. & Helsper, E. (2007) Gradations in digital inclusion: Children, young people and the digital divide. *New Media & Society*, 9(4), 671–696. doi: 10.1177/14614448 07080335.

Livingstone, S., Haddon, L., Gorzig, A. & Olafsson, K. (2010). *Risks and Safety on the Internet: The Perspective of European Children: Full Findings*. London: LSE.

Malliet, S. (2006). An exploration of adolescents' perceptions of videogame realism. *Learning, Media and Technology*, 31(4), 377–394.

Marr, N. & Field, T. (2001). *Bullycide: Death at Playtime* (1st edn). Didcot: Success Unlimited.

Mascheroni, G. and Ólafsson, K. (2014). *Net Children Go Mobile: Risks and Opportunities*. Milan: Educatt.

Mason, K.L. (2008). Cyberbullying: A preliminary assessment for school personnel. *Psychology in Schools*, 45(4), 323–348. Doi: 10.1002/pits.20301.

Ngo, A.D., Ross, M.W. & Ratliff, E.A. (2008). Internet influences on sexual practices among young people in Hanoi, Vietnam. *Culture, Health Sexuality*, 10, S201–S213.

Ólafsson, K., Livingstone, S. & Haddon, L. (2013). *Children's Use of Online Technologies in Europe: A Review of the European Evidence Base*. London: LSE.

Olson, C.K. (2004). Media violence research and youth violence data: Why do they conflict? *Acad Psychiatry*, 28, 144–50.

Olson, C.K., Kutner, L.A., Warner, D.E., Almerigi, J., Baer, L., Nicholi, A.M. (2007). Factors correlated with violent video game use by adolescent boys and girls. *Journal of Adolescent Health*, 41, 77–83.

Olson, C.K., Kutner, L.A., Warner, D.E. (2008). Development: Boys' perspectives the role of violent video game content in adolescent. *Journal of Adolescent Research*, 23, 55–75. doi: 10.1177/0743558407310713.

O'Moore, M. (2012). Cyberbullying: The situation in Ireland. *Pastoral Care in Education: An International Journal of Personal, Social and Emotional Development*, 30(3), 209–223.

Pellegrini, A.D. (2003). Perceptions and functions of play and real fighting in early adolescence. *Child Development*, 74, 1522–1533.

Pellegrini, A.D. & Smith, P.K. (1998). The development of play during childhood: Forms and possible functions. *Child Psychology and Psychiatry Review, 3*, 51–57. doi: 10.1111/1475–3588.00212.

Piaget, J. (1981). *Intelligence and Affectivity: Their Relationship During Child Development.* Palo Alto, CA: Annual Reviews.

Prensky, M. (2001). Digital natives, digital immigrants. Part 1. *On the Horizon, 9*(5), 1–6.

Rubin, K.H., Bukowski, W. & Parker, J. (2006). Peer interactions, relationships, and groups. In N. Eisenberg (ed.), *Handbook of Child Psychology* (6th ed.), *Social, Emotional, and Personality Development.* New York: Wiley.

Scarlett, W.G., Naudeau, S., Salonius-Pasternak, D.E. & Ponte, I.C. (2004). *Children's Play.* Thousand Oaks, CA: Sage.

Scharrer, E. & Leone, R. (2006). I know you are but what am I? Young people's perceptions of varying types of video game influence. *Mass Communication and Society, 9*, 261–286.

Scheidt, L.A. (2006). Adolescent diary weblogs and the unseen audience. *Digital Generations: Children, Young People, and the New Media*, 193–210.

Schmitt, K.L., Dayanim, S. & Matthias, S. (2008). Personal homepage construction as an expression of social development. *Developmental Psychology, 44*(2), 496.

Slonje, R. (2011). The nature of cyberbullying in Swedish schools: Processes, feelings of remorse by bullies, impact on victims and age and gender differences. Unpublished Ph.D. thesis, Goldsmiths, University of London.

Slonje, R. & Smith, P.K. (2008). Cyberbullying: Another main type of bullying? *Scandinavian Journal of Psychology, 49*, 147–154.

Slonje, R., Smith, P.K. & Frisen, A. (2012). The nature of cyberbullying and strategies for prevention. *Computers in Human Science.* Retrieved from: www.melissaagnes.com/wp-content/uploads/2012/10/Slonje-Cyberbullying.pdf.

Smith, P.K., Mahdavi, J., Carvalho, M., Fisher, S., Russell, S. & Tippett, N. (2008). Cyberbullying: Its nature and impact in secondary school pupils. *Journal of Child Psychology and Psychiatry, 49*(4), 376–385.

Subrahmanyam, K. & Greenfield, P.M. (2008). Online communication and adolescent relationships. *Future Child, 18*, 119–146.

Suler, J. (2004). The online disinhibition effect. *CyberPsychology and Behavior, 7*(3), 321–326. Doi: 10.1089/1094931041291295.

Uden, L. & Dix, A. (2000). Iconic interfaces for kids on the Internet. Proceedings of IFIP World Computer Congress, Beijing, 279–286.

Valkenburg, P.M. & Peter, J. (2007). Online communication and adolescent well-being: Testing the stimulation versus the displacement hypothesis. *Journal of Computer Mediated Communication, 12*, 1169–1182. doi: 10.1111/j.1083–6101.2007.00368.x.

Valkenburg, P.M. & Peter, J. (2009). Social consequences of the internet for adolescents a decade of research. *Current Directions in Psychological Science, 18*(1), 1–5.

Valkenburg, P.M., Schouten, A.P. & Peter, J. (2005). Adolescents' identity experiments on the Internet. *New Media & Society, 7*(3), 382–402.

Valkenburg, P.M., Peter, J. & Schouten, A.P. (2006). Friend networking sites and their relationship to adolescents' well-being and social self-esteem. *CyberPsychology & Behavior, 9*(5), 584–590.

Vandebosch, H. & Van Cleemput, K. (2008). Defining cyberbullying: A qualitative research into the perceptions of youngsters. *CyberPsychology & Behavior, 11*, 499–503.

Varjas, K., Henrich, C.C. & Meyers, J. (2009). Urban middle school students' perceptions of bullying, cyberbullying, and school safety. *Journal of School Violence, 8*(2), 159–176.

Villani, S.V., Olson, C.K. & Jellinek, M.S. (2005). Media literacy for clinicians and parents. *Child and Adolescent Psychiatric Clinics of North America, 14*, 523–544.

Vygotsky, L.S. (1976). Play and its role in the mental development of the child. In J.S. Bruner, A. Jolly & K. Sylvia (eds). *Play – Its role in Development and Evolution*, 537–554. New York: Basic Books.

Willard, N. (2004). *Educator's Guide to Cyberbullying: Addressing the Harm Caused by Online Social Cruelty*. Retrieved from: www.asdk12.org/MiddleLink/AVB/bully_topics/Educators Guide_Cyberbullying.pdf.

Ybarra, M.L. (2004). Linkages between depressive symptomology and Internet harassment among young regular Internet users. *CyberPsychology and Behavior, 7*, 247–257.

Ybarra, M.L. & Mitchell, K.J. (2004). Youth engaging in online harassment: Associations with caregiver child relationships, Internet use, and personal characteristics. *Journal of Adolescence, 27*, 319–336.

4 | Psychology and technology

18 Human–Computer Interaction

Andrew Errity

CHAPTER OVERVIEW

This chapter commences with a brief coverage of the history of Human-Computer Interaction (HCI) and the current state of the field, in particular addressing the variety of terminology used and the variety of disciplinary perspectives. It will then look at how HCI principles are applied in practice and provide appropriate examples. There will then be a discussion on the relationship between HCI and cyberpsychology, noting the key contributions each field can make. The chapter will conclude with a summary of the key points for students and attempt to set the context for future developments.

KEY TERMS

The field of HCI is concerned with the study, design and testing of interactive computer systems that exist at the point where humans and computers meet. This point, the **interface**, is typically a **Graphical User Interface** (GUI) that uses elements including text, icons, buttons and windows to communicate information to the user and allows the user to interact with the interface using devices such as a mouse, keyboard, touchscreen, etc. It is vital to consider both the **usability** and **User Experience** (UX) of an interface. Usability refers to the extent to which users can achieve specified goals with effectiveness, efficiency and satisfaction using an interface, while UX specifically refers to how a user feels when interacting with an interface.

INTRODUCTION

What is Human–Computer Interaction?

The goal of HCI is to create interactive Computer Mediated experiences that are satisfying, effective, efficient and useful. Those working in the field study the ways in which humans interact with computers in order to develop new and better interaction paradigms, models and theories.

The use and meaning of the term Human–Computer Interaction has evolved over its history. It has beginnings rooted in the more general terms 'human–machine interaction' and 'man–machine interaction' that refer to the interaction of humans and some form of physical machine – for example, in a manufacturing plant. With the growth of computing the more specific term Human–Computer Interaction emerged. The following is a classic and useful definition of the term: 'Human–computer interaction is a discipline concerned with the design, evaluation and implementation of interactive computing systems for human use and with the study of major phenomena surrounding them' (ACM SIGCHI, 1992, p. 5).

As someone reading a cyberpsychology textbook this will likely sound somewhat familiar. The fields of cyberpsychology and HCI have much in common. Both involve studying interactions involving humans and technology; however, with cyberpsychology the focus is on the human, rather than the technology, whereas in HCI this balance may be more heavily weighted towards the computer (Norman, 2008).

To provide some context, it is worth considering some typical HCI projects. One example would be the design, implementation and testing of the **interface** of a mobile app for an online social network. There are three key factors that are vital to consider in this, and any other, HCI project:

1   The user: who will be using this interface, what are their characteristics, capabilities and limitations?
2   The computer: what computer system will the user be interacting with, what affordances does it provide (e.g. input and output devices) and what constraints does it impose (e.g. small screen size)?
3   The task: what does the user need from the system; what functionality should it provide?

Not paying sufficient attention to any one of these factors may result in an interface that fails to be *useful* (allows the user to perform a required task), *usable* (the user can perform the task in an efficient manner, e.g. without error, delay, etc.) and *used* (provides an experience that users will want to use, e.g. be satisfying, fun, etc.) (Dix, *et al.* 2004). Each of these three factors could be evaluated during the HCI process in order to gauge the success of the mobile app interface design.

HCI projects can also be more research-focused and experimental in nature. For example, a HCI research project could involve the design, implementation and testing of multiple **prototype** keyboard layouts for text entry on a touchscreen display. Again, the user, computer and task must all be considered in this process. In this case the evaluation could involve measuring the number of words typed per minute or the number of spelling errors made per minute in order to determine which of the prototypes was best and/or to develop some model of human typing performance on a touchscreen display.

The ramifications of producing a poor human–computer interface can be significant. Take the social networking app discussed above as an example. If this app provides an unsatisfactory, frustrating experience the network's customers may move to a competitor, costing the company money. Similarly, if the app is not usable and causes users to make errors – e.g. sharing photos publicly rather than with selected friends – it may have negative consequences for the user. These hypothetical damages may be significant, but the cost of bad HCI can be even more extreme. One classic example of the catastrophic consequences that can result from a poor interface is the partial meltdown that occurred at the Three Mile Island nuclear power plant on 28 March 1979. A number of user interface problems were found to be among the factors contributing to the cause of this event (Stone *et al.*, 2005). For example, Norman (1983) points out that an important instrument that needed to be monitored was mounted on the rear of a control panel.

Who is involved?

HCI is a multidisciplinary field involving a range of areas such as human factors, computer science, cognitive psychology, sociology, communication, design, engineering, information science and – as highlighted above – cyberpsychology. This mix of disciplines makes HCI an extremely interesting, if at times complex, field to work in. When working on HCI projects, one often finds oneself having to read and conduct research in an area outside of one's own specialism. Similarly, such projects often involve working with interdisciplinary teams – e.g. consisting of a software engineer, psychologist, graphic designer and sociologist. Collaborating with individuals from such varying backgrounds and viewpoints can prove a challenge, but can also be a very enjoyable and educational experience.

Going forward, there are likely to be significant opportunities for collaboration between the fields of cyberpsychology and HCI. The knowledge of the human mind and behaviour in the context of human–technology interaction brought to the table by cyberpsychologists will be a useful complement to the skills and knowledge of those working on human–computer interfaces. Cyberpsychologists can provide an insight into the real and potential psychological effects of interface design decisions on the users of these interfaces.

The origins of Human–Computer Interaction

Naturally, the emergence of the HCI field is closely linked to the invention and exponential growth of computers. In order to understand how the HCI field developed and provide some context for its current state, it is useful to consider some of the key milestones in the history of HCI.

Vannevar Bush: as we may think

The roots of the field of HCI can be traced back as far as Vannevar Bush's seminal 1946 article 'As we may think' (Bush, 1945). This article was written at a time before the invention of personal computers, when there were only a small number of early computers in existence, each of which were the size of entire rooms. In 'As We May Think' Bush presents a prescient vision of a future in which computers augment the intellectual ability of humans.

J.C.R. Licklider: man–computer symbiosis

The year 1960 saw the publication of one of the most influential papers in the history of HCI and computer science, Joseph Carl Robnett Licklider's 'Man–computer symbiosis' (Licklider, 1960). In this paper Licklider, a psychologist and computer scientist, stressed the importance of a close, interactive relationship between humans and computer systems. His view was that rather than computers replacing human intelligence, computers could be used to amplify human intellect and free us from mundane tasks. Licklider's ideas would appear much later in the shape of modern GUIs and spoken language systems such as Apple's Siri, a technology that allows users to interact with their computing devices using natural speech.

Ivan Sutherland: Sketchpad

One of the key concepts of the GUIs we are familiar with today is that the user's input is performed directly on the system's output. This is known as direct manipulation and makes the interface much easier to use. This innovation was first implemented by Ivan Sutherland (1963) in his Sketchpad system. Sketchpad allowed a user to use a light pen to draw directly on an oscilloscope display. The graphical objects displayed on the oscilloscope display could also be directly manipulated using the light pen input device, a feature that would later make its way into more modern user interfaces where a mouse would be used rather than a light pen.

Douglas Engelbart: The Mother of All Demos

The ideas of Bush and Licklider were later pursued by inventor and engineer Douglas Engelbart. In 1968 Engelbart gave a lecture at the Fall Joint Computer Conference in San Francisco that has been retroactively named 'The Mother of All Demos'. In this lecture Engelbart gave a live demonstration of a computer system called the oN-Line System (NLS) that contained many of the fundamental elements of modern computer systems and interfaces including bitmapped screens, windows, the mouse, collaborative editors and video conferencing. This demonstration had a massive influence on computing and inspired many similar projects in the future.

Alan Kay and Xerox PARC: Dynabook and Xerox Star

In 1972, Alan Kay proposed (Kay, 1972) a portable personal computing device, named Dynabook, to act as an educational aid to children. This device built on the ideas of Engelbart and early cardboard prototypes of the Dynabook were developed in a tablet form factor that was unachievable in practice using the technologies of the time. Working at Xerox Paulo Alto Research Center (PARC), Kay and others developed this idea over a number of years. This work culminated in 1981 with the release of the Xerox Star, the first commercial system to incorporate elements such as icons, folders, windows, the mouse, Ethernet networking, file and print servers, and email.

Birth of the field

With the advent of the personal computer era in the late 1970s and early 1980s computers became more readily available and spread beyond commercial research labs and university campuses into people's homes and businesses. Computers and humans were beginning to interact on a scale and in a manner that had never been seen before. Thus, the need for the field of HCI became extremely important. This period saw the release of one of the first books on the topic, Ben Shneiderman's (1980) *Software Psychology*, and saw the first conference on Human Factors in Computing Systems take place in the US in 1982 (this would later become the annual **ACM SIGCHI** conference) marking what some consider the formal foundation of the HCI field (Lazar & Feng, 2010). A more detailed account of the history of HCI is provided by Grudin (2012).

The current state of the field

Technological shifts

The field has evolved since the early days described in the previous section. More recent technological advances such as the Web, touchscreens, gestural interfaces, speech recognition and synthesis, virtual reality displays, wearables, augmented reality and gaze tracking have posed new questions and opened new avenues in HCI design and research. One current trend is a move away from GUIs towards **Natural User Interfaces** (NUIs) (Montuschi *et al.*, 2014). The goal of these NUIs is to replace the artificial interfaces we are used to – e.g. using a mouse to manipulate graphical windows on a screen, with natural interfaces that are essentially invisible. For example, spoken language dialogue systems like Apple's Siri and gestural interfaces like Microsoft's Kinect are steps towards this goal of a NUI. A similar, complementary, trend is the rise of ubiquitous computing (also know as pervasive computing). This is the concept of computers becoming embedded everywhere and anywhere within our lives – for example, on our bodies, in our appliances and distributed throughout our environment.

Philosophical shifts

Initially, HCI focused on the **usability** of computer applications, defined by ISO9241–11 (1998) as the 'extent to which a product can be used by specified users to achieve specified goals with effectiveness, efficiency and satisfaction in a specified context of use'. However, in the mid-1990s there was a growing consideration of the broader UX of a product, incorporating the range of feelings and emotions a human has when interacting with the product. This change in focus saw the emergence of a new field, called **Interaction Design** (IxD), defined by Preece *et al.* (2015, p. 8) as 'designing interactive products to support the way people communicate and interact in their everyday and working lives'. This new field is wider in scope than traditional HCI, encompassing the design of any interactive experience. The rising use of these new terms – along with the term 'cyberpsychology' – from the mid-1990s onwards can be seen in Figure 18.1 (Michel *et al.*, 2011).

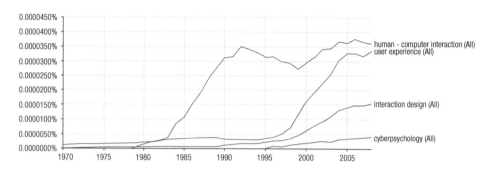

FIGURE 18.1 Number of occurrences of the terms 'human–computer interaction', 'user experience', 'interaction design' and 'cyberpsychology' in books published between 1970 and 2008

HUMAN–COMPUTER INTERACTION IN PRACTICE

The process of designing interactive experiences

As discussed above, the field of HCI is ever-changing: new technologies emerge (changing the 'computer'), users' attitudes, knowledge, experience, expectations, etc. shift (changing the 'user'), and new functionalities and activities are required to be modelled (changing the 'task'). As a result there is no single, universally applicable model for HCI. However, most HCI projects involve a number of fundamental activities (Preece *et al.*, 2015):

1   gathering requirements;
2   designing a solution(s);
3   constructing a prototype(s);
4   evaluating.

These activities are all described in detail in the existing HCI literature but may be discussed in a different order and/or may be referred to using different terminology (Preece *et al.*, 2015; Dix, 2004; Mayhew, 1999).

One key characteristic of this process is that it is iterative. For example, following evaluation a flaw may be identified in the interface. This may require returning to the design stage and continuing from there, or if necessary returning back to the requirements gathering stage and continuing through all four stages again. Another important feature of the process is that each stage provides an input to the next. For example, a prototype constructed at step 3 will be evaluated in step 4. A visual representation of this process is shown in Figure 18.2.

Modern HCI projects often apply a **User-Centred Design (UCD)** approach. UCD involves placing the user at the heart of the design thinking and ensuring that the system designed will fit the needs of the user, rather than the user having to adapt to fit the needs of the system. The nature of this user-centredness varies with each step in the process and will depend on the techniques used at each step. The following sections outline each of the four steps.

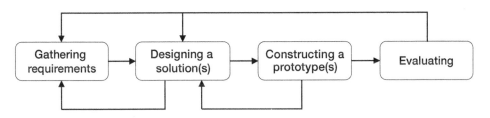

FIGURE 18.2 A process for designing interactive experiences

(adapted from Preece *et al.*, 2015)

Gathering requirements

It is essential to understand each of the three key factors in any HCI project – user, computer and task – before attempting to build the interface. Thus, the initial phase of the project typically involves gathering data about each of these three factors and using this data to inform the subsequent activities.

Task

Before proceeding with the design of an interface we must clearly establish what it is that the interface should do. There may be an obvious need that the interface is addressing or it may require some work to elicit the needs of the user. Preece *et al.* (2015) suggest a range of techniques for establishing requirements, including: interviews, questionnaires, focus groups, direct observation, indirect observation (e.g. getting users to keep diaries) and researching similar products. For example, after holding focus groups with users we may find that some of the requirements of an online dating website include the ability to create a profile, search for a suitable partner, accept or decline a request for a date, control who can see a user's profile and what data can be seen, etc.

When designing an interface to allow the user to perform tasks one must also understand the characteristics of these tasks. Who performs this task? When do they perform it? How frequently is the task performed? What tasks occur before/after this task? Is this task made up of subtasks? If so, how are these subtasks organised? Answers to these questions should be elicited using the techniques listed above. Having established the requirements and these task characteristics it is useful to model and document the task structure, often referred to as the task organisation model. Common approaches to this include: writing an 'informal narrative description' called a **scenario** (Carroll, 2000, p. 41), using the software engineering approach of use cases and use case diagrams (Jacobson *et al.*, 1992), or using the Hierarchical Task Analysis (HTA) approach (Hornsby, 2010).

User

Taking a user-centred approach we must gain an understanding of the characteristics of our target users in order to make optimal design decisions for these users. A key mantra to remember is: 'you are not the user; design for the user not for yourself'. Mayhew (1999) identifies four types of characteristics that should be considered:

psychological characteristics (e.g. attitude and motivation), knowledge and experience (e.g. computer proficiency and task experience), job and task characteristics (e.g. frequency of use and task structure), and physical characteristics (e.g. physical impairments). Data relating to these characteristics is typically gathered using questionnaires distributed to actual users, interviews with actual users, interviews with people knowledgeable about the user population, or ethnographic research (Mayhew, 1999).

Once this user profile data has been gathered, it must be analysed in order to draw high-level conclusions from the data. In some cases it may be evident from the data that there are distinct subgroups with the user population and each may need to be considered separately – e.g. in a hospital, doctors, nurses and administrative staff may display significantly different characteristics. One popular approach to summarising the data for each user group is to construct **user personas**. A user persona is a hypothetical user with the same characteristics, motivations, and goals as the real user population (Calabria, 2004). By giving personas names and photographs our minds can extrapolate to create a coherent picture of a whole person that can be used in our thinking when making design decisions. For example, one hypothetical user persona for an online dating website could be: '35-year-old Jack, whose busy job in the financial sector makes it difficult for him to find time to meet new people . . .' A real persona would flesh out these details to provide a more complete view of this particular type of user.

Computer

Having built a picture of the human, it is necessary to consider the computing **platform** they will be interacting with – i.e. the computer hardware and software that the interface being developed must run on. Both the capabilities and constraints (Mayhew, 1999) of the computing platform should be analysed. For example, if developing a mobile app for a smartphone the capabilities may include: multi-touch screen; high-resolution display, microphone, speaker, haptic feedback (vibration), etc. Whereas the constraints of this platform could include: 5-inch screen size, 8-hour battery life, no mouse, limited multi-tasking, etc. These characteristics of the computing platform have a fundamental impact on the interface that can be implemented.

Designing and prototyping

Once the characteristics of the user, computer and tasks have been established, the iterative process of interface design and prototyping can begin. However, it should be noted that these activities are not isolated away from the previous phase. While designing the interface it may become clear that some requirements have not been adequately captured and it may be necessary to gather more data.

Design guidelines and heuristics

Interfaces are not designed in an intellectual vacuum. The existing wealth of knowledge that has been generated in the HCI field over decades of research studies and commercial interface development projects should be taken into account when designing any new interface. Thankfully, work has been done to examine this large pool of knowledge and derive a set of usability principles, known as **heuristics**, that can be used as 'rules of thumb' (Nielsen, 1995) for interface design. One commonly used set of heuristics were originally developed by Nielsen (1993) based on an analysis of 249 usability problems and later revised to the following (Nielsen, 1995):

1   Visibility of system status.
2   Match between system and the real world.
3   User control and freedom.
4   Consistency and standards.
5   Error prevention.
6   Recognition rather than recall.
7   Flexibility and efficiency of use.
8   Aesthetic and minimalist design.
9   Help users recognise, diagnose and recover from errors.
10 Help and documentation.

In addition to these general usability principles, there may be specific design guidelines that apply to the platform the interface will run on. For example, both Google (2015) and Apple (2015) provide interface design guidelines that should be followed when designing for Android and iOS, their respective mobile platforms. Designing an interface that does not follow these platform guidelines risks breaking the 'consistency and standards' heuristic stated above. Work has been also been done to adapt heuristics such as those listed above to more niche application areas – e.g. virtual reality (Sutcliffe & Gault, 2004).

Prototyping

The design and prototyping tasks go hand-in-hand. Initially, only a **conceptual model** of the interface will be designed. This conceptual model incorporates high-level design decisions such as the overall structure of the interface and the basic interaction paradigm to be used. Once this has been evaluated and validated, as described in the next section, the design can proceed to consider more low-level details such as icons, fonts, menus and graphics.

At each stage of this iterative design process it is vital to construct a manifestation of the design to allow the designer to get a real sense of the interface and, arguably more importantly, they can be given to users for evaluation throughout the HCI process. The manifestation, or prototype, can take many forms – e.g. simple sketch on paper, cardboard mock-up, **low-fidelity prototype** (see example in Figure 18.3), **high-fidelity** prototype, etc. It is common to see a range of different prototypes produced, often starting with low-fidelity prototypes (that don't really resemble the final product, usually built using a different material or technology, as shown in Figure 18.3) and gradually moving to higher-fidelity prototypes (that closely resemble the final interface). The advantages of starting out with low-fidelity prototypes are that they are quicker to construct, promote exploration and facilitate rapid redevelopment. Having users interact with simple low-fidelity paper mockups, known as paper prototyping (Rettig, 1994), is a widespread and valuable technique.

Evaluation

Having constructed an interface it is time to test its usability and the UX it provides. The goals to be tested will vary from project to project but will typically be defined

FIGURE 18.3 An example of a low-fidelity prototype for a mobile social networking app

(created with Balsamiq Mockups: http://balsamiq.com/products/mockups)

in advance. Goals can be categorised as usability goals (e.g. can users perform tasks quickly, without making errors, etc?) and UX goals (e.g. do users find the interface fun and enjoyable to use?).

Preece *et al.* (2015) define three categories of evaluation techniques:

1   *Controlled settings involving users*, for example:
    Usability testing: tests are conducted in a laboratory-style setting. Users are typically given test tasks to perform and data is collected using a range of methods – e.g. questionnaires, observations and interviews. This is a fundamental approach in HCI and many authors have described ways to conduct such tests (Preece *et al.*, 2015; Rubin & Chisnell, 2008; Dix, 2004; Mayhew, 1999). The controlled-nature of the environment also facilitates additional data collection methods such as eye tracking and physiological measurements (e.g. heart and respiration rates).

2   *Uncontrolled settings involving users*, for example:
    Diary studies: users are asked to log their activities in a diary on a regular basis (Lallemand, 2012). These entries may include positive and negative reactions to elements of the interface.

    Field studies: users are observed performing tasks in the real context of use; an investigator will take notes and possibly also make video recordings.

    Online field studies: similar to the above; however, users are observed in virtual, online worlds such as World of Warcraft (Bainbridge, 2010), message boards, etc.

3   *Any settings not involving users*, for example:
Heuristic evaluations: the interface's adherence to a set of usability principles – e.g. Nielsen's (1995) ten heuristics listed above is measured by one or more expert evaluators.

   Models: primarily used to test alternative interfaces for the same system – e.g. the optimal arrangement of user interface elements on-screen, by predicting user behaviour. One classic predictive model is Fitts' law (1954), which predicts how long it will take a user to reach a particular on-screen target using a pointing device, based on the size of the object and the distance to it. A number of other predictive models such as the GOMS model and keystroke-level model are available (Card *et al.*, 1983).

CYBERPSYCHOLOGY AND HUMAN–COMPUTER INTERACTION

Psychology has played a key role in the field of HCI, beginning with classic work by Norman (1980) and Card *et al.* (1983). In a review of the psychological aspects of HCI, Olson and Olson (2003) explain that psychology has attempted to provide an understanding of 'the involvement of cognitive, perceptual and motor components in the moment-by-moment interaction a person encounters when working at a computer'. Having an understanding of a person's ability to multi-task, maintain attention, recognise and recall information, learn, reason, perceive their environment, etc. helps inform the design of an interface that will take advantage of a person's abilities while compensating for their limitations. A number of models and theories from cognitive psychology have been used in HCI, including distributed cognition, information processing and mental models. An exploration of these is beyond the scope of this chapter; however, a thorough explanation of these models and theories is provided by Carroll (2003).

   The emergence and growth of the field of cyberpsychology is closely linked to these previous crossovers between psychology and HCI. As the interactions between humans and technology became more intimate, more frequent and more immersive, there was a need for a field – cyberpsychology – to study the psychological phenomena surrounding these interactions. As previously mentioned, HCI and cyberpsychology have much in common, both involving the study of humans and technology, but with cyberpsychology placing a greater emphasis on the human (Norman, 2008). Given this strong link between the two fields, there is great potential for collaboration and sharing of knowledge.

   HCI can contribute decades of theory relating to the usability and UX of user interfaces. Practical elements of HCI such as design and prototyping may also be useful when constructing interactive experiences to test cyberpsychology theories or to attempt to apply lessons from cyberpsychology in real systems. The range of evaluation techniques used in HCI may be applicable in areas of cyberpsychology research and practice. For example, the online field studies mentioned in the Evaluation section above are extremely relevant to cyberpsychology.

   Similarly, cyberpsychology can make significant contributions to HCI. HCI is not explicitly concerned with the psychological effects of an interface on a human. There is a role for cyberpsychologists to provide input into the HCI design process, to ensure interfaces result in the desired psychological effect and/or avoid an undesirable effect. Similarly, cyberpsychologists will have a role to play in performing interface evaluations and experiments to build theories of the psychological phenomena surrounding HCIs. This will be particularly relevant when it comes to new and emerging technologies.

CONCLUSION

As computers become increasingly involved in all aspects of our lives, the importance of creating satisfying, efficient and effective interactive experiences between humans and computers increases. Similarly, as these interactions become more intimate and mediate more of our social interactions, it is becoming more and more important to understand the effects of such interactions on our psyche and to incorporate knowledge from the field of cyberpsychology into the HCI design process. In the future, as new technologies emerge, the fields of HCI and cyberpsychology will have a vital, collaborative role to play in ensuring that these new developments improve our quality of life and sense of well-being, augment our intellect and help us achieve our goals.

ACTIVITY

Imagine you are tasked with the design of a mobile app that aims to teach the user about some facet of cyberpsychology.

- Produce a low-fidelity paper prototype of your app.
- Observe a number of people using the prototype and encourage them to comment.
- How would users rate the usability and UX of the app?
- Based on their feedback, how could you improve the app in the next design iteration?

DISCUSSION QUESTIONS

1 Do you think J.C.R. Licklider's (1960) dream of 'Man–Computer Symbiosis' has been achieved? If so, what examples can you provide to support your view? If not, what developments need to take place to reach this fabled symbiosis?
2 In recent years the concerns of HCI have moved beyond usability to issues of UX such as emotion. Can you think of some interfaces that are particularly fun and enjoyable to use? What do these interfaces have in common?
3 The decisions made when designing a human–computer interface could have a significant psychological impact on its users. Can you think of any examples where such design decisions have had a negative psychological impact?

4 Discuss the various ways in which cyberpsychologists could work with people from other disciplines to contribute to a project involving the design, implementation and evaluation of a human–computer interface.

RECOMMENDED READING LIST

This is a comprehensive and practical introduction the field of interaction design.
Preece, J., Sharp, H. & Rogers, Y. (2015). *Interaction Design* (4th edn). Hoboken, NJ: Wiley.

A classic work that presents vivid, relatable examples of good and bad design and provides some fundamental principles of designing for people.
Norman, D. (2013). *The Design of Everyday Things* (revised and expanded edn). New York: Basic Books.

Practical interaction design tips from authors with real-world experience.
Allen, J. & Chudley, J. (2012). *Smashing UX Design Foundations for Designing Online User Experiences*. Chichester: Wiley.

A comprehensive introduction to the field of HCI, expanding on many of the topics outlined in this chapter.
Shneiderman, B. & Plaisant, C. (2010). *Designing the User Interface: Strategies for Effective Human–Computer Interaction* (5th edn). Reading, MA: Addison-Wesley.

GLOSSARY

ACM SIGCHI   Association for Computing Machinery's Special Interest Group on Computer–Human Interaction.

Conceptual model   Developed early in the interface design process, the conceptual model incorporates high-level design decisions such as the overall structure of the interface and the basic interaction paradigm to be used.

Graphical User Interface (GUI)   This is the layer between the human and the computer. The graphical user interface may consist of icons, buttons, text, windows and other visual indicators.

Heuristics   A set of guidelines or rules of thumb used to guide the design and/or evaluation of an interface.

High-fidelity prototype   Similar in look and behaviour to the desired finished product. Typically computer-based, allowing the user to interact with the prototype using a mouse, touchscreen, etc.

Human–Computer Interaction (HCI)   Refers to the field that studies the design and testing of interactive computer systems that exist at the point where humans and computers meet.

Interaction Design (IxD)   A field similar to HCI, but wider in scope, incorporating any interactive experience.

Interface   The boundary between the human and the computer through which the two parties exchange information. Most commonly, this is represented on screen via a graphical user interface and the human provides commands by clicking or touching on-screen interface elements such as icons or buttons.

Low-fidelity prototype   Often used early in the interaction design process, these prototypes are far from the finished product and may be developed using simple materials such as paper, offering no real user interaction.

Natural User Interface (NUI)   Interfaces that are essentially invisible. Such interfaces should be intuitive and easy to learn. Examples include interfaces that allow users to interact with computers using speech and/or gestures.

Platform   The combination of hardware and software making up a computer system.

Prototype   A sample or model constructed to test an interface concept.

Scenario   A description of one particular interaction a potential user may have with a system. For example, in an online dating site may involve a new user signing up and creating their profile.

Usability   The extent to which users can achieve specified goals with effectiveness, efficiency and satisfaction using a product.

User-Centered Design (UCD)   A design philosophy that focuses on the needs, desires and capabilities of the actual users of the product, rather than focusing on business goals, technologies or other aspects.

User Experience (UX)   Involves a user's emotions and attitudes about interacting with a product.

User persona   A description of a hypothetical user with the same characteristics, motivations and goals as the target user.

REFERENCES

ACM SIGCHI (1992). Curricula for human–computer interaction. Retrieved from: http://sigchi.org/cdg.

Apple (2015). iOS human interface guidelines. Retrieved from: https://developer.apple.com/library/ios/documentation/UserExperience/Conceptual/MobileHIG/.

Bainbridge, W. (2010). *The Warcraft Civilization: Social Science in a Virtual World.* Cambridge, MA: MIT Press.

Bush, V. (1945). As we may think. *The Atlantic Monthly, 176,* 101–108. Retrieved from: www.theatlantic.com/magazine/archive/1945/07/as-we-may-think/303881/.

Calabria, T. (2004). An introduction to personas and how to create them. Retrieved from: www.steptwo.com.au/papers/kmc_personas/.

Card, S., Moran, T. & Newell, A. (1983). *The Psychology of Human–Computer Interaction.* Hillsdale, NJ: Lawrence Erlbaum Associates.

Carroll, J. M. (2000). Introduction to the special issue on scenario-based systems development. *Interacting with Computers, 13*(1), 41–42.

Carroll, J. M. (ed.). (2003). *HCI Models, Theories, and Frameworks Toward a Multidisciplinary Science*. San Francisco, CA: Morgan Kaufmann.

Dix, A. J., Finlay, J. E., Abowd, G. D. & Beale, R. (2004). *Human–Computer Interaction* (3rd edn). Harlow: Pearson Education.

Fitts, P. M. (1954). The information capacity of the human motor system in controlling the amplitude of movement. *Journal of Experimental Psychology*, *47*(6), 381–391.

Grudin, J. (2012). A Moving Target: The evolution of Human-computer Interaction. In J. Jacko (ed.), *Human–Computer Interaction Handbook: Fundamentals, Evolving Technologies, and Emerging Applications*. (3rd edn). Boca Raton, FL: CRC Press.

Google (2015). Android design guidelines. Retrieved from: https://developer.android.com/design/index.html.

Hornsby, P. (2010). Hierachical task analysis, *UX Matters*. Retrieved from: www.uxmatters.com/mt/archives/2010/02/hierarchical-task-analysis.php.

ISO9241–11 (1998). Ergonomic requirements for office work with visual display terminals (VDTs) Part 11: Guidance on usability. Geneva: ISO.

Jacobson, I., Christerson, M., Jonsson, P. & Overgaard, G. (1992). *Object-oriented Software Engineering – A Use Case Driven Approach*. Harlow: Addison-Wesley.

Kay, A. C. (1972). A personal computer for children of all ages. In Proceedings of the ACM Annual Conference (ACM '72). New York: ACM.

Lallemand, C. (2012). Dear diary: Using diaries to study user experience, *User Experience Magazine*, *11*(3). Retrieved from: http://uxpamagazine.org/dear-diary-using-diaries-to-study-user-experience/.

Lazar, J. & Feng, J. (2010). *Research Methods in Human–Computer Interaction*. Chichester: Wiley.

Licklider, J. (1960). Man–computer symbiosis. *IRE Transactions on Human Factors in Electronics HFE-1*, 1, 4–11.

Mayhew, D. (1999). *The Usability Engineering Lifecycle: A Practitioner's Handbook for User Interface Design*. San Francisco, CA: Morgan Kaufmann.

Michel, J., Shen, Y. Aiden, A., Veres, A., Gray, M., The Google Books Team, Pickett, J., Hoiberg, D., Clancy, D., Norvig, P., Orwant, J., Pinker, S., Nowak, M. & Aiden, E. (2011). Quantitative analysis of culture using millions of digitized books. *Science*, *331*, 176–182.

Montuschi, P., Sanna, A., Lamberti, F. & Paravati, G. (2014). Human–computer interaction: Present and future trends. *IEEE Computing Now*, *7*(9). Retrieved from: www.computer.org/web/computingnow/archive/september2014.

Nielsen, J. (1993). *Usability Engineering*. Boston, MA: Academic Press.

Nielsen, J. (1995). 10 usability heuristics for user interface design. Retrieved from: www.nngroup.com/articles/ten-usability-heuristics/.

Norman, D. (1983). Some observations on mental models. *Mental Models*, *7*(112), 7–14.

Norman, D. (1988). *The Design of Everyday Things*. New York: Doubleday.

Norman, K. (2008). *Cyberpsychology: An Introduction to Human–Computer Interaction*. New York: Cambridge University Press.

Olson, G. M. & Olson, J. S. (2003). Human–computer interaction: Psychological aspects of the human use of computing. *Annual Review of Psychology*, *54*, 491–516.

Preece, J., Sharp, H. & Rogers, Y. (2015). *Interaction Design* (4th edn). Hoboken, NJ: Wiley.

Rettig, M. (1994). Prototyping for tiny fingers. *Communications of ACM, 37*(4), 21–27.

Rubin, J. & Chisnell, D. (2008). *Handbook of Usability Testing How to Plan, Design, and Conduct Effective Tests* (2nd edn). Indianapolis, IN: Wiley.

Shneiderman, B. (1980). *Software Psychology: Human Factors in Computer and Information Systems.* Cambridge, MA: Winthrop.

Stone, D., Jarrett, C., Woodroffe, M. & Minocha, S. (2005). *User Interface Design and Evaluation.* Amsterdam: Elsevier.

Sutcliffe, A. & Gault, B. (2004) Heuristic evaluation of virtual reality applications. *Interactive Computing, 16*(4), 831–849.

Sutherland, I. (1963). *Sketchpad: A Man-Machine Graphical Communication System* (doctoral dissertation). Retrieved from: www.cl.cam.ac.uk/techreports/UCAM-CL-TR-574.pdf.

19 Gaming

Andrew Errity, Brendan Rooney and Conall Tunney

CHAPTER OVERVIEW

Gaming has developed from a relatively niche activity to a pastime engaged in by a much wider cross-section of the population. The greater diversity of gaming platforms (such as smart phones and social networking sites), coupled with the greater social aspect of gaming has a psychological impact on users. This chapter will outline various definitions and types of games and describe key developments in the history of gaming. Following this, we will introduce the psychological theories and research that explore the motivations for and gratifications from playing video games, including the experience of presence and flow, and the use of 'gamification'. Finally, consideration will be given to problems associated with video game play such as intense forms of problematic use or 'addiction' and the debate about the link between violent video games and aggressive behaviour.

KEY TERMS

Games that are played on a computer system and allow the player to interactively control graphics on some form of display may be termed **video games**. The individuals who interact with and control the actions within a video game are frequently referred to as **gamers**.

AN INTRODUCTION TO VIDEO GAMING

Introduction

Video gaming has followed the exponential growth of computing, expanding from an activity initially engaged in by just a small number of the early computer hackers to one enjoyed by a diverse range of people from all ages and backgrounds. It is likely that you or someone close to you regularly play **video games**. This may involve spending hours at a time playing a massively multiplayer online role-playing game (MMORPG) such as World of Warcraft on a custom gaming computer, spending a few spare minutes playing a casual game such as Candy Crush on a mobile device, or game play somewhere between these two ends of the gaming spectrum. Given the growth of gaming, diversification of player demographics and increased social interaction facilitated by increased Internet connectivity, it is vital to consider the psychological impact of these games on the players. Prior to delving into these psychological aspects it is important to understand the context. What characteristics define a video game? How did games evolve to the diverse array of modern games we see today? What types of games are there? Who plays these games? This section aims to answer these questions.

What are video games?

Before attempting to define the characteristics of a 'video game', the term itself must be considered. Several alternative terms are also used, such as 'computer game', 'digital game' and 'electronic game'. The meaning of each of these terms may vary depending on the context and they are not always synonymous. For example, the term 'computer game' is sometimes used to refer to games played on personal computers while the term 'video game' sometimes refers exclusively to games on consoles such as the Sony PlayStation or Microsoft Xbox (Tavinor, 2008). For the purpose of clarity this chapter will use the term 'video game' to refer to games that are played on any computer system and allow the player to interactively control graphics on some form of display.

Defining the term video game is not as straightforward as one might first imagine due to the variety of games encompassed by the term and the rate at which games evolve. Some of the key characteristics that define 'traditional games' include conflict, rules, player effort and valued outcomes. Most video games embody these characteristics within software that provides an interface to control the game play. This interface is the point at which the computer and human meet and typically includes input elements (e.g. keyboard, mouse, gamepad, etc.) and output elements (e.g. speakers, screen, haptic feedback, etc.). More detailed discussions of what makes a video game have been provided by Wolf (2002), Wolf and Perron (2003) and Tavinor (2008).

The evolution of video games

William Higinbotham's Tennis for Two game, written in 1958 for an analogue computer and oscilloscope, is widely recognised as the first video game. It allowed two players to bounce a ball over a net on the oscilloscope display. Another notable early game, Spacewar!, was developed just three years later in 1961 by MIT student Steve

Russell on a PDP-1 computer. It took another decade for computer hardware costs to reduce to a point where video games were commercially feasible. In 1971 Nolan Bushnell released the first arcade video game, Computer Space, which was not a commercial success. However, Nolan persevered and in 1972 founded his own company, Atari, and produced a Ping-Pong simulation, with the help of engineer Al Alcorn, named Pong that became the world's first commercially successful arcade video game and launched the video game industry.

The video game industry has grown and evolved dramatically since these early days. A number of authors (Donovan, 2010; Kent, 2001; Rabin, 2011, pp. 3–40) have written detailed histories of video games, but the changes can be summarised in a few key categories:

- Hardware: The exponential improvements in computer hardware have had a huge impact on video games. Increasing memory sizes, improvements in graphics technologies, faster processor speeds and new storage media (e.g. CD-ROMs and DVDs) allowed games to move from 2D to realistic 3D graphics, and become larger and more complex. Reductions in the physical size of hardware devices have also facilitated the growth of mobile gaming.
- Interfaces: Linked to the improvements in computer hardware, the manner in which players interact with games has also evolved. Input devices evolved from simple joysticks, to mouse and keyboard, to touchscreens, to gesture controllers such as the Xbox Kinect. Similarly, output devices have developed from low-resolution monochrome displays, to modern high-definition displays, to virtual reality headsets like the Oculus Rift.
- Players: The demographics of **gamers** shifted from predominantly young males to a wider cross-section of the population.
- Connectivity: The growth of the Internet and increasing ubiquity of always-on high-speed Internet connectivity, both wired and wireless, has led to an explosion of online gaming, social gaming, mobile gaming, and casual gaming.
- Game design: Given the increasing diversification of the demographics of game players and game designers, new forms of game play are emerging to appeal to these different demographics.

What types of games are there?

As with other forms of entertainment such as film and music, video games can be categorised by genre, or in many cases assigned to multiple genres. As video gaming evolves the genres also change, thus it is impossible to give a definitive list of game genres that will not become outdated. However, Table 19.1 below, adapted from Rabin (2011, p.35–40), describes some of the most significant genres.

Who plays games?

The classic stereotype of a gamer is that of an adolescent male. However, the statistics show that this is a grossly inaccurate picture of the modern game playing audience. The Entertainment Software Association (ESA), whose members include many leaders of the video game industry, produces an annual report on the state of the US video

TABLE 19.1 Video game genres

Genre	Description	Example
Action	Quick and accurate reactions are required to succeed.	Pong
Adventure	Players, typically taking the role of a single character, can explore and interact with other characters and the game world. Gameplay focuses on puzzle solving and problem solving rather than action/combat.	Zork
Action–adventure	A combination of the two genres above.	The Legend of Zelda
Platformer	Run and jump from platform to platform to reach required goals.	Super Mario Bros
Fighting	Engage in combat, typically hand-to-hand, with other players or the computer.	Street Fighter
First-person shooter	The player's view of the world is from the perspective of the character they are playing.	Call of Duty
Strategy	Focus on planning, strategic thinking and decision-making. The player is typically given a top-down view of the game world. May be either real-time or turn-based.	Command and Conquer
Role-playing game (RPG)	Gameplay is based on traditional table top role-playing games.	Dungeons & Dragons
Massively multi-player online role-playing game	RPGs in which thousands of players simultaneously play in the same persistent virtual-world in real-time.	World of Warcraft
Simulation	Designed to simulate a real or imaginary reality.	Microsoft Flight Simulator
Rhythm	Require the player to match their actions to the musical beat, typically focusing on players playing simulated musical instruments or dancing.	Guitar Hero
Casual	Targeted at casual gamers, i.e. players who do not wish to commit large amounts of time and effort to playing games.	Angry Birds
Social	Involve an element of social interaction with other human players.	FarmVille

game industry. The 2014 ESA report (ESA, 2014) shows that in the US the average game player is 31 years old and 48 per cent of gamers are female. The report also reveals the size of the gaming industry, with 59 per cent of Americans playing games and total games sales of $15.4 billion in 2013. While this report only captures a snapshot of the video game industry in a single geographic region, it provides insight into trends that are evident in gaming globally. One such trend is the popularity and growth of social gaming. Among most frequent gamers, social games were found to be the most popular genre, increasing in popularity by 55 per cent from 2012 to 2013. With 66 per cent of gamers playing games with others, either online or in person, the social nature of gaming is evident. Another trend is the increasing popularity of smartphone and mobile gaming, increasing by 22 per cent and 37 per cent, respectively, over the previous year. Some people perceive games as a childish endeavour; however, the statistics above demonstrate that most US gamers are adults and a large portion of the population play games. With such a large and diverse audience it is key to consider the psychological impacts of gaming.

THE PSYCHOLOGY OF VIDEO GAMING

Why do people play video games?

Psychological gratifications

Since the rise in video games, media psychologists have tried to explain why people engage in such game playing activity. In general, research exploring the motivations for playing video games has referred to a number of common benefits or 'gratifications' that may contribute to the popularity of gaming. One of the major reasons proposed for video game play is that it can give a sense of satisfaction from achieving things in the game such as progressing up a level or defeating an opponent (Olson, 2010; Ryan, 2006; Sherry et al., 2006; Wan & Chiou, 2006; Wu et al., 2010; Yee, 2007). Another often cited gratification is that video games can provide cognitive and emotional escape from one's own life-problems or dealing with boredom (Olson, 2010; Sherry et al. 2006; Wan & Chiou, 2006; Yee, 2007) and at the same time, they offer the novelty of immersing oneself in another world of fiction or fantasy (Sherry et al. 2006; Wan & Chiou, 2006; Wu et al. 2010; Yee, 2007). Finally, researchers have talked about the social connectedness provided by games, from developing relationships with team-mates and collaborating on various tasks (Ryan et al. 2006; Sherry et al. 2006; Wan & Chiou, 2006; Wu et al. 2010; Yee, 2007).

The Self Determination Theory (SDT) (Przybylski et al., 2010) model of video game engagement encapsulates the above gratifications to explain the psychological benefits of video game play. The SDT model proposes that the popularity of a game is based upon its ability to satisfy basic psychological needs. According to SDT, people want to feel various degrees of competence (a sense of ability), autonomy (freedom and individuality) and relatedness (social connection), and so video games can be a way of providing them with some of these gratifications (Ryan et al., 2006).

Altered states of consciousness

Psychologists have also theorised about the benefits of video game play in terms of the altered states of consciousness it might produce. Playing video games commonly (and necessarily) alters a player's state of consciousness. When playing video games, players often lose awareness of their (real) surroundings and become engulfed in the world of the game. They may not notice the time go by or events that are taking place in the same room. However, even during particularly intense video game experiences, players will often retain some awareness (on some level) of their surroundings and the context in which they are engaging in the activity (Banos *et al.*, 2004; Singer & Witmer, 1999). This is necessary for their popularity, as an extreme dissociation from reality or hallucinogenic effect of video game play would be unusual and unsettling, if not traumatic.

The altered state of consciousness is an integral part of the way in which video games work, and has been explored in various different fields of study, including Psychology, Game Studies, Philosophy, Computer Science and User Experience (UX). This broad interest in the area has generated the use of various different terms for the changes in consciousness when playing. This can make studying the area tricky sometimes because these terms can be overlapping and yet have a slightly different focus.

One of the most common terms associated with the experience of video game play is '**presence**'. The term was first introduced as 'telepresence' by Minsky (1980) and in film studies has been referred to as the diegetic effect (Burch, 1979). Presence is a player's subjective sensation of 'being there' in the game (Barfield *et al.*, 1995; Clarke, 1997). Lombard and Ditton (1997) define it as 'a perceptual illusion of non-mediation' – that is, the extent to which a player is unaware that they are playing a game. Researchers exploring presence have distinguished between the contributing aspects of the medium (the video game or interface) on one hand and the psychological processes of the player on the other. These researchers have used a related but different term, '**immersion**', to define the characteristics of the technology. Immersive technologies are those that offer a higher quality or quantity of sensory information to the user (Slater, 1999). Thus, modern gaming experience is becoming increasingly immersive. So it would make sense if modern gamers are feeling more presence when they play; that there would be a relationship between the immersiveness of the game and the amount of presence that the player feels. Several empirical studies have demonstrated that feelings of presence tend to increase as the level of immersion increases (Hendrix & Barfield, 1996; IJsselsteijn *et al.*, 1998). However, Wirth *et al.* (2007) argue that we cannot assume such a relationship is simple and one way. They point out that there are other factors that affect feelings of presence such as the characteristics of the game (e.g. novelty or genre) and the individual gamer's preferences.

The state of '**flow**' is another common and overlapping psychological construct from the literature and while the term 'flow' is not solely reserved for video game play, it has become a useful construct for exploring the way in which gamers can engage with the activity. The term was coined by the Hungarian psychologist Mihaly Csikszentmihalyi (pronounced 'CHEEK-sent-me-hi-ee') and can be seen as a related concept to the idea of presence. To be in a state of flow is to be focused and engaged in game play (or another activity) and includes a feeling of enjoyment, being one with the game, and a distorted perception of time. It occurs in a moment when the player achieves a balance between the skill or effort required and the difficulty or challenge faced (Csikszentmihalyi & Csikszentmihalyi, 1988; Moneta & Csikszentmihalyi, 1996, 1999).

Despite the prevalence of enjoyable flow, playing a video game is not always a positive experience; games can cause us to feel a range of negative emotions such as anger, anxiety, disgust and fear (Funk *et al.*, 2006). Indeed, games that arouse negative emotions such as the game series Grand Theft Auto, Call of Duty and Assassins' Creed are among the most popular games currently available (VG Chartz, 2015). How do we explain enjoying a game that makes us feel negative emotion? Media psychologists such as Vorderer *et al.* (2004) and Oliver (1993) suggest that we enjoy the negative emotions associated with video game play, but only after the fact; that we enjoy reflecting on our negative experience. Thus it is proposed that experiencing all emotions (whether positive or negative) is enjoyable and beneficial.

Learning and honing adaptive skills

This idea is also in line with researchers such as Steen and Owens (2001) and Tan (2008), who have explored the evolutionary function of engaging with entertainment such as video games. They argue that playing video games is an 'adaptive activity'. In other words, humans are motivated to play video games, because they, in some way, contribute to human prosperity. According to Tan (2008), such activity allows us to learn and practice skills that are helpful for everyday life, in a way that is safe and enjoyable. What sort of skills? You would be forgiven for thinking that the average person would never need the skills of dragon-slaying or zombie-killing in their day-to-day lives. Of course! But embedded in these activities are opportunities to develop a range of other skills that are useful, such as problem solving, planning, social skills and emotion regulation (e.g. keeping calm in a stressful situation). Psychologists have argued that playing games might be beneficial because they allow us to hone skills in a way that is perhaps more enjoyable than, say, formally learning social skills from a textbook.

The idea that games make learning fun offers a possible explanation as to why people might engage in video game play. Furthermore, this idea offers an opportunity to capitalise on the popularity of gaming so as to increase engagement towards all sorts of activities. Nick Pelling (2011) referred to this activity by coining the term '**gamification**' in 2002. This is where an existing challenge or activity is redesigned with gaming principles or mechanics so as to make the task into an enjoyable game. For example, Recyclebank is an application that has gamified various tasks such as recycling, conserving water or online learning about sustainable living. Players earn points for these activities that can be redeemed for rewards like discounts on various products or services. More recently, some enterprising psychologists and other researchers have also begun to use gamification to bring about health and education benefits within entertaining video games. For example, O' Reilly *et al.* (2009) designed a video game called Pesky gNATs that supports the delivery of a Cognitive Behaviour Therapy (CBT) intervention for children experiencing anxiety or depression.

The negative aspects of computer gaming

As gaming in its various forms has become ubiquitous, the 'down-sides', or negative aspects, of gaming have been discussed heavily in the general media and scientific literature alike. The conversation ranges from anecdotes about people losing out on sleep after becoming immersed in a game, to stories of genuine addictive behaviours, and even to games being considered significant factors in acts of violence such as mass shootings in schools in the United States. A topic that reaches such a large cross-section of society, with such serious implications and emotions attached to it, has led to heated debate among psychologists. However, the field remains divided on key questions.

The debate

In essence, the debate surrounding video-game playing behaviour boils down to two questions:

1   Does playing for excessive lengths of time classify as an addiction or is it over-enthusiastic behaviour – i.e. is the behaviour pathological or problematic?
2   Does playing (violent) video games have a genuine and lasting effect on (aggressive) behaviour in real life?

Theories of how games affect people

Theoretical attempts to explain how gaming impacts players are largely the same as those that have been suggested for viewing violent or aggressive media. The foundational model is Social Learning Theory (Bandura, 1977), which posits that behaviour can be learned by modelling the observed actions of others, even without partaking in the behaviour itself. This theory has been applied to gaming where there is ample opportunity to learn from the behaviour of non-player characters (NPCs) and other players online. Building on this, Social Cognitive Theory (Bandura, 1986) suggests that exposure to violent or aggressive media leads to the priming of aggressive 'scripts', or pre-programmed ways of behaving. These theories also incorporate desensitisation, where a player becomes accustomed to violent stimulus, something that has been related to in-game violent behaviours that are common in many video games. While most of the published research supports the Social Cognitive and Social Learning theories (Bushman & Huesmann, 2014) the psychological literature is still divided and other theories must be considered, as the research is not yet conclusive. The competing theories are the Catalyst Model (Ferguson et al., 2008), which regards violent media as much less important than early social experiences, or Moral Panic Theory (Cohen, 1973), which would argue that the general fear of a new medium, though highly influential, is cyclical and will be replaced by fear of the next new medium.

Pathological or problematic behaviour?

Between the publication of the DSM-IV-TR (American Psychiatric Association, 2000) and the DSM-V (American Psychiatric Association, 2013), a wider debate about the legitimacy of behavioural addictions attracted much attention. This resulted in the creation of a new category of disorders called Behavioural Addictions. However, Internet Gaming Disorder has been added to section III of the DSM, which means that it is classified as a disorder that requires more research.

It is worth noting at this point that the debate on this issue is made less clear by the lack of coherent definitions in the literature. Spekman et al. (2013) offer a helpful critique of this problem, citing the use of pathological gaming, video game addiction, video game dependence and problematic gaming all being used as terms for similar behaviours among gamers.

Considering the lack of consistency in usage, the term 'problematic gaming' could be said to be the most helpful, as it offers the widest scope. In this context, Caplan (2003, 2005) attempts to explain generalised problematic Internet use within a cognitive-behavioural framework, a model that has been successfully applied to online gaming behaviour (Caplan et al., 2009). In Caplan's model problematic use, or use that leads to negative consequences, stems from a preference for online social interaction as opposed to face-to-face interaction. This preference can lead people to use the Internet for mood regulation, which in turn encourages deficient self-regulation of Internet use. In the final stage of this model it is deficient self-regulation that is predictive of negative outcomes for the user. When evaluated in a large sample of MMORPG players (Caplan et. al., 2009) results found the model to be effective in explaining negative outcome for online gamers. The psychosocial factors of the model were found to be more important than the comparatively less important factors of game mechanics.

Gaming and violence

The other key flashpoint around which researchers frequently clash is whether playing violent video games (VVGs) creates genuine violent trends in players, and therefore should they be considered a risk factor for committing acts of violence in the real world. As a research area with many studies it is possible to examine and compare various reviews that pooled the results of individual studies in meta-analyses. Strong meta-analytic research has suggested, taking into account all the published and unpublished literature available, that exposure to VVGs is a causal risk factor for higher levels of aggressive behaviour, aggressive cognition and aggressive affect, and for decreased empathy and pro-social behaviour (Anderson et al. 2010). However, this finding came after two previous meta-analyses observed minimal links between VVGs and violent outcomes for players (Ferguson, 2007; Ferguson & Kilburn, 2009). These reviews also commented on problematic aspects of the literature such as publication bias favouring significant findings and the use of unconventional measures in many experimental studies. In the wake of Anderson et al.'s (2010) paper, a series of tit-for-tat review and counter-review articles were produced (Bushman et al., 2010; Ferguson & Kilburn, 2010; Huesmann, 2010), leaving psychologists without a definitive result. More recently, Elson and Ferguson (2013) reviewed the 25 years of VVG research up to that point. They conclude that the empirical evidence is mixed at best, and that the strong claims of causal links between use and acts of violence cannot be supported by the literature.

Negative gaming behaviour

Aside from the above questions, which dominate the field and the media coverage, there are other negative aspects to gaming that run under the radar of large research projects. These negatives are behaviours like in-game cyber-bullying, **trolling** and griefing. Such behaviours can be considered to arise due to the anonymity created by the technological medium. This phenomenon is not a new discovery and has been noted in technologies such as CB radios in the 1970s, where communication without identifiable features or profiles allows people to communicate without repercussions.

CONCLUSION

The video game medium is one that is constantly evolving in tandem with technological advances and cultural shifts. The popularity of this medium is also increasing and finding new audiences beyond those that were typical in the past. Going forward, it will be increasingly important to study the psychological impact of game play on this diverse and growing population of gamers. Such studies should provide an insight into the psychological effects of game play and thus allow players to avoid the negative aspects of gaming and prioritise the potential positive elements. Similarly, game designers should be cognisant of the psychological factors at play when creating games.

ACTIVITY

If someone experiences 'flow' while playing a video game, their perception of time can be distorted (Nakamura & Csikszentmihalyi, 2009). To explore this yourself, ask someone to play a video game that they like (this is important if they are to experience flow) for a specific period of time, then stop them after a certain amount of time and ask them to estimate how long they have been playing. Make sure they don't know that you're going to ask them to estimate their playing time because knowing this might disrupt their ability to experience flow. You will also need to make sure that there is no time display feature as part of the game.

Did they experience flow? Was their estimate of elapsed time accurate? If not, was it longer or shorter than the correct amount? In other words, did time fly while they were having fun?

DISCUSSION QUESTIONS

1   Video games are good for society. Do you agree with this statement? Discuss the reasons why/why not.
2   Can you think of any reasons for playing video games that did not feature within the presented theories?
3   How much do you think the principles of gamification could be applied in formal education? Could everything in school be taught through a game?
4   Media reports on violent events in society, particularly those involving young males, often draw a link between video game violence and real-life violence. Discuss the evidence for and against this link.

RECOMMENDED READING LIST

This chapter from the *Oxford Handbook of Media Psychology* provides a comprehensive overview of the way in which digital games have been used to make positive changes for the player and society in areas such as health and education.

> Blumberg, F. C., Almonte, D. E., Anthony, J. S. & Hashimoto, N. (2013). Serious games: What are they? What do they do? Why should we play them? In K. Dill (ed.). *Oxford Handbook of Media Psychology* (pp. 334–351). New York: Oxford University Press.

This book provides a review of the psychology of video game motivation and engagement, addressing both the positive and negative aspects of game play. It is based on years of research with thousands of gamers.

> Rigby, S. & Ryan, R. (2011). *Glued to Games: How Video Games Draw Us In and Hold Us Spellbound*. Santa Barbara, CA: Praeger.

This article reviews the theoretical arguments that explore why people engage with entertainment (including video games) and then proposes a theoretical model to explain how and why people feel strong emotions towards entertainment that they know is fabricated and fictional.

> Tan, E. S. H. (2008). Entertainment is emotion: The functional architecture of the entertainment experience. *Media Psychology*, *11*(1), 28–51.

Game researcher Nick Yee has used player surveys, psychological experiments and in-game data to study online fantasy game play.

> Yee, N. (2014). *The Proteus Paradox: How Online Games and Virtual Worlds Change Us – and How They Don't*. New Haven, CT: Yale University Press.

GLOSSARY

Flow   A positive psychology theory proposed by Csikszentmihalyi (1990) which can help to explain optimal experience online. A flow state is a heightened state of engagement with a video game activity (or other activity) that is characterised by feelings of presence, energised focus and enjoyment, and being at one with the game. Flow typically involves distortions of time perception.

Gamer   A video game player.

Gamification   The application of game principles or mechanisms to a task or problem so as to encourage increased engagement with the activity.

Immersion   An objective characteristic that describes the quality or quantity of sensory information provided to a person from a video game (or other audio-visual technology).

Presence   The subjective feeling of being in a virtual environment (such as a video game or virtual reality); an illusion that renders the viewer unaware of the technological medium through which the environment is presented.

Trolling   Negative behaviours in online environments (such as social media and gaming) designed to provoke a reaction such as inducing annoyance or disruption.

Video game   Games that are played on any computer system and allow the player to interactively control graphics on some form of display.

REFERENCES

American Psychiatric Association. (2000). *Diagnostic and Statistic Manual of Mental Disorders* (4th edn, text rev.). Washington, DC: APA

American Psychiatric Association. (2013). *Diagnostic and Statistic Manual of Mental Disorders* (5th edn, text revised). Washington, DC: APA.

Anderson, C. A., Shibuya, A., Ihori, N., Swing, E. L., Bushmann, B. J., Sakamoto, A., Rothstein, H. R. & Saleem, M. (2010). Violent video game effects on aggression, empathy, and prosocial behaviour in Eastern and Western countries: A meta-analytic review. *Psychology Bulletin, 136*(2), 151–173.

Bandura, A. (1977). *Social Learning Theory*. New York: General Learning Press.

Bandura, A. (1986). *Social Foundations of Thought and Action*. Englewood Cliffs, NJ: Prentice Hall.

Banos, R. M., Botella, C., Alcaniz, M., Liano, V., Guerrero, B. & Rey, B. (2004). Immersion and emotion: Their impact of sense of presence. *CyberPsychology and Behavior, 7*, 734–741.

Barfield, W., Zeltzer, D., Sheridan, T. & Slater, M. (1995). Presence and performance within virtual environments. In W. Barfield & T.A. Furness (eds), *Virtual Environments and Advanced Interface Design* (pp. 473–513). New York: Oxford University Press.

Burch, N. (1979). *To the Distant Observer*. Berkeley, CA: University of California Press.

Bushman, B. J. & Huesmann, L. R. (2014). Twenty-five years of research on violence in digital games and aggression: Reply to Elson & Ferguson (2014). *European Psychologist, 19*(1), 47–55.

Bushman, B. J., Rothstein, H. R. & Anderson, C. A. (2010). Much ado about something: Violent video game effects and a school of red herring: Reply to Ferguson and Kilburn (2010). *Psychology Bulletin, 136*(2), 182–187.

Caplan, S. E. (2003). Preference for online social interaction: A theory of problematic Internet use and psychosocial well-being. *Communication Research, 30*, 625–648.

Caplan, S. E. (2005). A social skill account of problematic Internet use. *Journal of Communication, 55*, 721–736.

Caplan, S. E., Williams, D. & Yee, N. (2009). Problematic Internet use and psychosocial well-being MMO players. *Computers in Human Behaviour, 25*, 1312–1319.

Clarke, A. (1997). *Being There: Putting Brain, Body, and World Together Again*. Cambridge, MA: MIT Press.

Cohen, S. (1973). *Folk Devils and Moral Panics*. St Albans: Paladin.

Csikszentmihalyi, M. (1990). *Flow: The Psychology of Optimal Performance*. New York: Cambridge University Press.

Csikszentmihalyi, M. & Csikszentmihalyi, I. (1988). *Optimal Experience: Psychological Studies of Flow in Consciousness*. Cambridge: University Press.

Donovan, T. (2010). *Replay: The History of Video Games*. Hove: Yellow Ant.

Entertainment Software Association (ESA). (2014). 2014 essential facts about the computer and video game industry. The Entertainment Software Association. Retrieved from: www.theesa.com/wp-content/uploads/2014/10/ESA_EF_2014.pdf.

Elson, M. & Ferguson, C. J. (2013). Twenty-five years of research on violence in digital games and aggression: Empirical evidence, perspectives, and a debate gone astray. *European Psychologist*, 1–14.

Ferguson, C. J. (2007). The good, the bad and the ugly: A meta-analytic review of positive and negative effects of violent video games. *Psychiatric Quarterly*, *78*, 309–316.

Ferguson, C. J. & Kilburn, J. (2009). The public health risks of media violence: A meta-analytic review. *Journal of Pediatrics*, *154*, 759–763.

Ferguson, C. J. & Kilburn, J. (2010). Much ado about nothing: The misestimation and overinterpretation of violent video game effects in Eastern and Western nations: Comment on Anderson et al. (2010). *Psychology Bulletin*, *136(2)*, 174–178.

Ferguson, C. J., Rueda, S. M., Cruz, A. M., Ferguson, D. E., Fritz, S. & Smith, S. M. (2008). Violent video games and aggression causal relationship or byproduct of family violence and intrinsic violence motivation? *Criminal Justice and Behavior*, *35*(3), 311–332.

Funk, J. B., Chan, M., Brouwer, J. & Curtiss, K. (2006). A biopsychosocial analysis of the video game playing experience of children and adults in the United States. *SIMILE: Studies in Media Literacy and Information Education*, *6*(3), 1–15.

Hendrix, C. & Barfield, W. (1996). Presence within virtual environments as a function of visual display parameters. *Presence: Teleoperators and Virtual Environments*, *5*(3), 274–289.

Huesmann, L. R. (2010). Nailing the coffin shut on doubts that violent video games stimulate aggression: Comment on Anderson et al. (2010). *Psychology Bulletin*, *136(2)*, 179–181.

IJsselsteijn, W., de Ridder, H., Hamberg, R., Bouwhuis, D. & Freeman, J. (1998). Perceived depth and the feeling of presence in 3DTV. *Displays*, *18*(4), 207–214.

Kent, S. (2001). *The Ultimate History of Video Games*. Roseville, CA: Prima Publishing.

Lombard, M. & Ditton, T. (1997). At the heart of it all: The concept of presence. *Journal of Computer-Mediated Communication*, *3*(2).

Minsky, M. (1980). Telepresence. *OMNI Magazine*, June, 45–51. Retrieved from: https://web.media.mit.edu/~minsky/papers/Telepresence.html.

Moneta, G. B. & Csikszentmihalyi, M. (1996). The effect of perceived challenges and skills on the quality of subjective experience. *Journal of Personality*, *64*, 274–310.

Moneta, G. B. & Csikszentmihalyi, M. (1999). Models of concentration in natural environments: A comparative approach based on streams of experiential data. *Social Behavior and Personality*, *27*, 603–638. doi:10.2224/sbp.1999.27.6.603.

Nakamura, J. & Csikszentmihalyi, M. (2009). Flow theory and research. In C.R. Snyder & S. Lopez (eds), *The Oxford Handbook of Positive Psychology*, pp. 195–206. Oxford: Oxford University Press.

Oliver, M. B. (1993). Exploring the paradox of the enjoyment of sad films. *Human Communication Research*, *19*, 315–342.

Olson, C. K. (2010). Children's motivations for video game play in the context of normal development. *Review of General Psychology*, *14*, 180–187.

O'Reilly, G., McGlade, N. & Coyle, D. (2009). *Gnatenborough's Island.* University College Dublin.

Pelling, N. (2011). The (short) prehistory of gamification . . . . Retrieved from: http://nano dome.wordpress.com/2011/08/09/the-short-prehistory-of-gamification/.

Przybylski, A. K., Rigby, C. S. & Ryan, R. M. (2010). A motivational model of video game engagement. *Review of General Psychology, 14,* 154–166.

Rabin, S. (2011). *Introduction to Game Development* (2nd edn). Andover: Cengage Learning.

Ryan, R. M., Rigby, C. S. & Pezybylski, A. K. (2006). The motivational pull of video games: A self-determination theory approach. *Motivational Emotions, 30,* 347–363.

Sherry, J. L., Lucas, K., Greenberg, B. & Lachlan, K. (2006). Video game uses and gratifications as predictors of use and game preference. In P. Vorderer & J. Bryant (eds), *Playing Computer Games: Motives, Responses, and Consequences* (pp. 213–224). Mahwah, NJ: Lawrence Erlbaum.

Singer, M. J. & Witmer, B. G. (1999). On selecting the right yardstick. *Presence, 8,* 566–573.

Slater, M. (1999). Measuring presence: A response to the Witmer and Singer questionnaire. *Presence, 8,* 560–565.

Spekman, M. L. C., Konijn, E. A., Roelofsma, P. H. M. P. & Griffiths, M. D. (2013). Gaming addiction, definition, and measurement: A large-scale empirical study. *Computers in Human Behaviour, 29,* 2150–2155.

Steen, F. F. & Owens, S. A. (2001). Evolution's silent pedagogy: An adaptationist model of pretense and entertainment. *Journal of Cognition and Culture, 1,* 289–321.

Tan, E. S. H. (2008). Entertainment is emotion: The functional architecture of the entertainment experience. *Media Psychology, 11*(1), 28–51.

Tavinor, G. (2008). Definition of Videogames. *Contemporary Aesthetics, 6.* Retrieved from: http://hdl.handle.net/2027/spo.7523862.0006.016.

VG Chartz (2015). Software charts – Global top sellers for 27th December 2014. Retrieved from: www.vgchartz.com/#Global.

Vorderer, P., Klimmt, C. & Ritterfeld, U. (2004). Enjoyment: At the heart of media entertainment. *Communication Theory, 14,* 388–408.

Wan, C. S. & Chiou, W. B. (2006). Why are adolescents addicted to online gaming? *CyberPsychology and Behavior, 9,* 762–766.

Wirth, W., Hartmann, T., Böcking, S., Vorderer, P., Klimmt, C., Schramm, H., Saari, T., Laarni, J., Ravaja, N., Gouveia, F. R., Biocca, F., Sacau, A., Jäncke, L., Baumgartner, T. and Jäncke, P. (2007). A process model of the formation of spatial presence experiences. *Media Psychology, 9*(3), 493–525.

Wolf, M. (2002). *The Medium of the Video Game.* Austin, TX: University of Texas Press.

Wolf, M. & Perron, B. (2003). Introduction. In Wolf, M. & Perron, B. (eds), *The Video Game Theory Reader* (pp. 1–24). New York: Routledge.

Wu, J. H., Wang, S. C. & Tsai, H. H. (2010). Falling in love with online games: The uses and gratifications perspective. *Computers in Human Behavior, 26,* 1862–1871.

Yee, N. (2007). Motivations of play in online games. *Journal of Cyberpsychology and Behaviour, 9,* 772–775.

20 Psychological applications of Virtual Reality

Gráinne Kirwan

CHAPTER OVERVIEW

Virtual Environments (VEs) are a prominent aspect of cyberpsychology, both in relation to desktop software (such as immersive games) and dedicated three-dimensional (3D) viewing technologies, such as head mounted displays (HMDs). After a brief description of some of the equipment used in Virtual Reality (VR), this chapter will describe the phenomenon of **presence**, a sense of immersion in the virtual environment that is essential for many of the research, therapeutic, diagnostic and educational applications which are then described.

KEY TERMS

(VR) can broadly be defined as the use of computer technologies to create three-dimensional virtual worlds or objects which users can interact with. The user often inhabits a virtual body, known as an **avatar** within this world, and they can interact with other individuals or **agents** (characters controlled by the computer). Because of the 3D nature of these worlds they are often more immersive than VEs which are depicted via traditional, two-dimensional monitors. Consequentially, users may experience an increase in **presence** – a sensation of being immersed in a virtual world. Recent years have seen the development of relatively cheap HMDs targeted at a consumer audience, and this has resulted in the technology receiving increased attention from both the media and the general public, despite a lull in general interest since the term was initially popularised decades ago.

VIRTUAL REALITY EQUIPMENT

The most commonly used type of VR equipment are HMDs, but there is a variety of other display and interaction technologies which can also be utilised. Some of these will be briefly described in this section.

Head Mounted Displays

HMDs are relatively lightweight headsets, often incorporating headphones for sound (an example of one is shown in Figure 20.1). Most HMDs require a computer to run the virtual environment, the visual portrayal of which is then presented in the headset. Alternatively, some HMDs use smartphones to both run and display the virtual world, with the smartphone slotting into a space within the headset.

HMDs induce a sensation of three-dimensional viewing by presenting slightly different images to each of the users' eyes. This mimics vision in the real world, where each eye sees a slightly different view because of the small distance between the eyes. In this way the HMD fools the brain into thinking that the two-dimensional image being portrayed actually depicts 'normal' three-dimensional space. The HMD (or an

FIGURE 20.1 Virtual Reality Head Mounted Display with related equipment

(courtesy of Virtual Reality Medical Institute)

incorporated smartphone) also includes devices which detect the position and orientation of the user's head, and adjusts the image that is seen accordingly. This means that if a user decides to look over their shoulder, or down to the floor, the technology will detect this, and ensure that the image portrayed reflects this changed visual orientation.

For many of the psychological applications described later in this chapter, it is helpful if the researcher or therapist is able to determine exactly what the user is looking at throughout their experience. For this reason, they will often use a traditional monitor to show this, as can be seen in the left monitor in Figure 20.1. For certain purposes, such as treatment of anxiety disorders, it is also helpful for the therapist to be able to examine if the stimuli in the virtual world elicited a physiological reaction – there are physiological monitoring devices attached to the user in Figure 20.1, and their output is displayed on the monitor on the right-hand side of the image.

Other Virtual Reality equipment

While HMDs are one of the most common types of VR devices, they are far from the only technology used. Other VR display systems include projection-based systems, or systems similar to those used within cinemas to show 3D films. Such devices usually require the user to wear special sets of glasses which, combined with the display, allow different images to be portrayed to both eyes in a similar manner to that described above for HMDs. Such projection systems allow the user to still view aspects of the real world (such as their own body) while experiencing the virtual world. However, projection-based systems are expensive and difficult to transport, and this type of VR may feel less immersive to some users.

It should be noted that whichever device is used, it is important that the technology is also capable of replicating sound in three dimensions. If this is not achieved, the user will consciously or unconsciously realise that there is a mismatch between the auditory and visual stimuli, which may reduce their sensation of presence. Other senses, such as touch, smell and taste, have received less attention from researchers in VR. Datagloves and other haptic devices provide one possible method of allowing touch sensations to be transmitted to the user, but the added complexity in the virtual world that this requires, along with the additional costs of the equipment, mean that these are rarely utilised. Indeed, it may be possible for researchers and therapists to add tactile cues without the technological requirements of haptic devices – as early as 1997, Carlin, Hoffman and Weghorst used a furry toy spider in addition to a VR environment to treat a woman with a spider phobia (arachnophobia) – a technique known as **tactile augmentation**. Such a technique can greatly reduce the costs and technological requirements of adding the extra tactile sensations. Some centres specialising in the treatment of aviation phobias will also ask clients to sit in actual airplane seats in order to enhance the sense of realism.

The user of a virtual world can interact with it in many ways. These can include remote controls (sometimes called 'wands') and other devices such as keyboards, control panels and even a normal computer mouse. Depending on the system, the user might also be able to explore the virtual world by physically walking around real space and having their movements tracked – such a system allows an enhanced sense of realism and freedom to explore the virtual world, although care must be taken to ensure that the user does not walk into a wall or trip over an obstacle as their visual perception of the real world is blocked by the VR headset.

When using VR, users should always be conscious of a phenomenon known as **cybersickness**. This is a form of motion sickness caused by discrepancies between visual and proprioceptive cues, and is very similar to carsickness or seasickness. Symptoms include nausea, vomiting, postural instability and disorientation, but often the earlier stages of cybersickness can be identified by carefully observing the user for other symptoms, such as pallor or even yawning. Cybersickness can occur in any user, and in any virtual world, but it can be more common in virtual worlds which do not respond sufficiently quickly to user movement (lag) or those with misaligned optical components or slow frame refresh rates. In the vast majority of cases, simply turning off the VR or removing the person from the simulation will resolve any cybersickness within moments. However, care should also be taken with any potential VR users who have certain medical conditions, such as epilepsy, vestibular problems or some heart conditions. It is advisable that such individuals seek advice from a medical professional before being exposed to any VR environment.

Augmented reality

While not specifically VR, the related concept of **augmented reality** (AR) is also worth describing here. In AR, virtual objects are used to supplement a real scene using technologies such as cameras and screens. There are several smartphone applications which allow users to experience AR, and these have been particularly popular for tourism, where the user can view information about buildings, monuments and other tourist attractions by pointing their phone at the landmark. It has also been used for some museum exhibits – at a dinosaur exhibition at the Museum of New Zealand Te Papa Tongarewa in Wellington, visitors could interact with an AR dinosaur which would pace around the person (although the dinosaur was only visible on a giant monitor nearby and not in the real space surrounding the visitor).

While a variation on AR is frequently depicted in science fiction and superhero films as presenting 3D holographic type objects floating over tables in laboratories, in current consumer level AR the object is normally only viewable on a computer-generated screen, such as a smartphone display or computer monitor. While wearable devices such as smartwatches are becoming quite popular, so far this popularity has not extended to the initial glasses-type wearables which had the potential to display AR components in a more natural fashion. It is possible that should such devices become less intrusive – such as by replacing the glasses design with contact lenses – then they might enjoy greater success. HMDs which utilise smartphones may employ the camera within the device to created LAR scenes.

While AR will not be examined in detail in this chapter, it is worth noting that there are many practical psychological uses for the technology. For example, it has been used as a method of inducing the mirror box illusion for individuals experiencing phantom limb pain following amputation (see, for example, Desmond *et al.*, 2006; Ortiz-Catalan *et al.*, 2014). It is also possible that AR could be used as an alternative to VR for many of the purposes outlined below – for example Botella *et al.*, (2010) examined the potential of AR in the treatment of cockroach phobias, and Baus and Bouchard (2014) discuss the potential issues and benefits of AR in exposure-based therapy.

PRESENCE

It is interesting to attend cinemas full of individuals watching horror movies, if only to see the audience physically jump or crouch down in their seats as the tension builds. Sometimes their reaction is more subtle, such as holding their breath or an increase in heart rate, sometimes more obvious, such as hiding behind their popcorn or a cushion. Rationally, they know that what is happening on screen is not real, and that the villain, monster or other malevolent creature cannot actually harm them. But the film has drawn them in, causing them to feel fear, which has observable effects on their behaviour and physiology. The individual is experiencing a sense of immersion in the film, a phenomenon more commonly identified in VR literature as **presence**. In short, presence is the extent to which the person allows themselves to be convinced that they are somewhere other than their actual physical location. Riva *et al.* (2014, p.10) suggest that the sensation of presence requires three components:

1   That the multimodal input from the virtual world is combined so as to be experienced as a reality.
2   That the integration occurs from an egocentric perspective – specifically that the user feels that they are within the environment, rather than observing it from an external vantage point.
3   That the virtual experience is recognised as having meaning and relevance.

Consider again the fear that emerged from watching the film in the cinema – to experience such terror the viewer needs to set aside the knowledge that the events portrayed are not actually occurring at that moment, in that location. They need to ignore the fact that they are in a cinema, with other people, watching the events occur on the screen. In essence, in order to experience presence, the viewer needs to enter the world of the film and to have 'an illusion that [the] mediated experience is not mediated' (Lombard & Ditton, 1997, paragraph 1). Various occurrences can break that illusion – for example, a phone might ring during the film, or some other patrons may start talking, and part of the annoyance that occurs in the viewer as a result of these experiences is likely due to the disruption of the sensation of presence.

Other factors can also disrupt presence – such as the cybersickness or lag problems mentioned above. It is also helpful if the VR used has a sufficient 'field of view' – the proportion of the visual field on which the virtual world is displayed. If the field of view is too small, then the user may be distracted by stimuli in the real environment. This can be partially addressed by using larger screen sizes in HMD, but some newer HMDs counter the problem by designing the headset so that it fits snugly to the face, preventing the user from seeing external stimuli while it is being worn.

Presence is necessary for many of the psychological applications of VR to be effective – the user needs to feel immersed in the environment portrayed. The remainder of this chapter will briefly describe some of the psychological applications of VR, particularly those related to treatment, diagnosis, pain management and psychological research.

VIRTUAL REALITY AS A TREATMENT TOOL

Virtual Reality has opened up new possibilities in the treatment of several conditions. Most notably these include anxiety disorders and addictions, although researchers and therapists have also identified other conditions which might be effectively treated with VR.

Anxiety disorders

When VR technologies were still very new, many therapists identified them as potential aids in the treatment of various psychological conditions. This was particularly true for anxiety disorders such as phobias and Post-Traumatic Stress Disorder (PTSD), where VEs could be used to elicit anxiety responses in clients undergoing therapy. Such responses can also be elicited using other techniques, such as in-vivo exposure (where the client confronts the feared situation or object in real life) and imaginal exposure (where the client visualises the feared situation or object). However, both of these techniques have limitations which in-virtuo (VR) exposure can help to overcome (Wiederhold & Wiederhold, 2014). Many clients are too afraid to face their fear during in-vivo treatments, or may never seek such treatment due to the anxiety that they know it will bring. Clients may also have problems visualising the feared object or situation in sufficient detail for imaginal exposure to be effective. However, potential clients are more open to facing their fears in virtual worlds and do not have to visualise the stimulus themselves.

It is important to note that the virtual world is not an alternative to traditional therapy, but rather should be seen as an adjunct to it. The presence of the therapist remains as important as it is for other forms of treatment, as they provide guidance to clients on how to manage their responses and overcome their phobias as they explore the virtual world. While in the virtual world, the therapist helps the client to extinguish their initial response to the feared object or situation by repeatedly exposing them to cues related to their fear, preventing them from avoiding the feared situation, and providing them with techniques which help them to face the situation when it occurs. As these techniques are learned, and the urge to flee is extinguished, the client learns to manage and overcome their fears.

The images in Figures 20.2 and 20.3 display some examples of what such virtual worlds look like. Figure 20.2 shows a room filled with spiders, suitable for the treatment of clients with arachnophobia. In virtual worlds such as this one, the environment can be adapted to best treat the client. For example, early stages of the therapy might involve a single virtual spider at the far end of the room, or one enclosed within a glass box. As the client masters their fear, then the number of virtual spiders can be increased, and their proximity to the client in the virtual world can be adapted.

Figure 20.3 is taken from a larger suite of virtual worlds designed to reduce aviophobia (fear of flying). This image is of the security clearance section of an airport,

FIGURE 20.2 A virtual world for the treatment of arachnophobia

(courtesy of Virtual Reality Medical Institute)

with signs for passengers to follow to reach the gates. As those who have a fear of flying might begin to associate general airport stimuli with flying, this might result in anxious reactions occurring in response to environments such as this. Again, the phobia therapy can be tailored to the client – for individuals who show no fear response to this part of the flying experience, such a virtual environment could be skipped, with the treatment progressing quickly to virtual worlds simulating the aircraft and flying experience itself.

In addition to phobias, VR therapy has also been successfully utilised in the treatment of other anxiety disorders, including PTSD, generalised anxiety disorder, panic disorder and obsessive–compulsive disorder (see Wiederhold & Bouchard, 2014 for a review of this area).

FIGURE 20.3 A simulation of an airport security check

(courtesy of Virtual Reality Medical Institute)

Addictions and eating disorders

The treatment of addictions and some eating disorders using VR follows a similar basic premise to that of anxiety disorders. The client is exposed to cues in the virtual world (objects or situations) which would normally elicit a reaction in the real world. For example, an individual with problematic drinking behaviours might associate specific environments, such as hotels, bars and restaurants, with consuming alcoholic beverages. They may also find their cravings increase as they are exposed to certain cues, such as advertisements or items on display at supermarkets or other public places. In a similar way to the treatment of phobias and other anxiety disorders, **Virtual Reality Exposure Therapy** (VRET) can be used to reduce the client's responses to these cues by displaying them in a carefully controlled virtual environment and providing the client with techniques for managing, resisting and reducing their cravings.

Many studies have examined first the potential for virtual reality cues to induce cravings in individuals (cue-reactivity), and then the use of VR as a method of reducing those cravings. These papers have considered the potential of VR in the treatment of smoking addictions (see, for example, Pericot-Valverde et al., 2014; Thompson-Lake et al., 2015), problem drinking (see, for example, Lee et al., 2007; Traylor et al., 2011) illegal drugs (see, for example, Saladin et al., 2006; Wiederhold et al., 2014) and even pathological gambling addiction (see, for example, Bouchard et al., 2014).

Similar methodologies can be employed in the treatment of eating disorders. For example, Bordnick et al. (2011) describe the potential for VR research in the assessment and treatment of obesity. Other studies have examined the potential of using VR in the treatment of anorexia and bulimia (Gorini et al., 2010). However, later research has found that food cravings elicited by virtual food are not significantly different to those elicited by picture cues, and cravings elicited by real food are significantly greater (Ledoux et al., 2013), so the value of VR over other methods is less clear. Nevertheless, review papers such as that by Ferrer-Garcia and Gutierrez-Maldonado (2012) suggest that there is potential in the use of VR for eating disorders in non-clinical samples, despite methodological issues in some studies, particularly relating to small sample sizes.

VIRTUAL REALITY AS A DIAGNOSTIC TOOL: PARANOIA AND ATTENTION DEFICIT HYPERACTIVITY DISORDER

While VR has been demonstrated to be an effective treatment tool for many conditions, there are some psychological conditions for which it can also be used as a diagnostic tool. These include paranoia and Attention Deficit Hyperactivity Disorder (ADHD).

When assessing a client who may have unusually high levels of paranoia, it is sometimes difficult to be certain if their actions and reactions are actually warranted. For example, a person complains that others are especially impolite towards them, or take advantage of them, and this may be a delusion or an accurate observation. Questionnaires and even some clinical interviews may have problems in differentiating between these circumstances. It is helpful if we can observe the client's reactions to other individuals, but it is difficult to sufficiently control such circumstances so that the other individuals maintain a standardised response to the client. Researchers such as Daniel Freeman have used VR simulations of a library and an underground train to assess the cognitions of individuals regarding the computer-controlled agents within those worlds (see, for example, Fornells-Ambrojo et al., 2015; Freeman et al., 2010). While many users see the agents in these worlds as benevolent or neutral, some users demonstrated paranoid appraisals of the agents, despite seeing them react in exactly the same way. When users show such paranoid appraisals, it may be an indication of an underlying condition.

In a similar way, Albert 'Skip' Rizzo and his colleagues developed an immersive VR classroom which is designed to assess symptoms of ADHD in children (see, for example, Bioulac et al., 2012; Parsons et al., 2007). The virtual classroom resembles a traditional classroom, including a teacher and a board, and the child is required to perform a task related to the content on the board. Occasional distractions are introduced into the environment (such as a paper airplane and passing vehicles) and the child's reactions to these distractions are noted, as well as their effects on the child's scores on the task.

VR can also be used as a therapeutic tool for paranoia and ADHD, and the interested reader can review the work of Freeman, Rizzo and others to see the developments in these areas. The technology also has therapeutic value in realms other than psychological disorders, and its use as a distractor for pain is considered in the following section.

VIRTUAL REALITY AS PAIN MANAGEMENT

Have you ever noticed a bump, cut or bruise on your body that you have no memory of receiving? The probability is that at the time that you received that injury, you were either asleep, or you were distracted. For some people, the knowledge that they are about to experience pain (for example, while receiving a vaccination) can lead to a heightened state of anxiety, which might result in an intensification of the pain experience.

Such phenomena were noticed by early researchers of pain and integrated into a model known as the Gate Control Theory of pain, which was developed by Melzack and Wall (1967). This theory suggests that the perception of pain is complex, and the severity of the pain experienced can vary depending on factors such as the extent of the injury, the emotional status of the person and the extent to which the person is distracted. The use of VR in pain management depends on this last factor, providing sufficient distraction to the user so that their experience of pain is reduced. This distraction might be used in addition to, or as an alternative to, pharmacological analgesics.

The use of VR in the diagnosis and treatment of psychological conditions as outlined in the previous sections relies on the virtual world recreating an environment containing specific cues which will elicit precise reactions from the user – such as the fear in anxiety disorders or the craving in substance abuse. In contrast, the use of VR in the management of pain often does not require cues specific to the condition, but rather the distraction from the non-virtual world instead, so while the content of the world might be tailored to the user's condition, it does not have to be. For example, the

FIGURE 20.4 The Enchanted Forest Virtual Reality world is used by the Virtual Reality Medical Institute as a pain distraction technique

(courtesy of Virtual Reality Medical Institute)

Virtual Reality Medical Institute uses a virtual world called the 'Enchanted Forest' (see Figure 20.4) during pain management.

An example of a virtual world which has been specifically designed for the type of pain that the user is suffering from is 'SnowWorld', which was developed by Hunter Hoffman and his colleagues for the distraction of burn pain (see, for example, Hoffman *et al.*, 2011). SnowWorld, the Enchanted Forest and other virtual worlds for pain distraction have demonstrated potential in reducing the subjective discomfort of individuals undergoing painful procedures, as described in a 2014 special issue of the journal *Cyberpsychology, Behavior and Social Networking* as well as many other articles. In a similar way, VR has also been demonstrated to affect the perception of the passage of time in patients undergoing intravenous chemotherapy (Schneider *et al.*, 2011), with patients tending to underestimate the duration of the treatment when experiencing VR.

VIRTUAL REALITY IN PSYCHOLOGICAL RESEARCH

A final application of VR for psychology is the potential for the use of virtual worlds in psychological research. In perception research an experimenter can fully immerse a participant within a virtual world, where there are no other visual or auditory distractions. If the experimenter decides that they do want to see how the participant's scores change when subjected to distraction, they can add very specific additional stimuli into the visual field, and these stimuli will appear in exactly the same place at exactly the same time for each participant.

VR can also be used in social psychological research, allowing for high levels of experimental control over relatively realistic environments (see, for example, Blascovich *et al.*, 2002). While this can be used to examine traditional topics in social psychology, the nature of the virtual environment can also allow new phenomena to be uncovered. For example, Yee and Bailenson (2007) noted that participants' behaviour 'conforms to their digital self-representation independent of how others perceive them' (p. 271), with individuals who were assigned taller or more attractive avatars proceeding to act more confidently and intimately respectively. Yee and Bailenson termed this the **Proteus Effect**, and it has been identified across a variety of behaviours (see, for example, Blascovich & Bailenson, 2011; Fox *et al.*, 2013). As this effect has been demonstrated to last for some time after immersion in a virtual world, these findings are of immense importance in the potential of VR to alter human behaviours.

CONCLUSION

As is evident from the research presented in this chapter, psychology has long appreciated the potential for VR in research, assessment and therapy. As the technologies become more affordable and mainstream, it is possible that these developments will increase in number and potential. It should also be noted that VR has a wide variety of uses that are not described here, including engineering, architecture, entertainment, data visualisation, training and education. However, up to now, VR therapy has generally been used as an additional tool in conjunction with a human therapist, and it will be interesting to see if Artificial Intelligence technologies might in the future be incorporated into VR devices in order to allow the client to progress independently of the therapist. The psychological applications of Artificial Intelligence will be considered in the next chapter.

ACTIVITIES

1   Consider when you have felt the most presence in a film, book or video game. What was your subjective experience of that immersion? What elements of the media enhanced that sense of immersion?
2   While most VR equipment is still relatively expensive to purchase, you can experience the phenomenon with relatively little cost by combining a smartphone with kits such as Google Cardboard. See www.google.com/get/cardboard/ for information on how to create a VR headset using cardboard, lenses, magnets, and some other inexpensive items.

DISCUSSION QUESTIONS

1 What other psychological applications might virtual reality have?
2 Considering the Proteus Effect identified by Yee and Bailenson, what are the ethical and practical implications of research in this field?
3 So far, the psychological applications of Augmented Reality have mostly been restricted to the treatment of phobias of small animals, such as insects. What other conditions might it also benefit?
4 What other psychological conditions might virtual reality be useful in the diagnosis of?

RECOMMENDED READING LIST

Wiederhold and Bouchard compile chapters from some of the leading authors in the field of virtual reality in this book examining how VR can be used in the treatment of anxiety disorders. It also includes chapters examining related concepts such as presence and sickness in virtual worlds.

> Wiederhold, B.K. & Bouchard, S. (eds) (2014). *Advances in Virtual Reality and Anxiety Disorders*. Berlin: Springer.

Blascovich and Bailenson's book, *Infinite Reality* describes broader psychological research in VR, with particular focus on the person as an avatar in virtual worlds.

> Blascovich, J. & Bailenson, J. (2011). *Infinite Reality: Avatars, Eternal Life, New Worlds, and the Dawn of the Virtual Revolution*. New York: HarperCollins.

In June 2014, the journal *Cyberpsychology, Behavior and Social Networking* published a special issue examining the use of VR in the distraction of pain. It includes a series of articles and guest editorials on the topic.

> *Cyberpsychology, Behavior, and Social Networking* (2014, June). *17*(6), 331–424.

Wiederhold, Riva and Wiederhold consider how VR could be used in reducing the misuse of prescription opioid drugs in this editorial column.

> Wiederhold, B.K., Riva, G. & Wiederhold, M.D. (2014). How can virtual reality interventions help reduce prescription opioid drug misuse? *Cyberpsychology, Behavior and Social Networking, 17*(6), 331–332. Retrieved from: http://online. liebertpub.com/doi/pdfplus/10.1089/cyber.2014.1512.

GLOSSARY

Agent   Virtual world characters controlled by the computer.
Augmented reality (AR)   The visual portrayal of virtual objects over real world displays using technologies such as cameras and screens.

Avatar An online representation of a user, especially in three-dimensional virtual worlds.

Cybersickness A form of motion sickness caused by discrepancies between visual and proprioceptive cues.

Head Mounted Displays (HMDs) Virtual reality technology where the environment is presented to the user via screens in a headset.

Presence The subjective feeling of being in a virtual environment (such as a video game or virtual reality): an illusion that renders the viewer unaware of the technological medium through which the environment is presented.

Proteus Effect Proposed by Yee and Bailenson (2007), this refers to a change in online and offline self-perception based on the features or behaviours of a user's avatar.

Tactile augmentation Using a real item to induce a sensation of touch when a user is in a virtual world.

Virtual Reality (VR) The use of computer technologies to create three-dimensional virtual worlds or objects which users can interact with.

Virtual Reality Exposure Therapy (VRET) The use of VR to present cues or stimuli to a user to treat a psychological condition such as an anxiety disorder or addiction.

REFERENCES

Baus, O. & Bouchard, S. (2014). Moving from virtual reality exposure-based therapy to augmented reality exposure-based therapy: A review. *Frontiers in Human Neuroscience, 8*, 112. doi: 10.3389/fnhum.2014.00112.

Bioulac, S., Lallemand, S., Rizzo, A., Philip, P., Fabrigoule, C. & Bouvard, M.P. (2012). Impact of time and task on ADHD patients' performances in a virtual classroom. *European Journal of Paediatric Neurology, 16*(5), 514–521.

Blascovich, J. & Bailenson, J. (2011). *Infinite Reality: Avatars, Eternal Life, New Worlds, and the Dawn of the Virtual Revolution*. New York: HarperCollins.

Blascovich, J., Loomis, J., Beall, A.C., Swinth, K.R., Hoyt, C.L. & Bailenson, J.N. (2002). Immersive virtual environment technology as a methodological tool for social psychology. *Psychological Inquiry: An International Journal for the Advancement of Psychological Theory, 13*(2), 103–124.

Bordnick, P.S., Carter, B.L. & Traylor, A.C. (2011). What virtual reality research in addictions can tell us about the future of obesity assessment and treatment. *Journal of Diabetes Science and Technology, 5*(2), 265–271.

Botella, C., Bretón-López, J., Quero, S., Baños, R. & García-Palacios, A. (2010). Treating cockroach phobia with augmented reality. *Behaviour Therapy, 41*(3), 401–413.

Bouchard, S., Loranger, C., Giroux, I., Jacques, C. & Robillard, G. (2014). Using Virtual Reality to provide a naturalistic setting for the treatment of pathological gambling. In C.S. Lanyi (ed.) *The Thousand Faces of Virtual Reality* (pp. 6–21). Rijeka: InTech Europe.

Carlin, A.S., Hoffman, H.G. & Weghorst, S. (1997). Virtual reality and tactile augmentation in the treatment of spider phobia: A case report. *Behaviour Research and Therapy, 35*(2), 153–158.

Desmond, D.M., O'Neill, K., De Paor, A., McDarby, G. & MacLachlan, M. (2006). Augmenting the reality of phantom limbs: Three case studies using an augmented mirror box procedure. *Journal of Prosthetics and Orthotics, 18*(3), 74–79.

Ferrer-Garcia, M. & Gutierrez-Maldonado, J. (2012). The use of Virtual Reality in the study, assessment and treatment of body image in eating disorders and nonclinical samples: A review of the literature. *Body Image, 9*(1), 1–11.

Fornells-Ambrojo, M., Freeman, D., Slater, M., Swapp, D., Antley, A. & Barker, C. (2015). How do people with persecutory delusions evaluate threat in a controlled social environment? A qualitative study using virtual reality. *Behavioural and Cognitive Psychotherapy, 43*(1), 89–107.

Fox, J., Bailenson, J.N. & Tricase, L. (2013). The embodiment of sexualised virtual selves: The Proteus effect and experiences of self-objectification via avatars. *Computers in Human Behaviour, 29*(3), 930–938.

Freeman, D., Pugh, K., Vorontsova, N., Antley, A. & Slater, M. (2010). Testing the continuum of delusional beliefs: An experimental study using virtual reality. *Journal of Abnormal Psychology, 119*(1), 83–92.

Gorini, A., Griez, E., Petrova, A. & Riva, G. (2010). Assessment of the emotional responses produced by exposure to real food, virtual food and photographs of food in patients affected by eating disorders. *Annals of General Psychiatry, 9*(1), 30.

Hoffman, H.G., Chambers, G.T., Meyer III, W.J., Arceneaux, L.L., Russell, W.J., Seibel, E.J., Richards, T.L., Sharar, S.R. & Patterson, D.R. (2011). Virtual Reality as an adjunctive non-pharmacological analgesic for acute burn pain during medical conditions. *Annals of Behavioural Medicine, 41*(2), 183–191.

Ledoux, T., Nguyen, A.S., Bakos-Block, C. & Bordnick, P. (2013). Using virtual reality to study food cravings. *Appetite, 71,* 396–402.

Lee, J.H., Kwon, H., Choi, J. & Yang, B.H. (2007). Cue-exposure therapy to decrease alcohol craving in virtual environment. *CyberPsychology & Behavior, 10*(5), 617–623.

Lombard, M. & Ditton, T. (1997). At the heart of it all: The concept of presence. *Journal of Computer Mediated Communication, 3*(2). DOI: 10.1111/j.1083–6101.1997.tb00072.x.

Melzack, R. & Wall, P.D. (1967). Pain mechanisms: A new theory. *Survey of Anaesthesiology, 11*(2), 89–90.

Ortiz-Catalan, M., Sander, N., Kristoffersen, M.B., Håkansson, B. & Brånemark, R. (2014). Treatment of phantom limb pain (PLP) based on augmented reality and gaming controlled by myoelectric pattern recognition: A case study of a chronic PLP patient. *Frontiers In Neuroscience, 8.* DOI: 10.3389/fnins.2014.00024.

Parsons, T.D., Bowerly, T., Buckwalter, J.G. & Rizzo, A.A. (2007). A controlled clinical comparison of attention performance in children with ADHD in a Virtual Reality classroom compared to standard neuropsychological methods. *Child Neuropsychology: A Journal on Normal and Abnormal Development in Childhood and Adolescence, 13*(4), 363–381.

Pericot-Valverde, I., Secades-Villa, R., Gutierrez-Maldonado, J. & Garcia-Rodrigues, O. (2014). Effects of systematic cue exposure through Virtual Reality on cigarette craving. *Nicotine & Tobacco Research, 16*(11), 1470–1477.

Riva, G., Mantovani, F. & Bouchard, S. (2014). Presence. In B.K. Wiederhold and S. Bouchard (eds) *Advances in Virtual Reality and Anxiety Disorders* (pp. 9–34). New York: Springer.

Saladin, M.E., Brady, K.T., Graap, K. & Rothbaum, B.O. (2006). A preliminary report on the use of Virtual Reality technology to elicit craving and cue reactivity in cocaine dependent individuals. *Addictive Behaviours, 31*(10), 1881–1894.

Schneider, S.M., Kisby, C.K., & Flint, E.P. (2011). Effect of Virtual Reality on time perception in patients receiving chemotherapy. *Supportive Care in Cancer, 19*(4), 555–564.

Thompson-Lake, D.G.Y., Cooper, K.N., Mahoney III, J.J., Bordnick, P.S., Salas, R., Kosten, T.R., Dani, J.A. & De La Garza II, R. (2015). Withdrawal symptoms and nicotine dependence severity predict Virtual Reality craving in cigarette-deprived smokers. *Nicotine & Tobacco Research, 17* (7), 796–802. DOI: 10.1093/ntr/ntu245.

Traylor, A.C., Parrish, D.E., Copp, H.L. & Bordnick, P.S. (2011). Using Virtual Reality to investigate complex and contextual cue reactivity in nicotine dependent problem drinkers. *Addictive Behaviours, 36*(11), 1068–1075.

Wiederhold, B.K. & Bouchard, S. (eds) (2014). *Advances in Virtual Reality and Anxiety Disorders.* New York: Springer.

Wiederhold, B.K. & Wiederhold, M.D. (2014). Introduction. In B.K. Wiederhold and S. Bouchard (eds) *Advances in Virtual Reality and Anxiety Disorders* (pp. 3–8). New York: Springer.

Wiederhold, B.K., Riva, G. & Wiederhold, M.D. (2014). How can Virtual Reality interventions help reduce prescription opioid drug misuse? *Cyberpsychology, Behaviour and Social Networking, 17*(6), 331–332.

Yee, N. & Bailenson, J. (2007). The Proteus Effect: The effect of transformed self-representation on behaviour. *Human Communication Research, 33*(3), 271–290.

21 The psychology of Artificial Intelligence

Gráinne Kirwan

CHAPTER OVERVIEW

Artificial Intelligence (AI) plays an important, yet often invisible, role in our online lives. Interactions such as searches, online recommendations and gaming are often based on AI. The role of **Non-Player Characters** (NPCs) in gaming is a clear example – the realism of these characters and their responses to player actions can have a significant impact on the perceived quality of a game. The rise in the quality of '**chatbots**' (interactive communicative agents), and their use in customer/user interfaces on websites is an interesting development, as is the inclusion of such **chatbots** as interaction devices on smartphones and mobile devices. The potential use of artificially intelligent robots as companion devices is explored, and the observed effects on specific populations is examined. The potential future role of artificial intelligence in human life is considered.

KEY TERMS

Several definitions of **Artificial Intelligence** (AI) have been proposed, including 'the science and engineering of making intelligent machines, especially intelligent computer systems' (McCarthy, 2007, p. 2) and 'the field that studies the synthesis and analysis of computational agents that act intelligently' (Poole & Mackworth, 2010, p. 3). Often AI is associated with **robotics,** the creation of programmed machines which may or may not have some degree of autonomy, although many AIs do not have robotic forms. Some researchers are particularly interested in robots that can interact socially with other robots or humans with some degree of adherence to social and/or cultural norms, a field known as **social robotics.**

Despite the prevalence of features of AI in modern society, there are many problems in defining an agreed standard of AI. Also, individuals may demonstrate the **AI effect,** where they refute the existence of intelligence in some technologies that actually demonstrate one or more elements of AI.

DEFINING AND TESTING ARTIFICIAL INTELLIGENCE

One of the main problems in defining artificial intelligence (AI) comes from the definition of 'intelligence' itself. Even within humans, there are many types of intelligence. For example, maybe you have a friend who is extremely good at languages and who can help you when you need to proofread or translate a document. But it might be a different friend who is the most help if you need to build a wall, or navigate a route that you've never travelled before. Gardner (1983) suggests that there are multiple intelligences that people can have, including linguistic, musical, logical–mathematical, spatial, bodily–kinaesthetic and personal intelligences. While some individuals may have high levels of many of these intelligence types, sometimes people differ widely on their levels, being exceptionally good at some, while being quite poor in other areas.

Often when we see artificially intelligent beings portrayed in science fiction, they demonstrate high intelligence across many of the types that Gardner suggests (although almost always their 'personal' intelligences are relatively low). Because of this, it is somewhat unsurprising that most people fall victim to the AI effect with regard to current technologies. It is extremely difficult to build a physically agile robot which is also capable of creativity, learning, natural language processing, planning, perception, decision making, problem-solving and holding vast quantities of knowledge. Nevertheless, it is worth considering how far AI has come in a relatively short period of time. In 1967, AI researcher Marvin Minsky said 'within a generation . . . the problem of creating "artificial intelligence" will substantially be solved' (Minsky, 1967, as cited by Crevier, 1993, p. 109). With the benefit of hindsight it is easy to think that Minsky was overly optimistic, yet the advances that have been made in this field should not be underestimated. While we may not yet have the types of AI displayed in science fiction movies, we do now have self-driving cars, autonomous robots, chatbots with natural language processing, and AI agents on our smartphones and tablets which can interpret our requests and complete a wide variety of tasks.

Probably the most famous test to determine if we have actually achieved artificial intelligence is known as the **Turing test** (although when originally conceived by Turing in 1950, he proposed it as the 'Imitation Game'). This test determines that if a computer can have a conversation with a human without the human knowing that they are talking to a machine, then the AI is deemed to have passed the test. There have been many attempts to create machines with this goal in mind, and competitions are held annually to assess entries.

There are arguments against the validity of the Turing test as a measure of artificial intelligence, the most famous being the 'Chinese room argument' developed by John

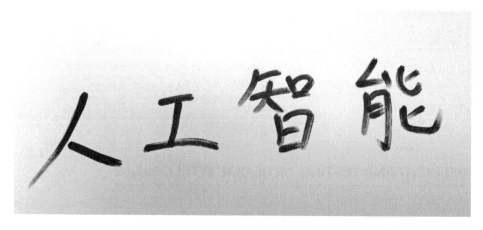

FIGURE 21.1 Searle's 'Chinese room argument' is a critique of the validity of the Turing test as a measure of artificial intelligence. The characters in this image are those for 'artificial intelligence' and were prepared by Ng Yin Lu

Searle in 1980. It offers the example of a person inside a room who does not speak Chinese, but who does have a library of 'if . . . , then . . .' rules which indicate which character strings are the appropriate response to other written strings of characters (similar to those in Figure 21.1). These inputs can be submitted to the room by people outside. If the person in the room follows the 'if . . . , then . . .' rules, they can provide responses in such a way that it appears that they understand the conversation, even though they have no idea what they are communicating about. In short, Searle argues that a computer could pass the Turing test while only having **Weak AI** (i.e. only a simulation of intelligence) rather than **Strong AI** (where the computer actually possesses the intelligence that it appears to have).

There are, of course, further counterarguments against Searle's position. For example, we accept that many of the people that we meet on a daily basis have true intelligence based only on the responses that they give during conversations. We make judgements about people based only on what we can see, and the Turing test suggests a similar goal for machine intelligence. This is a topic of much philosophical argument within the field, and further elaboration can be found in texts such as Epstein *et al.* (2008).

SOCIAL ROBOTICS

While the philosophy of AI is a very interesting topic, psychologists are frequently more interested in how humans interact with the AI, particularly when the AI is embedded in a robot. **Social robotics** examines how humans interact socially with robots, and even how robots interact with each other. A prominent example of a research group in this area is the Massachusetts Institute of Technology Personal Robots Group, which develops social robots and assesses how users interact with them and what their potential applications might be.

However, social robotics can also consider many of the higher-end commercially available toys that simulate pets and contain a certain degree of AI (for example, they may learn behaviours, or adopt certain personalities depending on how they are treated by their owners). Heerink *et al.* (2012) examined how children experienced and interacted with a robot dinosaur, noting that their interactions with it were prevalently social, rarely treating the robot as an object. Similarly, Díaz *et al.* (2011) noted that when children interacted with different types of robots, the robots' appearance and performance altered the interactions that children engaged in with them, including affecting attachment.

Our interactions with robots are obviously dependent on our interpretations of the robot's actions and intentions. Correct interpretations are not always easy to achieve, at least immediately (Erden & Tapus, 2010). However, it is possible that our interpretations of the robot's actions can affect how we feel about interacting with the robot. For example, Park *et al.* (2012) found that when interacting with robots that were programmed to demonstrate facial expressions associated with either introverted or extroverted personalities, users tended to be most comfortable around robots with similar personalities to themselves.

Of course, our interactions with other humans, and even animals, are rarely one-sided – the other communicator must work with us to develop mutual understanding, and they will often infer our intentions from relatively subtle and sometimes ambiguous cues. Ideally, future robots will have these abilities, especially if it is a collaborative working environment (Breazeal *et al.*, 2011). Similarly, Salah *et al.* (2012) recognise how robots need to be able to interpret human behaviours and respond to them appropriately.

Social robotics is a very important topic when psychologists consider the role of AI in human interactions, and we will return to consider some aspects of this in more detail when discussing the potential for companion robots below. However, it should be remembered that in cutting-edge research it is sometimes better for investigators to know how a human would engage with a robot before they start to programme the AI itself (hence they know how to design the robot better, or what features to focus on, or they can test features that are not yet technically possible). To allow this, some research is conducted as a **'Wizard of Oz'** study, where the robot or agent is not actually autonomous, but is instead controlled by the researchers so that it acts in a way that the agent actually would if it was developed. There are obviously some ethical implications with studies of this type – if the participant knows that they are really engaging with a human being they may behave differently than if they think that they are interacting with a robot. However, they may also make personal disclosures to an entity that they think is artificial which they would not to a human researcher, or they may believe themselves to be alone and engage in behaviours that they would not do if another person (rather than just a robot) was present.

APPLICATIONS OF ARTIFICIAL INTELLIGENCE

There are many applications of AI. Sometimes we are conscious that we are interacting with an AI agent, while sometimes the application that we are using utilises a basic level of AI without our realising it. Here we will consider various reasons why psychologists have an interest in artificial intelligence. These include gaming, customer service/user interfaces, psychotherapy and companionship. However we will start with a brief explanation of how AI can aid psychologists develop a greater understanding of cognitive psychology.

Cognitive psychology

Cognitive psychologists try to understand how human cognition works. They wish to determine why we make the decisions that we do, how we solve problems, how we perceive the world, and how we store and retrieve items in our memories. Unfortunately, the methods by which these processes occur can be quite difficult to accurately determine. We can observe a person encountering a situation where they have to make a choice, but even if we encourage them to talk out loud while they are making their decision, it is possible that we will miss steps in their cognitive processing (and indeed, by asking them to talk through their reasoning, we may alter the decision that they will make).

Early cognitive psychologists developed theories to help to understand what happened while people underwent cognitive processes, but these could be vague and quite difficult to test. They then began to develop flowcharts – a diagram describing a process in terms of questions, responses and outcomes, which included more detail on the stages involved. The accuracy of these flowcharts could be tested by coding them into computers using AI languages. The researchers could then provide the computer with the same input that they gave human participants. If the computer model came up with the same response that humans made, then it was likely that the model predicted by the flowchart was correct. Of course, for this to be true, the computer program needed to make the same type of errors that the human participants did. The researchers were not looking to create a computer that would always provide the 'correct' answer – instead, they attempted to create a computer that provided the same output that a human did given the same set of data. If this occurred, then the flowchart was likely an accurate depiction of how humans thought, perceived and reasoned as well.

Nevertheless, there are some cognitive processes that may be extremely difficult to programme. Friedenberg (2008) differentiates between 'computable' and 'uncomputable' processes. Solving a mathematical equation is a classic example of a computable process – we can clearly set out the steps that the person or computer needs to complete in order to find the solution. It is more difficult to identify the processes in generating an original fine oil painting or mood-evoking piece of music – creativity is very difficult to define in a cognitive flowchart. That is not to say that we will never know how to define creativity in a computable way, but for the moment it remains difficult to replicate artificially.

Gaming

While we don't often think about artificial intelligence while gaming, it contributes significantly to the feeling of realism that we experience. This is particularly so for non-player characters (NPCs) – characters within the game that the gamer does not control. These might be the opponents in a sports game, or the villains in an adventure or shooter game. They may also be 'helper' characters who form a team that you are leading, or who are designed to provide advice or help at various stages of a game. If designed well, they can enhance the game significantly, but if the NPC behaves in certain ways, it may break the player's sense of immersion (Johansson *et al.*, 2014).

There is some evidence that individuals can form attachments to such NPCs, depending on their personalities and motivations, as well as the behaviours and physical attractiveness of the NPC (Coulson *et al.*, 2012). To achieve higher quality of interaction and increase social relations it is necessary for the designers of the NPC to consider many psychological factors. Chowanda *et al.* (2014) describe how rules can be generated that guide the actions of NPCs, and that these actions could be dependent on aspects such as 'observed social and emotional signals, the agent's personality, and the social relation between agent and player' (p. 134).

In some ways we can consider the AI behind NPCs in gaming as a type of Turing test. The character needs to be able to respond in ways that convince us of their identity – as a helper, as an opponent, or as any other type of character. If the NPC behaves in ways that are incongruent with that identity, or converses in ways which a real-life person in the same circumstances would not, then it will have an effect on how we perceive the game and our relationship with the character.

Customer services and user interfaces

As chatbots grow closer to passing the Turing test, various potential commercial applications have been explored. Probably the most widely used of these are customer service chatbots and user interfaces on smartphones which utilise natural language processing to interpret user requests. These chatbots help users to find out information and carry out tasks in as natural a way as possible – as if they were asking a friend, colleague or human customer service agent to help them to achieve a goal. In some cases, it is even helpful to analyse similar human conversations in order to determine the best way to create and programme the chatbot (Jenkins *et al.*, 2007). However, there is little research evaluating the benefits of chatbots in customer service roles, and what does exist does not always show that such interaction agents are preferred to standard web-based interfaces (see, for example, May & Kirwan, 2014).

However, one way in which artificially intelligent user interfaces could surpass traditional ones is their ability to react and adjust to the user. For example, Saadatian *et al.* (2014) suggest the use of Probabilistic Mood Estimation (PME) to determine the user's mood through information such as location, physical activity, and so on. This could then be used to alter the behaviour of an AI virtual companion on a smartphone (which could feasibly include the user interface AI), so that it behaves in a manner which complements the user at that time (e.g. happy, relaxed or sleepy). Similar research by Adam and Lorini (2014) suggests that an agent which can interpret user emotion could be used to suggest coping strategies (such as positive reinterpretation of events) to help the person to improve their well-being.

Psychotherapy

With enhanced conversational abilities, other opportunities arise for chatbots beyond customer service and user interfaces. There are various aspects of psychotherapy that

AI could be utilised in, such as clinical training, psychological assessment, clinical decision making and treatment (Luxton, 2014). As early as 1988, Binik *et al.* considered the potential for AI in therapeutic practice for clients with sexual dysfunction.

While never intended to actually conduct any psychotherapy itself, one of the first chatbots was created as a parody of a Rogerian psychotherapist. Her name was Eliza, and she was created by Joseph Weizenbaum (1966) to study natural language processing between humans and computers. Weizenbaum chose this persona for his chatbot because of the nature of conversation between a therapist and client. For example, a therapist might turn the last statement made by the client into a question, while adding little detail (e.g. a client might say 'I feel sad', while Eliza might respond 'why do you feel sad?'). Adopting such an identity for his chatbot allowed Weizenbaum to avoid providing the programme with vast quantities of general knowledge.

While quite basic by today's standards, Weizenbaum's chatbot still had an interesting effect on users. He later noted that his secretary held conversations with the chatbot, preferring to have these in private. This, along with similar observations, led to the development of the term the '**Eliza effect**' – defined by Hofstadter (2008) as 'the susceptibility of people to read far more understanding than is warranted into strings of symbols – especially words – strung together by computers' (p. 157).

Since Eliza there have been several other examples of chatbots imitating psycho-therapists, although often these have been designed to help in the training of psychotherapists rather than being intended to provide therapy themselves. For example, Gutiérrez-Maldonado *et al.* (2008) created a three-dimensional environment where trainee psychotherapists can interact with a group of AI clients. The trainee therapists are required to make a diagnosis based on the actions and statements of the virtual clients.

More recent reviews, such as that by Luxton (2014), highlight the advancements in AI for clinical psychological practice, while noting that there are some problems which clinicians need to be aware of. Certainly, AI programmes would have some advantages over human psychotherapists – for example, they would be immune to countertransference, and would have a memory for details that most human psychotherapists could only dream of. Nevertheless, they would also have failings – they may not be able to pick up on nuance or subtlety, and their inability to empathise may cause problems during therapeutic interventions. However, work continues in this field – for example, Lisetti *et al.* (2013) evaluated the potential of a virtual conversational agent in health interventions, with promising results.

Companionship

One of the main applications of social robotics is companionship, with research often specifically focusing on the use of robots as companions for older adults and children. While many positive aspects have been identified, there are also many concerns regarding such use.

Some researchers have investigated the use of therapeutic robots in hospitals and elder-care settings. Such robots are often designed to have the same advantages as are found in animal therapy, but without the risks of infection or injury which real animals bring. Some research has identified potential benefits (see, for example, Shibata & Wada, 2008), but there are indications that many elderly users might reject the robot, feeling it might be suitable for others who are more dependent or lonely than themselves (Neven, 2010). Still others admit the benefits of such robots, but indicate that the ethical concerns of their use, especially with patients with dementia, need to be carefully considered (Calo *et al.*, 2011).

It should be noted that the AI companion does not need to have a robotic form, and many 'virtual' pets are presented within games or smartphone apps. While these too have been shown to provide companionship, it is at a significantly lower level than real pets, and it is most effective with younger children (Chesney & Lawson, 2007; Lawson & Chesney, 2007). Nevertheless, it should be remembered that whether or not the AI is housed in a robot form can impact on how users interact with it. Segura *et al.* (2012) noted that participants preferred a robotic companion to a virtual agent presented on a normal screen when completing secretarial tasks, finding it to have greater social presence and to be less annoying. Similarly, Syrdal *et al.* (2013) noted that sharing physical space in real time might be important for companionship.

The use of AI as companions may also pose problems. For example, Borenstein and Peterson (2013) discuss Child-Robot Interaction (CRI), arguing that while a robotic companion for children might have many benefits, there are ethical issues which may impact on the healthy emotional development of the child. It has already been evidenced that children can attribute emotions and human-like rights to robots (see, for example, Beran *et al.*, 2011; Kahn *et al.*, 2012). The ethical difficulties are not limited to the reactions of children. Wilks *et al.* (2015) describe the development of CALONIS, a companion for a veteran with damage to the brain resulting in memory problems. In a Wizard of Oz type study they found that the robot enhanced communication with the patient, but that ethical issues arose regarding the relationship between the companion and the patient, and the dissemination of the patient's communications to their caregiver.

Scheutz (2012) queries whether humans might become emotionally dependent on social robots, particularly as a result of the 'unidirectional emotional bonds' that could occur, where humans have feelings regarding the robots, while the robots do not have any emotions at all. Similarly, Sharkey and Sharkey (2012) discuss several ethical concerns regarding the use of robotic care for the elderly, including loss of privacy, deception, loss of control and a potential reduction in human contact. However, they do note that robots could improve the lives of the elderly and reduce dependence, provided that they were implemented carefully. Borenstein and Pearson (2010) also consider robots as caregivers, but emphasise that they may not be flexible enough to predict what a patient might do, and that they would fail to offer emotional support, while use of the technology might also lead to erosion of the relationships between human caregivers and the patients.

ARTIFICIAL INTELLIGENCE IN THE FUTURE

Many of the sections above have considered the short-term developments that we can likely expect in psychological applications of AI. Many philosophers, authors and researchers also consider the longer-term possibilities, such as what will happen when AI reaches and surpasses human intelligence (e.g. Barrat, 2015; Bostrom, 2014; Kurzweil, 2005). For some, it is a moment to be feared, while others are hopeful that at such a time it will be possible for humans to attain immortality by being able to upload themselves into a machine. Researchers in AI refer to a time in the future known as the **singularity,** although sometimes with different definitions. Some authors take it to be the point in time when the advances in AI become uncontrollable, some take it to be the time when AI surpasses human intelligence in every way and becomes a **superintelligence**. Predictions for what will happen after the singularity are hypothetical, although it has often been noted that humanity will need to be prepared for such an event, and that care needs to be taken in the development of AI to ensure that a positive outcome is reached. Psychologically, it will be of interest to discover how humans and robots interact when such an event occurs, and particularly what rights such AIs will enjoy.

CONCLUSION

This chapter has considered the relationship between psychology and AI. In particular, it has examined how AI is defined, and the applications of AI with psychological relevance – especially gaming, user interfaces, customer service agents, psychotherapy, companionship and the greater understanding of cognitive science. While there are notable benefits to AI in all of these areas, it is clear that a greater understanding of how humans interact and behave around AI will be extremely useful as the technology develops.

ACTIVITY

Find two or three chatbots online and have a conversation with each (you can find them easily by using the word 'chatbot' in a search engine). Try to include Eliza among them, as well as one or two newer chatbots. What are the techniques used by each chatbot? Does it have a personality? What does it do when faced with a question or statement that it does not have an appropriate answer for? Does the more recent chatbot feel qualitatively different to Eliza, or are they broadly similar?

DISCUSSION QUESTIONS

1   Is the Turing test an accurate measure of AI?
2   What role might companion robots have to play for older adults and children in the future? Will they have a similar role to play for younger adults?
3   AI is playing a more significant role in customer service and user interfaces. What features might make them more liked or accepted by users?
4   Should AI be used in place of human psychotherapists?

RECOMMENDED READING LIST

Alan Turing's 1950 paper proposing the 'Imitation Game' (later known as the 'Turing test') is accessible, even to those without a technical or strongly mathematical background.

> Turing, A. M. (1950). Computing machinery and intelligence. *Mind, 49*, 433–460.

Jay Friedenberg's textbook has particular focus on how AI can help us to understand cognitive science, examining what an artificial person would need to be able to do, and how close technology is to achieving this.

> Friedenberg, J. (2008). *Artificial Psychology: The Quest for What it Means to be Human.* New York: Psychology Press.

Kevin Warwick's primer is an excellent introduction to artificial intelligence as a field, including information on philosophy and robotics.

> Warwick, K. (2012). *Artificial Intelligence: The Basics.* Abingdon: Routledge.

David Duffy's humorous, touching and thought-provoking book explores what can happen when a group of researchers attempt to recreate the conversational style of a human in an android. It is an easy read, yet encourages us to consider what the future may hold.

> Duffy, D. (2012). *Losing the Head of Philip K. Dick: A Bizarre but True Tale of Androids, Kill Switches and Left Luggage.* Oxford: Oneworld Publications.

GLOSSARY

AI effect   A phenomenon where users discount technologies which include some degree of AI as not really being intelligent.

Artificial Intelligence (AI) The creation of intelligent machines and computer systems.

Chatbots   Artificial agents that can hold conversations with a user.

Eliza effect   A phenomenon where people read understanding into computer-generated actions and communications.

Non-Player Characters (NPCs)   Characters in games which are controlled by the computer rather than the gamer.

Robotics   The creation of programmed machines which may or may not have autonomy.

Singularity   A future time where advances in AI become uncontrollable or where AI becomes a superintelligence.

Social robotics   Research examining how robots interact socially with other robots or humans.

Strong AI   A computer which actually possesses the intelligence that it appears to have.

Superintelligence   A level of intelligence reached by an AI where it surpasses human intelligence in every way.

Turing test   A standard of AI proposed by Alan Turing, where the computer is deemed to have passed if a human conversing with it cannot tell that it is not human.

Weak AI   A simulation of intelligence, where no real intelligence exist.

Wizard of Oz study   A research methodology common in AI where it appears that a robot or computer is behaving intelligently, but instead it is being controlled by a human.

REFERENCES

Adam, C. & Lorini, E. (2014). A BDI emotional reasoning engine for an artificial companion. In J. M. Corchado, J. Bajo, J. Kozlak, P. Pawlewski, J. M. Molina, B. Gaudou, V. Julian, R. Unland, F. Lopes, K. Hallenborg & P. G. Teodoro (eds) *Highlights of Practical Applications of Heterogeneous Multi-Agent Systems: The PAAMS Collection* (pp. 66–78). New York: Springer International Publishing.

Barrat, J. (2015). *Our Final Invention: Artificial Intelligence and the End of the Human Era.* New York: St Martin's Press.

Beran, T. N, Ramirez-Serrano, A., Kuzyk, R., Fior, M. & Nugent, S. (2011). Understanding how children understand robots: Perceived animism in child-robot interaction. *International Journal of Human-Computer Studies, 69*(7–8), 539–550.

Binik, Y. M., Servan-Schreiber, D., Freiwald, S., & Hall, K. S. (1988). Intelligent computer-based assessment and psychotherapy: An expert system for sexual dysfunction. *The Journal of Nervous and Mental Disease, 176*(7), 387–400.

Borenstein, J. & Pearson, Y. (2010). Robot caregivers: Harbingers of expanded freedom for all? *Ethics and Information Technology, 12*(3), 277–288.

Borenstein, J. & Pearson, Y. (2013). Companion robots and the emotional development of children. *Law, Innovation and Technology, 5*(2), 172–189.

Bostrom, N. (2014). *Superintelligence: Paths, Dangers, Strategies.* Oxford: Oxford University Press.

Breazeal, C., Gray, J. & Berin, M. (2011). Mindreading as a foundational skill for socially intelligent robots. In M. Kaneko & Y. Nakamura (eds) *Robotics Research* (pp. 383–394). Berlin Heidelberg: Springer.

Calo, C. J., Hunt-Bull, N., Lewis, L. & Metzler, T. (2011, August). *Ethical Implications of Using the Paro Robot.* In 2011 AAAI Workshop (WS-2011–2012). San Francisco, CA.

Chesney, T. & Lawson, S. (2007). The illusion of love: Does a virtual pet provide the same companionship as a real one? *Interaction Studies, 8*(2), 337–342.

Chowanda, A., Blanchfield, P., Flintham, M. & Valstar, M. (2014, January). ERiSA: Building Emotionally Realistic Social Game-Agents Companions. In T. Bickmore, S. Marsella and C. Sidner (eds) *Intelligent Virtual Agents* (pp. 134–143). New York: Springer International Publishing.

Coulson, M., Barnett, J., Ferguson, C. J. & Gould, R. L. (2012). Real feelings for virtual people: Emotional attachments and interpersonal attraction in video games. *Psychology of Popular Media Culture, 1*(3), 176–184.

Crevier, D. (1993). *AI: The Tumultuous Search for Artificial Intelligence.* New York: Basic Books.

Díaz, M., Nuno, N., Saez-Pons, J., Pardo, D. E. & Angulo, C. (2011, March). Building up child-robot relationship for therapeutic purposes: From initial attraction towards long-term social engagement. In Automatic Face & Gesture Recognition and Workshops 2011 IEEE, Santa Barbara, CA.

Epstein, R., Roberts, G. & Beber, G. (eds) (2008). *Parsing the Turing Test: Philosophical and Methodological Issues in the Quest for the Thinking Computer.* New York: Springer.

Erden, M. S. & Tapus, A. (2010, June). *Postural Expressions of Emotions in a Humanoid Robot for Assistive Applications.* Robotics Science and Systems-RSS Workshop on Learning for Human–Robot Interaction Modeling. Zaragoza, Spain.

Friedenberg, J. (2008). *Artificial Psychology: The Quest for What it Means to be Human.* New York: Psychology Press.

Gardner, H. (1983). *Frames of Mind: The Theory of Multiple Intelligences.* New York: Basic Books.

Gutiérrez-Maldonado, J., Alsina, I., Ferrer, M. & Aguilar, A. (2008, June). *Virtual Reality and Artificial Intelligence to Train Abilities of Diagnosis in Psychology and Psychiatry.* Paper presented at the World Conference on Educational Multimedia, Hypermedia and Telecommunications, Chesapeake, VA.

Heerink, M., Diaz, M., Albo-Canals, J., Angulo, C., Barco, A., Casacuberta, J. & Garriga, C. (2012, September). A field study with primary school children on perception of social presence and interactive behaviour with a pet robot. Paper presented at RO-MAN 2012 IEEE, Paris, France.

Hofstadter, D. R. (2008). *Fluid Concepts and Creative Analogies: Computer Models of the Fundamental Mechanisms of Thought.* New York: Basic books.

Jenkins, M. C., Churchill, R., Cox, S. & Smith, D. (2007). Analysis of user interaction with service oriented chatbot systems. In J. A. Jacko (ed.) *Human–Computer Interaction: HCI Intelligent Multimodal Interaction Environments* (pp. 76–83). Berlin Heidelberg: Springer.

Johansson, M., Strååt, B., Warpefelt, H. & Verhagen, H. (2014). Analyzing the social dynamics of non-player characters. In S. A. Meijer & R. Smeds (eds) *Frontiers in Gaming Simulation* (pp. 173–187). New York: Springer International Publishing.

Kahn Jr, P. H., Kanda, T., Ishiguro, H., Freier, N. G., Severson, R. L., Gill, B. T., Ruckert, J. H. & Shen, S. (2012). 'Robovie, you'll have to go into the closet now': Children's social and moral relationships with a humanoid robot. *Developmental Psychology, 48*(2), 303–314.

Kurzweil, R. (2005). *The Singularity is Near: When Humans Transcend Biology.* London: Penguin.

Lawson, S. & Chesney, T. (2007). The impact of owner age on companionship with virtual pets. Proceedings of the European Conference on Information Systems 2007, Geneva, Switzerland, Paper 26. Retrieved from: http://aisel.aisnet.org/cgi/viewcontent.cgi?article=1170&context=ecis2007.

Lisetti, C., Amini, R., Yasavur, U. & Rishe, N. (2013). I can help you change! An empathic virtual agent delivers behavior change health interventions. *ACM Transactions on Management Information Systems (TMIS), 4*(4), 19. doi. 10.1145/2544103.

Luxton, D. D. (2014). Artificial intelligence in psychological practice: Current and future applications and implications. *Professional Psychology: Research and Practice, 45*(5), 332–339.

McCarthy, J. (2007). What is Artificial Intelligence? Retrieved from: http://jmc.stanford.edu/articles/whatisai/whatisai.pdf.

May, P. & Kirwan, G. (2014). Virtual Assistants: Trust and adoption in telecommunication customer support. In A. Power & G. Kirwan (eds) *Cyberpsychology and New Media: A Thematic Reader* (pp. 75–90). Hove/New York: Psychology Press.

Neven, L. (2010). 'But obviously not for me': Robots, laboratories and the defiant identity of elder test users. *Sociology of Health & Illness, 32*(2), 335–347.

Park, E., Jin, D. & del Pobil, A. P. (2012). The law of attraction in Human–Robot Interaction. *International Journal of Advanced Robotic Systems, 9*(35). doi: 10.5772/50228.

Poole, D. L., & Mackworth, A. K. (2010). *Artificial Intelligence: Foundations of Computational Agents.* New York: Cambridge University Press.

Saadatian, E., Salafi, T., Samani, H., De Lim, Y. & Nakatsu, R. (2014). Artificial Intelligence Model of a smartphone-based virtual companion. In Y. Pisan, N. M. Sgouros & T. Marsh (eds) *Entertainment Computing–ICEC 2014* (pp. 173–178). Berlin Heidelberg: Springer.

Salah, A. A., Ruiz-del-Solar, J., Meriçli, C. & Oudeyer, P. Y. (2012). *Human Behavior Understanding.* Berlin Heidelberg: Springer.

Scheutz, M. (2012). The inherent dangers of unidirectional emotional bonds between humans and social robots. In P. Lin, K. Abney & G. A. Bekey (eds) *Robot Ethics: The Ethical and Social Implications of Robotics* (pp. 205–221). Cambridge, MA: MIT Press.

Searle, J. R. (1980). Minds, brains, and programs. *Behavioral and Brain Sciences, 3*(3), 417–457.

Segura, E. M., Kriegel, M., Aylett, R., Deshmukh, A. & Cramer, H. (2012, January). How do you like me in this: User embodiment preferences for companion agents. In Y. Nakano, M. Neff, A. Paiva & M. Walker (eds) *Intelligent Virtual Agents* (pp. 112–125). Berlin Heidelberg: Springer.

Sharkey, A. & Sharkey, N. (2012). Granny and the robots: Ethical issues in robot care for the elderly. *Ethics and Information Technology, 14*(1), 27–40.

Shibata, T. & Wada, K. (2008). Robot therapy at elder care institutions: Effects of long-term interaction with seal robots. In S. Helal, M. Mokhtari and B. Abdulazarak (eds) *The Engineering Handbook of Smart Technology for Aging, Disability, and Independence* (pp. 405–418). Hoboken, NJ: John Wiley & Sons.

Syrdal, D. S., Dautenhahn, K., Koay, K. L., Walters, M. L. & Ho, W. C. (2013). Sharing spaces, sharing lives – the impact of robot mobility on user perception of a home companion robot. In G. Herrmann, M. J. Pearson, A. Lenz, P. Bremner, A. Spiers & U. Leonards (eds) *Social Robotics* (pp. 321–330). New York: Springer International Publishing.

Turing, A. M. (1950). Computing machinery and intelligence. *Mind, 49*, 433–460.

Weizenbaum, J. (1966). ELIZA – a computer program for the study of natural language communication between man and machine. *Communications of the ACM, 9*(1), 36–45.

Wilks, Y., Jasiewicz, J. M., Catizone, R., Galescu, L., Martinez, K. M. & Rugs, D. (2015). CALONIS: An artificial companion within a smart home for the care of cognitively impaired patients. In C. Bodine, S. Helal, T. Gu & M. Mokhtari (eds) *Smart Homes and Health Telematics* (pp. 255–260). New York: Springer International Publishing.

Glossary

Abnormal psychology   The scientific study of abnormal behaviour.

ACM SIGCHI   Association for Computing Machinery's Special Interest Group on Computer–Human Interaction.

Addiction   The state of being enslaved to a habit or practice or to something that is psychologically or physically habit-forming.

Advance fee fraud   A type of online fraud where a user is promised a significant financial reward should they meet what initially appear to be minor demands and fees.

Agent   Virtual world characters controlled by the computer.

AI effect   A phenomenon where users discount technologies which include some degree of AI as not really being intelligent.

Anonymity   Nobody can identify you online.

Anonymous   Your identity is hidden from others.

Artificial Intelligence (AI) The creation of intelligent machines and computer systems.

Assessment   Any process by which learning is judged. It may lead to accreditation.

Asynchronous communication   Communications where it is expected that the users are not simultaneously communicating.

Attention   Means directing the mind to any object of sense or thought.

Augmented reality (AR)   The visual portrayal of virtual objects over real world displays using technologies such as cameras and screens.

Avatar   An online representation of a user, especially in three-dimensional virtual worlds.

Behavioural addictions   Involve a repeated compulsion to perform a particular behaviour.

Bite   This is what a troll wants a person to do, to rise to the bait and react to the bait.

Blended (hybrid) learning   Learning through a combination of classroom based (face-to-face) learning and online learning.

Boundaryless mindset   This is the mindset of staff that are not restrained by traditional organisational boundaries. They may work collaboratively across teams and as part of multidisciplinary teams.

Boundaryless organisations   In these organisations the barriers between internal and external functions have been reduced. Organisational layers are reduced in the hope of achieving greater organisational efficiency and effectiveness.

Brand awareness   The ability to recognise and recall the brand from a relevant cue.

Bring your own devices (BYOD)   Learners bring their own devices to the learning space.

Broadcasting   One-to-many with the primary flow outwards from the one.

Captology   Field of using computers as persuasive technologies.

CBT-(IA)   Cognitive behavioural therapy – Internet Addiction.

cCBT   Computerised CBT.

Chatbots   Artificial agents that can hold conversations with a user.

Cognitive Behavioural Therapy (CBT)   A short-term psychotherapy developed by Aaron Beck and Albert Ellis.

Collective identity   Describes how people are similar to each other, when the psychological connection between the individual self and the social group the individual is a member of is considered.

Communicating   Involves one-to-few with reciprocal exchanges.

Communication Privacy Management (CPM)   A theory developed by Sandra Petronio (2002) describing how individuals view and share their private information.

Compliance   Public adherence to the requests of others.

Computer Mediated Communication (CMC)   Human communication that relies on the medium of computer technology.

Computer Supported Co-operative Work (CSCW)   The use of computing technology to support work by groups.

Conceptual model   Developed early in the interface design process, the conceptual model incorporates high-level design decisions such as the overall structure of the interface and the basic interaction paradigm to be used.

Conditions of learning   The set of internal and external conditions that influence learning (Gagné *et al.*, 1992).

Conformity   Change in our opinions, perceptions, attitudes and behaviour that can be observed when we want others to believe that we agree with others around us.

Constant connectedness   This is a consequence of twenty-first-century technology. Often there is an expectation of fast responses to requests and being available 24 hours a day.

Consumer–brand relationship   What consumers think and feel about a brand and experience with a brand.

Contact hypothesis Allport's idea of how to reduce bias by encouraging contact as equals between two individuals or groups.

Cookies See 'Internet cookies'.

Criminological psychology A branch of psychology which deals mostly with understanding and reducing criminal behaviour.

Cues-filtered out A description of Computer Mediated Communication (CMC) as a medium where there are limited non-verbal cues available (see also **lean medium**).

Customer segmentation Dividing a customer base into groups of individuals who are similar in specific ways such as by demographics, lifestyle and values, or by psychological factors such as personality and motivations.

Cyber obsessional pursuit (COP) Using technology-based stalking behaviours to harass someone or demand intimacy from them.

Cyberbullying Various types of bullying that occur using technology.

Cyberchondriasis The condition where individuals misinterpret common symptoms of often minor illnesses as serious, life-threatening signs of disease, having researched their symptoms on the Internet.

Cybercrime Any unlawful act which is conducted using computing technologies.

Cyberdeviant A form of maladjusted Internet use at work that may be perpetuated by the lack of supervision in staff that work virtually.

Cyberpsychology The branch of psychology that examines how we interact with others using technology, how our behaviour is influenced by technology, how technology can be developed to best suit our needs, and how our psychological states can be affected by technologies.

Cybersickness A form of motion sickness caused by discrepancies between visual and proprioceptive cues.

Cyberslacking This is use of the Internet at work for personal reasons – for example, social networking, shopping, surfing the net, gambling, etc. Managers often fear that this can lead to loss of productivity and ultimately cost the organisation money.

Deindividuation Process by which you don't feel personally accountable for actions due to being part of a group.

Distance learning Learning with teachers and learners are in different physical spaces.

Distraction Anything that prevents someone from concentrating on something else.

Door in the face technique Two-step compliance technique where the person is initially asked with a large request, which is then followed by a second, more modest, request.

DSM-5   The *Diagnostic and Statistical Manual of Mental Disorders*, 5th edition (DSM-5).

Educational technology   The technological artefacts and devices used in education; how the technologies are used in education and learning, and the context for their use (Selwyn, 2011).

eLearning   Learning with electronic technology.

Eliza effect   A phenomenon where people read understanding into computer-generated actions and communications.

eLoyalty   A favourable attitude towards an online business influencing the intention of the consumer to repurchase from a company, and the likelihood of them recommending the brand to someone else.

Emojis   Variation of emoticons.

Emoticons   The use of symbols to demonstrate facial expressions in communication.

Exergaming   The activity of playing interactive games consoles, such as the Wii and WiiFit.

Experiential learning   Learning through a cyclical process of doing, reflecting on action, identifying learning and applying the new learning (Watkins *et al.*, 2002) .

Experiment   A research situation or activity that has been specifically designed and controlled so as to allow researchers to establish causal inference (i.e. the role of some condition or characteristic in causing some outcome).

Face-to-face learning (f2f)   Teachers and learners are in the same physical space in classrooms, lecture theatres, labs and studios.

Flaming   When personal insults are exchanged online.

Flipped classroom   Learners access concepts and ideas in their own time using video lectures, readings and the classroom (face to face) becomes a space for discussion and analysis enabling critical thinking and creativity.

Flow Theory   A positive psychology theory proposed by Csikszentmihalyi (1990) which can help to explain optimal experience online. A flow state is a heightened state of engagement with a video game activity (or other activity) that is characterised by feelings of presence, energised focus and enjoyment, and being at one with the game. Flow typically involves distortions of time perception.

Fluidity   In Computer Mediated Communication (CMS), refers to content that can be changed easily and frequently.

Focus groups   A variant of the interview method conducted with small groups of people, that allows for discussion to answer the interviewer's questions.

Foot in the door technique   Two-step compliance technique where the person is first asked a small request which is then followed up with a second, much larger, request.

Forensic psychology   A branch of psychology which encompasses legal and criminological psychology.

Formal learning   Learning that takes place in formal settings such as schools and colleges or through courses. It often leads to accreditation.

Gamer   A video game player.

Gamification   The application of game principles or mechanisms to a task or problem so as to encourage increased engagement with the activity.

Gaming   The use of video games online or offline.

Global Positioning System (GPS)   A system that involves satellite tracking to plot the movement patterns of objects. GPS devices used in sport are typically smaller than a mobile phone and are positioned in a pouch within the training gear of the athletes, usually on the back, between the shoulder blades.

Graphical User Interface (GUI)   This is the layer between the human and the computer. The GUI may consist of icons, buttons, text, windows and other visual indicators.

Graphics (pictures)   Static items such as illustrations, drawings, charts, maps, photographs and dynamic items such as animation and video.

Group norms   The rules individuals are expected to obey as members of a particular group.

Group roles   The parts that individuals play within a group or the positions they fill within a group (formal or informal).

Groupthink   'The tendency for cohesive groups to become so concerned about group consolidation that they fail to critically and realistically evaluate their decisions and antecedent assumptions' (Park, 1990, p. 229).

Halo effect   A cognitive bias that occurs when one element of the dating profile, usually the photograph, influences the observer's impressions of the profile as a whole.

Head Mounted Displays (HMDs)   Virtual reality technology where the environment is presented to the user via screens in a headset.

Heuristics   A set of guidelines or rules of thumb used to guide the design and/or evaluation of an interface.

High-fidelity prototype   Similar in look and behaviour to the desired finished product. Typically computer-based, allowing the user to interact with the prototype using a mouse, touchscreen, etc.

Homophily   The tendency for people to like others similar to themselves.

Human-Computer Interaction (HCI)   Refers to the field that studies the design and testing of interactive computer systems that exist at the point where humans and computers meet.

Hyperpersonal communication   A model by Walther (1996) describing how Computer Mediated communication can lead to enhanced feelings of intimacy.

Identifiable   Your identity can be seen by others.

Identity   Recognition of one's potential and qualities as an individual, especially in relation to social context.

Identity formation   Where young people reassess their childhood identifications as their awareness of societal values increases.

Immersion   An objective characteristic that describes the quality or quantity of sensory information provided to a person from a video game (or other audio-visual technology).

Implicit Association Test   Test which measures attitudes that the person is unaware of or unwilling to admit to having.

Impression management   Selectively self-presenting or editing messages to reveal socially desirable attitudes and dimensions of the self.

Informal learning   Learning that takes place when someone decides to learn something from a book, a video or from another person generally from interest or need.

Instruction   All the events that affect learning.

Instructional design   The systematic design of instruction to support learning (Gagné *et al.*, 1992).

Interaction Design (IxD)   A field similar to Human-Computer Interaction, but wider in scope, incorporating any interactive experience.

Interface   The boundary between the human and the computer through which the two parties exchange information. Most commonly, this is represented on screen via a graphical user interface and the human provides commands by clicking or touching on screen interface elements such as icons or buttons.

Internet Addiction Disorder   A disorder associated with the overuse of the Internet.

Internet cookies   Data used by websites to record user activity.

Internet gamers   Gamers who play online video games.

Internet-enabled cybercrime   Crimes for which offline equivalents exist, but which Internet technologies enable or extend.

Internet-specific cybercrime   Cybercrimes for which offline equivalents do not exist.

Interview (research)   A method of data collection where questions are asked by the interviewer so as to collect information from the interviewee.

Knowing-doing gap   A situation where the user knows what the most secure behaviour is, but fails to behave in a way which promotes such security.

Lean medium   A description of CMC as a medium where there are limited non-verbal cues available.

Learning A change in behaviour.

Lecture capture Multimedia lectures in classrooms can be created as audio/video recordings.

Legal psychology A branch of psychology which deals with the process of law.

Listserv Email discussion list.

Low-fidelity prototype Often used early in the interaction design process, these prototypes are far from the finished product and may be developed using simple materials such as paper, offering no real user interaction.

Massive open online courses (MOOCs) These are courses available on the Internet that are open to all who register at little or no charge and often taken by large numbers of students.

Mastery of learning Achieved when learners are successful at learning tasks (Gagné *et al.*, 1992).

Mental disorders Cover a wide range of mental health issues. These include anxiety, stress, mood disorders and addiction.

Mental health Defined as a state of well-being in which every individual realises his or her own potential, can cope with the normal stresses of life, can work productively and fruitfully, and is able to make a contribution to his or her community (WHO, 2007).

Mental preparation A broad term used to describe the ways in which athletes 'ready' themselves, mentally, to participate in their sport.

Mindfulness Means paying attention in the present moment, on purpose and non-judgementally.

mLearning Mobile learning using mobile devices such as phones and tablets.

Mobile computing The use of smartphones, tablets, laptops and other mobile devices as computers.

Multimedia Any material that contains words and graphics.

Multimodality The use of multiple modes of communication, such as text with video, images or sound.

Multitasking Involves doing more than one thing at once.

Natural User Interface (NUI) Interfaces that are essentially invisible. Such interfaces should be intuitive and easy to learn. Examples include interfaces that allow users to interact with computers using speech and/or gestures.

Negative automatic thoughts Thoughts that are unhelpful and negative.

Nomophobia The term refers to the fear of being out of mobile phone contact, a run-down battery or losing the phone itself.

Non-Player Characters (NPCs) Characters in games which are controlled by the computer rather than the gamer.

Non-Reactive Data Collection (NRDC)   When the researcher collects data using an unobtrusive observation method.

Observation (research)   A non-experimental research method whereby the researcher observes behaviour.

Offender profiling   The creation of profiles of criminal suspects, sometimes by forensic psychologists

Online counselling   The delivery of therapeutic interventions over the Internet.

Online dating   Searching for a romantic or sexual partner on the Internet, typically via a dedicated website.

Online disinhibition   The online disinhibition effect was coined by Suler (2004). It refers to a loosening or removal of social inhibitions when interacting online, that would normally be present in face-to-face communication.

Online gaming   Playing video games over a computer network, often with other players.

Online learning   Use of communication networks for educational purposes mediated by the Web.

Ostracism   When one is excluded or isolated from a group.

Paralanguage   Modifying meaning through the use of volume, intonation or other adjustments.

Peer pressure   Pressure to fit in with those we spend time with.

Persuasion   An attempt to bring about a change in attitude or behaviour.

Phishing   Emails which appear to be from a reputable source which are designed to elicit sensitive information from a user, leaving them vulnerable to identity theft.

PIU   Problematic Internet Use.

Platform   The combination of hardware and software making up a computer system.

Prejudice   General term for any negative attitude towards a social group.

Presence   The subjective feeling of being in a virtual environment (such as a video game or virtual reality); an illusion that renders the viewer unaware of the technological medium through which the environment is presented.

Primary research   When the researcher collects original data, specifically for their research project.

Privacy   The state or condition of not having personal information disclosed in public or semi-public settings.

Protection Motivation Theory   A theory proposed by Rogers (1975, 1983) which identified several factors which might trigger engagement in protective behaviours.

Proteus Effect   Proposed by Yee and Bailenson (2007), this refers to a change in online and offline self-perception based on the features or behaviours of a user's avatar.

Prototype   A sample or model constructed to test an interface concept.

Psychopathology   The scientific study of mental disorders.

Questionnaire   A series of predefined questions or other statements distributed so as to collect information from respondents.

Research   The systematic process of collecting and analysing information in an effort to make a contribution to knowledge of a particular phenomenon.

Research population   The entire group of people (or animals or other things), with the characteristic(s) a researcher wishes to explore; the whole group of interest.

Research sample   A subset of the population, from which the researcher can collect data so as to make claims about the population.

Robotics   The creation of programmed machines which may or may not have autonomy.

Scenario   A description of one particular interaction a potential user may have with a system. For example, in an online dating site may involve a new user signing up and creating their profile.

Secondary research   When the researcher collects, reviews or synthesises existing research.

Self   A person's essential being that distinguishes them from others, especially considered as the object of introspection or reflexive action.

Self-presentation   A strategic negotiation of how one presents one's self to audiences.

Singularity   A future time where advances in Artificial Intelligence become uncontrollable or where AI becomes a superintelligence.

Skype   A software application and online service that enables voice and video phone calls over the internet.

Smileys   Variation of emoticons.

Social and emotional development   Experience, expression and management of emotions and the ability to establish positive and rewarding relationships with others.

Social Categorisation Theory   Putting people into groups on the basis of some shared attribute.

Social Identity Theory   Theory which seeks to explain intergroup discrimination and how we form in-groups/ out-groups.

Social influence   How we are affected by the real or imagined presence of others.

Social loafing Describes the reduction in effort exerted by some individuals when they are performing as part of groups.

Social media Websites, applications and online social networks which individuals use to make contact with others and to communicate and share information online.

Social networking The use of social media.

Social networking sites (SNSs) See 'social media'.

Social robotics Research examining how robots interact socially with other robots or humans.

Spyware Software that enables a user to obtain covert information about another's computer activities.

Strong AI A computer which actually possesses the intelligence that it appears to have.

Superintelligence A level of intelligence reached by an Artificial Intelligence where it surpasses human intelligence in every way.

Synchronous communication Communications where it is expected that users are simultaneously communicating, such as instant messaging.

Tactile augmentation Using a real item to induce a sensation of touch when a user is in a virtual world.

Teaching A key part of instruction where teachers (also called instructors) organise and plan the instruction for students and classes.

Technology Acceptance Model (TAM) Designed to explain why people do or do not use technology in the context of the workplace. However, because online shoppers are also technology users, it has also been used to explain people's inclination to adopt technology in online shopping.

Technology-enhanced learning The use of technology to support learning.

Telecommuters Those who work independently from the 'hub' and touch base only when necessary. Telecommuters stay connected to the workplace by using a variety of digital technologies.

Text Words printed on a screen or spoken.

Theory of Reasoned Action (TRA) The TRA examines people's intention to adopt certain behaviours, and that intention is determined by their attitude towards the behaviour and by subjective norms about the behaviour.

Trolling Negative behaviours in online environments (such as social media and gaming) designed to provoke a reaction such as inducing annoyance or disruption.

Turing test A standard of Artificial Intelligence proposed by Alan Turing, where the computer is deemed to have passed if a human conversing with it cannot tell that it is not human.

Twitter   A microblogging tool and online social network, where individuals post short messages (tweets) of up to 140 characters that their 'followers' can read, favour and retweet.

Uncertainty reduction   Strategies used at almost every stage in a relationship to reassure a person about aspects of their partner or relationship. Can include information seeking.

Usability   The extent to which users can achieve specified goals with effectiveness, efficiency and satisfaction using a product.

User Experience (UX)   Involves a user's emotions and attitudes about interacting with a product.

User persona   A description of a hypothetical user with the same characteristics, motivations and goals as the target user.

User-Centred Design (UCD)   A design philosophy that focuses on the needs, desires and capabilities of the actual users of the product, rather than focusing on business goals, technologies or other aspects.

Video game   Games that are played on any computer system and allow the player to interactively control graphics on some form of display.

Viral   A marketing technique where consumers voluntarily pass a marketing message about a company to others.

Virtual Environments (VE)   A computer-generated three-dimensional representation of a setting or situation.

Virtual identity suicide   The removal of an online profile, sometimes to increase privacy.

Virtual Learning Environments (VLEs)   Also called Learning Management Systems (LMS) or Course Management Systems (CMS) (Moore *et al.*, 2011) are web-based courses that support formal learning in schools and colleges.

Virtual organisation   Members work for the same company but are geographically distant from each other and communicate by information technology.

Virtual Reality (VR)   The use of computer technologies to create three-dimensional virtual worlds or objects which users can interact with.

Virtual Reality Exposure Therapy (VRET)   The use of VR to present cues or stimuli to a user to treat a psychological condition such as an anxiety disorder or addiction.

Virtual teams   A virtual team is made up of a number of different people who work together collaboratively using web-based technologies. They may never meet in person.

Warranting principle   People are more likely to trust information online if it cannot be easily manipulated.

Weak AI   A simulation of intelligence, where no real intelligence exists.

Web 2.0   A term used to describe the increased interactivity online, particularly in relation to social media and other user-generated content.

Web-facilitated   Where learning is supported by online course materials and activities.

Wikis   Collaborative websites.

Wizard of Oz study   A research methodology common in AI where it appears that a robot or computer is behaving intelligently, but instead it is being controlled by a human.

Word of mouth (WOM)   Communication by a consumer to others actively influenced or encouraged by an organisation.

Working memory   The system for temporarily storing and managing the information required to carry out cognitive tasks such as learning and comprehension.

World Wide Web   An application of the Internet which allows the linking of documents online.

Index

References to non-textual matter such as figures or tables are in italics.